Children and Reading Tests

Advances in Discourse Processes
Roy O. Freedle, Series Editor

Children and Reading Tests

Clifford Hill and Eric Larsen
Teachers College
Columbia University

Ablex Publishing Corporation
Stamford, Connecticut

Printed in the United States of America

Library of Congress Cataloging-in-Publication Data

Hill, Clifford.
    Children and Reading Tests / by Clifford Hill and Eric Larsen.
    p. cm. — (Advances in discourse processes ; v. 65)
    Includes bibliographical references and index.
    ISBN 1-56750-444-2 (cloth) — ISBN 1-56750-445-0 (pbk.)
    1. Reading—Ability testing. 2. Reading comprehension—Ability testing. 3. Children—Books and reading. I. Larsen, Eric. II. Title. III. Series.
LB1050.46.H55   2000
372.48—dc21
                              99-19364
                                   CIP

Ablex Publishing Corporation
100 Prospect Street
P.O. Box 811
Stamford, CT 06904-0811

To Jeremy
for teaching us
who the child reader is
and to Kathleen
for teaching us
who the child reader becomes

Contents

Part I.   Introduction

Part II.   Testing Reader Parsimony

Acknowledgments

We would like to thank the following individuals for their help:

Roy Freedle, who early on made a commitment to our work and has been patient in waiting for us to deliver it;

Walter MacGinitie, who first gave us the idea for the study, provided the background material we needed, and answered many questions about how standardized tests of reading comprehension are constructed;

Neal Grove, who helped to prepare the initial proposal that was funded by the National Institute of Education;

Robert Aronowitz, Gayle Cooper, Alexander Dietrichson, Sharon Goldstein, Maurice Hauck, Lori Langer de Ramirez, Marie Keem, Daniella Olibrice, Kate Parry, Enid Pearsons, Susan Price, and Paula Schwartz, who provided many different kinds of help in carrying out the research and preparing the manuscript; and Meredith Phillips who has been patient and supportive in seeing the book through production.

In addition, we would like to thank the many graduate students at Teachers College, Columbia University, who conducted interviews and experimental probes with children. You are too numerous to name here, but we bear a special debt of gratitude to each of you for the ingenuity and commitment that you brought to your work with children.

Finally, we would like to thank the hundreds of children in metropolitan New York who participated in the study over these many years. We hope that their participation has helped them to become more skilled at taking standardized tests of reading comprehension, but even more importantly, more skilled as readers.

Preface

During the past couple of decades there has been a good deal of policy debate about the role of standardized testing in American education. This debate has been recently centered on whether a reading test should be developed at the national level for children in the fourth grade. Those who support such a test argue that high standards cannot be maintained nationwide unless there is some means to enforce them. If a national reading test were put in place, children who did not pass it could be held back and placed in specialized reading programs designed to provide them help. The test would thus have an important diagnostic role to play: it could identify not only individual children who need help but also schools in which there is a disproportionate number of such children. Both individuals and institutions could be targeted for the special help that they need.

Those who oppose a national test make two different kinds of arguments. First of all, there is the politically based argument that a nationally developed test violates a basic principle that education should be controlled at the local level. Second, there is the educationally based argument that a high stakes test would have negative effects on classroom practice. Given the high stakes attached to such a test, teachers would be required to spend a good deal of classroom time on test-taking skills, which have limited value in developing children's capacity for reading comprehension. Indeed, those who make this argument claim that such skills often run counter to the constructivist curricula being used in many programs of early childhood education.

This last argument is based on a rather negative assessment of reading tests for children. Those who make this argument, however, generally do not provide evidence for why they hold this view. Indeed, the policy debate on a national reading test has proceeded with virtually no attention to how reading tests actually work and how children respond to them. This neglect is symptomatic of a problem that inheres in educational policy debates: attention is generally focused on the broad consequences of a particular program or activity rather than on the program or activity itself. Although these consequences are important in a policy debate, they should be considered in the context of a substantive review of the particular program or activity under consideration. In the case of testing, such a review should consist of close attention not only to representative test material but also to test takers' responses to it.

In the research reported in this book, we have taken a close look at a corpus of test material and children's responses to it. In conducting this research, we have drawn on Hymes' (1962) model for examining language in social context. This model, known as the *ethnography of communication*, is used to investigate not only oral communication but also written communication in a range of settings.

In order to understand what goes on when children respond to a reading test, we developed a framework in which we investigated how such a test reflects the interpretive norms of the larger tradition in which it is embedded. Within this framework, we also investigated the interpretive norms that children bring to the experience. We used a range of methods not only for understanding how a reading test functions as institutionalized text, but also how children draw on their own ethnocultural norms of language, thought, and experience in responding to it.

In analyzing test material as text, we used a range of tools that allowed us to examine the material at both a macro-level and a micro-level. At the macro-level, we drew on various tools of analysis to examine logical and pragmatic properties of meaning. At the micro-level, we drew on various tools of analysis to examine syntactic and semantic properties of meaning. In this way, we were able to identify problems not only within individual test units but also those that run across the units. Problems associated with the genre of reading tests hold a particular interest for us, and they are brought together in the concluding chapter of this volume.

At the same time, we had to take apart children's responses to the test material. This was not easy to do since most of the processes involved in reading cannot be directly observed. We thus resorted to various methods that allowed us to make plausible inferences about how children were responding. Many of these methods were developed from our analyses of the test material. Whenever we uncovered particular problems in the material, we worked out tasks that would shed light on how children handled them. The construction of these tasks has been a major feature of our research.

Another major feature of our research has been its focus on children. Over the years we have worked with hundreds of children from diverse ethnocultural backgrounds as they responded to the corpus of test material. We were often surprised by children's responses as they brought their own ethnocultural knowledge and experience to bear on the test material. Many children raised possibilities of meaning that we—and presumably the test makers—had not anticipated. The sheer richness of children's responses to the test material constitutes one of the most valuable lessons in this book.

When it was time to give a name to our book, we decided that it would be better to put *children* before *reading tests*. Not only does this title sound better—we will have occasion in this book to discuss linguistic reasons for placing a shorter term before a longer one—but, more importantly, this ordering reflects the emphasis on children in our research. We hope that this emphasis will be increasingly reflected in the world of educational practice where it is often the reading tests that are placed before children.

Part I

Introduction

In Chapter 1 we describe the context of this study of children's responses to reading tests. We begin with the larger context by characterizing the emergence of standardized testing in this century. Working from a historical perspective, we present its initial promise of greater equity and efficiency in dealing with a large and culturally heterogeneous population. We also delineate various problems that came to be associated with this approach as it became widely deployed in American education.

We next turn to the immediate context of the study and describe its various stages: the major goals we set out to accomplish, the corpus of test material we put together, and the methods we used to analyze this material and children's responses to it. We end the chapter by providing different kinds of apparatus that orient the reader to the chapters that follow.

chapter I

Context of the Study

The genre with which this book is concerned—the short texts followed by multiple-choice questions that are used on standardized tests of reading comprehension—has a fairly brief history. It is the product of a movement during the early years of the 20th century that sought to apply scientific principles to the measurement of human abilities. This new approach was first used on a mass scale during the First World War, when various kinds of aptitude and intelligence tests were constructed to help in the assignment of nearly two million army recruits. It was not long before the new tests made their way into education, where they were used in managing the large and heterogeneous body of students that had been produced by universal schooling. During the 1920s, the Stanford-Binet tests were widely used at both primary and secondary levels to place students in homogeneous groups, which were regarded as the most effective way to deliver instruction. The practice of using tests with young children was thus initiated, and it has continued until the present time.

It was during the same decade that tests were first developed that could be used to measure educational achievement in different areas. Among these, tests that measure reading comprehension have always been regarded as the most basic. Indeed, reading scores are still commonly used as measures of the overall effectiveness of schools and curriculums. This practice can be traced to the common-sense view that any individual who lacks reading skills is unable to function effectively in a modern society.

From the standpoint of the new science of testing, there were two main difficulties with traditional testing of reading comprehension, which required students to write essays on culturally valued texts they had been assigned to read: (1) there was no way of determining the

3

effects of real-world knowledge and writing skill on an individual's performance; and (2) there was no way of assuring that evaluation would be consistent from one teacher to another.

One solution that addressed both problems was the multiple-choice format, an innovative technology in which a question is accompanied by the correct answer, with the latter being concealed among more or less plausible alternatives. The multiple-choice technique made it possible to measure reading ability without the use of writing, and it purportedly removed the subjective element from scoring by producing answers that were clearly right or wrong. An additional advantage was that scoring could be done quickly and inexpensively, especially after machines that could do the job were introduced in the 1930s.

It is important to note that the reading comprehension measured by the new tests deviated not only from traditional practices but also from our everyday sense of what reading is for. In the real world, we feel it is important to understand what we read because we may need to use the information at a future time. In administering a test of real-world reading, we might ask students to read a text, then take it away, and ask them what they have retained; or we might even ask them to read a text on one day and then on another day ask them to use the information in solving a problem. From the standpoint of the new testing paradigm, these practices would be undesirable, because we wouldn't be able to determine whether a poor performance was due to lack of comprehension or to faulty recall strategies. We might, as a consequence, give students instruction in comprehension, when what they really need is help with retention (though it is not clear how these two processes can be easily separated in practice). Thus, tests of reading comprehension are usually "open book," with the relevant text available while the tasks are being completed, whereas in everyday life we are often faced with a situation in which we must depend on our memory of a pertinent text.

Another major innovation of the new testing paradigm was the use of statistics in selecting the most effective test material and in establishing norms. Prospective test units[1] are typically pilot tested and those that fail to perform well for one reason or another are discarded. One important technique for evaluating test units is biserial correlation, which compares how test takers perform on a particular unit with how they perform on a larger sample of test units. A unit, for example, in which readers who do well on other units tend to get the wrong answer, and readers who do poorly on other units tend to get the right answer, would not be used in the final test, because it would work against the differentiations among readers established by the other units. The overall objective is to produce an instrument in which a test taker moves gradually from units that nearly everyone gets right to units that only a few are able to handle, for this is the pattern that produces the maximum differentiation with the minimum number of units.[2]

When a test has reached final form, it is given to a sample of the target population, and their performance is used to establish norms against which future takers of the test will be measured. Thus, these tests have come to be referred to as NORM-REFERENCED, or simply *normed*, or more generally as STANDARDIZED. Norms are widely misunderstood by the public, which often assumes that they represent some well-established, stable standard of how well, say, a third grader should read. Indeed, one often reads about educators who establish such goals as "every third grade child will read at grade-level or above," which is reminiscent of Garrison Keillor's Lake Wobegon, a town where "all the children are above average." By definition, half the children who take a normed test will be above grade-level and the other half below. If the nation did manage to improve reading significantly over a period of years, the improvement would disappear as test makers updated their norms. Given the confusion engendered by normed achievement tests, it has often been suggested that they be replaced by what are called CRITERION-REFERENCED tests, that is, tests which compare test takers to some established standard rather than to each other, but this proposal has received little attention from either those who produce tests or those who make use of them.

Over the last 25 years, there has been increasing criticism of standardized tests from a number of perspectives. One of the most frequent criticisms is that these tests discriminate against students whose ethnocultural background differs from that of the test makers and the norming group. Certainly statistical data indicate that such students, even those who perform relatively well in school, are less able to perform well on these tests (for a recent report on such data, see Jencks & Phillips, 1998). A similar criticism has been made in the case of female students, since statistical data show that they, too, often perform less well on these tests. A particularly dramatic case has been the Scholastic Achievement Test (SAT), which is designed to predict how well individual students will perform in college. Despite the avowed purpose of this test, it consistently underpredicts the grades that women receive in college courses (Clark & Grandy, 1984; Dorans & Kulick, 1983; Rosser, 1989; Sims-West, 1996).

Another major criticism concerns the effect that these tests have on curriculum and instruction. A curriculum is often distorted by the need to prepare students for multiple-choice testing: they end up spending a disproportionate amount of time reading practice test passages rather than books or, at least, well-sequenced excerpts designed to promote learning. Such test-dominated instruction has long been criticized (e.g., Hoffman, 1964), and yet few teachers are able to resist it; not only do parents and administrators judge them according to student performance, but the students themselves often insist on getting prepped for an important test. Given the high-stakes nature of many tests, conscientious teachers feel responsible for getting students ready to take them.

A further problem is how to ensure that the administration of a given test is fair. The purpose of a standardized test is to provide a reliable means of evaluating large numbers of students in many different places; but for such evaluation to be accurate, the students must be working in the same basic conditions—the same amount of time for the test and the same degree of help, or lack of it, from the person in charge. These conditions are, however, difficult to control. Even when test administrators follow all the instructions, the physical conditions in which a test is taken—the weather, the adequacy of furniture and lighting, the amount of disturbance from outside the room—may vary so much as to give some test takers an unfair advantage over others.[3]

The greatest advantage of all is to be gained by cheating. Because standardized testing has become so important, it is not uncommon that the security of a major test is breached. In a recent scandal in New York City, answers to the Regents Exams were leaked, and when state officials failed to take immediate action, one newspaper even printed some of the answers on the front page. Even when there is no overt cheating, administrators sometimes attempt to protect the reputation of their schools. One practice is to arrange for weaker students to be absent on the days that the tests are to be administered.

Despite all these criticisms, the reliance on standardized testing continues to increase in American education. Using a survey conducted by the National Center for Fair and Open Testing, Medina and Neill (1990) estimate that more than 100,000,000 standardized tests of achievement were administered to nearly 40,000,000 students during the academic year 1986–1987. Included in this number were nearly 40,000,000 diagnostic tests for students in special education programs, 2,000,000 tests to screen children in preschool programs, and nearly 7,000,000 other tests administered by programs such as the General Equivalency Diploma (GED) and the National Assessment of Educational Progress (NAEP). Despite this barrage of standardized tests, the national debate about improving American schools often calls for an even greater reliance on such tests. This debate suggests that the public as a whole is still willing to take the tests pretty much at face value. *The New York Times,* for example, annually publishes scores on citywide tests according to school district and even individual schools. A major consequence is that the public reputation of an individual school rises or falls in accordance with its place in the overall standings.

RESEARCH BACKGROUND

The research reported in this volume had its inception in the late 1970s when researchers from the Educational Testing Service and Teachers College, Columbia University, met together in a seminar on reading assessment sponsored by the Institute for Urban and Minority Education. Members of the seminar were concerned that, despite the widespread criticism of standardized tests, there had been relatively little close analysis of what these tests call for and how students respond to them. The initial efforts attempted to uncover how students from varying ethnocultural backgrounds responded to material selected from various reading tests used in metropolitan New York (see Freedle, 1977; Hill, 1977a, 1977b; Nix & Schwartz, 1979).

While the seminar was in progress, we were offered test material that had been pilot-tested for the second edition of the Gates-MacGinitie Reading Tests, but which was subsequently not used in the published tests. This offer was attractive for several reasons. First of all, the material was designed for use at the third-grade level, the first level at which passages combined with multiple-choice tasks are used to test children's reading comprehension. This material thus provided us an opportunity to study children's responses before they developed various kinds of test-taking strategies. This level is also the focus of national debates about the best policies for teaching children to read: in the third grade, children are viewed not simply as learning to read but developing the knowledge and skills that enable them to read in order to learn.

Moreover, we welcomed the opportunity to analyze material that was not part of a published test since we had experienced difficulties in publishing close analysis of material from published tests. Over the years these difficulties have been numerous: either test publishers have refused permission outright or have granted it but then withdrawn it when they discovered the nature of our research. In fact, in order to publish one study, we were forced to take out the exact words of the test material we were analyzing and make do with a description of it in our own words. Since we are trained as linguists to attend closely to exact wording, the test publisher's prohibition vitiated crucial points in our analysis. Given these experiences, the chance to do research on material that had been vetted in a published test—and yet could be reproduced freely—lessened our concern that we might ultimately be prevented from presenting our findings in the most compelling way.

Finally, the offer was attractive because statistical data were available on responses of representative African American and European American children to this test material. The pilot testing had been conducted with samples of students in large urban areas such as Houston. We tend to be more cautious about such data than test makers usually are since generic descriptors such as *African American* can be quite misleading in modern American society, where cultural identity is inherently complex. We prefer to characterize such identity from a transcultural perspective; that is to say, one that is sensitive to the various cultural influences at work in a single individual. Such complexity is reflected not only in cultural aspects of identity but also in other aspects such as gender and socioeconomic class.

Nevertheless, we believed that the pilot data would help us to focus attention on certain test units where the gap in performance between the two ethnocultural groups was especially pronounced. As the research developed, this concern with ethnocultural differences was broadened so that we dealt with other groups such as Latinos and Asian Americans. At the same time, we dealt with developmental factors alongside the ethnocultural ones. No matter which ethnocultural background children come from, they are often confronted with test material that make cognitive demands they are not prepared for.

After examining the pilot-tested material, we developed a research proposal and received funding from the National Institute of Education. Our overall goal in this research was to examine test material for third-grade children as comprehensively as possible from three complementary perspectives:

1) a linguistic approach in which we would combine the microlevel analysis of traditional linguistics with attention to such macrolevel concerns as the logical and pragmatic relationships between propositions;
2) a genre approach in which we would utilize a relatively large corpus to gain an understanding of the general structure and function of the material used on reading tests; and
3) a discourse approach in which we would seek to understand not only what is on the page but what goes through the heads of different children as they read and respond to the page.

In dealing with written language, we use the term DISCOURSE to describe reader interaction with text rather than simply text itself. In effect, we view discourse, whether constituted by oral or written language, as fundamentally interactive.

As we submitted our report of this research in order to meet the funding deadline (Hill & Larsen, 1983), we were left with some intriguing questions that we wished to explore further. In particular, we wanted to build on the work of researchers such as Trabasso (1981) and Collins, Brown, and Larkin (1980) to characterize more precisely the inferences that children make in responding to the material in our corpus. Working with a distinction between TEXT BASE and SITUATION MODEL (van Dijk & Kintsch, 1983), we developed a framework for characterizing these inferences. To illustrate this framework, we here introduce sample material from our corpus:

> The fawn looked at Alice with its large, gentle eyes. It didn't seem at all frightened. "Here, then! Here, then!" Alice said, as she held out her hand and tried to stroke it. It moved back a little and then stood looking at her again.

> A. How did the fawn's eyes look?
>   sad   gentle
>   tired   frightened

> B. What did Alice try to do to the fawn?
>   help it   pet it
>   hug it   hide it

The text base of this passage includes not only overtly stated propositions (e.g., Alice tried to stroke the fawn) but also inferences that are directly entailed by them (e.g., Alice did not manage to stroke the fawn). We use the term AUTOMATED to describe this kind of inference.

As children work with a text base, they naturally construct a situation that takes into account the propositions and automated inferences that it contains. This conversion of text into meaning is a complex process that necessarily involves a good deal of inferencing. As children read the above passage, for example, they must construct a physical scene (presumably one where undomesticated animals roam about) in which a human being (presumably a young girl) interacts in a rather personal way with one of these animals (presumably one that she has never met before). Even in a relatively short passage, inferences multiply rapidly as words are converted into a world.

Officially, what is to be comprehended on a reading test is the passages, but in actual practice the situation models that children construct are often influenced by material in the tasks, especially the potential answers that are supplied. Ideally, a test taker exits a passage with a well-formed interpretation that is clearly matched by only one of the available choices. But if this doesn't happen, each choice becomes a candidate for inclusion in the situation model that the reader has constructed, perhaps altering it substantially. This book provides many examples of how children use these choices to construct trial situation models as they respond to tasks.

Our framework identifies three kinds of inferences—motivated, invited, and extended—each of which is associated with a corresponding situation model. MOTIVATED INFERENCES are those that while not logically entailed by the text base are nevertheless directly stimulated by it: for example, certain children, cued by one of the choices in task (A), inferred that the fawn was frightened because it "moved back a little" when Alice tried to stroke it. Some of these children found further support in the statement "It didn't seem at all frightened," reasoning that this assertion implied that the fawn actually *was* frightened. Many readers would, no doubt, recognize the merit of this inference, even if they did not make it themselves as they read the passage.

INVITED INFERENCES have a more problematic relation with the text base: a number of children, for example, cued by a choice in task (B), inferred that Alice was trying to help the fawn. They were then able to return to the passage and find some support: not only did Alice speak to the fawn in a friendly way but she even tried to stroke it. Even though this inference goes beyond what the text base strictly supports, it is associated with some of the information it contains.

It is not always easy to distinguish motivated and invited inferences. In general, invited inferences are more loosely associated with the text base. In some ways, they resemble the inferences commonly made in conversation, where one person says something that can stimulate another to move beyond what was actually said: for example, if we bring up the subject of food, our listeners, given certain interactional norms, may well infer that we are hungry. In certain traditions of literacy— especially those embodied in reading tests—readers are expected to resist making such inferences and restrict themselves to those that can be strictly justified.

Since real-world knowledge is used in creating both kinds of inferences, it cannot be used to distinguish between them. Indeed, in our ordinary experience of comprehension, what we read and what we know tend to form a seamless web. When children are encouraged to talk about their understanding of a passage, they often have difficulty in sorting out why they made a particular inference—for example, that the fawn was frightened. The children who focused on passage information when explaining this inference may have done so because they knew that this is the way to explain what one does on a test. In their actual experience, however, knowing that a fawn is likely to be frightened by people may have functioned as a crucial lens which highlighted certain parts of the passage.

Let us now consider EXTENDED INFERENCES. In reading about Alice and the fawn, a number of children inferred that the fawn must have been hurt in some way (e.g., one child said that "the fawn had a broken leg"). Obviously such an inference extends the text base a good deal more than the inference that Alice was trying to help the fawn. Yet even in making this extended inference, certain children found ways of put-

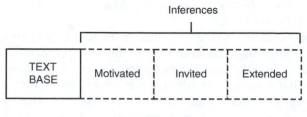

FIGURE 1.1

ting together their real-world knowledge—the fawn is an animal that ordinarily runs away from human beings—with one bit of passage information—this particular fawn did not run away from Alice. Once these two pieces of information were joined, the children were then in a position to infer that something must have happened to the fawn to prevent its running away. Just as a motivated inference cannot be sharply differentiated from an invited one, so an invited inference cannot be sharply differentiated from an extended one. Ultimately, the three kinds of inferences are best viewed as operating along a continuum (Figure 1.1), and judgments as to how to characterize a particular inference may well vary among people with different kinds of knowledge and experience.

The three kinds of inferences can be used to characterize three different situation models. Thus, a situation model that contains only motivated inferences can be considered a MOTIVATED SITUATION MODEL. Similarly, a situation model that contains at least one invited inference can be thought of as an INVITED SITUATION MODEL. Finally, an EXTENDED SITUATION MODEL is one that contains at least one extended inference.

As we continued to develop our framework, our thinking was enriched by other researchers who were beginning to use techniques of discourse analysis to take a close look at how children respond to reading tests (see, for example, Aronson & Farr, 1988; Freedle & Duran, 1987; Garcia, 1988; Haney & Scott, 1987; Johnston, 1984; Langer, 1987; Pearson & Valencia, 1987). Many of these researchers shared our concern with how ethnocultural norms of language, thought, and experience affect children's performance on these tests. During this period, we continued to conduct seminars in which graduate students helped us explore questions that had remained unanswered in the original research report. As students worked with this framework, we continued to refine it so that eventually it became a tool used to analyze reader interaction with other test material not only in this country but also abroad. A good deal of this research was brought together and presented from a policy perspective in a volume *From Testing to Assessment: English as an International Language* (Hill & Parry, 1994).

The objective of the present volume is to gather together and integrate all the work that has accumulated around the original corpus of test material. This undertaking has forced us to rethink much of the material so that it more faithfully reflects the broader policy perspective on testing and assessment that we have developed. At the conclusion of this volume we formulate a policy position on the basis of the research we have carried out. This position has been formulated in light of a recent proposal for a national reading test at the fourth-grade level. Such an ambitious plan raises basic policy questions that we address in the concluding chapter: Should such a national test be developed? If so, to what degree should it be based on the multiple-choice format? Or does such a test need to be supplemented with, or perhaps even replaced by, other forms of assessment?

METHODOLOGICAL REMARKS

We began the original research project in a graduate seminar that included students from various ethnocultural backgrounds. Our initial work was two-fold: (1) comprehensive textual analyses of the test units that had been pilot-tested at the third-grade level, and (2) exploratory interviewing of children after they had responded to the units. On the basis of the textual analyses, we developed various notions about why certain units might be difficult for children. The interviewing lent support to some of these notions, led us to modify or discard others, and uncovered other difficulties that we had not anticipated: there were more things in children's heads than were dreamt of in our text analyses.

We were then faced with the task of synthesizing what we had learned from these two activities. This took a good deal of time, for we were working out, unit by unit, the key issues that we would explore during the main stage of our research. It was during this period that we narrowed our group of units from 46 to a research corpus of 22. One reason for selecting 22 units was that this is the number of units used on a Gates-MacGinitie test at the third-grade level. We would thus be able to create a mock exam which we could administer to children who participated in the research. In addition, our experience during the exploratory interviewing had made it clear that children of this age can deal with only a limited number of units.

We followed two principles in narrowing down our corpus. First, we wanted to highlight those units in which developmental or ethnocultural problems were especially pronounced. In order to focus on such units, we used the results not only of our textual analyses and exploratory interviewing but of the initial pilot testing as well: for example, we tended to select units where the gap in performance between African American children and European American children had been especially pronounced. Second, we wanted a balanced representation of the range of units included on standardized tests of reading comprehension at this grade level. In selecting a unit, we thus attended to (1) the nature of the passage (e.g., whether it was narrative, descriptive, or expository); (2) the nature of the tasks (e.g., whether they were classified as literal or inferential); and (3) the interaction between passage and tasks (e.g., whether a narrative passage was followed by literal or inferential tasks).

In addition to these formal principles, we were guided by what we had learned informally about the individual units during the exploratory interviewing. We had discovered that certain units were more useful than others at uncovering what children do. We were not always able to explain why a particular unit was effective: with some, it was perhaps a matter of lively content; with others, it may have been the sheer difficulty that forced children to attend to how they responded. Whatever the reasons for children's greater engagement, we did select units that had, as it were, carried their weight during the exploratory interviewing.

Once we had established our final corpus, we were ready for the main stage of our research in which we (1) interviewed individual children to document various ways in which they responded to units in our corpus, and (2) administered experimental probes to representative groups of children to explore how widespread certain of these responses might be.

Hundreds of children have participated in this research over the years. Our primary means of contacting these children was through teachers who enrolled in research seminars at Teachers College. Sometimes they provided us direct access to children in their classrooms. At other times teachers who were familiar with our research methods conducted the interviews or probes themselves. Everyone who conducted research observed a basic principle: individual children who were interviewed did not participate in group probes. In this way the integrity of children's responses could be maintained, whether they were participating in an individual interview or a group probe.

Interviewing

Our interviewing usually involved three steps:

1) A mock exam of 22 units (see Appendix A) was administered without any set time limit.

2) While the child relaxed, the interviewer looked over the answers to see which units were most promising for exploration.

3) The child was interviewed, with a focus on the units that had been identified in step 2.

We began with notions about interviewing that owed much to Piaget. We were sympathetic to his reactions against experimental psychologists' demands that a standardized format of exactly worded questions be followed to insure comparability of results. Duckworth has conveniently summarized Piaget's reactions to these demands:

> Piaget and his researchers engage in a rather loose discussion with a child. The researcher has a number of key questions in mind, to be brought up in the standard order. But the phrasing of the questions and the ensuing discussions with the child depend on the child's reactions. Piaget is criticized by many psychologists for not having a standardized format—a fixed set of questions phrased in a fixed way so that exactly the same words are used with each child. The point of this standardization is to guarantee that each child is dealt with in the same way. But from Piaget's point of view standardizing the words has little to do with standardizing the problem for the children. The words are only a way to get the thinking going. There is no guarantee that the same words will cue in the same way for every child. It is important to vary the words used until they make contact with the child's thinking. Reaching the child is what has to be standard. Sticking rigidly to a fixed formula can almost guarantee a lack of standardization. (1987, p. 27)

At the beginning of our interviewing, we too were strongly committed to the notion of having "key questions in mind, to be brought up in the standard order." In fact, we developed questions and tasks to be explored with the child. It was understood, of course, that a certain flexibility was needed in order to take account of each child's responses. Questions varied, for example, according to whether the child selected the target response or one of the distractors. Here is the initial interview guide for the unit about Alice and the fawn, which we have already presented (see p. 9):

1) Ask children to read the passage aloud.
2) Ask children to retell the story without looking at the passage.
3) Ask children to read (A) and (B) and respond to each.
4) Returning to (A), ask children why they picked the answer they did.
5) Explore the process by which children arrived at their response by asking follow-up questions. Some possibilities are:
   a) Does the story say so or did you just know?

b) Do you think any of the other answers are good ones?

c) What does the word *it* refer to in the story?

d) What does *she* refer to?

e) When did the fawn's eyes look _____?
   (insert in the blank the word(s) chosen by children)

6) Now explore the process by which children arrived at the answer to (B). Possible follow-up questions include the following:

   a) Does the story say so or did you just know?

   b) Are any of the other answers good ones?

   c) What does *stroke* mean? Can you use it in a sentence?

   d) Do you know what a fawn is?

7) When you think you have obtained as much information as you can with specific questions, ask broader questions such as the following:

   a) If there were no answers here to choose from, if there was just the question by itself, what answer would you give? (first for (A) and then for (B))

   b) Do you remember ever reading this story before?

   c) What does the story say about the fawn's eyes?

   d) What do you think the fawn's eyes really looked like?

   e) What does the story say that Alice tried to do to the fawn?

   f) What was Alice really trying to do to the fawn?

We found such guides to be invaluable, but as we progressed with the interviewing, we became less concerned with bringing up "key questions" in a "standard order." We increasingly came to rely upon the interpersonal relations that emerged with the individual child. We came to appreciate that the kinds of questioning that were productive with some children were not necessarily appropriate for others. We also came to realize that many children were aware of whether we were responding to what they had experienced or were merely working through our list of questions. In analyzing our interviews, we became aware that we often lost valuable information when we attempted to pursue a list of questions rather than working with what children gave us.

Moreover, we became aware that children have a limited capacity for reflecting upon their own experience. While they may at first be attracted to a certain kind of adult talk, they soon lose patience; and so we began to concentrate on those areas where children seemed to have access to their experience. This meant that other areas simply had to be ignored. We were still committed to the notion that, as interviewers, we should be maximally aware of all the problems inherent in the test unit under discussion, but we realized that our interviewing would be more effective if we were free to pursue whatever emerged with the individual child. Moreover, at the end of such interviewing, we found that we had often managed to deal with the key questions, but that they had emerged collaboratively. Once our control had been lessened, it was the children who often brought up the questions that we were concerned with.

We should note here our sympathy for the ethnomethodological critique of interviewing within a traditional paradigm of research—that such interviewing does not sufficiently draw on the indigenous categories of those being interviewed (Briggs, 1986; Mischler, 1986). Accommodating these categories is clearly fundamental to interviewing; and yet we have reservations about the strong version of the ethnomethodological position, namely, that interviewers are to eschew their own categories, working only with those provided by the interviewees. This position is virtually impossible to maintain whenever those being interviewed lack well-developed categories about the subject matter at hand. Third graders have not done much thinking about how a reading test works, even though many are quite aware of the powerful influence it can have on their lives. But even in the best of circumstances total avoidance of one's own categories is a methodological fiction and even to pursue it as an ideal may only lead interviewers to introduce their own categories more deviously. Moreover, those being interviewed may well perceive such avoidance as violating the give-and-take norms of conversation and so avoid introducing their own categories as well. An interview is, after all, a form of conversation, and any radical deviation from the norms of everyday talk may have unwanted effects (see Hill & Anderson, 1993 for more detailed discussion of these matters).

We would like to discuss two additional problems we encountered in our interviewing. First, we soon became aware that children, when questioned about a particular answer, tend to assume that it was wrong. As a consequence, they often take up a defensive stance or even shift to another answer—at times, the target response—right on the spot. This assumption of a wrong answer was, in fact, warranted, since our research strategy was to focus on tasks for which children had selected what we refer to as a SYMPTOMATIC DISTRACTOR (i.e., one that may reveal a broader pattern in the child's approach to test-taking). In order to counteract this tendency, we began by explaining to them that we weren't interested in "whether they got the answer right but how they went about choosing it." We would then question them about one or two tasks where they had selected the target response. In this way we could help them build up confidence in their own thinking before we moved on to tasks where they had selected a distractor.

Our second problem had to do with the natural inclination of the interviewer to function as a teacher. We were initially committed to the principle of working strictly with what children brought to the test unit: hence if they did not understand a unit, we attempted to resist our instincts to guide them toward a better understanding. As we analyzed the exploratory interviews, we became aware of the subtle ways in which our pedagogical instincts came naturally into play. Rather than attempting to banish those instincts, we reconciled ourselves to them. Investigating children's differing capacities for gaining help from an interview became a matter that concerned us, and we have occasion to analyze such differences when we present the results of our research. In our concluding chapter, we refer to a model that Feuerstein (1977) describes as DYNAMIC ASSESSMENT, in which test takers' capacities to work with such help is part of what is evaluated.

One final word about interviewing: we have no illusions that children—or, for that matter, adults—can report comprehensively on what takes place when they read. Reading is such a complex activity that most of it is necessarily conducted out-of-awareness; readers are thus not in a position to reconstruct what happens during their actual experience of reading. Even if children could perform such reconstruction, they would not necessarily be able to talk about it during an interview. An interview makes its own demands on what is said and what is left unsaid, and these demands are radically shaped by the interaction between the child and the interviewer. Despite all these constraints, we still find that children's struggle during an interview to reconstruct their initial act of reading provides rich information; and if this information is used judiciously, it opens up possibilities of understanding their reading that can be gained in no other way.

Group Probes

We conducted two major kinds of experimental probes with groups of children:

1) those concerned with what children *know* about some particular feature of a unit (hereafter referred to as KNOWLEDGE PROBES); and
2) those concerned with what children *do* when a test unit is presented in a different way (hereafter referred to as PERFORMANCE PROBES).

The first kind of probe deals primarily with children's REAL-WORLD SCHEMAS, the second with their TEXTUAL SCHEMAS.

We can use the unit about Alice and the fawn (see p. 9) to illustrate these two kinds of probes. As to a knowledge probe, we asked children who had not seen the unit to define words like *fawn* and *stroke*. In probing for children's knowledge of *stroke*, we used two different approaches. We used a relatively unstructured probe, simply asking children to use the word *stroke* in a sentence. We also used a more structured probe to find out whether children would find a sentence acceptable in which the

Here are some sentences that contain the word *stroke*. Circle the number of each sentence that uses this word in a correct way.

1. Homer's granddad had a stroke.
2. Homer went out on the golf course to practice his strokes.
3. Homer ate all the delicious strokes on his plate.
4. Homer's mother told him to stroke the kitten gently.
5. The recipe said to beat the cake batter 100 strokes.

FIGURE 1.2

word *stroke* is used in the same way as it is in the test passage (Figure 1.2).

As to a performance probe, we presented an altered task (B) in which the underlying intent was expressed straightforwardly:

What did Alice try to   →   In the story, the word
do to the fawn?   "stroke" means _____.

We presented this performance probe in two versions. In one version four choices were provided, but in the other children filled in the blank on their own.

To give a further sense of the difference between knowledge probes and performance probes, we provide here a representative sample of each kind (children generally responded to both kinds of probes in writing, though, on occasion, we did audiorecord oral responses):

Knowledge probes

1) Children focus on the meaning of a word (as illustrated by the probe on *stroke*).
2) Children tell what they know about some feature of punctuation such as quotation marks.
3) Children interpret what a particular sentence means.
4) Children evaluate whether a particular sentence sounds all right, and if not, try to explain why it doesn't.
5) Children tell what they know about a particular topic.
6) Children draw a picture or describe a picture in relation to what they have read.

Performance probes

1) Children respond to a task with some feature changed in it (as illustrated by the probe for task (B) above).
2) Children read the initial portion of a passage and then complete it.
3) Children read the passage and then extend it.

4) Children recall a passage and/or tasks.
5) Children make up tasks after reading the passage.
6) Children draw the scene they imagined while reading.

A final word of caution about our use of probes—so many of them were conducted that we were unable to insist upon the standards that would be used in administering more formal experiments. We were generally not able to pilot test them in order to improve their substance or design; nor did we select participants according to random procedures. Rather we conducted probes with children in metropolitan New York as various opportunities developed. Typically, a teacher would administer a probe in a single classroom, and so the number of children involved is generally around 25 to 30. At times, a probe was administered to a single group of European American children in order to provide some kind of a baseline. At other times, a probe was administered to contrasting ethnocultural groups in the same school (e.g., African American children and European American children). At other times, a probe was administered to a similar ethnocultural group in contrasting socioeconomic settings (e.g., African American children in both an inner-city school and a suburban school). In certain instances, we administered a probe not only to third and fourth graders but also to older children or even adults so that we could establish a baseline from which to evaluate the younger children's responses. The adult probes were conducted with graduate students in language and literacy courses at Teachers College, Columbia University. We focused on the responses of native speakers of English, though occasionally we examined the responses of non-native speakers, especially when they shed light on relevant background knowledge needed to respond to a specific unit.

We caution the reader to bear all these factors in mind when evaluating the results of the various probes. They were designed to provide working ideas about what children know and can do with respect to our corpus of test units. Used judiciously, they can provide insights into possible differences, on the one hand, between children and adults and, on the other, between children who belong to different groups, as defined by features such as gender, ethnocultural identity, and socioeconomic class. As already observed, such broad categories cannot capture the complexity of individual identity and so must be used with great care.

THE FORMAT OF STANDARDIZED READING TESTS

At this point a brief characterization of the format of standardized reading tests may be helpful. The Gates-MacGinitie Reading Tests are one of a handful of testing programs that have been widely used to compare the reading achievement of individual students, classes, schools, and school districts with national norms. One reviewer has suggested that they are "a prototype of the contemporary standardized reading test" (Calfee, 1987, p. 593). The range of tests provided in the Gates-MacGinitie program can be found in Table 1.1.

The units that constitute our corpus were prepared for the comprehension section of Level C, which is intended primarily for use with third graders or beginning fourth graders, but is also used "out of level" with older children whose reading is below average. This section consists of 22 passages, each followed by two multiple-choice tasks. The test is not intended to reward speed. It has been formulated so that in the 35 minutes allowed "most children will have time to try all the units" (MacGinitie, 1978b, p. 30). The comprehension sections of Levels D, E, and F are similar except that they contain fewer passages and the number of tasks per passage varies. Form 2 of Level F, for example, contains 14 passages and there are from two to five tasks for each. Considering the difference in reading speed between third graders and high school students, it is surprising that the total number of words in the passages in Level F(2) is only slightly higher than the total for Level C(1)—1,272 as opposed to 1,098. Clearly, even a slow reader will use only a fraction

TABLE 1.1

Test Level (Forms)	Designed for Grade	Number of Tasks		Testing Time (in minutes)
R (1,2)	1,0–1,9	54		About 65 minutes (given in 2 sessions)
A (1,2)	1,5–1,9	Vocabulary	45	20
		Comprehension	40	35
B (1,2)	2	Vocabulary	45	20
		Comprehension	40	35
C (1,2)	3	Vocabulary	45	20
		Comprehension	44	35
D (1,2,3)	4–6	Vocabulary	45	20
		Comprehension	43	35
E (1,2,3)	7–9	Vocabulary	45	20
		Comprehension	43	35
F (1,2)	10–12	Vocabulary	45	20
		Comprehension	43	35

Source: MacGinitie, 1978b, p. 59.

of the time available in the initial reading of the passages. The bulk of the time spent on a test is taken up with reading the tasks, considering alternative answers, and rereading the passages for crucial information.

The format of a standardized reading test is a compromise between several objectives. The fundamental goal is that the test be valid and reliable. Other things being equal, the validity and reliability of a test increase when there are more units and a greater variety of unit types, since the result depends less on any particular unit. Pressures to make tests longer and more complex are counterbalanced, however, by practical considerations. To maintain reliability, a test must be uniformly administered by teachers who have no special training beyond the directions in the manual, and this is more likely to be achieved if a test uses a simple format that is familiar to teachers and students. With respect to length, the longer a test becomes, the more difficult it is to fit it into the school routine. The ideal is a test that takes no longer than a class period, including the 10 to 15 minutes necessary for distributing materials, giving instructions, and completing practice units.

One effect of these various constraints on format is that the texts to be comprehended are extremely brief. If it has been determined that there must be 44 tasks and that there should only be two tasks per unit and that they must be completed in 35 minutes, there is no alternative. The average length of a passage in Forms 1 and 2 of Level C is just under 50 words, with the longest containing 73 words and the shortest only 23 words.

The passages used are intended to reflect the "kinds of material that most communities hope their children will learn, will read, and will enjoy reading." (MacGinitie, 1978b, p. 31) The subject matter of the passages has been distributed at different test levels according to the general plan summarized in Table 1.2.

Narrative-descriptive is presumably a cover term for fictional passages. In the plan outlined above, the amount of narrative-descriptive material

TABLE 1.2

Content Area	Percentage of Comprehension Passages					
	A	B	C	D	E	F
Narrative–Descriptive	85	70	55	40	32.5	32.5
Social Sciences	10	15	20	27.5	32.5	32.5
Natural Sciences	5	15	20	27.5	25	25
The Arts	0	0	5	5	10	10

Source: MacGinitie, 1978b, p. 59.

decreases with each level, while the amount of expository material from the social sciences, the natural sciences, and the arts increases. From our point of view, this plan confounds two different principles of classification: one based on discourse mode—narrative, descriptive, expository—and one based on the status of the information conveyed—fictional or factual. We would prefer a system of classification that keeps these two principles separate, as shown in Figure 1.3. This classification makes clear that while expository passages can be presumed to be factual, narrative-descriptive passages are not necessarily fictional. Indeed, the historical anecdote, which is both narrative and factual, appears frequently on reading comprehension tests, probably because it is a form that can be kept brief.

The tasks in the Gates-MacGinitie Tests are divided into two categories, literal and inferential. A literal task is concerned with "something that is explicitly stated in the passage; it involves a restatement or a paraphrase." An inferential task, on the other hand, is concerned with "something that is only implied in the passage" (MacGinitie, 1978b, p. 32). The two kinds of tasks have been distributed so that the proportion of inferential tasks increases with each level, as shown in Table 1.3.

These two categories are widely used in describing comprehension tasks, and yet the criteria used to decide which category a task belongs in are not obvious. When we have asked graduate students to categorize test units according to the definitions above, there has been a marked lack of agreement. Greater unanimity would, no doubt, be possible if they were given specific training in applying the criteria. Nevertheless, their difficulties do point to a fuzziness in this commonly held distinction. As indicated by our earlier discussion of text base and situation model, we have developed a more fine-grained approach to inferencing in this study.

We should note that the Gates-MacGinitie tests use the distinction between literal and inferential only as a guide in preparing units. They do not use these categories to produce separate scores, as do other test-

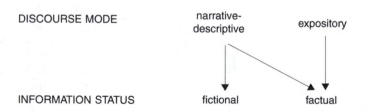

FIGURE 1.3

TABLE 1.3

	Percentage of Questions					
	A	B	C	D	E	F
Literal	90	80	65	55	55	55
Inferential	10	20	35	45	45	45

Source: MacGinitie, 1978b, p. 59.

ing programs that provide subscores not only for literal and inferential skills but even other skills such as finding the main idea. Such schemes are suspect on at least two grounds: the subscores are based on too few units to be reliable, and the units used are not valid measures of specific skills (Calfee, 1987). For a discussion of difficulties that arise from the use of such diagnostic schemes with multiple-choice tests, see Hill and Parry (1988, 1989).

AUTHENTICITY OF THE CORPUS

Having described the corpus and the context for which it was prepared, we are now in a position to address the question of how the units in the corpus differ from the ones actually used in the published tests. Or to pose the question more pointedly, is there some way in which the units in the corpus differ from those in the published tests that might affect the outcome of our research?

After exploring this question from various points of view, we eventually came to the conclusion that the majority of the units in our corpus were not found to be deficient but were simply left over. To understand how this might come about, we need to look at the unit-selection process from the test makers' point of view.

To begin with, we need to think about three different kinds of criteria that are involved:

1) goals for passage content and task type (implementing the benchmarks for Level C covered in the preceding section would produce a test in which 12 of 22 units would be narrative-descriptive, 4-5 would be devoted to social science, 4-5 to natural science, and one to the arts, and in which 29 of 44 tasks would be literal and 15 inferential);
2) tasks that are free of psychometric flaws or cultural bias; and
3) tasks that represent the range of difficulty required to achieve maximum differentiation (in the published tests, tasks range from those

which were answered correctly by 87 percent of the norming group to those that were answered correctly by only 11 percent).

While the test makers would try to satisfy all these criteria when writing units and selecting those to be pilot tested, they would not know whether they had succeeded in developing enough units to satisfy all the criteria until after the pilot testing. We can imagine situations in which they end up with an abundance of social science passages and a paucity of natural science passages. To avoid such problems, one could write and pilot test a much larger number of units, but the extra time and expense involved makes this impractical. In fact, test makers look at potential units very closely before pilot testing; only those that are regarded as serious candidates for the final test are included.

The great majority of the passages supplied to us were bunched towards the upper levels of difficulty required by the test design. It is not that they were more difficult than some of the units used on the published tests but rather that there were relatively few slots available for units of such difficulty. Hence, they were not used because few units of such difficulty were required. In addition, they may have been passed over because they deal, say, with social science and five such units had already been selected, or they have two literal tasks, and the guidelines required a unit with one literal and one inferential task.

Given the complexities involved, it is not surprising that even adults who are experienced in writing for third graders might tend to produce units that are more difficult than intended. In any case, this difficulty largely disappears with more mature readers. With one notable exception, the units in our corpus were answered correctly by virtually all of the adults who tried them. In addition, these units demonstrated face validity during the research; no one, either a child or an adult, ever questioned their authenticity. In fact, adults often volunteered something to the effect that these units were just like the ones they remembered puzzling over in elementary school.

Now to answer the question with which this section began:

1) The average difficulty of the units in the corpus was substantially higher than that of the units used in the published tests.

2) Two or three of the units showed a sufficiently large gap in the performance of African American and European American children during the pilot testing that they would probably not have been used.

3) Two or three units showed such a low biserial correlation that they would probably not have been used.[4]

4) One unit is clearly flawed, as indicated by adult readers' difficulties; the defect is, however, well camouflaged, and it is not clear that any of the ordinary procedures for selecting units would have excluded it.

Thus, the most distinctive feature of the units in the corpus is their high average difficulty, and we eventually came to think of this as an advantage. As the research progressed, we were continually surprised at what the children were able to communicate during the interviews. We became increasingly aware that it was the difficulty of the units that led to such remarkable struggles for comprehension and to the corresponding richness of the recalls. Researchers into the writing process who use think-aloud techniques have reported a similar phenomenon: unconventional writing assignments produce richer and more complete protocols (Flower & Hayes, 1980). Evidently, more familiar tasks activate largely automatic processes which remain out of awareness and thus unavailable for report.

Although we were concerned about the authenticity of our corpus in the early stages of the research, there came a point at which this question receded. As the research developed, we became increasingly confident that the results of individual interviews and group probes were not confined to the particular units in our corpus but rather represented patterns that were inherent in the use of the multiple-choice technique to assess something as complex and as context-sensitive as reading comprehension.

DEFINITION OF TERMS

There is no agreed upon terminology for referring to the machinery of reading comprehension tests. We have introduced certain terms of our own while retaining others that are commonly used. We refer to the combination of an individual text and the questions that follow it as a TEST UNIT, or simply a UNIT. We have introduced this term in order to call attention to a feature of reading tests that is often overlooked: it is the passage and the tasks together—and not just the passage in isolation—that constitute the text to be comprehended. Many test makers, who use the term *item* to refer to a task, end up using the cumbersome term *item set* to refer to the passage and tasks as a whole. In actual practice, those who talk about tests seldom use this term; rather they use *item* indiscriminately to refer to both the individual task and the combination of a passage and tasks.

As for the two major parts of the test unit, we use the terms already established in this chapter—PASSAGE and TASKS. We distinguish between the two tasks in a unit by referring to them simply as (A) and (B). As for the two parts of the task, the first part we call the STEM, whether it is a question or a sentence to be completed. The second part—the suggested answers—we generally refer to as CHOICES. We call the choice designated as correct by the test makers the TARGET RESPONSE (the term *key* is often used); the choices they designate as incorrect we call DISTRACTORS. Figure 1.4 shows the relationships between these basic terms.

From a formal point of view, the various tasks can be divided into two groups: (1) COMPLETION TASKS, in which the student is given the initial part of an incomplete statement and the four choices represent possibilities for completing the statement; (2) and QUESTION TASKS, in which the student is asked a question and the four choices represent possible answers. The following unit provides an example of each type:

> The trap-door spider lives in a burrow that it digs in the ground. It lines the burrow with silk that it has spun. A tightly fitting door of silk and mud closes the burrow at the entrance.
>
> A. This spider lines its burrow with
>
> mud   grass
> silk   cotton
>
> B. What part of the burrow gives this spider its name?
>
> the entrance   the floor
> the web   the lining

In completion tasks the word or phrase used to complete the stem is called the COMPLETER. When the target response is used as a completer, the stem and the completer together form the TARGET PROPOSITION. The target proposition for (A) above would be:

> This spider lines its burrow with silk.

Correspondingly, when a distractor is the completer, the incomplete statement and the distractor form a DISTRACTOR PROPOSITION. The three possible distractor propositions for (A) above are:

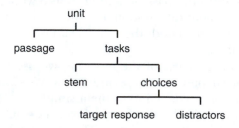

FIGURE 1.4

This spider lines its burrow with mud.
This spider lines its burrow with grass.
This spider lines its burrow with cotton.

With a question task, the target proposition consists of the "long answer" that contains the target response (i.e., the answer that is maximally redundant). For (B) above the target proposition would be:

The entrance is the part of the burrow that gives this spider its name.

The distractor propositions for (B) would be:

The floor is the part of the burrow that gives this spider its name.
The web is the part of the burrow that gives this spider its name.
The lining is the part of the burrow that gives this spider its name.

In addition to these terms for referring to the basic machinery of reading tests, we have developed a distinctive terminology for describing various features of text structure and reader response. Some of these terms have already been used (e.g., those having to do with inferencing on pages 9–11). All technical terms are printed in small capital letters when they are introduced; they can also be found in the Glossary (see page 401).

PRESENTATION OF THE RESEARCH

For each of the test units in our corpus, we have attempted to bring together various kinds of data collected over the years and weave them into a coherent account. We generally begin with data relevant to the passage: (1) where it came from (e.g., if it was excerpted from published material, how it was adapted for the test), (2) what kind of genre it belongs to, (3) how it is rhetorically structured, and (4) which features—both local and global—are difficult for young readers. We then turn to the tasks and weave together various kinds of relevant data: (1) contrasts in the performance of African American and European American children during the pilot testing, (2) excerpts from interviews with individual children, and (3) results of experimental probes conducted with children and, in certain instances, with older students and even adults.

One advantage of presenting the data in close proximity to the unit that stimulated them is that a considerable amount of detail can be included without putting too much burden on the reader. Another advantage of such presentation is that it allows us to bring to the surface and examine closely all the fine detail that ordinarily remains out of awareness during reading. From our own perspective, this complexity sheds a useful light on the gap between what takes place during everyday comprehension and what constitutes comprehension on a reading test.

Our extended analysis of each test unit is also a useful reminder of the many different kinds of response that a short text can engender in children from various ethnocultural backgrounds. One of the most valuable aspects of this research is that it allows us to observe hundreds of children reading the same corpus of test material.

There is, however, a disadvantage in presenting the units one by one: material relevant to a particular issue in testing or reading comprehension may appear in more than one place. We have sought to alleviate this difficulty by judicious cross-referencing, thorough indexing, and the inclusion of a glossary of special terms. We have also included a summary chapter in which the most important findings of the study are brought together and presented from a policy perspective. To facilitate cross-referencing, we have given each unit a name based on a salient aspect of its content. These names are always printed in small capital letters (e.g., ALICE AND THE FAWN). Readers should bear in mind that these names are for mnemonic purposes and are not part of the actual test units.

In all, we have provided comprehensive accounts of 18 of the 22 units in our corpus. The 4 remaining units, which were less productive, are discussed briefly in connection with one of the main units. The 18 main units have been divided into two groups. The 8 units in which the passage is a fictional narrative are presented in Part II, Testing Reader Parsimony, which focuses on the ways that children respond to various kinds of incompleteness. The remaining 10 units—6 of which can be classified as expository, 2 as descriptive, and 2 as historical narrative— are presented in Part III, Testing Reader Flexibility, which focuses on children's capacity to handle certain textual complexities that test makers have come to rely on when developing test units.

In presenting our research to various audiences, we have found that an effective approach is to begin by asking members of the audience to respond to one or more of the test units to be discussed. By stimulating them to produce their own data, we encourage them to abandon the role of observer and become a participant, both as a reader and as a researcher. Each of the accounts in this book begins with the text of the unit to be discussed. We hope that readers will pause to interact with each unit, maintaining as much awareness as possible of how they respond to it. This initial bit of self-produced data provides a useful starting point for considering what many other readers—children and adults alike—have made of the same text. We encourage any reader who would like to simulate the child's experience of a reading test to turn to Appendix A and respond to all 22 units (target responses are identified in Appendix B, which contains the results of the pilot testing).

NOTES

1. We use the term *test unit*, or simply *unit*, to describe the combination of a passage and multiple-choice tasks. In a later section of this chapter, Definition of Terms (p. 25–27), we provide a rationale for our use of this term.
2. Computer-based testing can speed up the process of differentiation by using a test taker's performance on one test unit to determine whether the following one should be easier or more difficult.
3. In a study of coaching schools in Taiwan, Lin (1993) reported a range of strategies that are taught to improve student performance on the TOEFL. One of the more ingenious strategies was teaching candidates to mail their applications from certain areas within Taiwan in order to increase their chances of being assigned to test taking centers that not only had superior playback equipment but also the least amount of external noise (e.g., it was particularly important to avoid a center near the international airport that could seriously interfere with student performance on the listening component of the test).
4. It is difficult to be precise on points (2) and (3), since exact cut-off points were not established with respect to either ethnocultural differences or biserial correlation.

Part II

Testing Reader Parsimony

In Chapter 1 we remarked on the brevity of the passages used in the units of our corpus. We suggested that this brevity results from an effort to achieve a balance between two antithetical goals: the psychometric goal of maximizing validity and reliability and the practical goal of providing a test that can be administered in a single class period. In Part II of this study, we present eight units from our corpus that contain narrative passages. We will begin by considering how narratives can be made brief enough to fit the test format.

The shortest of the eight passages is only 37 words long, while the longest contains 78 words. A question that naturally occurs is "What kind of story can you tell in 78 words, let alone 37?" A brief answer is "Not a very exciting one." But before we consider the consumer's point of view, let us speculate on the options open to those who prepare test units.

Ideally, test passages should represent the kinds of reading that children are expected to do in school and at home. Since narratives of less than a hundred words are not common in these environments, passages are frequently taken from longer pieces. There are two possibilities. One is that a passage will consist of the beginning of a longer narrative. Here is an example:

> One day many years ago, Dr. Wye came along the Salem Road. Dust was all over the buggy top, all over the big gray plodding horse, and all over the doctor's hat and coat. He was tired and drowsy, but you would not have guessed it, for he sat up straight and solid.

The formulaic *One day many years ago* clearly marks this passage as the inception of a narrative. The total effect is to set a scene:

Time:	many years ago before automobiles were common
Place:	a rural area
Protagonist:	Dr. Wye, the kind of man who sits up straight even when nodding off

Setting up the scene leaves little space for actual narration and so the reader is left wondering what might happen next. We describe this kind of passage as TRUNCATED and present two examples of it in Chapter 2.

The second possibility for drawing a test passage from a longer piece is that it will represent something other than the beginning:

> Hans found himself in a pretty pickle in the chimney. The soot got into his eye and set it to watering, and into his nose and set him to sneezing, and into his mouth and his ears and his hair. Still he struggled on, up and up. "Every chimney has a top," said Hans to himself, "and I am sure to climb out somewhere or other."

Here readers may wonder not only what will happen next but what has already happened. Certainly they are justified in feeling they should have been told how Hans came to be in this predicament. We use the term EXCERPTED to refer to passages like this one that cause the reader to wonder what has already happened. We present three examples of excerpted passages in Chapter 3.

An alternative to selecting a test unit from a larger narrative is to construct one that seems to be complete. Here is a passage that manages to convey the sense of a whole story—beginning, middle, and end:

> Using wires, magnets, and electric batteries, Alexander Graham Bell began to build models of an invention he called the telephone. None of his ideas worked. Then one day Bell's assistant happened to pull a small spring connected to their latest model. In another room, listening into the receiver, Bell heard a faint "twang." It was the first sound ever heard over a telephone line.

We cannot be certain whether the test makers wrote this passage from scratch or adapted it from existing material. Whichever strategy they followed, the result is much the same: the kind of narrative often referred to as an anecdote. First, a background situation is sketched in from which the reader must infer who Alexander Graham Bell is—the inventor of the telephone—and when all this took place—before there were telephones, whenever that was. The reader is then told about a specific action—pulling a small spring—and why this action is remembered—it was the first sound ever heard over a telephone.

Clearly something must be sacrificed if the semblance of a complete story is to be achieved with so few words. What tends to be left out is the kind of connecting detail that a reader is accustomed to. Consider, for example, the relations between the first two sentences. Sentence 1 reports that Bell began to build models of a telephone. The use of *began to* leads a reader to expect to be told something about what these models were like, how they differed from each other, or at least to find out how long Bell worked on them. But sentence 2 does not build on these expectations; instead it reports only that none of Bell's ideas worked. It is as though a large gap emerges between the two sentences, one that a reader must fill in. As the writer moves ahead at a rapid pace, a comparable gap emerges between sentences 2 and 3, and the reader must suppress any expectation of finding out why nothing worked. We use the term GAPPED to refer to passages that omit information a reader, based on previous experience with similar texts, has been conditioned to expect. We present three examples of gapped passages in Chapter 4.

We might note here that the term gapped, depending as it does on such variables as what writers decide to include and what readers tend to expect, must be understood in relative terms. With respect to our corpus, the passages are so brief that all of them can be seen as gapped in one way or another. Generally speaking, truncated and excerpted passages do manage to provide the kind of sensate detail a child needs in order to imagine the physical scene. In the truncated passage above, dust is everywhere:

> all over the buggy top, all over the big gray plodding horse, and all over the doctor's hat and coat.

In the excerpted narrative, it is soot that is everywhere:

> The soot got into his eye and set it to watering, and into his nose and set him to sneezing, and into his mouth and his ears and his hair.

There is virtually no room for this kind of elaboration in gapped passages.

chapter 2

Truncated Narratives

I n describing our three-way classification of narrative passages—
truncated, excerpted, and gapped—we did not mean to imply that
it would always be easy to decide which category to place a particular passage in. Certain passages seem to straddle two categories. Consider, for example, whether the following passage is better viewed as
truncated or excerpted:

> The thunder rumbled again, almost as though it were in the earth instead
> of the sky, making the house tremble a little. And then slowly, one by one,
> as if someone were dropping pennies on the roof, came the raindrops. A
> noise of wind stirred in the leaves, and then the rain burst strong and loud
> upon the world.

This passage can be viewed as simply beginning a story and thus be classified as truncated. It can also be viewed as an internal paragraph, which
would make it excerpted. Many writers try to capture a reader's attention by starting in the middle of things and only then do they give the
background information that is needed for a fuller understanding. On
the basis of the available evidence, we are not able to decide which is the
better classification.

There is not likely to be any disagreement about how we have classified the first narrative in this chapter; the second one, however, may
occasion some disagreement. In the final analysis, what is important is
not what a passage is, but rather how individual readers take it, what
they do in response to its inherent incompleteness.

SHOP SIGN

We begin with a truncated narrative that was particularly difficult for children:

Its first appearance sent a flutter of excitement through the street. It was only a shop sign, made up of white lettering on a sky-blue background. It announced that Mrs. Doyle was a dealer in candies, homemade taffies, confectionery, and sundries. The "sundries" was a mystery to most of the admirers of the sign, but they assumed it meant something at least as delicious as caramel.

A.   What was the mystery?
   an appearance   the caramel
   a woman   a word

B.   The story is mainly about
   candies   a shop
   a sign   Mrs. Doyle

Rather than telling a story, this passage only manages to get one underway. In fact, the entire passage can be viewed as an example of a fictional technique that is commonly used to launch a story. A single object—in this instance a shop sign—is introduced, leaving readers to wonder why. Their curiosity may be heightened by the way in which the object is presented. It is evoked in the first sentence, but not actually named until the second. Moreover, the message conveyed by the shop sign is rather obscure. The final word on the sign—*sundries*—is described as *a mystery to most of the admirers of the sign*. This bit of mystery is perhaps emblematic of larger ones circulating in the air: just who is Mrs. Doyle, and why has she become a dealer in candies?

Just as their curiosity is aroused, readers find that they are at the end of the story. In (A) they are asked "What was the mystery?" For this task, the pilot testing conducted by the test makers yielded the results shown in Table 2.1. The African American and European American children's patterns of response were quite similar. Both groups viewed the three distractors, particularly *the caramel* and *an appearance,* as representing more of a mystery than the target response *a word*. The proportion of children in both groups who selected the target response was well below chance on both tasks in this unit (i.e., less than 25 percent in a unit with four choices).[1]

There are several characteristics of (A) that might help account for these results. To begin with, the task itself is elliptical. A fuller form would make clear that the question has to do with the point of view of

TABLE 2.1

	African American	European American
an appearance	36%	31%
the caramel	36%	34%
a woman	22%	20%
a word	7%	16%

the townspeople, perhaps something like "What did the admirers of the sign think was a mystery?" The elliptical form of the task apparently encouraged some children to take the word *mystery* as referring to their own experience. The form of the verb—the fact that *was* is used rather than *is*—should prevent this interpretation, but children often will not pick up on such a low-profile signal.

Once we take the perspective of a reader rather than that of the townspeople, the story bristles with possibilities for mystery. Indeed, the fact that the story is unfinished leaves everything up in the air. At first glance, a woman might be seen as representing the most mystery, given that the owner of the shop is so provocatively described. Some children, however, were not able to relate *a woman* to Mrs. Doyle, probably because of the elliptical nature of this distractor. A more explicit version—something like "a woman named Mrs. Doyle"—would have made this connection clearer. Even if children could make the connection, they were likely to be puzzled by the various things that Mrs. Doyle was a dealer in. If so, the word *dealer*, left standing on its own, would be suggestive to children who watch TV, especially those who live in the inner city. In fact, an irreverent adult reader, pointing out that sundries can be pins and needles, suggested that Mrs. Doyle might well be supplying needles not used to sew on buttons or darn socks.

From a certain vantage point, *an appearance* represents the least mysterious element in the narrative. Readers are directly told about the shop sign and what it says. Still, a number of children seemed to align the words *mystery* and *appearance*, as illustrated by the following exchange between an interviewer (I) and a child (C):[2]

I   Why did you choose *an appearance?*
C   In the passage it was mentioned that *sundries* was a mystery. It means mystery was what *sundries* is, and this means the appearance of the sundries was a mystery. People tried to find out an appearance of *sundries*—what it is.

I   Do you know the meaning of *sundries?*
C   No, not quite.
I   Can you guess?
C   Well, it might be something as delicious as caramel, right?

Certainly, the manner in which the sign conveys information is mysterious. Most of the townspeople do not know the word *sundries,* and we might guess that some of them, like the children we interviewed, have trouble with *confectionery.* In any case, there doesn't seem to have been any mystery before the sign, so its appearance can well be taken as causing the mystery—which, of course, is not very far from *being* the mystery. In any case, it is more inclusive of the possibilities for mystery than any of the other choices. One boy told us that he chose *an appearance* "because the mystery was the whole thing—the woman, the sign, everything."

We are, once again, dealing with an elliptical distractor. Shortening *the appearance of a shop sign* to *an appearance* made it possible for some children to interpret this response as referring not to the advent of the sign in the town but rather to the physical appearance of the sign. When one child was asked why she made this choice, she answered "Well, I think that sign had a very strange appearance." She then talked about its coloring, but finally referred to the information it contained. She viewed *sundries* as only one among many mysterious words on the sign.

Another child related her choice of *appearance* to her lack of knowledge of the word *sundries:*

I chose *appearance* because I didn't know what *sundries* meant....I thought it was a type of candy that was sort of like caramel....They said it as if it was a separate kind of candy.

When the interviewer asked her why she hadn't chosen *caramel,* she replied:

I chose *appearance* because mostly the admirers of the sign—they were looking at the appearance of the sundries....In some way they were mystified by the appearance of the word sundries.

As indicated by her language, she is rather grownup in her choice of words; indeed, one might speculate that she was partly attracted to *appearance* because of its sophisticated sound. Certainly, the word is in keeping with the overall tone of the passage. Throughout this study we will have ample opportunity to observe children choosing a word because it, as one of them put it, "sounds like a word used on a test." We can describe such children as using a SOUNDS-RIGHT STRATEGY.

Finally, we were able to observe some children as interpreting *an appearance* in the context of such words as *mystery, flutter,* and *excitement.* They seemed to view these words as signifying something not quite real. As one child explained:

> It says here that "Its first appearance sent a flutter of excitement"—and you don't know what it is. That's the mystery.

The mystery that children found in *the caramel* was of a very different kind. A number of them stumbled over this word when they were asked to read the passage aloud. Many were familiar with the word in spoken form, but they often pronounced it as a two-syllable word ['kar·məl] and could not easily connect it with the three-syllable written form.

Children may have also been drawn to this distractor for a mechanical reason: it is the only one of the choices that is preceded by *the* rather than *a* or *an.*[3] It appears that test takers are more prone to select any choice that differs formally from the others. This may be simply because it is thereby more salient, but then, too, they are likely to suspect that it differs for some reason. Certainly coaching manuals encourage test takers to pick the longest response if they have no idea of which way to go, on the assumption that a target response tends to be longer than its distractors since it requires greater precision. Of course, test makers have read these manuals too, and on a professionally prepared test, test takers are unlikely to improve their score with this particular rule of thumb.

Another mechanical procedure—in the sense that it is dependent upon form rather than meaning—that some children used is to select a response that repeats material from the passage. We call such a practice REPETITION STRATEGY. There are two examples in the task under discussion, *an appearance* and *the caramel,* and the fact that they repeat words used in the passage undoubtedly contributed to their being selected much more often than the other two responses.

There are two strategies[4] that can lead children to select a repetition response. The first may be described as a DESPERATION STRATEGY. Children can become so confused by a passage that they have no idea of what a task calls for and latch on to any word repeated from the passage. Even children who lack effective decoding skills can use visual-matching techniques to identify a choice as having already occurred in the passage. It may be that a rather long word like *caramel* or *appearance* is particularly noticeable and thus easier to match up in this way.

The selection of a repetition response can also result from a STICK-TO-THE-PASSAGE STRATEGY. In preparing children for tests, teachers often admonish them to work only with what is in the passage. This advice is based on a good deal of experience, for children are prone—as this study amply documents—to expand passage content as they respond. Some children may, however, carry this advice further than intended and develop a strategy based on the principle that a choice containing a word from the passage is to be preferred to one that doesn't.

We have been discussing what might have attracted children to the various distractors in (A). Certainly an important element in why so many of them chose *the caramel, an appearance*, and, to a lesser extent, *a woman* is that there was something that actively discouraged them from selecting the target response *a word*. Or perhaps it should be put more strongly: whenever a target response falls well below chance, we can presume that there were certain factors that led children to eliminate it.

In principle, there are two basic ways that readers can arrive at the answer in a multiple-choice task. They can look for the response that confirms their sense of what the passage means and what the task is asking for. Or, they can proceed by ruling out the wrong responses and ending up with the right one. Certainly most choices involve an intricate mixing of these strategies. Presumably readers lean more on the former when the task is easy, and more on the latter when it is difficult. With a task such as (A), in which few children were successful, many must have been driven to the latter strategy. In fact, some must have gone through the four choices and found them all unsatisfactory. When test takers are in this situation, they either give up and move on to the next task, or they begin a weighing of alternatives that is periodically interrupted by trips back to the passage searching for a crucial insight. If that insight remains elusive, the test taker ends up having to decide which is the best of an unpromising lot.

What were the impediments that prevented children from choosing *a word*? The interviews suggest that there were four different levels of blockage. Most basic is the failure to understand the relevant part of the passage. Many children were unable to process the final sentence:

> The "sundries" was a mystery to most of the admirers of the sign, but they assumed it meant something at least as delicious as caramel.

Some of them took *it* as referring to *shop sign*, like the three previous uses of *it* in the passage, rather than *sundries*. Some even associated *they* with *sundries* rather than with *admirers of the sign*.

The inability to connect *mystery* as it is used in the task stem with *mystery* as it is used in the passage represents a second level of blockage. This is understandable enough—the word *mystery* is typically applied to larger patterns of meaning; it is surprising to find it used, rather than some term like *unfamiliar*, to refer to a single word. As already pointed out, there are several elements in the passage that fit quite well with the more conventional uses of this word. The use of the word *what* in the stem may have also contributed to the tendency to understand *mystery* in a more holistic way, since this question-word also tends to be content-oriented. In effect, (A) seems to ask about larger matters but must be answered with what is only a local detail in the passage.

A third level of blockage is represented by children who processed the final sentence fairly well (i.e., who equated *mystery* with *sundries*) but who failed to see that the passage was treating the word as a mystery rather than the things the word stands for. These children were prepared to understand *mystery* as referring to something small, but they were operating on the level of content, not of wording, and were thus unable to see *a word* as a correct response. This is complicated by the fact that, strictly speaking, it was not the word that was a mystery to the townspeople, but rather its meaning. If the passage had been really explicit, it would have read:

> The meaning of the word "sundries" was a mystery to most of the admirers of the sign.

It is interesting to speculate how performance on this task would have differed if the target response had been *the meaning of a word*.

The fourth level of blockage occurred with the few children who understood that the mystery was the word *sundries*, but still could not connect this word with the elliptical response *a word*. As test takers search through possible responses for one that validates their understanding of the task, the easiest to recognize is one that uses the same wording as the passage—what we have referred to as a repetition response. If this is lacking, they look for a response that can be considered synonymous in some way. In (A), the target response is in a superordinate relationship to the passage word with which it must be matched, that is, *a word* identifies a larger category to which *sundries* belongs. Here are interviews with two children who understood the equation of *sundries* and *mystery* in the passage, but were unable to see how *a word* could be the answer to their problem. The strategy that both adopted was ingenious: since the townspeople assumed that *sundries* was like *caramel*, they inferred a relationship between these two terms; and as they scanned the choices for something to match up with *sundries*, which they understood to be the mystery, the only possibility they could see was *caramel*, and they chose it, although evidently unwillingly. When they went over the test unit again with an interviewer, they were able to see how *a word* could be the correct answer:

(1)

C I have *caramel* underlined, but I think it would be "sun-dries."
I That's pronounced "sundries."
C Sundries.
I All right. But what is that? It's not here in your choices.
C I know, so I would say *a word*.
I Why is it that you circled *caramel* first?
C Because they were all assuming it was caramel and that was a mystery to them.
I Is that what it says, that caramel was a mystery?
C No, no, but it was a mystery what *sundries* was.
I So why did you circle *caramel*?
C Because they didn't have anything saying *sundries*.

(2)

I Why was the caramel a mystery?
C Because—mmm—probably the *word* is. I have it as *caramel* but I think it's *a word*.
I Which word?
C *Sundries*.
I What made you pick *caramel* the first time?
C Because it said, *at least as delicious as caramel*. But it—so I thought it was something like a caramel. That's what I thought.
I Do you know what *sundries* means?
C No.

By way of contrast, one child who had picked *a word* the first time around began to waffle during the interview:

It was about a shopping sign that was in a man's window and it said that he was selling candies. And people were puzzled about a word—*sundries*. I picked *a word* because—oh, it's *caramel*.

A short while later, he was able to recover his equilibrium:

Because the people thought it was caramel, but they weren't puzzled over caramel. They were puzzled over the word.

From an adult perspective, (A) seems to be a relatively straightforward task. The passage does, after all, use the word *mystery* to refer to the word *sundries*: *The "sundries" was a mystery to most of the admirers of the sign.* Moreover, there are two overt cues that the mystery was simply a word rather than what the word itself refers to: (1) the placing of *sundries* in quotation marks, and (2) the use of *was*—a singular form of the verb—after the word *sundries*.

These cues are not, however, necessarily available to an inexperienced reader. Although quotation marks can be used in a number of different ways, children tend to associate them with a single function. We asked 30 children what quotation marks are used for, and 26 of them mentioned only quoted speech, while 4 said they didn't know. By the same token, the use of the singular verb can pass by unnoticed. Possibly some children thought of *sundries* as being like *series*, singular even though it ends in *-ies*. But more generally, children of this age are not attentive to formal cues such as quotation marks and number agreement.[5]

Actually, quotation marks—or, as in this book, italics—are a fairly weak signal that a word is being used as a word, and so writers typically use an additional cue. Notice the differences in the following sentences:

1) Hey, the word *books* shouldn't have a *c* before the *k*.
2) Hey, the *books* shouldn't have a *c* before the *k*.
3) Hey, *books* shouldn't have a *c* before the *k*.

In (1) the meaning is unmistakable. Most people find (3) to be clearer than (2). The combination of *the* plus a nominal in (2) encourages readers to think of a real-world entity rather than a linguistic one, a reading that quotation marks may or may not prevent. In comparison to (1) and (3), (2) seems somewhat ill-formed. It is interesting to speculate whether *word* was present before *sundries* but was removed in order to make (A) more difficult. If so, it would have been better to remove *the* too.[6]

Most children did not have any idea of what the word *sundries* means. Hence, they processed the word more at the level of form than of meaning. When first reading the passage orally, several children pronounced *sundries* as "sundaes" and went on to mention various kinds of ice-cream concoctions (e.g., hot fudge sundaes). One child said:

They sound like something you treat yourself to on Sunday.

Other children pronounced the word as "sun-dries," so that it rhymed with *mudpies*. Some children associated this word with dried fruit:

It sounds like some kind of fruit. I don't know. I saw this kind of dried fruit, you know. It comes in these packs.

One child said that Mrs. Doyle wanted to sell dried fruit so that "parents wouldn't get angry about all that candy."

A number of children associated "sun-dries" more specifically with raisins for a reason that we will shortly disclose. Here are four examples of children who made this association:

(1)

I   What does "sun-dries" mean? (The interviewer adopts the child's pronunciation.)
C   Dry in the sun.
I   Uh-huh. Okay, how could that word be the mystery?
C   'Cause some people don't know how the raisins was dried.[7]

(2)

C   It's like a kind of candy, I guess, and it's dried by the sun probably.
I   Have you heard this word before or was this the first time?
C   Probably the first time, but it probably means "raisins."

(3)

I   What are sundries?
C   "Sun-dries" is something like raisins. They are dried in the sun. Grapes are dried in the sun. Raisins are "sun-dries" because raisins are dried in the sun. That's why they call raisins "sun-dries."

(4)

I   What made you think of raisins?
C   I just remembered how I know it means "raisins." That's the name of the raisins my sister eats—"Sun-dries."

This child was evidently thinking of the brand *Sun Maid*. Later, while discussing another test unit, he suddenly said:

> I just remembered something. Now I know why else I knew "sun-dries" meant "raisins." It's the only thing I know besides tobacco that dries in the sun.

This association of "sun-dries" with raisins clearly comes from more than the children's imagination. While taking the mock-test, they encountered SHOP SIGN just after dealing with RAISINS, a unit whose major theme is how grapes are *dried* in the *sun* in order to produce *raisins*. None of the children actually mention this unit, even though the child in (3) uses one of its central predicates (i.e., *dried in the sun*). In fact, she uses this predicate in three consecutive sentences and thus links together the words that function as subject in these sentences: *sundries*, *grapes*, *raisins*. It is as if she is actively working out the connection among these three. In this study, we will have a number of occasions to observe children making such connections and will refer to this phenomenon as UNIT LEAKAGE. We suspect that the brevity of test units conspires with time constraints to produce a good deal of such leakage. Indeed, the effects of such leakage on children's performance is probably much greater than is generally recognized.

Before leaving this task, we would like to observe that certain adults also use the pronunciation "sun-dries." We asked 30 adults to write down how they pronounce *sundries* and then provide a definition of the word with an example of its use. Among the 19 who provided a decipherable pronunciation, 2 did use the "sun-dries" pronunciation. Among the 24 who provided a definition and example, 13 provided an acceptable definition and 16 an acceptable example. We might note that a surprising number of adults, especially women, focused on either toiletries or beach articles. Clearly this word can be quite slippery for many adults.

Let us now turn to the second task: *The story is mainly about* _____. The question that immediately occurs is, "What story?" An obvious answer is, "The story about Mrs. Doyle and her candy shop that was begun in the passage." But the test makers mean something quite different. In this context, *the story* is meant to be synonymous with what we have been referring to as the passage. Moreover, its use in other units in our corpus makes clear that *the story* can refer to passages that are either narrative or expository, either fictional or factual (see (A) in MINNESOTA, and (A) in JAYS AND CROWS). These units reflect usage in many elementary classrooms, where any piece of prose, short or long, is called *a story*.[8] Unsatisfactory as it may be to use the word in this way, it is difficult to suggest an alternative. When we were developing terminology for the present study, we could think of only a few possibilities for referring to the "text" part of a test unit; though none of them seemed quite right, we finally settled on the word *passage*. Yet this word would be unfamiliar to too many young children to be functional in a third-grade test.

No doubt teachers want to keep things simple for children by avoiding words they might find confusing. Yet maintaining a usage that differs from that in the larger world can also be confusing. We have sometimes encountered college students who maintain the elementary pattern and refer to the essays in a book of expository prose as "stories." Since children are dealing with various genres, not just in writing but also in audiovisual media, they need a vocabulary to help them conceptualize the differences. Becoming familiar with the adult use of *story*, which strongly implies "narrative" and somewhat less strongly "fictional," would be a significant step in this direction.

Another significant word in the stem is *mainly*. It implies that the "story" is about more than one thing, and that deciding between them may require some weighing of alternatives. The responses presumably represent the test makers' estimation of what are the leading possibilities. If we assume that the story in question is the one that the passage has initiated, what are the relative probabilities that *candies, a sign, a shop,* and *Mrs. Doyle* will figure prominently in it? *Mrs. Doyle* is clearly a strong candidate. After all, most stories are about people; there is also a fairly high probability that Mrs. Doyle will turn out to be the protagonist and that we will follow her fortunes right through to the end. On the other hand, many people would probably agree that the least likely candidate for "mainly about" would be *a sign*. It's hard to imagine a narrative that would focus extensively on such an inanimate entity. In fact, the probability seems quite high that the sign is just a device for initiating the narrative and that it will not be mentioned again. The other two choices, *candies* and *a shop*, occupy a middle ground between these two extremes, with the latter perhaps being more likely to figure in the rest of the narrative, because it may well be the scene of much of the action.

The results of the pilot testing for this task are shown in Table 2.2. The numbers for both groups tend to follow our scenario, with *Mrs. Doyle* being the most frequent choice and *a sign*, the target response, being below chance.

The interviews brought out some of the thinking that children went through to arrive at their answers. One child, when asked what the story was mainly about, quickly replied, "Oh, the lady that makes candy for the kids." Another defended his choice by saying that "the whole story is about her." She went on to say that "they [presumably the test makers] made up a story for her. She is a dealer in candies, dealing candies." One child even justified his choice of *Mrs. Doyle* by saying that she was "the one who invented that sign." He went on to claim that she had also "invented a new name for some ice cream" (like the children mentioned earlier, he associated *sundries* with *sundaes*).

Although there is no firm evidence in the interviews, more than one interviewer had the impression that some children picked *candies* because the passage had stimulated their sweet tooth. One child pic-

TABLE 2.2

	African American	European American
candies	23%	28%
a shop	22%	14%
a sign	23%	17%
Mrs. Doyle	32%	40%

tured "several big jars of candies in the shop." Somehow he even managed to locate "the sign which says *sundries* on one of the jars." Other children were able to cite evidence for their choice of *candies* from the passage:

I   What made you pick *candy*?

C   'Cause it said Mrs. Doyle was a dealer *in* "candies, homemade taffies, confectionery, and sundries." And sundries was a mystery "as delicious as caramel"—that's candy.

The interviewer then turns to the other choices:

I   What if somebody said it was mainly about a shop?

C   No, it probably wouldn't be about a shop.

I   Why not?

C   Because they have more written about candies than about a shop.

I   Okay. What if someone said it was about a sign?

In responding to this question, the child, once again, works himself back to *candies*:

No, 'cause there's plenty of other subjects that are in the story, so how could it be just about a sign? Mrs. Doyle? You could say it was about Mrs. Doyle, but I said it was about candies, because it's Mrs. Doyle's candies.

Another child explained that she was initially attracted to *candies*, but then decided that *Mrs. Doyle* was just as attractive. She finally selected *a sign*. When questioned about this, she sketched a spatial image with her hands that represented her sense of the relationships in the passage (Figure 2.1). In effect, *candies* and *Mrs. Doyle* were grouped together, while *a sign* formed a separate group. She was using a well-known rule of thumb for handling multiple-choice tasks: if two or more choices have an equal claim, then the correct answer must be something else. We refer to this as an ELIMINATE-IF-EQUAL STRATEGY.

FIGURE 2.1

To get some sense of how mature readers would respond to this question, we asked a group of adults[9] to read the passage and respond to (B) with the multiple choices removed. Out of 22 replies, 12 referred to the appearance of the sign, 8 to the opening of the shop (sometimes including the townspeople's reaction), and 2 to candies. What is striking about these reactions is that almost all of them focus on events; for these readers it was what happened that was important. If we look at the choices supplied with (B), we find that they refer to one person and three things. In effect, the dynamic aspects of the passage are not represented in these choices. Certainly, if *the appearance of a sign* and *the opening of a shop* had been given as choices, selecting a response would have been a very different process. A perverse aspect of the multiple-choice format is that material which seems central and relevant when reading a passage may be rendered marginal by a particular constellation of choices.

Tasks like (B), which deal with the "main idea"[10] of a text, are thought of as being concerned with meaning. Certainly test makers include them because they think that they test whether children can handle a certain kind of meaning adequately. In fact, however, our ability to answer such questions depends not so much on our knowledge of meaning relationships in the real world, or in the imaginative world activated by a text, as on our sensitivity to how a text is written. Our sense of what a text is "mainly about" depends on its rhetoric, that is, on the order in which information is presented and on the relationships that are set up. In the passage in question, the shop sign is placed at the top of an implied hierarchy, and our knowledge of Mrs. Doyle, the shop, and the candies is made to depend upon it, as shown in Figure 2.2. Part of the flair in this passage is that the writer has been imaginative enough to think of an unhackneyed way to introduce a character and a setting.

The paragraph could have been written more conventionally so that it focused on Mrs. Doyle, perhaps following her as she makes the candies, cleans the shop, and letters the sign. Or it could have been used to set the scene: the shop on Main Street, Mrs. Doyle working away inside, the heaps of delicious candies, the sign in the window. In these two hypothetical versions, the bits of information we receive would not have

FIGURE 2.2

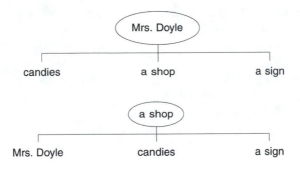

FIGURE 2.3

changed, but our sense of what the passage was mainly about would shift significantly (Figure 2.3).

Our sense of what a text is about depends not only on the hierarchies it sets up but also on how pervasive and prominent the various strands of information it conveys are. Figure 2.4 shows how the shop sign is kept in focus by the way the text is worded.[11] In effect, this one bit of information is carried by five elements spread over four sentences; two of them are nominals and the other three are pronominals. The use of a pronominal assumes that there is a nominal in the text with which it can be connected. In the passage, the first two pronominals—*its* and *it*—cannot be interpreted by readers until they get to the phrase *a shop sign*. Cohesive relationships in which the pronominal precedes its nominal in

SENTENCE	INITIAL POSITION	OTHER POSITIONS	
1	Its		
2	It	a shop sign	Cataphoric
3	It		
4		the sign	Anaphoric

FIGURE 2.4

this way are referred to as CATAPHORIC. In sentence 3, however, the pro-nominal *it* follows its nominal, namely, *a shop sign*. Cohesive relation-ships that depend upon this kind of retrieval are referred to as ANAPHORIC. In sentence 4 *the sign* is also anaphoric, because *the* signals old information; in other words, *the sign* in sentence 4 refers to the same entity as *a shop sign* in sentence 2.

This analysis demonstrates that *a shop sign* is both more pervasive and more prominent in the passage than any of the other choices. It is more pervasive in that it is distributed throughout the passage; and it is more prominent in that each of the first three sentences opens with a pro-nominal referring to the sign. Moreover, the cataphoric pattern estab-lished by the first two sentences provides a dramatic focus for *a shop sign*; or to use a term frequently used by discourse analysts, it is the shop sign which is STAGED within the passage.

Here is a less technical explanation from a fifth grader:

It is all over the place. Here it says, *Its appearance*. Here it says, *It was a shop sign*. Here it says, *It announced*. That's what it's mainly about.

This somewhat older child was clearly able to carry out the kind of cohe-sion analysis that we have displayed above. In interviewing younger chil-dren, we discovered only one child who seemed to have access to this kind of analysis:

Well, they mostly just talk about the sign and things in the sign, about the sign. So I chose *a sign*. It's also about candies but more about a sign.

Even in the midst of the child's analysis, one gets a hint of his attraction to candies.

A cohesion analysis provides a principled way to confirm our sense that the passage is "mainly about" a sign. Such analysis, however, pre-supposes that readers have developed skills that enable them to attend not only to what is expressed—the meaning—but also the way it is expressed—the wording. Attention to wording is associated more with written language than with spoken language, in part because written language is more stable and easier to review. As has often been pointed out (e.g., Olson, 1977), most people develop their written language abil-ities in connection with schooling. Third graders have not, however, had a chance to get very far in this process. Most of their attention to word-ing is a by-product of learning to read and spell isolated words. They have had little chance to develop the facility with larger expanses of text, as this task demands.

In closing this discussion, we would like to return briefly to (A) and note that it, too, forces children to operate on the level of wording rather than of meaning. In responding to (A), children must know that the presence of quotation marks around *sundries* indicates that it refers to a word rather than a thing (there is the added complication that this word is on the shop sign they are reading about rather than on the page they are actually reading); and in responding to (B), they must focus upon *sign* as the primary lexical vehicle within the passage. In both instances, children must attend to the mediating structure of language rather than to what is mediated. It is for this reason that these tasks can be classified as METALINGUISTIC: that is to say, language is used to explore language structure itself. Young children are not accustomed to carrying out this kind of operation, and it is thus not surprising that they perform dismally on these tasks.

LEAVING HOME

Here is another unit in which the passage presents a truncated narrative:

Jim and his family were going away for a week. They took a bus across town to the train station and then settled down for a long trip. First they passed by many tall buildings and busy streets. Later they went by farms and woods. They went through other cities, too, before they reached the little town near the sea.

A. Where is Jim's home?
     by the sea   on a farm
     in a little town   in a city

B. Most of the trip was by
     train   car
     bus   boat

The passage describes the journey of someone named Jim—whom most children take to be a young boy[12]—and his family from a city to a small town near the sea. It opens with an orienting sentence and then moves on to describe the journey itself in four sentences. The first two of these sentences describe only the inception of the journey. By way of contrast, the last two sentences describe the rest of the journey, including the family's arrival at the little town near the sea. In effect, there is a marked discontinuity between textual space and the geographical space it represents—the initial pair of sentences describes only a short bit of the journey (presumably only a few miles), whereas the final pair describes the great bulk of the travel (perhaps even hundreds of miles). Such discontinuity can be motivated, at least for adult readers, on different grounds: to begin with, the inception of the trip, given a traveler's anticipation, is generally vivid and intense; moreover, it often consumes a good deal of time and practical energy, as anyone knows who has struggled even a relatively brief distance through urban congestion to catch a train or plane. In some instances, it can even take longer to travel a few miles to an airport than hundreds of miles on the plane itself. In the case of child readers, they are obviously less able to use pragmatic knowledge in negotiating the discontinuity under consideration—one between textual space and the geographical space represented. We will have occasion to show how this discontinuity became a source of confusion.

Once the passage has described the journey, it comes to a rather abrupt end, with no mention of what Jim and his family did in the little town near the sea. It is, of course, possible for a story to be only about a journey—indeed, writers often put together a rather lengthy book just about the making of a journey. In this instance, however, the journey is not at all eventful; we are simply told that Jim and his family saw the most predictable scenery as they went along. This blandness predisposes a reader—at least one who is attempting to establish meaning—to regard the train trip as mere prologue and to anticipate the real story as unfolding only after Jim and his family arrive in the little town.

As we shift from the passage to the two tasks, we can observe a couple of features that are somewhat unusual. To begin with, these tasks violate a kind of unwritten rule that they should contrast with each other in some significant way (e.g., it is common that one task deals with content and the other with some aspect of vocabulary; or if they both deal with content, one may require that information be recycled and the other that it be inferred). In this unit, however, the two tasks are similar in that they both require children to use their powers of inference, to use directly stated information to derive other information that is not.

These tasks are also unusual in that they do not maintain a consistent frame—the first uses the present tense, whereas the second shifts to the past tense:

A. Where *is* Jim's home?
B. Most of the trip *was* by _____ .

Following a narrative passage, both tasks are ordinarily in the past tense. Presumably (A) has been put in the present tense because it is not part of the narrative sequence but is rather concerned with background information. On the other hand, this task would work perfectly well if it were put in the past tense:

Where was Jim's home?

It is not clear what, if any, are the effects of this shift in tense.

With respect to ethnocultural variation, this unit is of particular interest. During the pilot testing, European American children performed significantly better than African American children on both tasks. Table 2.3 shows the proportions of children selecting the target response for each. In analyzing children's responses to these tasks, we will be concerned with showing how ethnocultural norms affect their understanding of the passage.

Before we undertake such an investigation, we would like to call attention to a relation between passage and tasks that can be commonly found in test units. Whereas the passage presents bits and pieces of

TABLE 2.3

	African American	European American
(A) in a city	24%	35%
(B) train	43%	56%

information in a relatively dispersed form, a task, by virtue of its particular configuration of choices, forces readers to fit them into a relatively tight schema, which, in many instances, can be quite reductive. To use a familiar metaphor from literary criticism, a task functions as an interpretive filter. Test takers are often encouraged to avail themselves of these filters by reading the tasks before they read the passage.

To illustrate the point we are making, we can focus on two pairs of opposing choices—*in a city* and *in a little town* in (A), *bus* and *train* in (B)—and show how they lead readers to set up the kind of schema shown in Figure 2.5 for the journey that Jim and his family make. Jim and his family's trip begins with a specified sequence—home, bus across town, train station—all of which must be conceived as located within a city. They then switch to a train—though the switch is unspecified—and the next segment of their trip is viewed as taking place from the train station to the city limits (*they passed by many tall buildings and busy streets*). After leaving the city, they are pictured as passing through countryside (*farms and woods*) and other cities, which, within the working schema, can be easily expanded to something like the following: they went through an unspecified sequence of two or more cities interspersed with space that was non-city (e.g., countryside or towns). Not surprisingly, most children seemed unable to activate such a detailed schema, though

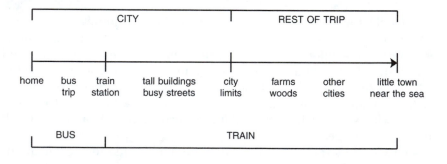

FIGURE 2.5

some, as we will see, were able to construct a simpler one that accorded with their own sense of place and travel.

In order for readers to select *in a city*, the target response for (A), they should, in principle, establish two points:

1) Jim's home is in the place he starts out from.
2) This place is more appropriately characterized as a city than as a little town.

There is a good deal of textual evidence for these two points, especially the second one; it is, however, dispersed throughout the passage, and readers, as we have suggested, have little or no motivation to bring it together until they encounter the task itself. Moreover, their capacity to bring such evidence together depends upon their having access to bodies of knowledge that many children simply do not possess.

The information needed for the first point—namely, that Jim's home is where he starts from—can be found in the initial sentence of the passage:

Jim and his family were going away for a week.

To go away ordinarily indicates 'moving from a home base.' In this case, the absence is to be a temporary one, lasting only *for a week*. Hence readers can infer that where Jim is leaving from is more permanent than where he is going to—and so his originating point should be considered 'home.'

The expression *going away* did not, however, function in this way for many children. We can identify a number of potential reasons for their failure to focus on its intended meaning. To begin with, they are probably most familiar with the verb *go away* when it is used, often in anger, to command someone to leave. In such usage, the notion 'departure from home base' is not necessarily presupposed; if anything, quite the opposite is true. The person being addressed has little or no permanent claim on the space in which the words are uttered. Moreover, the function of *go away* within the passage, despite its location within the initial sentence, may have contributed to its lack of saliency. In this position it is simply providing background information for the story rather than information within the story itself. When we asked children to recall the content of the passage, they tended to leave out this initial information, presumably because it is not included in the narrative sequence (see Black & Bower, 1980, for evidence that background information in a story is more difficult to recall than the story information itself).

We might further note that *going away*, even when describing a departure, has a more specific meaning than 'moving from home base.' In New York City, for example, it is a common way of referring to a vacation. During the early part of the summer, one often hears the question, "When are you going away?" For readers who are familiar with this use, the succeeding details in the passage concerning the trip and its seaside destination mesh neatly within a vacation schema. Some children did work with such a schema. Consider the following exchange with an African American boy:

C   The first sentence says, *They were going away*—must have been to vacation.
I   So what do you understand by the phrase *going away*?
C   Leaving your home to go on vacation.
I   Do you think Jim's family was going on vacation?
C   Mmhmm, maybe to vacation or camp out.

An African American girl also drew on a vacation schema, but allowed for other possibilities as well.

I   What does *going away* mean?
C   It means going away on vacation or if something has happened in their family: for example, if someone died, or is sick or got hurt, they would go to see that person.

From inside a vacation schema, it is easy to see that 'home' is where Jim started out from. But for those readers who speak of "taking a vacation" rather than "going away," the situation is not as immediately clear.[13]

One particularly skillful 10-year-old test taker selected *in a little town* as her response to (A). In defending her choice, she says that she

was thinking they were at a grandmother's house or an aunt's or something and they were going home.

The interviewer then focuses on *going away* in the first sentence and she responds:

Going away from wherever; it didn't have to be their own home....If you're at your house and you say, "I'm going away," then you, you know, you're going away from home. If you're at your grandma's house and you say, "I'm going away," then you know you're going home.

Clearly this girl did not possess the restricted meaning for *going away* that the test makers assumed. She also did not possess the restricted meaning for *home* that the test makers assume in constructing (B), a point to which we will return.

The passage provides three separate sources of information for the second point that must be established in order to answer (A), namely, that where Jim leaves from is a "city" rather than a "town."

Sentence 2:	They took a bus across town to the train station....
Sentence 3:	First they passed by many tall buildings and busy streets.
Sentence 5:	They went through other cities, too....

The first source of information, though it consists of two cues, is not as strong as the others. The first of the two cues—*bus across town*—is subject to a good deal of confusion; for it is, ironically, this expression that suggests Jim is starting out from a city rather than a little town. Certainly, the possibility of using the expression *across town* in reference to a small town cannot be excluded. One can well imagine using the expression with reference to, say, a service station:

Do you know where Tom's service station is?
It's across town on Highway 316.

Since *across town* is associated with *bus*, however, it brings to mind, at least for seasoned Manhattanites, the familiar expression "crosstown bus," which, in turn, brings to mind a city (these associations are especially strong for anyone accustomed to living in a gridlike urban space). One African American boy seemed to work with such a schema:

I   Where do you think the train station was?
C   On the other side of the town.

He placed special stress on "the other side" and extended his arms to reinforce the notion that Jim's family had to go from one end of town to the other.

Yet certain children took the mere presence of the word *town* in the passage as cueing an answer that contained the word itself. One child who made this literal interpretation said:

Because it says *across town*. That means they're crossing his little town to the train station in the city.

Another child even used the expression *across town* to defend a change in his answer from *by the sea* to *a little town*:

> But I think it's a little town now. It says: "Jim and his family were going away for a week. They took a bus across town." If it was in the city, it would say "take a bus across the city."

One child who made a literal interpretation of *across town* still rejected *in a little town* as an answer, since he reasoned that a town can be located in a city (note how he breaks up the idiom by inserting *the* into *across town*):

> *In a town* might be an answer, because in the passage it was mentioned that they took a bus across the town. Jim's home might be in a town, but town is also in a city, so I canceled it out.

The literal interpretation of *across town* was made even by children who lived in Manhattan and presumably were quite familiar with expressions like "crosstown bus," "uptown train," or "downtown subway." Consider, for example, the following response of a third grader at a private school on the upper east side of Manhattan:

> I   So why didn't you pick the city?
> C   I don't know. 'Cause they took a bus across town. A town isn't a city.

By way of contrast, some children took the mere fact that a bus was talked about as precluding *a small town*. One African American child reflected his rural origins with the following claim:

> You know, well, not many of little towns have very big buses. They have— they haven't buses. They use cars.

He also used the second cue in sentence 2, pointing out that a little town doesn't have a train station either.[14]

This child was also able to make use of the cues in sentence 3, as indicated by his response to the interviewer's probing for other cues:

> I   Anything else make you think of a city?
> C   Many tall buildings. A lot of tall buildings and busy streets.

At this point the interviewer switched to another topic, so we do not know whether this child would have gone on to spell out the cue in sentence 5 as well. As a reader, he was particularly attuned to making sensible inferences based on his real-world knowledge. Unfortunately, these inferences, as we will shortly see, can work against choosing the target response.

There were children who did manage to specify the cue in sentence 5; here, for example, is how one third-grade child used this cue:

I   Well, where did they start?

C   In the city. 'Cause they went through other cities. That means different ones.

Clearly, she viewed the journey in the way that the test makers seem to have envisioned it:

city → countryside → other cities → little town near the sea

A girl who was in a gifted class at her school and who was able to recall the passage nearly verbatim drew the picture of Jim's journey shown in Figure 2.6 to justify her choice of *in a city*. As can be seen, she cleverly integrates words and images to represent Jim's journey in four stages. In the third stage, she places triple underlining under the word *other*, presumably in order to emphasize the importance of this cue in selecting *in a city* as a response to where Jim lived.

There were children, however, who saw Jim and his family as departing from a small town and only reaching a city once the train trip was well underway. Figure 2.7 shows a drawing made by an African American boy who chose *in a little town*. The schema that this child seems to have constructed for the passage is represented in Figure 2.8. We might

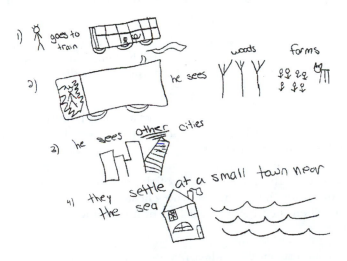

FIGURE 2.6

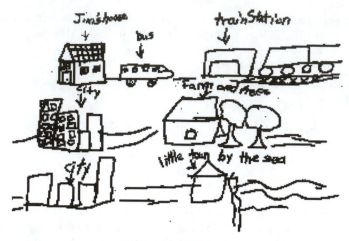

FIGURE 2.7

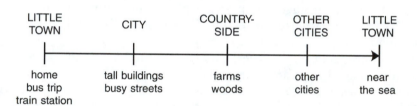

FIGURE 2.8

note that certain aspects of the text structure encourage the construction of this schema:

Sentence 2:   [bus across town]   +   [settled down for a long trip]
Sentence 3:   first   +   [tall buildings and busy streets]
Sentence 4:   later   +   [farms and woods]
Sentence 5:   [other cities]   +   too

As shown in Figure 2.9, sentence 2 describes the departure (it pictures Jim and his family settling down for the trip), and then sentences 3-5, structured with the connectives *first*, *later*, and *too*, describe three major segments of the journey itself.

With respect to this interpretation of the passage, the responses of one African American fourth grader who chose *in a small town* for (A) are revealing. When the interviewer asked him to tell what he had just read, he replied:

It was about a summer day when Jim was going camping with his—um— father and mother. And they had a very long trip. First, they had to take

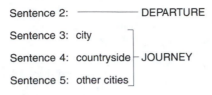

FIGURE 2.9

the bus to the train, and a train all the way out to the house—out by the sea.

He placed particular stress on *all the way*, making a sweeping gesture with his hand to indicate what a long trip it was.

The interviewer, herself African American, then posed a question in which she assumes the child's point of view, namely, that Jim and his family started in a town:

So when you were thinking that he was on the bus and they said he went on—they said he went—"passed by many tall buildings and busy streets"— was he outside of the town at that point or was he still....

The child interrupts her question with a firm answer:

C   He was outside of the town.
I   And outside of the town was what?
C   Like in a big city.

It is clear that this child viewed Jim and his family as passing through a big city along the way. Hence, for him the expression *other cities* referred back only to a city they traveled through rather than to the point they started from (Figure 2.10).

There were European American children who envisioned the journey in a comparable way. One young girl, who regularly went with her family to a summer home on Fire Island, felt that Jim and his family saw the tall buildings and busy streets only after they had settled down on the

FIGURE 2.10

train and the trip was well underway. Incidentally, she chose in *a little town*, even though she felt, in her own case, that her real home was in Manhattan rather than on Fire Island:

> I always used to ask, as soon as we'd get there [Fire Island], when we'd be going home again.

Apart from all the above difficulties, we should note that terms like *town* and *city* have relative and overlapping meanings that are not clearly differentiated. What one person calls a town another may very well call a city. Besides this, there are many special usages that carry these words beyond their normal meaning. The Town of Hempstead on Long Island has nearly a million inhabitants, while Vatican City is exceedingly small, to choose two extreme examples; and as we pointed out earlier, the word *town* is actually used in the passage to refer to the city where Jim lives.

The difficulty of sorting out these two words was poignantly expressed by a ten-year-old boy who lives on the lower east side of Manhattan:

> I'm not sure exactly where Jim's house is. It may be where he left from or where he went to. I know that he went to a small town, but I don't know the real size of the place he left. It may have been a city or a town. If I choose *town* as an answer, my chances of getting it right seem better.

This child evidences a keen sense of strategy: Since he thinks home could be located at either the starting point or end point, he rightly chooses *in a little town,* since he can be certain that the end point was, in fact, a town:

> Starting point: town or city
> End point: town

This inability to distinguish clearly between 'city' and 'town' apparently contributed to the popularity of two distractors during the pilot testing, as shown in Table 2.4. Some of the children we interviewed were just as comfortable choosing *in a little town* as *in the city*. When we pressed them to distinguish the two, they felt no need to do so, and hence the set of cues in sentences 3, 4, and 5 simply passed them by.

TABLE 2.4

	African American	European American
by the sea	32%	23%
in a little town	32%	34%

On the other hand, there were children who considered the two choices to be so similar that they were forced to look elsewhere. Hence they arrived at *by the sea* by using an eliminate-if-equal strategy (see p. 47 in SHOP SIGN), which might be formalized in the following way:

IF in a city = in a little town, THEN SELECT *by the sea*.[15]

This same strategy, ironically enough, led other children to the target response. Since the passage says that the trip ended *in a little town near the sea*, these children reasoned that the distractors *in a little town* and *by the sea* were equal in that they refer to the same location. Consequently, they selected *in a city* as their answer:

IF in a little town = by the sea, THEN SELECT *in a city*.

During the interviewing, we came across several children whose understanding of this unit was affected by whether they tended to view their own home as in a city or in a small town. For those who live in a small town, a city may well be viewed as a place to visit rather than to live in. But for those who live in cities, the question seems to be more complicated. One might think that they would view the city as the place where home is and a small town, particularly one by the sea, as the place for a holiday. Because of distinctive patterns of sociocultural experience, however, some children who live in the city do not think of it as home, at least not in the sense that a person has just one home, a sense that is assumed by this task.

The word *home* itself is not always used to describe an urban apartment, at least not in Manhattan. When we asked children what expressions they use to invite friends to where they live, they used *place*, *house*, and *apartment* more than *home*. However, some children whose parents own country houses did report themselves as using the word *home* whenever they invite friends to these places. It is possible that they are simply adopting speech patterns that can be found in the places where the country houses are located. Moreover, some of these children viewed the country house, often located in a "little town near the sea," as their true home. Adopting the cultural values of their parents, they viewed their city apartment as simply a *pied-à-terre*. One of the members of the research team asked his high-school daughter, who regularly goes to a country house, to respond to the various units on the mock-test. She did all of them rapidly without any problem except for this one task. When he asked her why she had circled *in a little town*, she used the expression *country house* in referring to the place *near the sea*. Invoking the eliminate-if-equal strategy, he asked her how she had decided between *in a little town* and *by the sea*. She said that this had worried her, but she finally resolved it by figuring out that *by the sea* had been included as a "trick choice." She pointed out that Jim's home was "just near the sea and not actually by it." When he asked her whether she thought tests actually force such refined distinctions upon the reader, she responded with a rather disdainful "Of course."

It is particularly interesting to examine the notion of home among African American children. Many of those we interviewed belong to families who maintain strong ties with relatives in small towns and thus, no doubt, hear expressions such as "going back home." During the interviewing we discovered that a number of them do go back home during the summer months. We also discovered that for these children the experience of an extended family is so strong that they do not necessarily possess the notion of a single home that this task assumes.

To illustrate their thinking about home, let us examine what one African American girl said when asked to recall what was in the passage:

C   Jim and his family, they was in the city and they was going to go to his home. So they took the bus to the train station and took the train through little towns and cities[16] until they got to their town.
I   Why did you decide he was going home?
C   I guess he was going home. They was going away[17] for a week so they was either going to his mother's house or his grandmother's house or his relative's house.
I   But what were they doing in the city?
C   I don't know.

At this point the interviewer, reflecting his own ethnocultural vantage point, asks for clarification:

I   Do you have any idea why you thought he was going home?
C   Probably he was going to visit his family.
I   Then he goes to visit his family, would you think of that as home?
C   Mmhmm.
I   Even relatives? Can a person have more than one home?
C   Mmhmm.
I   So do you have more than one home?
C   Mmhmm.
I   How many?
C   I have a lot of homes—my grandmother's, my mother's, my aunts', my cousins', my grandfather's house.

This child's litany of homes was so dramatically enunciated that it brought the interviewer's line of questioning to a rather abrupt halt.

Other African American children also worked with the notion of 'multiple homes':

> I have different homes—in New Brunswick where I now live with my mom and sisters; in Georgia where my dad's family lives. I have aunts and uncles there. That is where I used to live.

Some African American children drew on such a notion in interpreting what the phrase *Jim's family* means:

> The story only says *Jim's family*. It might not be his parents; he could be with his aunt or uncle; and Jim, he is travelling to go to visit them for a week in the summer. So his uncle and aunt may be living in a town by the sea. Jim could also have gone with his aunt or uncle to stay with them, because maybe his parents went away for a week.

Another child said that *family* is

> not only parents, but also relatives and friends, neighbors, and anyone who treats you well.

The interviewer then asked, "In your understanding, what is *family*?" The child replied, "Someone who cares for you, loves, feeds, and dresses you."

We do not wish to suggest that only African American children operate with the notion of multiple homes. Certain European American children whom we interviewed worked with a similar notion, though, typically, one of dual rather than multiple homes. Consider, for example, the following exchange with a boy whose parents owned a country house:

> I   Why did you say *by the sea*?
> C   'Cause it said in the last sentence. I thought that meant they had a home there.
> I   Is that the only home Jim has?
> C   No. He also has one in the city.

As the interview continued, the boy became aware that *in the city* was the desired response, but he remained attached to the notion of more than one home:

> C   This is getting me mixed up. They went through other cities, they went across town, and then it says before they reached the little town near the sea. It's nuts.

I   Well, where did they start?
C   In the city. 'Cause they went through other cities. That means differ-
    ent ones.
I   So they started in the city and went to....
C   To another home in the little town by the sea.
I   So they had two homes?
C   Yes. A country house and one in the city.

The idea that home is just not one place was as strong for this European American boy as it was for the African American girl. For each of
them, it was rooted in a distinct pattern of life in American cities. In the
case of the girl, this pattern involved her moving from one place to
another within an extended family, and her own ethnocultural values
led her to use the word *home* for each place where a member of her
larger family lived. In the case of the boy, this pattern involved his moving back and forth between a city apartment and a country house—and
for him the word *home* applied equally well to each.[18] These patterns are
quite different from each other; yet, taken together, they dramatize that
ethnocultural norms of language, thought, and experience affect all children and that these norms can run counter to those assumed by test
makers in constructing tasks. Certainly, in contemporary society, with its
high rate of divorce, children from a wide range of ethnocultural backgrounds are accustomed to calling more than one place *home* and thus
are not in a position to readily adopt the notion 'a single home' that the
task assumes.

Judging from the results of the pilot test, we suspect that these distinctive norms led to greater confusion for African American children on
this particular task. In order to get a better idea of how they think about
the word *home*, we gave 20 third graders at a school in Harlem the task
in Figure 2.11. Ten of the children answered *yes*; four wrote *2*, two wrote
3, and four wrote *4*. In effect, at least six of these children seemed to be
carrying around in their heads a notion much like the little girl's—home
is where various members of your extended family live.

Given these results, we gave the same task to 20 African American and
European American children in a suburban school and found that less
than a third answered the question *yes*. Moreover, these students, except

Do you have more than one home?
If your answer is "yes," how many places do you call home?

FIGURE 2.11

for one African American child, wrote that they had only two homes. When we questioned them about their second home, they focused either on a vacation home or the fact that their parents were divorced.

Before leaving (A), we would like to report an intriguing example of ethnocultural influence documented by two Japanese graduate students. They administered this test unit to Japanese adults as well as children and discovered that both groups—the children even more so—preferred the response *in a little town* to (A). What was particularly intriguing was that two distinct cultural schemas contributed to this response, one having to do with the departure and the other with the destination. As for the departure, certain Japanese respondents pictured Jim and his family as living outside the city and coming into the city to catch a train, since Japanese cities, at least when compared to American cities, are less likely to include residential areas. As for the destination, certain Japanese respondents pictured Jim returning to the place where he grew up. In Japanese culture, the most basic word for 'home,' *uchi*, is strongly associated with the place where one grew up and where one's parents often continue to live (indeed, this word can refer to 'family' as well as to 'home'). Hence many of those who selected *in a little town* saw Jim as an adult returning to visit the place where his parents live. One child, when asked who would be living in the little town by the sea, answered, "Mother and father"; and as one of the adults put it, "Why else would Jim be taking the train to the little town?"

One of the Japanese graduate students administered the test material with a Japanese name in place of *Jim*. Under this condition, Japanese respondents were even more likely to select *in a little town*. Such a result provides further evidence for the strength of the two cultural schemas that we have described above.

Let us now turn to (B). As reported earlier, about half of the children selected the target response *train* during the pilot testing, though there was a substantial gap between African American (43 percent) and European American (56 percent) children. The main distractor was *bus*, which was chosen by 27 percent of both groups. The power of this distractor obviously results from a striking gap in sentence 2 of the passage:

> They took a bus across town to the train station and then settled down for a long trip.

The reader begins this sentence with the protagonists on a bus and ends with them preparing themselves for a long trip. From the destination of the bus—the train station—and from the fact that these characters are experiencing locomotion in the succeeding sentence, a reader must infer that they somehow managed to carry out a number of activities between the compound predicates in sentence 2—getting off the bus, walking through the station, and getting on the train.

From the vantage point of the test makers, such an inference is best viewed as an automated one (i.e., one goes to a train station in order to get on a train). From the results of the pilot testing, it is clear that this inference was not automated for all children. In fact, some children simply assumed that Jim and his family stayed on the bus when they reached the train station. As one child put it, "They went to the train station but they never got off the bus." Unfortunately, the interviewer did not follow up on why Jim and his family bothered to go to the train station if they were going to stay on the bus. There were apparently children who worked with a schema that might be described as 'transportation station'—a place where people are able to arrive and depart by means of either a bus or a train. One child, apparently drawing on personal experience, thought that the trip was made by some combination of bus and train:

They might have spent 5 hours on a bus and maybe 15 minutes on a train.

A writer cannot, of course, tell everything; an important aspect of skillful writing is knowing what must be said and what it is safe to leave out. The omission in this sentence, however, seems perverse. There were children who, in fact, expressed annoyance at this gap; as one of them put it, "Something's messed up here." Other children seemed willing to tolerate the gap as simply a necessary evil in taking a test; as one of them commented rather acerbically, "You don't go to a train station to do nothing."

It seems fairly obvious that the missing information was withheld in order to provide the foundation for the second task. As we analyze other passages in forthcoming chapters, we will have occasion to observe how information was apparently withheld so that a task could be constructed. Indeed, such withholding will be viewed as an example of a larger pattern that discourse analysts (e.g., Fillmore & Kay, 1983; Hill & Parry, 1989) have documented: namely, the tendency to violate normative patterns of prose in order to create tasks that have a certain discriminatory power. Such violations can be especially problematic for inexperienced readers who, when confronting test material, are often confused about how to approach it. In the case of withheld information, for example, they are not at all sure about supplying it since they have often been warned by teachers, parents, and other well-meaning adults that they must stick to what is on the page in order to perform well on a test.

In closing our discussion of this task, we would like to note a pattern of real-world experience that may have had particularly adverse effects on the performance of many inner-city children. For them, the implied transfer from bus to train is, ironically, counter to the one they are likely to make. When they leave the city, they generally take the train (i.e., the subway) to the bus terminal and then take a bus to the small town where their relatives live (a trip, incidentally, which is often described as "going home"). In fact, since long-distance travel by train is largely moribund in our culture, this unit probably strikes many children as old-fashioned. We will speculate on how such a perception might affect their reading comprehension as we present BLACK BONNET, the first unit in the next chapter.

NOTES

1. This happened only rarely on the tasks in our corpus. The other cases are (B) in LEARNING TO READ, (A) in GREEN CEDARS, and (B) in MOTHER ALLIGATOR.

2. In reporting on the interviews, we will use the neutral term *child*, except when gender or ethnocultural identity seems relevant to understanding what the child says. Age will be indicated for interviewees who are not third or fourth graders.

3. The general principle is that *the* marks old information, that is, information that is thought of as familiar to the audience. Presumably in answering questions about a text, one uses *the* if one assumes that the questioner has read the text and otherwise *a* or *an*. In this case, it would not have been possible to use *the* with *word*, since there are many words in the text that might be referred to. In any case, using *the* would have marked the target response formally, which test makers are careful to avoid. It would be possible to use *the* with *appearance* and *woman*, but these choices have been made so elliptical that they no longer connect easily with the text and *a/an* seems altogether more comfortable. On the other hand, it is not possible to be consistent and use *a caramel*, because the word is not used as a count noun in the passage (though it can, of course, be so used in other contexts to refer to an individual chunk of candy). It might have been less confusing to signal the mass-noun status of caramel by using it without any determiner.

4. We should make clear at the outset that our use of the term *strategy* does not imply that we think children plan all that they do or are even necessarily conscious of it.

5. For some African American children, the cues for subject-verb agreement in standard English may not be particularly salient, since they speak a dialect that signals this agreement in other ways (e.g., *He go to the candy shop*).

6. In writing this text, we are assuming a sophisticated readership. Yet, similar to (1) above, we have typically inserted *the word* before italicized terms to insure against even a momentary misapprehension. In the last two sentences above, however, this procedure would have resulted in the awkward

phrases "the word *word*" and "the word *the*," so, similar to (3) above, we decided to rely on italics alone.

7. We see here an instance of the point made earlier about differing patterns of subject-verb agreement in certain varieties of African American speech (i.e., the use of *was* with *raisins*).

8. This claim should perhaps be confined to classrooms in the United States. Two of our interviewers who had been educated in England failed to select the target response because they could not conceive of *the story* as being equivalent to *the passage*.

9. Throughout this study we report data gathered in group probes with adult subjects. Generally speaking, these adults were students in programs that deal with language and literacy at Teachers College, Columbia University. In evaluating their performance, it is important to bear in mind that they are probably more analytic in their approach to language than the average adult.

10. At the elementary level, the main idea is usually considered to be the subject matter that a text is focusing on. In higher grades, the subject matter of a text is usually referred to as the *topic* which is typically expressed by a nominal (e.g., *smoking*). The term *main idea* is often restricted to assertions that can be discussed and supported, which are typically expressed by propositions (e.g., *Smoking should be banned*). In any case, *topic* and *main idea* are quintessentially expository terms, and any use of them with narrative text inevitably leads to difficulties.

11. This display is based on the model of COHESION developed by Halliday and Hasan (1976). In essence, this model is concerned with the various kinds of presupposing relations that run through a text.

12. Most of the children we interviewed were prone to view the 'dramatis personae' in the test passages as fairly young children. This appears to be a further reflection of what we talked about in SHOP SIGN; namely, that many children respond to the passages from a highly personal point of view. As one African American child put it, "Jim was maybe about 9 or 10—like me." In this instance, the children's view of Jim as a young boy is probably quite sound. For one thing, the expression *Jim and his family* points toward this interpretation. Moreover, the narrative style embodies a child's point of view, though it may, of course, simply reflect adaptation to the intended audience.

13. It has been our experience that these contrasting usages often reflect contrasting lifestyles. New Yorkers who *go away* usually end up in a pleasant, quiet place, often the same place year after year, in which they proceed to vegetate. People who *take a vacation*, on the other hand, are likely to take a trip in which they cover a good deal of terrain.

14. To verify whether a train station is associated predominantly with cities, we asked 28 children to identify whether it is found primarily in a town or a city; only 6 of them associated it with a town.

15. A question of theoretical interest is whether in most languages the unmarked representation of movement is from home base to some other point, or vice-versa. There are cogent arguments for either view that we

cannot enter into here. If unmarked representation is, however, 'return' rather than 'departure'—and we think that it is—it might contribute, in some measure, to the surprising number of readers who selected *by the sea* as well as *in a little town*. In effect, we picture ourselves more easily as returning rather than leaving—it is as if we view ourselves, when reporting motion, as trying, much like Odysseus, to get back home (Hill, 1992).

16. Notice the merging of *little towns* and *cities* in her recall; this might provide evidence for a point that we established earlier: in picturing the train moving through other cities, readers must picture not simply the cities but intervening landscape that is non-city (unless, of course, they have the schema of a megalopolis where cities stretch end-to-end).

17. At this point, she actually uses the expression *going away*, but it does not affect her notion of where home is, presumably because she sees both the departure point and the destination point as home.

18. We might note that such usage has been particularly encouraged by real estate advertising in which the words *home* and *house,* for reasons that are not hard to imagine, have become virtually synonymous.

chapter 3

Excerpted Narratives

A s we pointed out in the introduction to Chapter 2, LEAVING HOME may occasion some disagreement as to how it should be categorized. We suspect that it was written for the test rather than taken from a longer narrative, and one can think of it as telling a complete story, though certainly not a very compelling one. It would have thus been possible to classify it as gapped. When we talked to children, however, we found that many regarded it as a preamble. They were left to wonder what happened after Jim and his family got to the little town near the sea. As already suggested, our classification scheme is basically built around how readers respond to the inherent incompleteness of a narrative.

The first narrative in this chapter could have been classified as truncated. Like LEAVING HOME, it can be viewed as just getting a story underway. On the basis of children's responses, however, we think it is better classified as excerpted. We also think that the way it is written provides subtle evidence that it is not an initial paragraph. The other two narratives in this chapter are not likely to occasion any disagreement—both are clear examples of starting out *in medias res*.

BLACK BONNET

Our first example of an excerpted passage presents a train scene:

The train stopped. Miss Esther stood far back to get away from the smoke and roar. As the cars pulled away, she took a few steps forward to scan the platform. There was no black bonnet with a worn lace veil, no old lady with a burden of bundles. There were only the station master, a boy or two, and a clean-faced bent old man with a bird cage in one hand and an old carpetbag in the other.

A.   What did Miss Esther expect to see?
    a lot of people   an old man
    a black bonnet a bird cage

B.   Miss Esther stepped forward when the
    crowd left   crowd arrived
    train left   train arrived

This scene, like the one in LEAVING HOME, comes from a world that no longer exists. The two differ, however, in the way in which they evoke this world. LEAVING HOME is written in a colorless style and provides readers little detail with which they can establish an earlier world. Here that world is captured by sensate detail: the train, for example, emits *smoke and roar*; and Miss Esther—the name itself is dated—searches for an old lady wearing a *black bonnet with a worn lace veil*. The very language used to render the detail itself evokes the past, at least for a reader accustomed to certain kinds of literary evocation.

These two units, despite stylistic differences, illustrate test makers' tendency to avoid contemporary material. This avoidance is presumably in the interests of fairness and neutrality, but in light of the pilot test results, one might question whether these interests are served. European American children seem to have an advantage in dealing with such material. Consider, for example, how readily a suburban child went from the detail of smoke to a dated world: "It was an old-fashioned train because they'd have smoke." European American children seem to have greater access to the ethnocultural norms represented in passages such as BLACK BONNET and LEAVING HOME. During the interviewing, we discovered several children who could talk about the old-fashioned trains pictured in storybooks such as *The Little Red Caboose* or *The Little Engine That Could*.

The sensate detail, important in establishing the dated setting, is not particularly helpful in supporting the central point of the passage—the contrast between what Miss Esther expected to see (described in sentence 3) and what she actually saw (described in sentence 4). Most of the children whom we interviewed had difficulty in retrieving this point. It tended to get lost in the "smoke and roar" of peripheral detail, as their performance on a recall task clearly indicates. The passage was displayed on a screen for 30 seconds, and then 34 children wrote down what they could recall of the passage (the number of children who mentioned the various bits of sensate detail is placed in parentheses):

Miss Esther's standing back and/or stepping forward (18)
bird cage and/or carpetbag (16)
smoke and/or roar (15)[1]
black bonnet (9)

Among these various details, the one recalled least frequently—black bonnet—is the one most closely linked to the central point. Moreover, only two children actually mentioned the contrast most central in the passage:

The lady didn't saw a black bonnet all the lady saw was a oldman a bird cage and a carpetbag.

She didn't see the black bonnet. She only saw a stationmaster and a bend old man with one hand in the bird cage and the other in the old bag.[2]

Neither child reproduced the parallel existential statements that anchor this contrast in the passage: *there was no/there were only*. Instead each rendered the contrast by referring to Miss Esther and her act of seeing: *she didn't see/she only saw*. We might note that the sheer bulk of detail some children managed to get down on paper made their omission of this contrast even more striking. One girl, for example, wrote the following:

The train was coming and the train stopped and she steped back so the smoke and the roar won't bother her. And she steped forward and steped in the train. she saw a man with a bird cage in his hand and a bag in his other hand. And she saw two boys with clean face.

We then asked 34 adults to do the same recall task. In general, they focused on the central contrast rather than the peripheral detail. Thirty-two of them mentioned this contrast, and several even used some form of the word *expect*, as illustrated by the following response (note the discursive commentary that often emerges in adult recall):

Miss Esther was waiting at the train station. She was expecting an elderly lady (probably a widow, if we can guess from her dress) and instead saw an old man carrying a bird cage and another object. This probably took place sometime early in this century or in the last, as it appears to be a steam locomotive that is pulling the train.

More than half of the adults, however, preserved some form of the oblique language in the passage. Ten of them, in fact, produced verbatim the *there was no/there were only* contrast:

> There was no black bonnet with wilted yellow lace worn by a figure burdened with candles. There were only the stationmaster and a boy or two.

Just why did children—as opposed to adults—have so much trouble in recalling the central point of the passage? Clearly, a number of factors are at work. To begin with, although children are drawn to sensate detail—as evidenced by their responses to the recall task—they are less inclined to establish pattern in that detail. Perhaps an even more basic factor is the oblique manner in which sentences 4 and 5 express the central point. These sentences contrast sharply with the previous three, which represent events and actions (i.e., train stopped, Miss Esther stood back, train left, Miss Esther stepped forward) from what might be called an external point of view.

This point of view, however, suddenly vanishes, and an internal one—presumably belonging to Miss Esther—emerges in its place. Sentence 4 merely registers the absence of a certain person and the reader is left to make two closely related inferences: first, that Miss Esther did not see the old lady, and second, that she had been expecting to see her. If the external point of view had been maintained, these propositions might have been overtly expressed (e.g., *She did not see the old lady whom she had been expecting*); and sentence 5, of course, would have begun with *she saw only* rather than *there was only*. It is obvious that children would have understood the passage better if sentences 4 and 5 had maintained *she* as the subject. It is noteworthy that the two children who actually recalled the contrast did, in fact, represent it in just this way.

Children's difficulties, however, did not arise merely from the shift between the first three sentences and the last two. Many of them came directly from the internal complexity of these last two sentences. We have already pointed out how sentence 4 parallels sentence 5 in order to convey the central contrast, as shown in Figure 3.1. In addition, the complement of each sentence consists of parallel nominals, as shown in Figure 3.2. Notice that the nominals vary in size and complexity, with the last nominal—one that has nothing to do with Miss Esther's expectations—being the most complex.

As young readers attempt to process all this embedded detail, they tend to lose their grip on the larger whole that the two sentences

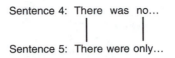

Sentence 4: There was no...

Sentence 5: There were only...

FIGURE 3.1

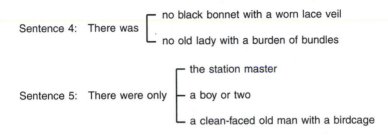

Sentence 4: There was
- no black bonnet with a worn lace veil
- no old lady with a burden of bundles

Sentence 5: There were only
- the station master
- a boy or two
- a clean-faced old man with a birdcage

FIGURE 3.2

express. By the time they wade through all the lace and bundles, the birdcage and the carpetbag, they may no longer be aware of the over-arching frame signaled by the contrast between *there was no* and *there were only*. That frame does, after all, extend over a good deal of syntactic space and is not easily processed (i.e., *there was no* and *there were only* are quite distant from each other).

Added to all the foregoing complexity is the fact that sentence 4 can be interpreted in two ways. From a pragmatic point of view, it is clear—at least to an adult reader—that this is a familiar kind of literary parallelism in which a person is first described synecdochically (i.e., a part stands for the whole), and then the figurative language is explicated by an appositive, as shown in Figure 3.3. From a strictly linguistic point of view, however, there is nothing to prevent a reader from assuming that the parallel nominals refer to separate entities, as shown in Figure 3.4. One child, for example, wrote:

She was looking for a black bonnet with blue lace and veil and a lady with bags.

Given this confusion, we decided to test which interpretation children would make when faced with a comparable parallelism. We gave the task in Figure 3.5 to 24 children in the fourth grade. Twelve answered that

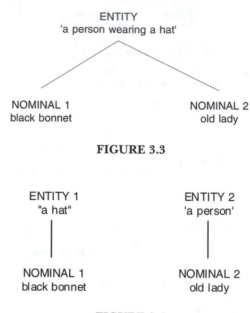

ENTITY
'a person wearing a hat'

NOMINAL 1
black bonnet

NOMINAL 2
old lady

FIGURE 3.3

ENTITY 1
"a hat"

NOMINAL 1
black bonnet

ENTITY 2
'a person'

NOMINAL 2
old lady

FIGURE 3.4

Read the following sentence. How many children did Mrs. Smith see on the merry-go-round?

Mrs. Smith smiled as she saw that red cap, that little boy waving from the blue horse on the merry-go-round.

FIGURE 3.5

she saw two children, 10 that she saw one child (the other 2 wrote *red cap* and *I don't know*). These results suggest that children of this age do not readily understand this kind of parallelism (though the wording *how many children* in the task may have led to a greater choice of two children).

There are thus two major sources of complexity that prevent children from grasping the central point of the passage:

1) the shift from an external perspective (sentences 1-3) to an internal perspective (sentences 4-5); and
2) the shift from appositonal parallelism (sentence 4) to nonappositional parallelism (sentence 5).

In responding to (A), the task concerned with what Miss Esther expected to see, European American children selected the target response—*a black bonnet*—more frequently than African American children did (35 percent to 21 percent). We should note, at the outset, that setting up *a black bonnet* as the target response is extremely misleading, given that test makers ordinarily construct tasks that require children to take a literal approach to figurative language. Hence *an old lady*, which was not actually provided as a choice, would have been more appropriate in that it describes the actual target of Miss Esther's expectations. Many of the children we interviewed made this very point. Certain of them were, in fact, incredulous upon discovering what the target response was:

C   What was she expecting to see? A whole load of people—first I put *black bonnet*, but you don't expect to see a bonnet.
I   What did you expect?
C   Somebody wearing a bonnet so that couldn't be right.

As the exchange continued, the child gradually became aware that *a black bonnet* was, in fact, the target response:

C   You mean it's black bonnet, don't you? Boy, is that stupid.

Another child expressed similar incredulity:

I   The correct answer is *a black bonnet*. I'm telling you the truth. The people who made the test up....
C   (interrupting angrily): It was *a black bonnet*?
I   Yes.
C   That's so queer.
I   Why?

The child answered with a heavy tone of sarcasm:

C   Well, they say, "There was no black bonnet with a torn [sic] lace veil." It doesn't mean that she actually has to see a black bonnet, that the old lady's going to come up to her and say, "Here's a black bonnet," and then run away.

As the girl continued to complain about this question, the interviewer suddenly asked:

I   Can you give me an idea of what you think would be a better question?
C   Well, like something that would be easy, like...uh..."What do you think Miss—Mrs. Esther felt like?" and then go (a), (b), (c), (d)—blah, blah, blah, blah.

I   Okay. What words would you use?
C   *Frightened, sad, happy, glad.*

During the interviewing we noticed that African American children, in particular, seemed to think that the choice *a black bonnet* was designed to be a trap (one even started referring to it as "a brown bonnet"). Consider, for example, the wariness of a ten-year-old girl:

I   Was there anything in the passage that mentions what she was expecting to see?
C   A black bonnet was in there, but I don't think she was expecting to see a black bonnet.

She went on to explain, somewhat derisively, that Miss Esther was not expecting to see a black bonnet, but rather an old lady wearing one. Many African American children, particularly the girls, knew what a bonnet is because their mothers and grandmothers are accustomed to wearing one to church. As one girl put it,

Grandma has lots of different bonnets—she wears a black one when somebody dies.

What is particularly striking about these children's failure to select the target response is that they did, in fact, understand the figurative language of the passage. They felt, however, that merely recycling this bit of language would be misleading, for it would indicate that Miss Esther was really looking for just a black bonnet. These children seemed to have developed some sense of a test norm that might be stated in the following way: whenever a passage uses figurative language, any task dealing with that language has to, as it were, defigure it. The target response should have been something like *an old woman.*

On the other hand, some children selected the target response, and yet did not understand the figurative language in the passage. When we asked one child about his choice of *a black bonnet,* he said that Miss Esther had expected to see a black bonnet "somewhere on the platform." Upon further questioning, he was unable to explain why she might expect to see an unattached bonnet there, even though, as indicated by the following exchange, he did know what a bonnet is:

I   Well, what do you think a bonnet is?
C   It's like, it's a hat, like, and with a cloth attached to the top of it and you can pull it. You can put it up over the hat or down to cover your face.

One child did try to motivate Miss Esther's search for a black bonnet:

> Well, Miss Esther, the old woman, arrived at the station. She got off the train and looked for the black bonnet. I guess her bonnet was blown away by the wind so she tried to find it.

This child views Miss Esther and the old woman as the same person; once he fused the two women into one, he pictured her as on the train rather than in the station.

Another child who chose *a black bonnet* resorted to a sequence of causal propositions in explaining his choice:

I   Okay, why did you choose a black bonnet?
C   Because in the passage they said, "There was no black bonnet," so instead of seeing a black bonnet Miss Esther saw an old man with a bird cage. So she was expecting to see *a black bonnet.*

The interviewer asked him to reread the passage and then asked him again about the black bonnet:

C   I think it might refer to a person because a thing cannot wear a worn lace veil.
I   Do you think *black bonnet* refers to an old lady?
C   Yes, maybe.
I   Did you think that when you were first taking the test?
C   No, I didn't think about that.

We came across a particularly interesting example of ethnocultural influence in the choice made by a Turkish girl who had recently moved to New York City. When she was asked whether Miss Esther was looking for someone wearing a black bonnet, she answered:

> No, because everyone could wear a black bonnet.

Apparently she was picturing the headdress of women in her own Muslim culture. She was then asked to justify her choice of *a black bonnet*, and she responded: "Maybe Miss Esther had lost it."

Even though none of these children selected the target response for the reason envisioned by the test makers, each would receive full credit in a normal testing situation. On the basis of our interviewing, we have discovered that children often choose—or, for that matter, avoid—the target response for a reason that the test makers were not able to foresee.

Let us now turn to the distractors shown in Table 3.1 and begin by observing that African American and European American children were

TABLE 3.1

	African American	European American
a lot of people	25%	35%
an old man	32%	16%

pulled in opposing directions during the pilot testing (when we come to (B), we will see a similar pattern of opposition). Usually children in the two groups are most attracted, though to a different degree, to the same distractor (see pp. 36–37 in SHOP SIGN, where we point out that the four choices are roughly parallel for the two groups).

Let us first consider European American children's greater attraction to *a lot of people*. As we observed in LEAVING HOME, they may have more experience of train travel than African American children do, and so are more likely to be misled by what an experienced train traveler knows—a train station tends to be crowded at the moment a train arrives. In fact, a number of European American children used this bit of real-world knowledge to justify their choice of *a lot of people*. Here are some examples of how they were misled by this knowledge:

(1)

I   So why do you think she was expecting to see a lot of people there?
C   'Cause at the train station usually there's a lot of people.

(2)

I   Why did you pick that *[a lot of people]*?
C   Well, if there is—if—usually on trains, there's a lot of people waiting.

(3)

I   Why did you think a lot of people were there?
C   Because there was a train and most trains have a lot of people there.

(4)

I   So why were there a lot of people there?
C   There are a lot of cars so if there's a lot of cars, there should be a lot of people that—aaah—come to use cars.

Certain children interpreted the particular attention to the lonely few at the station as itself indicating that Miss Esther had, in fact, anticipated a crowd. Consider, for example, the following exchanges:

(1)

I   Well, where did you get *a lot of people*?

C   Because there were only the station guy and this other guy—the clean old man—she was expecting to see a lot more people, right?

(2)

C   The answer to (A) is *a lot of people.*
I   Why?
C   There were only the station master, a boy or two at the train station. There was supposed to be a lot of people. Miss Esther expected to see a lot of people at the train station.

(3)

I   Now in—in (A)— what did you—you say she was expecting to see?
C   A lot of people.
I   Okay. Now what made you think she was expecting to see a lot of people?
C   (reads from passage) 'Cause *There was no black bonnet with a worn lace veil, no old lady with a burden of bundles. There were only the stationmaster, a boy or two, and a clean-faced bent old man with a bird cage in one hand and an old carpet bag in the other.*
I   Now, let me stop you a second.
C   *There was only*—that means that there weren't many people, and she was expecting a lot of people.
I   Okay, okay. So that's how you read it. You saw the word *only* and so you felt she was disappointed.
C   Yeah.

This child interprets the word *only* in a normative way—that Miss Esther was, in fact, expecting to see a lot of people.

Finally, some children—African American as well as European American—seem to have selected *a lot of people* as a last resort, eliminating, one by one, the other choices. One child articulated this BACKING-INTO-THE-ANSWER STRATEGY by saying that the answer couldn't be *an old man* or *a bird cage*, because Miss Esther did not "really see them"; and it couldn't be *a black bonnet*, because the idea of looking for a bonnet was "crazy." He then concluded that it had to be *a lot of people*, but gave no reason for his choice.

African American children's preference for *an old man* is probably best traced to two sources. First they may have responded more to the incipient dramatic structure of the passage. The old lady, presented first, is barely sketched in; and then the station master and the boy or two are given short shrift. Finally, the old man is described as if he is somehow the main point of the story, as if whatever drama is about to unfold will center around him as the major character. He is described as *clean-faced, bent,* and *old*; and he carries *a bird cage in one hand and an old carpetbag in the other.* For the child attentive to the dramatic function of language, surely it must be the old man whom Miss Esther was expecting to see.

Second, certain African American children seem to have been influenced by the multiple uses of *old* in the passage—*old lady, old man, old carpetbag* (even the *lace veil* is described as *worn*). It is as though they saw *old* everywhere and so wanted to pick a choice that included it—if not *old lady*, at least *old man*. We will have other occasions to observe how children can be misled by an oft-repeated word or concept.

Let us now turn to (B) and first note that it, like (A), is best described as a recycling task; that is to say, one that calls for information in the passage. In the case of (B), however, this information must be rephrased (*cars pulled away = train left*), whereas in (A) it needs only to be repeated. In this instance, African American children (49 percent) selected the target response more frequently than European American children did (43 percent). The latter's weaker performance can be traced to their substantially greater attraction to the distractor *crowd left*. When we examined the two most frequently selected distractors, we discovered that European American children were more strongly pulled toward this distractor (as shown in Table 3.2).

If European American children work with the schema 'a crowd welcomes a train,' they tend to assume that the relatively empty platform indicates that a crowd has left. But there is an even more compelling reason for their choice of this distractor: if they take *cars* as referring to automobiles rather than individual parts of the train, they can simply assume that all the people got in their cars and drove away from the station. Here's how one European American third grader explained his choice of *crowd left*:

I   Why did you choose when the crowd left on (B)?
C   'Cause it said, *When the cars pulled away.*
I   What kind of cars are these?
C   (a bit indignant) I'm not sure, because this story isn't realistic, and I haven't seen if this story is realistic. So how can I tell you what the cars are?
I   What did you picture about the cars? You thought there were a lot of people in the cars?

TABLE 3.2

	African American	European American
crowd left	12%	35%
train arrived	23%	9%

C   Yeah. If there's going to be some cars going away, there has to be at least a little bit of a crowd.
I   So did you think about cars like cars that drive on the street?
C   Yeah.
I   Do you know what else can be called cars?
C   Yes, of course—a train.
I   What if this is talking about train cars?
C   Well, then it would be when the train left.

Certainly this child has a point—the test makers could have avoided a great deal of confusion by following his suggestion. But then they would not have been in a position to create the kind of task that they need, one in which a certain proportion of test takers select a distractor.

We were curious to know to what degree European American children's association of *car* with "automobile" rather than "train part" may have contributed to their selecting *crowd left*. In checking up on what they knew about this word, we consulted *The Living Word Vocabulary*, a reference work on children's vocabulary compiled by Dale and O'Rourke (1976). This work states that 92 percent of children at the third-grade level know that *car* can refer to a "train part." We found this figure somewhat high, given that only 94 percent are listed as knowing that *car* can refer to an "automobile." We decided to give 20 children the task shown in Figure 3.6. Nearly half—9 children—filled in the second blank with an answer that contained the word *car*:

cars (3)	ox cars (1)	carrier cars (1)
box cars (2)	flat cars (1)	freight cars (1)

Given that they actually had to produce the word *car*, this is a relatively high proportion (consider, for example, that only 13 wrote *engine* in the first blank).

We then gave the receptive task in Figure 3.7 to the same children and found that all but one associated *car* with (b)—the number choosing

Here is a sketch of the train. Please label each part.

FIGURE 3.6

Which parts of a train are called cars? Circle the letter above each part that you choose.

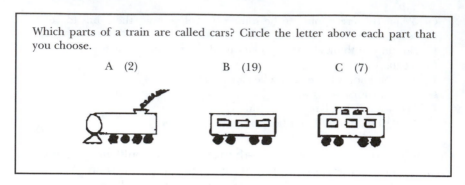

FIGURE 3.7

each letter immediately follows it. We were thus left with an intriguing question: if European American children are comfortable using the word *car* to refer to a part of a train, why did so many of them interpret it as referring to an automobile? If they think of *cars* as referring to automobiles, they can picture a sequence in which passengers who have rapidly descended from the train are whisked away by waiting cars, while Miss Esther, trying to orient herself, scans the platform; or they can imagine a scene in which the cars are driven by people who have brought to the station passengers who wish to board the train and that the drivers have not waited for the train to leave before they themselves leave the station. They can even imagine a scenario that combines elements of the above two. Whatever scene they imagine, the station is likely to resemble those in suburbia, where an adjacent parking lot makes arriving, waiting, or departing automobiles seem an integral part of the station. Indeed, it is this unit, perhaps more than any other in our corpus, that demonstrates how ethnocultural norms of language, thought, and experience can be as misleading to European American children as to African American children.[3]

There is an additional reason why certain children were confused by this task: they pictured Miss Esther as being in the train rather than on the platform. When reading this passage, most adult readers picture Miss Esther as standing on the station platform, mainly because of the words *Miss Esther stood far back*. For them, she could not be inside the train, because they do not conceive the aisle of a train as sufficiently wide to allow her to stand far back. Nevertheless, a reader can construct a scenario in which Miss Esther stood inside the train, far back from the exit, to avoid the smoke and roar. Certainly the passage opening—the short sentence *The train stopped* followed directly by a sentence that opens with *Miss Esther*—can lead a reader to position her in the train, particularly since stories and movies often focus our attention on the person(s) who arrive rather than the one(s) waiting for the arrival. To test how readers respond to the particular opening of this passage, we presented only the first two sentences of the passage to 30 children and then asked them where they pictured Miss Esther as standing: 18 of them pictured her as standing inside the train.

Once children commit themselves to this schema, they may hold on to it as they continue reading the passage. Consider, for example, what one child said as the interviewer questioned him about Miss Esther's location:

I   What was the relationship between smoke and roar and where she stood?

C   It went past the window.

I   Oh so you thought she was inside the train.

C   Yeah....She had to be in the train because mostly the smoke doesn't get—Have you ever seen an old-fashioned train in the movies—the smoke doesn't—It never goes in the place where the people are sitting down.

FIGURE 3.8

I   No, you're right about that.

C   It always goes the other way round; and that's why they have stations on one side and some on the other.

I   O.K. I think we need to draw pictures on this one.

The child and the interviewer then proceeded to draw pictures of the scene that each had imagined. The child's drawing is shown at the top of Figure 3.8, the interviewer's drawing at the bottom.

If Miss Esther is pictured as arriving on the train, there is a further indeterminacy as to whether she gets off at the station or stays on the train. If she does get off, then her few steps forward are on the platform; if not, they are inside the train itself. One child reasoned that she must have stayed on the train since the old lady had not come to meet her. The various possibilities for Miss Esther's location and movement are displayed in Figure 3.9.

None of these interpretations, in and of itself, prevents a reader from selecting the target response for (B)—or even for (A). Nevertheless, we have often observed that even the slightest indeterminacy in a passage can lead inexperienced readers to think that they are failing to understand something that they should. It is as if one blurred detail can cause the whole picture to go out of focus. As we move on to consider other units, we will have other occasions to observe how children can be thrown off track by a seemingly insignificant detail that they are unable to figure out.

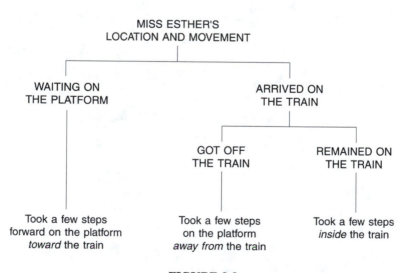

FIGURE 3.9

ALICE AND THE FAWN

We can verify that the following unit contains an excerpted narrative, since four sentences have been taken from Lewis Carroll's *Through the Looking Glass* with only slight modifications.

The fawn looked at Alice with its large, gentle eyes. It didn't seem at all frightened. "Here, then! Here, then!" Alice said, as she held out her hand and tried to stroke it. It moved back a little and then stood looking at her again.

A.   How did the fawn's eyes look?
   sad   gentle
   tired   frightened

B.   What did Alice try to do to the fawn?
   help it   hug it
   pet it   hide it

It is instructive to compare the excerpted passage with the original. The paragraph from which the passage was taken follows. It includes (1) brackets to indicate the beginning point and end point of the excerpt, and (2) italics to indicate the various points at which changes were made.

Just then a Fawn came wandering by: [*it* looked at Alice with its large, gentle eyes, *but* didn't seem at all frightened. "Here then! Here then!" Alice said, as she held out her hand and tried to stroke it; *but* it *only started* back a little, and then stood looking at her again.]

The changes, except for those involving punctuation, are listed in Figure 3.10.

The changes seem to be designed not only to make the text more readable for young readers but to reduce any sense they might have that

	Original	Test Passage
Sentence 1	It	The fawn
Sentence 2	but	Ø
	Ø	it
Sentence 4	but	Ø
	only started	moved

FIGURE 3.10

the fawn was frightened. For example, the *but* removed from sentence 2 seems to have signaled that the *large, gentle eyes* would be thought of as *frightened*. As we will see, many children restore the *but* when they recall what was in the passage. In addition, the verb *started* is replaced with *moved: started* carries the sense of sudden movement and, by virtue of phonetic similarity, is readily associated with *startled*.

During our interviewing, we came across a few children who knew that this passage was taken from *Through the Looking Glass*. One child whose father is a professor of English literature was even able to locate just where in the larger story this scene occurs. One African American boy talked about reading *Alice in Wonderland*, though he seems to have fused it, given his description of the fawn, with some classical tale:[4]

> I read a story about Alice and the Wardrobe, right, and then she went into this wardrobe, that's like a key passing through time or something like that and she finded a faun and the faun had some horns on his head. It had two horns. And starting at the neck or back was like a horse or goat and then its neck and head; it was human.

The interviewer then asked:

I   And you remember how that word *faun* was spelled in that story?
C   Yes.
I   How?
C   F-A-W-N.

One child, recently arrived from Jamaica, talked about having seen a movie entitled *Alice and the Fawn*. The interviewer tried to find out more about this movie, but did not have much success. From the description that the child provided, it may have been *Bambi*.

Most children are not familiar with the larger story from which the passage has been excerpted but still are led to invent a context in which to place the brief encounter between Alice and the fawn. Indeed, the nature of the detail, and the imaginative manner in which it is reported, leads most children to thicken the texture of the encounter, and as we will see, such thickening can lead children to pass over the target response and select a distractor in each of the tasks.

The tendency to expand this passage can be traced to three main sources, which will be considered in turn:

1) internal relations among the various actions and states that are reported;
2) children's real-world knowledge of how a fawn behaves in the presence of a human being; and

3) children's textual knowledge of what constitutes a narrative.

As to the first source, the following sequence of actions and states is represented in the passage:

1) The fawn looks at Alice.
2) The fawn does not seem frightened.
3) Alice speaks and acts:
   a) She says, "Here, then! Here, then!"
   b) She tries to stroke the fawn.
4) The fawn moves back.
5) The fawn looks at Alice again.

These actions and states seem innocuous, and yet when placed together they are likely to activate children's real-world knowledge that an undomesticated animal is likely to be skittish in the presence of a human being. This knowledge, in turn, leads them to view the fawn as frightened of Alice. Such an interpretation provides a dynamic connection—one involving cause-and-effect relations—between actions and states that would otherwise be viewed as static and without any real point. Hence readers are likely to draw upon a familiar narrative frame for binding the various elements in the passage together:

Confrontation:	A girl meets a young deer that appears not to be frightened.
Action:	The girl tries to pet the deer.
Result:	The deer now appears as frightened to the girl.

This frame is simple and yet has ample generative power. Consider, for example, the relation between the confrontation and the action: the first can be viewed as providing a motive for the second. The girl acted in the way that she did because she thought the fawn really was frightened, even though it seemed not to be. Or consider the relation between the action and the result: what the little girl did enabled her to confirm her original belief—the fawn was indeed frightened. Such fleshing out of the frame gives it the rounded contours that children experience when they are imaginatively engaged with a real story.

This frame is so powerful that children not only expand what is present but tend to extend it. Any real story would hardly end with a deer, frightened, stepping back from a little girl. Here's what one African American girl said when asked to recall what she had just read:

Once upon a time Alice was walking through the forest and she saw a fawn. It was beautiful and she saw how gentle it was looking at her. So she went over there and walked to it and tried to pet it. Then the fawn jerked back. She was wondering why did the fawn jerk back.[5] So she went over there and she went to get her friend. Her friends came. They all surrounded the fawn and then suddenly she got to it. And then she realized that the fawn had a broken leg.

The use of formulaic *Once upon a time* signals that this child wishes to produce a story of her own, not merely repeat what she has read; still she retains substantial detail from the passage, weaving it into a larger narrative. This child managed to select the target response for both tasks, even though her expanded narrative provided a context, which, in the case of many children, led to the choice of a distractor. It is as if her performance for the interviewer was one thing, her responses to the tasks quite another. When the interviewer asked her why she chose *gentle*, she simply replied: "Because that's what I read in the story." The distractor *frightened* may not have exercised much power, since she did not know that a fawn was a deer; in the context of the story she thought that it was a dog who would obviously be less frightened.

It was quite common that children did not know that the fawn was a deer. As we have seen, one thought that it was a faun, a mythical being. Some simply described it as an animal, although a number did try to specify its identity, describing it variously as "a person," "a forest animal," "an elephant," "squirrel of some kind," "like a bird," "like a duck," and "something like a goose." The child who described it as "like a duck" later talked about how Alice stroked "the fawn's feathers."

Following up on these confusions, we gave the task shown in Figure 3.11 to 160 third and fourth graders in two schools, one urban and one suburban (the numbers were relatively large because we wanted to contrast African American children with European American children in each setting). The proportions who selected *a baby deer* on this task are shown in Table 3.3. We can observe here two sharp contrasts: (1) considerably more European American children than African American children knew the word *fawn*, and (2) among African American children, many more children in the suburban school knew the word than in the urban school.

A fawn is most like

1. a small nest	3. a baby duck	5. a baby robin
2. a baby hamster	4. a baby deer	6. a mythical animal

FIGURE 3.11

TABLE 3.3

	African American	European American
urban	15%	82%
suburban	51%	87%

We then administered the actual test unit to these same children to determine whether there was any significant correlation between their knowledge of the word *fawn* and how they performed on the two tasks. We discovered no significant correlation, which supported what we had observed during the interviewing: for certain children, knowing what a fawn is adversely affected their performance on one or both of the tasks. Some of the children who selected *frightened* for (A) or *help it* for (B) were prone to talk about how a baby deer acts around people—it is frightened and so needs to be helped. Here, as in a number of other instances, we were able to see how children's real-world knowledge actively works against their selecting the target response.

Let us now turn to the tasks. (A), like the tasks in BLACK BONNET, can be described as an INFORMATION-RECYCLING TASK; it asks readers to affirm that the passage described the fawn's eyes as *gentle*. (B) can be termed a VOCABULARY-DEFINING TASK since its function is to determine whether readers know the meaning of the word *stroke*. Both of these tasks can be described as ACOMMUNICATIVE in that they ask readers to use language in a way that runs counter to everyday communicative norms. Thus, (A) requires readers to abandon their emerging understanding of the passage as a whole in order to locate and recycle a trivial detail. (B) requires readers to forsake meaning and focus on wording (i.e., to move from what is being said to how it is being said).

When information-recycling or vocabulary-defining do occur in everyday interaction, it is because someone has indicated in some way that communication has not taken place. Obviously, this is not the case with (A) and (B). They are examples of "teacher questions"—questions that arise not from a need to know, but from a desire to find out whether somebody else knows. As has frequently been pointed out, the psychological dynamics of such questions are different from anything that occurs in everyday interaction. The place where they flourish is a school setting, and it is, of course, the test that most perfectly embodies them.[6]

Sometimes the acommunicative nature of a test task is cued by the use of expressions like *In the story* or *The story says that*. Such locutions are evidently meant to imply that the answer should come from attending to the details, even the exact words, of the passage. Here, for example, is how (A) and (B) might have been written:

(A)   How did the fawn's   →   The story says that the fawn's
      eyes look?   eyes looked _____ .

(B)   What did Alice try   →   In the story, what does Alice
      to do to the fawn?   try to do to the fawn?

Notice that even with these cues readers still cannot be certain whether these tasks are information-recycling or vocabulary-defining. It is only when they get to the choices that they can tell one kind of task from the other. If there is a choice that recycles the relevant part of the passage, they select it as the target response. In the absence of such a choice, they must search for another kind of relationship with that part, namely, synonymy. Thus we could turn (A) into a vocabulary-defining task by substituting a synonym like *soft* for the target response *gentle*. Similarly, we could turn (B) into a recycling task by substituting *stroke it* for the target response *pet it*.

In the case of a vocabulary-defining task, one can introduce further wording that makes the vocabulary-defining status of the task clear. Consider, for example, how (B) might have been written:

What did Alice try   →   In the story the word
to do to the fawn?   "stroke" means _____ .

The presence of *the word "stroke" means* leaves no doubt as to what the point of the task is. The use of *in the story* also implies that the word *stroke* has several senses and that the one referred to is, in fact, the one that it has in the passage. In other words, the answer should be based on the passage rather than on general knowledge of word meanings. The fact that *stroke* has different senses is not, however, exploited in this task; that is, none of the distractors activates any alternative sense of *stroke*.

In our own thinking about the form of acommunicative tasks, we have found the terms *overt* and *covert* to be useful. We use OVERT to describe an acommunicative task that contains a formula, COVERT to describe one that does not. We use the terms FOCUSED and UNFOCUSED to describe the two kinds of overtness we have distinguished above. In Figure 3.12, these terminological distinctions are used to illustrate various transformations of (A) and (B).

Given the frequent use of formulaic material to cue an acommunicative response, its absence may not be as neutral as Figure 3.12 suggests. As children become familiar with the language used in standardized testing, they may come to rely on such cueing. If they then encounter a

Covert	Overt
The reader does not know that the task is acommunicative.	UNFOCUSED: *The reader can tell that the task is acommunicative but not whether it is information-recycling or vocabulary-defining.*
(A) How did the fawn's eyes look? →	The story says that the fawn's eyes looked _____.
(B) What did Alice try to do to the fawn? →	In the story what does Alice try to do to the fawn?
	FOCUSED: *The reader knows that the task is vocabulary-defining.*
(B) What did Alice try to do to the fawn? →	In the story the word "stroke" means _____.

FIGURE 3.12

task that lacks it, they may not recognize the acommunicative intent, particularly when a distractor has been included that fits with, indeed motivates, a communicative response. Both (A) and (B) provide such a distractor; and as shown by the table below, African American children, in comparison to European American children, were more drawn to it, at the same time that they were less drawn to the acommunicative target response, as shown in Table 3.4.

TABLE 3.4

		African American	European American
	Task (A)		
acommunicative target response	*gentle*	46%	64%
communicative distractor	*frightened*	25%	17%
	Task (B)		
acommunicative target response	*pet it*	26%	52%
communicative distractor	*help it*	47%	30%

Let us examine (A) in more detail. To select the target response *gentle*, the reader must locate the nominal *its large, gentle eyes* in the passage, realize that only a portion of it is relevant,[7] and be able to expand that portion into the target proposition: *The fawn's eyes looked gentle.* Such a recycling operation appears to be straightforward, but our work with children uncovered a number of difficulties. We have already pointed out one of them: that such a task, by its very nature, forces readers to work within an acommunicative framework, something that many third and fourth graders are unprepared to do.

Still another difficulty with (A) is its use of the word *looked*. This word is used twice in the passage, where it combines with the particle *at* to form a transitive phrasal verb. In (A), however, *looked* is a copula, meaning "seemed" or "appeared," that links *the fawn's eyes* with a predicate adjective. We found that some children, instead of taking *looked* as a copula, tried to use it in the same sense that they found in the passage. In other words, they thought the task was concerned with stating "how the fawn *looked at Alice*." They selected *frightened*, intending something like "The fawn looked at Alice in a frightened way." Some children who seem to have understood *look* in the same way selected *gentle*: for example, the girl who said in her recall of the passage (see p. 91):

It was beautiful and she saw how gentle it was looking at her.

We discovered, however, that the major stimulus for choosing *frightened* comes from motivated inferencing. Using the narrative frame provided on page 91, we can identify two separate points—stage 1 (confrontation) and stage 3 (result)—at which the fawn's eyes can be described as *frightened*. In interviewing children, we discovered that most who selected *frightened* were thinking of the fawn's eyes at stage 3. In describing the fawn's movement at this stage, African American children tended to use dramatic language, as illustrated by the following two uses of *jumped back*:

Then the fawn jumped back and looked at her.

So Alice reached out her arm to pet him but the fawn jumped back startled.

In the second example, the child's addition of *startled* comes close to Lewis Carroll's original phrase *started back*. This child, like many others, also restored the *but* that was removed from the original. We suspect that this restoration is a firm signal that a child views the fawn as frightened.

Three other children made the connection between the fawn's final movement and its frightened state quite explicit:

> It backed up as if it were frightened.

> It must have been frightened because when she tried to stroke her, he moved back.

> Because it kind of ran away. Animals run away usually when they are scared.

One child even speculated that the fawn moved back because it thought that Alice might be trying to hurt it:

> Maybe it thought that she was goin' to throw a stone and that's why it moved back.

At various points in our interviewing, African American children made interpretations that had to do with potentially aggressive behavior. It is important to note that this child's expansion of the passage content does arise from a crucial detail—the fawn's moving back—that invites speculation by virtue of its isolation at the end of the passage.

Certain African American children focused sharply on the fawn's eyes even at stage 3, adding detail that went beyond what the passage contains. One child pictured the fawn's eyes as "wide open" because of its fear:

> I   Why did you pick *frightened* as the answer to the first question?
> C   Because it say in the story when she tried to stroke it, it moved back and looked at her. His eyes, I think, were wide open so it must be frightened.

Another child, who had begun her written recall with the sentence *The fawn looked at Aliced with it's glorious eyes,* ended by focusing, once again, on the eyes:

> But the fawn stepped back 2 steps, But her eye's were a little frightened.

This girl was able to achieve a certain narrative unity with her sustained attention to the fawn's eyes (note that she also restored the original *but*).

There are good reasons for readers assuming that (A) is concerned with the appearance of the fawn's eyes at stage 3 rather than at stage 1. First, they might feel that the fawn's eyes have already been described at stage 1 and so there would be no point in repeating this description. Second, readers could assume that questions following a story tend to focus on the final state of affairs rather than some earlier state. If the passage and tasks are viewed as forming sequential discourse, then (A) immediately follows the statement that represents the fawn's second act of looking. In interviewing children, we have discovered that a "last-in, first-out" principle often accounts for the way they chunk information.

As noted in Chapter 1 (p. 10), the passage does provide information that allows a reader to infer that the fawn's eyes looked frightened at stage 1 as well as at stage 3. This interpretation opposes the actual state of the fawn's eyes to an apparent state. In effect, sentence 2—*It didn't seem at all frightened*—can be taken as a cue that it was, in fact, frightened. As one child who chose *frightened* put it, "It didn't look frightened but it was." She apparently interpreted (A) as concerned with how the fawn's eyes "really looked," since Alice, after attempting to pet the fawn, discovered that it was, indeed, frightened.

Moreover, the question is concerned with how the fawn's eyes appeared to Alice, the only person who was in a position to observe them (the task stem could be expanded to "How did the fawn's eyes look *to Alice?*"). If readers focus on Alice's point of view, they can readily interpret her actions as indicating that she herself thought the fawn was frightened. Most children, when reading the story aloud, utter her words, *Here then! Here then!*, with a soothing intonation.

Before leaving (A), we should note that many children, no doubt, selected *frightened* simply because it was present in the passage. There were children we interviewed whose only rationale for selecting this word was "'Cause it says so." As pointed out in SHOP SIGN (p. 39), test makers often include a repetition-distractor in the tasks they construct. In this instance, they included not only *frightened* but *tired*, which is closely related in graphic form to the word *tried* in the passage.

Let us now turn to (B), a task that also reflects a tension between an acommunicative target response and a communicative distractor. If we were to make explicit the intent of this task, we might paraphrase it as:

> Which of the following responses results in a proposition that would most closely parallel the one in the passage which states that Alice tried to stroke it (i.e., which contains a verb roughly synonymous to stroke)?

This metalinguistic intent, as already indicated, can be made overt by changing the task stem:

> In the story, the word "stroke" means _____.

Certain children were able to discern this metalinguistic intent, as evidenced by the following exchange:

I   What did Alice try to do to the fawn?

C   She tried to stroke it. *Stroke* is almost the same as *pet*, just in other words.

I   So you knew when you read these words that you were looking for something that was similar to the text itself?

C   Yes, *stroke* was almost another word for *pet*. That's my reason.

This child was able to use the lexical unit *try* in (B) to cue a search for a synonym, by returning to the passage where *to stroke* functions as the infinitival complement to the verb *try*. For more communicatively oriented children, the presence of *try* in (B) cued a search for a response that would represent what Alice was "actually trying" to accomplish when she stroked the fawn. In effect, these readers understood the task as embodying the following kind of question:

What was Alice trying to do for the fawn when she stroked it?

In response to this question, certain children, cued by the distractor *help it*, made what we are calling an *invited inference*: that is to say, they extended the text base by inferring that Alice was stroking the fawn in order to help it.

Here are a couple of examples of how African American children responded when asked why they thought Alice was trying to help the fawn:

(1)

C   Because it says right here—here it is [he then reads from the passage, replacing *stroke* with *help*].

I   How do you know she tried to help it?

C   She tried to stick her hand out for her to reach it.

I   How come you think that's a way of helping the fawn?

C   Save its life.

(2)

C   Because the fawn was hurt.

I   Does the story say that it was hurt?

C   No, but that's what I think.

This second child is aware that he is expanding the story but apparently feels justified in doing so.

We discovered other children who felt that the fawn was hurt. One child summarized the story in the following way:

A fawn got hurt and the girl is trying to help it. The fawn kind of ran away, got scared.

This child also chose *frightened* for (A). Indeed, many children who selected the communicative distractor for one task also selected it for the other one.

It is not altogether clear why a number of children thought that the fawn was hurt. As we mentioned in Chapter 1 (see pp. 10–11), they may have combined textual information—the fawn did not run away from Alice—with real-world knowledge—a fawn is the kind of animal that runs away from a human being—and made an extended inference that something was preventing the fawn from running away (i.e., the fawn was hurt in some way). No child provided us with such an explanation, but then it can be quite difficult to describe such subtle interactions between textual information and real-world knowledge.

The multiple senses of the word *stroke* provide another source of interference in children's responses to (B). The word can refer to a movement which is either "hard and quick" or "soft and caressing." Most dictionaries list the sense of hard, quick movement in the initial entries for *stroke* as a noun. For example, the *American Heritage Dictionary* initially defines *stroke* in relation to the more familiar word *strike*, an association which a number of children made:

1) an impact; blow; strike.
2) an act of striking.

This sense is reflected in such special uses as:

1) any of a series of movements of a piston from one end of the limit of its motion to another;
2) the sudden severe onset of a malady, as apoplexy or sunstroke.

This latter use would probably be salient for those whose primary experience of language is oral (e.g., "Be quiet now! You know Grandpa's had a stroke"). By way of contrast, the use of *stroke* as a verb to indicate "soft, caressing movement" would appear to occur more frequently in what can be described as a literate register. Children might, for example, encounter such use in a fairy tale:

And then Sir Gawain gently stroked the princess' golden hair.

During the interviewing, we discovered that many children did associate *stroke* with "a blow." One boy, for example, thought it meant "to grab something and push it forward." Another boy said: "Like when you row a boat, you stroke it." The interviewer then asked him to act out what stroking a fawn means, and he responded with a series of rapid, jerky gestures. When the interviewer asked whether it was "a nice action or a bad one," the boy replied, "A bad one." One child, while reading the passage orally, stopped and asked the interviewer:

C   *Stroking,* is that "to hit," right?
I   No.
C   No? But in a baseball bat, when you got to stroke somebody, you stroke him like that [takes a violent swing]. That's the meaning I have of *stroke.*
I   So that's what made you feel—
C   A stroke. Like this wood, and I stroke it at the tree or something. *Stroke* means like vroom, vroom, like that.

This child chose *help it* for (B). When asked for his reason, he replied:

Well, I think I just had to guess that word because I didn't find out about the stroke that I was thinking of.

Given these responses during the interviewing, we asked a group of 32 children what the word *stroke* means. Here's how they responded:

illness (13)[8]	paddle a boat (2)	pencil stroke (1)
swimming (5)	skim the water (2)	brush stroke (1)
a movement (3)	hit swiftly (1)	golf (1)
sunstroke (2)	12-stroke engine (1)	

Only two children defined *stroke* as roughly synonymous with *pet,* both using the expression "soft pat." During the interviewing, we discovered that the children who did know this meaning preferred *pat* to *pet* (i.e., they would make a vertical movement rather than a horizontal one to illustrate the meaning of *stroke*). It is as though the sense of piston-like movement lingers even in their understanding of *stroke* as a soft gesture. One girl freely mingled the soft and the hard as she tried to define *stroke:*

I   What does *stroke* mean?
C   *Stroke* means—sort of—"pet" or "pat"—sort of—very hard, something like that.
I   Can you describe it in words?
C   I could describe it as you stroke your bunny lovingly or dog lovingly.

In another attempt to find out how children understand *stroke,* we presented the task in Figure 3.13 to a group of 20 children (the number of children who placed a *C* in front of each sentence is placed in parenthe-

Here are some sentences that contain the word *stroke*. Circle the number of each sentence that uses this word in a correct way.

1. Homer's granddad had a stroke. (17)
2. Homer went out on the golf course to practice his strokes. (10)
3. Homer ate all the delicious strokes on his plate. (1)
4. Homer's mother told him to stroke the kitten gently. (2)
5. The recipe said to beat the cake batter 100 strokes. (10)

FIGURE 3.13

ses immediately after it). These two probes suggest that children of this age do not readily associate *stroke* with *pet*.

Finally, we should note that in our probe with African American children in urban and suburban schools, there was a significant gap in their performance on (B), as 59 percent of those in suburban schools but only 35 percent of those in urban schools successfully chose the target response. Unfortunately, we did not conduct a prior probe to explore their knowledge of the word *stroke*, but we suspect that there would have been a substantial difference. We also suspect that there would have been a strong correlation with their performance on this task. Knowing that *stroke* can be synonymous with *pet* is crucial in responding successfully to (B).

In closing our discussion of this unit, we would like to reproduce a story written by a ten-year-old African American child. He was an imaginative reader who talked freely about his approach to the various test units. When the interviewing was over, he voluntarily wrote down the following story:

> I was walking in the woods when suddenly I saw something move in the bushes. I went to see what it was and it was a deer it looked at me and it was a sad look. I looked back and saw it was caught in a trap, I jiggled the trap but it wouldn't open, so I took a rock and smashed it. I opened and the deer was free, it looked at me again and then it ran away.

This child selected a communicative distractor for both tasks on this unit—*sad* for (A) and *help it* for (B). These choices—taken together with his story—provide poignant commentary on his own experience as a test taker. Unfortunately, he lacked a rock that would allow him to smash the trap these tests set for him.

LEARNING TO READ

Let us now consider a third unit that contains an excerpted narrative:

> She looked at the calendar. "Only two more days and I go to school. In three days I can read!"
>
> Mama chuckled. "Not quite that soon, dear."
>
> "How many days?"
>
> "Some children learn to read in a few months. Some learn in about a year."
>
> A year? A whole year? Maybe not till she was seven? That would be awful!
>
> A.   How old is the girl in this story?
>
>   six   four
>
>   eight   seven
>
> B.   At first, how long did the girl think it would take her to learn to read at school?
>
>   three days   a few months
>
>   one day   a year

This passage differs from all others in our corpus in that it consists almost entirely of dialogue. It opens with an exchange between a "she" and a "Mama." The first statements in quotation marks are introduced by (1) *She looked at the calendar* and (2) *Mama chuckled* (we will hereafter refer to such sentences as INTRODUCERS). After the initial exchange, a second one ensues, but this time no introducers are used: there are simply two statements in quotation marks. The reader is able to attribute them to the daughter and mother respectively by drawing upon normative rules of turn-taking (and, of course, the content of the utterances). Then comes a statement that has neither an introducer nor quotation marks. In certain respects, it resembles direct speech (e.g., the use of fragments such as *A year? A whole year?*). In other respects, it resembles reported speech (e.g., the use of *she*). This hybrid statement—which we can describe as FREE INDIRECT SPEECH[9]—is used to represent not what the girl said but what she thought. The overall structure of the passage is summarized in Figure 3.14.

To experienced adult readers, this structure presents no real difficulty. We automatically make the various transitions from one utterance to the next; and when we come to the free indirect speech, we know that the writer is now reporting the girl's thoughts rather than her speech. But to children, the structure of the passage can present a number of problems. They are not able to make the various transitions with ease, and,

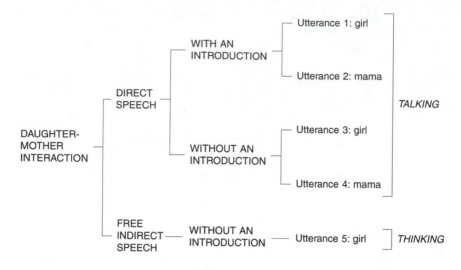

FIGURE 3.14

in fact, many are unable to make the final transition at all. Their oral experience of language has not prepared them to deal with the literary device—free indirect speech—used to represent the girl's internal reaction, and so they are not able to extract the information needed for responding to (A).

Most children were able to handle the direct speech without difficulty, whether or not an introducer was present. As we pointed out in SHOP SIGN, quotation marks are generally sufficient to cue even young readers that speech is being represented directly. We did discover a few children who seemed unable to work with the initial pair of introducers. It is as though they expected an introducer to contain a verb that refers to an act of speaking (e.g., *She said* or *Mama replied*). One child seemed to think Mama's chuckling constituted one speech act and the quoted words that follow a separate act to be attributed to the little girl.

Before considering children's difficulties with (A), let us first note its similarity to (B). Each calls for a response that involves a calculation. Neither calculation, in and of itself, is difficult: for (A), $7 - 1 = 6$, and for (B), $3 - 2 = 1$. What children find difficult is knowing that the tasks call for a calculation. During the interviews a number of children were surprised when they found out what the point of the tasks was. As one child exclaimed, "Oh, now I get it. This is like a logic test." He went on to explain that he expected to do "word problems" only on a math test.

This difficulty with tasks that call for calculation is illustrated by children's performance on another unit in our corpus which we refer to as CLASS ELECTION.

> The class became very quiet as Joan opened the last few ballots. The count was 17 to 17. Then she opened the final ballot. "Our new president," she said, "is Jason Brandt."

A. They were voting for
   a new club   class president
   club president   a class name

B. The final count was
   18 to 17   17 to 17
   Jason Brandt   Joan and Jason

In order to select the target response for (B), children must understand that when Joan "opened the final ballot," the count, which had been 17 to 17, became 18 to 17. In effect, they only need to perform the simplest of calculations:

$$\begin{array}{r} 17\text{ to }17 \\ +1 \\ \hline 18\text{ to }17 \end{array}$$

This calculation is obviously easy for children at this level, but for some reason most are not able to understand that this is the point of the task. During the pilot testing, only 19 percent of the African American children and 21 percent of the European American children selected this response. When we interviewed children, they were generally unable to focus on the need for the above calculation. Most children accepted the overt mention of *17 to 17* as representing the final count (on the whole, children seemed to be unfamiliar with the ballot-counting scene evoked by the passage). Since no numeral is used in reference to the final ballot, it may be difficult for children to integrate this information with the numerically encoded information that precedes it. In contrast, a math problem ordinarily specifies numerically all the relevant information needed to carry out the appropriate calculations.

To return to LEARNING TO READ, the difficulty of performing the required calculations was, no doubt, exacerbated by the particular nature of the passage. Upon encountering an intimate exchange between a daughter and mother, even experienced readers are not likely to feel the need to make explicit the information that these calculations lead to. They are more likely to wonder about, say, the relations between the mother and daughter or what they meant by what they said: for example, just what did the daughter have in mind when she said that she would be able to read in three days?

In order to determine to what extent readers make these calculations after an initial reading, we displayed this passage on a screen for 25 seconds to selected groups of adults and children. We then displayed the two tasks without the choices. Out of 18 adults, 10 were able to select the target responses, *six years* for (A) and *one day* for (B). Out of 34 children—17 African American and 17 European American—only two from each group selected the target response for (A), and no one selected it for (B). The superior performance of the adults may be traced to a number of factors. They are, as already pointed out, graduate students specializing in language study. Moreover, the test-like situation seems to have prompted them to process more low-level detail than they ordinarily would. Finally, the amount of time allotted, in principle, allows for at least one re-reading; and adults have learned how to use extra time in a testing situation to ferret out the kinds of detail they are likely to need.

Added to the unexpected nature of the two calculations is one other feature that makes them difficult for children. In selecting a response to (A), the wording *she was seven* is available at the end of the passage; and in selecting a response to (B), the wording *In three days I can read* is available at the beginning. If these expressions are considered apart from context, they can be viewed as justifying the choice of *seven* and *three days*, which were, in fact, the most popular distractors during the pilot testing. In effect, the tasks would be constituted as acommunicative—requiring only that information be recycled—rather than as communicative—requiring that an actual calculation be made.

The proportions of children who selected the acommunicative distractors during the pilot testing are shown in Table 3.5. As can be seen, the two groups of children did not differ in the degree to which they were attracted to an acommunicative distractor in (A). In (B), however, the European American children were somewhat more prone to constitute the task as merely a recycling one. Their stronger orientation to an

TABLE 3.5

	African American	European American
seven	41%	41%
three days	42%	49%

TABLE 3.6

	African American	European American
six	26%	40%
one day	19%	17%

acommunicative approach, which often works in their favor, may have led them to choose *three days*.[10]

The above pattern is reversed when one examines the proportion of children selecting the target response on the two tasks, as shown in Table 3.6. In this instance, it is (A) that reflects the ethnocultural difference—a significantly larger proportion of European American children selected *six*. With respect to (B), children in the two groups did not differ significantly. In fact, the proportion in both groups fell below chance, as was the case in SHOP SIGN.

As already pointed out, the information that (A) calls for is buried at the end of the passage in the free indirect speech that is used to represent the girl's internal reactions. We cannot here enter into the complex ways in which free indirect speech differs from, yet overlaps with, direct speech (see Banfield, 1982, and Quirk, Greenbaum, Leech, & Svartik, 1985, for such a discussion). Two mandatory shifts that take place whenever a writer moves from one mode to the other are illustrated in Figure 3.15. The first involves a shift from first to third person; the second is often referred to as BACKSHIFTING in that it parallels a shift from present tense to past tense (i.e., $\emptyset$ to *-d*). Both shifts are at the propositional core—subject and verb. At the adverbial periphery, *next year* could shift to *the following year*, but it doesn't have to.

Let us return to the passage and consider how these shiftings might have confused an inexperienced reader. The passage, until the final two lines, has included only two kinds of sentences:

1. those containing the features [+third person] and [+past tense] which describe actions

| Direct speech: | I | will + $\emptyset$ | come next year. |
| Free indirect speech: | She | [will + -d] = would | come next year. |

FIGURE 3.15

a) She looked at the calendar.
b) Mama chuckled.

2) those enclosed in quotation marks which represent speech
   a) "Only two more days and I can go to school. In three days I can read."
   b) "Not quite that soon, dear."
   c) "How many days?"
   d) "Some children learn to read in a few months. Some learn in about a year."

Hence, we may view the passage, until the final paragraph, as consisting only of narrative descriptions and direct speech.

Upon encountering the final paragraph, children may view the initial fragments *A year? A whole year?* as continuing the direct speech, even though no quotation marks are present. These fragments contain neither pronoun nor verb, so they cannot themselves signal the shift to free indirect speech; and, given the absence of pronoun or verb, they do not appear to be descriptive statements containing the features [+third person] and [+past tense]. Yet as readers move to the next fragment—*Not till she was seven*—they may assume, upon processing the two words *she was*, that the mode of descriptive statement has reappeared. On the surface, *she was* appears to be expressing past tense, much as *she looked* and *Mama chuckled* does. The likelihood of readers assuming this textual consistency is, no doubt, increased by their lack of familiarity with the use of verb backshifting to signal free indirect speech; and as we have already suggested, no introductory clause such as *she thought* alerts them to the presence of this mode.

What do children make of this final paragraph as they deal with these confusing signals? Some made very little of it, having no idea to whom it should be attributed. Others took the pronoun cue—*she* instead of *I*—as referring to the writer of the passage rather than to the characters:

C   I think it was the writer, probably.
I   Is there any way you can tell?
C   Because it said *she* and not *I*.

Still others used the same cue to ascribe the words to the daughter:

C   I think it's the girl in the story. She was just thinking this over in her mind or something.
I   She was thinking this over in her mind?
C   She was thinking, *A year? A whole year? Maybe not till she was seven?* She probably was thinking that in her mind.

It is possible that children could extract from the final paragraph the information needed for responding to (A), without attributing it to any one person. The words are, after all, the same, whether they are ascribed to the little girl, the mother, the writer, or to no one at all. The children we interviewed, however, were generally not able to make much use of any stretch of language that they could not meaningfully situate in the larger discourse.

Children's difficulty with this final paragraph is intensified by its fragmentary nature. In order to perform the calculation called for by (A), children have to combine the first two fragments—essentially conveying the same information—with the third. In effect, they need to know that together the three convey the following information:

> Maybe not till she was seven, a whole year [from now], [would she be able to read.]

Before discussing how a reader supplies the two bracketed bits of information to form a syntactic whole, we would like to note how unnatural either would have sounded if it had actually been in the final paragraph. As writers of imaginative fiction have long known, the technique of syntactic fragmentation is particularly appropriate for conveying the texture of the language we think in. Our thinking moves toward a state of pure predication, one in which words that convey old information are continuously suppressed.

In examining how the bracketed words represent old information, we must, of course, work from the little girl's perspective, for it is in her consciousness, at a particular point in the narrative, that certain information must be viewed as either new or old. The second bit of bracketed information—*would she be able to read*—has been provided by what the mother has just said, and so the little girl doesn't have to supply it. However, the first bit of bracketed information—*from now*—is not retrievable from the immediate discourse. Rather it expresses a frame of reference that human beings take for granted in both external and internal speech. Linguists such as Bennett (1976) and Fillmore (1997) have used the term DEICTIC to describe the use of one's own spatiotemporal location (i.e., the "here and now" of communication itself) as an unspecified reference point. We will, however, use the term ANCHORED rather than deictic, contrasting it with UNANCHORED, to distinguish the two modes of interpreting an utterance like "I'll do the job in a week." In the anchored mode, the point at which the job will be done is seven days from the speaker's now, but the job itself may take a day, a month, or any length of time. In the unanchored mode, however, the job itself will take a week to do, but it may be started the next day, a month later, or whenever. In effect, the anchored mode is inception-oriented, the unanchored mode extent-oriented:

Anchored: I'll do the job in a week [from now].
Unanchored: I'll do the job in a week [ø].

When we come to (B), we will see that both modes were used by children in interpreting the little girl's statement *In three days I can read.* Some anchored it in the little girl's now, but others, particularly the African American children, took this statement as describing the extent of the time period that the little girl thought would be required for learning to read.

There is an accumulating body of research that suggests European American children are more prone to use an anchored mode of interpretation than African American children (see Hill, 1998 for a review of this research). Hitherto this difference has been demonstrated in a spatial domain rather than a temporal one. European American children are more likely, for example, to work off their own "here" in making an utterance like *Hey, that's my pen in front of the telephone.* As shown on the left in Figure 3.16, they are prone to envision the pen as located in an orientational field that takes its source from the point where they are. African American children, however, are more prone to locate the pen in an orientational field that takes its source from the point where the telephone is, as shown on the right in Figure 3.16. We have collected evidence that suggests that African American children's lesser use of 'here' is paralleled by a lesser use of 'now.' If it is, this may help to

ANCHORED   UNANCHORED

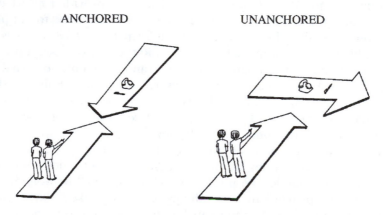

FIGURE 3.16

explain why they experienced more difficulty in dealing with the tasks in this unit.[11]

Apart from these ethnocultural differences, all children have difficulty in anchoring spatial and temporal phrases when they are reading. Such difficulty contrasts with the ease they display in supplying the 'here and now' in their oral experience of language. Consider, for example, the little girl's language in the passage. It provides three examples of anchored temporal phrases—*Only two more days, In three days,* and *A year? A whole year?*—and each fits naturally with what she is saying. As readers, we take such language use to be normal for a six-year-old child. Moreover, children of this age are competent in interpreting their interlocutors' anchored language (i.e., they can decenter to the 'here and now' of the person they are talking to).[12] This decentering skill, however, is less in evidence when they are reading, for children often fail to supply the 'here and now' that is needed to make sense of an anchored phrase (e.g., *A year? A whole year?*). It is as though children's decentering skills are limited to the immediate world of space and time that they experience during face-to-face communication.[13]

One other factor may have contributed to African American children's greater difficulty with (A). As research by Labov (1970) suggests, narrative style in African American speech communities tends to focus on external events, avoiding, for the most part, overt psychologizing within the narrative itself. Moreover, those who use this style will often report internal experience as though it were external (i.e., that which was merely thought will be reported as if it were spoken). In this sense, this narrative style resembles what can be found in traditional oral cultures: the story teller focuses on external events, leaving the audience to infer the characters' internal responses to these events. Upon completion of the narrative, however, members of the audience, along with the narrator, often explore just what these responses might be. Indeed, a major function of oral narrative is precisely to stimulate such exploration.

According to Labov, this style is embedded in a cultural system of communication that places greater reliance on bodies of shared information. This system also relies heavily on paraverbal and nonverbal channels in transmitting information concerning how people feel about experience. In effect, speakers directly display emotion, both their own and that belonging to the people they talk about, and so they have less need to encode it verbally.

Given these ethnocultural patterns, many African American children would be less familiar with the narrative structure of the passage, one that requires them to move from external events to internal ones; that is to say, from activities such as looking at a calendar, speaking, and chuckling—which are potentially available to any observer present at the scene—to an activity such as thinking, which is not directly available to such an observer.

Given all the difficulties we have delineated, we were not surprised to discover that many children whom we interviewed resorted to real-world knowledge in responding to (A): in effect, they ignored the final paragraph leading to the calculation and simply reasoned how old the little girl would be if she were starting school. In drawing on such knowledge, the age that children set up for the girl could vary considerably, according to whether they associated starting school with attending a prekindergarten program, kindergarten, or the first grade (it would, of course, be much easier for them to specify when they started first grade as opposed to school). Children's notion of 'starting school' can be quite vague, since it is subject to a range of factors in their own experience: for example, did they themselves attend a prekindergarten program? And if so, was it housed in the same building as the regular school programs?

During the interviewing, we became aware that certain African American children who had participated in prekindergarten programs such as Operation Head Start were prone to select the distractor *four*. Here is how one of these children justified this choice:

I   So why did you choose *four*?
C   'Cause at four years old you go to school.[14]

Some of these children further reasoned that *four* was a better choice than *six* since it would be consistent with the little girl not knowing how to read. As one of them put it:

If she's four, she maybe can't read.

This particular child went on to point out that if the little girl were six, she would already know how to read. Clearly he was able to use his real-world knowledge to make sensitive inferences about what he reads. In this instance, however, this skill led him to select what can be described as a REAL-WORLD KNOWLEDGE DISTRACTOR.

During the pilot testing, the distractor *four* had been somewhat more attractive to the African American children (23 percent as opposed to 14 percent for the European American children). In order to get a better sense of what African American children think about starting school, we asked 21 third graders (1) how old children are when they first go to school and (2) how old they were when they first went to school. Their responses are shown in Table 3.7. In responding to both questions, the great majority—85 percent—designated an age younger than the prototypical age—6 years old—associated with starting first grade.[15]

TABLE 3.7

	2-3 Years Old	4 Years Old	5 Years Old	6 Years Old
Question (1)	7	2	9	3
Question (2)	8	4	6	3

By way of contrast, many European American children we interviewed used the word *school* to describe postkindergarten experience. One girl, for example, made this point in explaining her rejection of the choice *four*:

> Because she would only be in kindergarten if she was four.

Other European American children actively justified their choice of *six* by identifying it as the age at which children begin school (i.e., enter first grade). One boy, for example, said:

> That means that she is going—like—to first grade; and if someone's got to go to first grade, they got to be six.

He went on to make the ingenious point that, in one sense, the little girl already knew how to read. When she looked at the calendar, she was able to "figure out what it said."

This task reveals quite dramatically two different ways in which the use of real-world knowledge can be used in interacting with a task: it can be used to justify either the target response or the distractor. In one instance, children receive credit for their response; in the other, they receive no credit at all. Yet in both instances, children have followed a similar pathway that can be characterized as PASSAGE-INDEPENDENT (we will use this term more extensively in Chapter 6 when we deal with tasks that accompany expository passages).

Let us move on to (B), bearing in mind the substantial comparison of the two tasks that has been already made. It should be remembered that, despite the apparent similarity of the two tasks, more children had difficulty with (B) during the pilot testing. The repetition distractor *three days*, as already shown, was particularly attractive to children in both groups. It was as if children, failing to understand the real point of the task, grabbed on to whatever they could.

The greater difficulty of this task may be partly attributed to its syntactic complexity. Whereas (A) has only one verb, (B) has four—*think, take, learn,* and *read*—each functioning at a different structural level. A version of the sentence somewhat closer to the deep structure would be:

> The girl thought that for her to learn to read would take so long.

An additional level of structure is represented by *at first*, the initial adverbial that modifies all of the remaining sentence.

In reading (B) aloud, a number of children were not able to render clearly the tone groups that signal the underlying syntactic relations. Evidently, the syntactic complexity prevented their chunking the words into meaningful groups. This was all the more striking in that all the individual words could be pronounced easily. All 18 of them—the most used in any task stem in our corpus—are monosyllabic words that can be found in the most ordinary kind of talk.

We have already pointed out how test makers tend to write a task as simply as possible (e.g., in SHOP SIGN, they wrote *What was the mystery?*, rather than, say, *What did the townspeople think was a mystery?*). It is thus interesting to speculate on why they made this one so complex. To begin with, they probably added *at first* so that children would focus on what the girl thought at the beginning of the passage rather than at the end. If the children focused on the end, they would choose *a year* rather than *one day*.[16]

Why then did they include *at school* at the end of the task? At first glance, this final spatial phrase seems less motivated than the initial temporal one. In fact, the test makers probably would have preferred—had it not made the task even wordier—another temporal clause like *once she went to school*:

> At first, how long did the girl think it would take her to learn to read once she went to school?

This version of the task manages to focus on what is crucial—the point in time at which she thought she would begin to learn to read.

We cannot be certain why the test makers included the final phrase *at school*, but we suspect that it had to do with their concern that children might anchor *how long* in the girl's now:

> How long [from the point at which she was talking] did the girl think it would take her to learn to read?

The form of the question, strictly considered, does not allow for such expansion, for the *how long* focuses only on the unanchored duration that the girl projects for learning to read. To allow for the above expansion, the task would have had to be written differently:

> How long [from the point at which she was talking] did the girl think it would be until she had learned to read?

It is not surprising, given this underlying complexity, that many children were confused about whether *how long* should be anchored or not.

When discussing (A), we pointed out a number of reasons why young readers tend to become confused about a temporally anchored statement. In this instance, there are a number of factors that heighten the possibilities for confusion. To begin with, *how long* focuses on an imagined temporal extent—as opposed to an actual one—and this fact alone may have led some children to anchor it. Given that the act of imagining is itself anchored in the little girl's 'now,' it is as if the content of that act comes, by a kind of osmosis, to be anchored there as well.

More important, however, is the fact that readers, in order to interpret *how long* at all, must anchor the two temporal phrases that the little girl uses in her initial utterance. In the case of the first, this anchoring flows naturally from the presence of *only...more*:

> Only two more days [from now] and I go to school.

The second phrase, however, contains no specific markers that call for anchoring:

> In three days I can read.

Rather anchoring is signaled by the position of *in three days*. This phrase, like the preceding one, receives tonic stress and, concomitantly, semantic foregrounding:

> *Only two more days* and I go to school.
> *In three days* I can read.

This parallelism leads the reader to process the two as a single unit of discourse, and so anchoring spreads from the first to the second:

> *Only two more days* [from now] and I go to school.
> *In three days* [from now] I can read.

We might note that, apart from the parallelism, the mere fact that *in three days* is frontshifted favors anchoring. Notice that the first sentence of the following pair is more likely to be anchored than the second:

(1) *In three days* I can read.
(2) I can read *in three days*.

Even in (1), however, the effects of frontshifting are at least partially offset by the presence of *can*. This auxiliary tends to block the anchoring of any concomitant temporal phrase. Notice, for example, how a simple change from *can* to *will be able* strengthens the possibility for anchoring:

(1) In three days I can read.
(2) In three days I will be able to read.

The echo of *from now* can be heard more strongly in (2), and it becomes even stronger when *in three days* is placed at the end of the sentence:

I will be able to read in three days [from now].

We suspect that *can* may, in fact, have been a factor in many children's choice of *three days* in (B). Inexperienced readers often allow a local cue to exercise more power than it should. It is only as readers place *can* in a larger context that they are able to suppress its misleading effects. We can represent this context by adding the preceding sentence initiated by *only two more days* to the following sentence that represents what the mother said (Figure 3.17). The fact that the mother uses *soon* rather than a word like *fast* shows that she herself treats the daughter's utterance as anchored (Figure 3.18).[17] Obviously this kind of cue is accessible only to a reader who is skillful in integrating various parts of this text. Most children were, of course, not even able to chunk the two sentences that the daughter uttered, as indicated by the exceedingly small number who were able to choose *one day* as a response in (B).[18]

Let us now turn to a set of problems much less technical than the preceding ones, but perhaps even more troubling to children in their approach to (B). These problems are best viewed as pragmatic, for they have to do with what readers think the little girl really meant when she uttered the words: *Only two more days and I can go to school. In three days I*

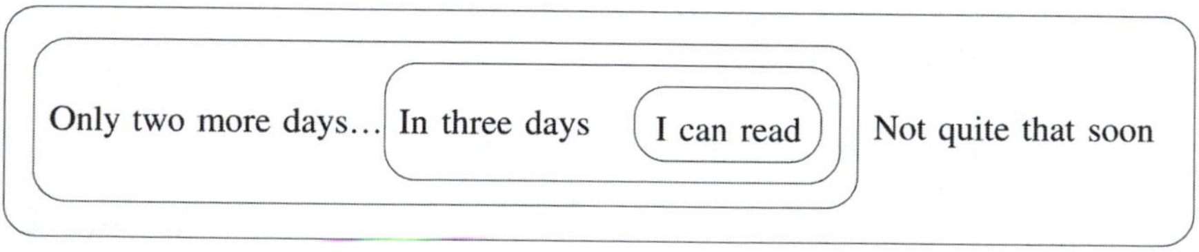

Only two more days... In three days I can read Not quite that soon

FIGURE 3.17

	DAUGHTER		MOTHER
Anchored	In three days [from now]	I can read.	Not quite that *soon*.
Unanchored	In three days [Ø]	I can read.	Not quite that *fast*.

FIGURE 3.18

can read! To adult readers experienced in dealing with literate—indeed, literary—representation of children's talk, the boldness of the little girl's utterance may itself be taken as a cue to what she meant—just to go to school is to be in the place where reading takes place; and so they are motivated to select *one day* even without performing the mental arithmetic of subtracting 2 days from 3. In fact, such a pragmatically oriented reader might even prefer a more reduced answer than *one day*, for it seems clear that the little girl is not really concerned with delineating a precise period of time in which the activity of learning to read will take place. Rather she is making a symbolic statement that simply passing through the school door is to enter the world of reading, and, in one sense, she is right, for school is the place whose *raison d'être* is to teach children how to read books.[19]

It is true that the mother does not respond to her daughter's words as being merely symbolic. She—as parents are wont to do—forces her daughter to face the literal import of her words (in this sense, she is embodying school practice itself, which can even lead a reader to wonder why she has not already taught her daughter to read); and it is further true that the daughter goes along with her mother's ploy. But even these two facts do not necessarily support what (B) forces the reader to assume: that the little girl, at the moment of speaking, was thinking she would be able to read after one day at school. We cannot ignore what ethnomethodologists have taught us about conversational meaning: that it is socially constituted (i.e., it resides in social interaction rather than in the minds of the speakers).[20]

Children who did not try to figure out what the little girl really meant by her words had an advantage in responding to (B). By accepting what this task assumes, they were then in a position to accept *one day* as simply expressing the little girl's naïveté. As one child put it, "That's crazy to think you can learn to read in one day." Focusing on the little girl's naïveté, however, led this child to choose the distractor *four*, on the assumption that a six-year-old child would not be so naïve to think that she could learn to read straightaway. As he put it, "Anybody who's been to kindergarten knows better."

One child even ignored the little girl's statement altogether, since it did not make any sense to him. In defending his choice of *a year*, he said:

> Because you cannot learn to read in one day, or in three days, or even in a few months. It took me a whole year to learn to read.

We can observe here what we described in (A): a child being led astray by real-world knowledge. Indeed, in this task, two of the distractors—a *few months* as well as *a year*—function as real-world knowledge distractors. Given this child's notion of 'learning to read,' he is led to select a response that involves a more extended period of time.

There were other ways in which children were led astray on this unit: for example, trying to figure out what the little girl really meant by "learning to read." The daughter of an English professor provides an interesting case in point. She failed to choose the target response for (B), selecting *three days* instead (this happened on only one other task in our corpus, and in that instance her failure, as we hope to convince you, is best viewed as a success). When she realized that she had not selected the target response, she was visibly disappointed. But she struggled gamely to make sense out of the little girl's initial statement:

> I guess she meant a word here and there, because you can't learn how to read a paragraph that fast. She was just thinking about a few tiny words like *it, the, art*.

It was her father who was conducting the interview, and even he was puzzled at her having included *art* in the list of easy words:

I *It, the,* and what?
C *It, the,* and *art*. A-R-T. Art.
I A-R-T. Art. I see. Uhmm.
C And small words like that. And her name.

She goes on to tell about her own experience of learning to read:

> I learned to read when I was about three-and-a-half. We had these easy reader books, like *Foot Book*. It is all about foot, like F-O-O-T; and it tells all about foot; and like the small words, you know, I learned how to read them even before I went to school. And so I was—I could read pretty clearly, but not really the hard words like, let's see, *units*, for example. But I could read small little words—*it, the, is, my*, and words like that.

The father then points out that he didn't know how to read when starting school, but thought he would learn to read automatically:

I thought a short time later I'd be able to read all the comic books.

The daughter cannot resist a mild reprimand:

Yes. Anyway, you shouldn't have even read comic books.

She uses this bit of parent–child exchange as a springboard for commenting on the fact that the mother in the story did not understand what her own daughter had meant when she was talking about learning to read:

The mother thinks the girl means that she could read some really hard book like that—like *The Count of Monte Cristo*.

In closing our discussion of this unit, we would like to suggest that any assessment of reading comprehension needs to take account of children's capacity to work out pragmatic meaning for what they read; and yet here the child's legitimate concern with such meaning led her away from the temporal detail that (B) calls for. In effect, her quest for pragmatic meaning obscured a certain kind of literal detail, one that did not mesh well with her understanding of what the little girl was really trying to say.

ADDENDUM

When we conducted the probe in which adults and children responded to the tasks without the choices provided, we came across other ways of chunking the two temporal phrases in the girl's utterance. First of all, each group included two individuals who responded to (B) with *five days*, a choice not among the four actually provided in the task. As shown in Figure 3.19, these individuals anchored the first temporal expression in the little girl's 'now' and the second at the point where the first temporal period ends (i.e., the girl's 'then'). We may describe this mode as NOW-THEN ANCHORING, thereby contrasting it with the NOW-ANCHORING that was called for.

The probe was also administered to 12 graduate students who were not native speakers of English. In this group, 4 students chose *5 days;* 3

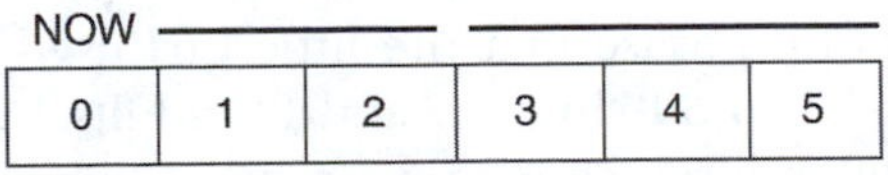

NOW —————— ——————————

0	1	2	3	4	5

FIGURE 3.19

of these students were speakers of an Asian language in which now–then anchoring is more frequently used. During an interview, a Korean child also showed a preference for five days:

> You know, there is a period after the first part, *Only two more days I can go to school.* So the second part, *In three days I can read,* is different from the first part. So she can go to school in two days and in three days after the school she can read. It covers five days.

This child was able to articulate clearly the way in which he held separate the two temporal expressions.

During the probe, there were also individuals—1 child and 3 adults—who provided the answer *two days* to (B). This is a rather strange response but it is possible that the individuals did manage to chunk the two phrases. If they did, they presumably anchored both phrases in the girl's "now," unlike the individuals who chose *five days*. They failed, however, to understand that *only two more days* and *in three days* actually point toward the same day—the little girl's first day at school. *Only two more days* refers to a point in time at the beginning of that day and *in three days* to a point at the end of it (readers can then subtract two from three in order to arrive at the target response *one day*—i.e., the amount of time actually spent in school). Hence, with respect to the school day itself, the two temporal phrases call for different interpretive modes. The first phrase calls for the EXCLUSIVE MODE displayed in Figure 3.20. The second calls for the INCLUSIVE MODE displayed in Figure 3.21. Presumably the individuals who chose *two days* used the inclusive mode for both temporal phrases, as shown in Figure 3.22. The use of the inclusive mode for both phrases would lead a reader to overshoot the first school day and land on a second one.

It is not surprising that children, when interpreting temporal phrases, are not certain about whether to include the day on which the counting begins (hereafter BD for "beginning-day") and the day on which it ends (hereafter ED for "end-day"). Many factors can determine whether these days are included in the counting: the time of day at which the utterance is assumed to take place, the time of day at which the predicated event is expected to take place, and, of course, the nature of the temporal phrase (we have pointed out the effects of *only…more* in the first phrase).

In order to get a clearer idea of how English speakers actually interpret the first temporal phrase that the little girl used, we gave the task shown in Figure 3.23 to 30 children and 30 adults. As shown in Table 3.8, the majority of children chose September 4, which means that they had to exclude both BD and ED from the counting (Figure 3.24). A

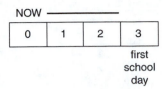

FIGURE 3.20

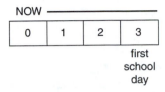

FIGURE 3.21

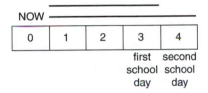

FIGURE 3.22

While looking at a calendar, a little girl says to her mother:

Only two more days and I can go to school.

The date on the calendar is September 1. On what date will the little girl start school?

FIGURE 3.23

TABLE 3.8

	Children	Adults
September 2	1	0
September 3	13	24
September 4	16	6

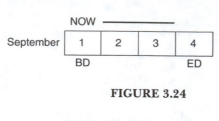

FIGURE 3.24

FIGURE 3.25

number of children were quite articulate about the fact that they were excluding BD. As one child put it,

> You wouldn't count the day you're speaking on. You always start with the next day. Only two more days after that day.

The child who chose September 2 presumably did just the opposite of what these children did. Ignoring the cue of *only...more*, he included both BD and ED in the counting (Figure 3.25). Working only with information available in the interview, we could not easily understand why he did this; his mother, however, reported that he is prone to foreshorten the time period involved in any event that he is looking forward to. In this way he is able to make the event seem closer than it actually is.

Those who chose September 3—the preferred choice among adults—had to exclude either BD or ED from the counting. If BD is taken as zero, as shown in Figures 3.19–3.22, then it is excluded. BD may, however, be included under certain pragmatic conditions. To explore its inclusion, we presented another version of the same task to 30 children, simply adding the words *One morning at the breakfast table*. Children were now more aligned with adults: they, too, preferred the choice of *September 3* (23 selected it). Given this precise cue, children were able to place the little girl's utterance at an early point in BD and thus include that day in the counting.

These probes helped us to uncover a more refined distinction that is often overlooked when linguists discuss now-anchoring: namely, whether the temporal unit representing 'now'—whether a day, a week, a month, or whatever—is actually included in the counting. We might note that there appear to be ethnocultural differences with respect to whether the now-unit is included: when speakers of Asian languages such as Chinese or Korean use now-anchoring, they are less likely to include the now-unit. This tendency not to include the now-unit is congruent with their lesser use of now-anchoring in spatial and temporal predication (see Hill, 1998, for further discussion of how Asian and African systems of communication make less use of immediate point of view than European ones).

It is difficult to imagine how this difficulty of actually counting the days might have affected children's performance on (B). It would not, of course, lead directly to a distractor, since a choice such as *two days* or *five days* is not available. However, it might, when joined with the complications already noted, lead children to avoid anchoring altogether and thus opt for the unanchored choice—*three days*.

At this point it might be useful to retrace our steps and summarize all the decisions that a reader has to make about how to chunk *in three days* with *only two more days*. We can represent these decisions in the flow-chart displayed in Figure 3.26. Readers may make a decision at any of three points that will lead them away from the target response *one day*. It is only at the first point that a distractor—*three days*—is actually provided; yet as we have seen, when children and adults are free to choose their own responses, they make decisions at both the second and third decision points that lead away from the target response.

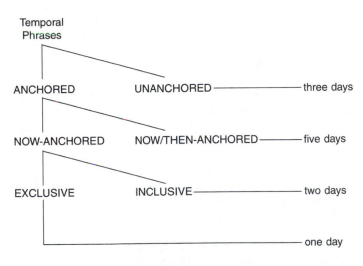

FIGURE 3.26

NOTES

1. One child mentioned the roar but mislocated its source: "The story was about a lady who got off the train and moved far back and roared."
2. In presenting children's writing, we do not correct errors in spelling or grammar.
3. In considering this fact, we should remember that a large number of European American children still managed to select the target response for both tasks. It is simply that ethnocultural experience seems to have strengthened the choice of a particular distractor on each task, thereby contributing to the salient divergence between the two groups.
4. He also fuses the title, replacing *Wonderland* with *Wardrobe*; he may have been thinking of C. S. Lewis' *The Lion, the Witch, and the Wardrobe.*
5. This child used a strong verb—*jerked back*—to express the fawn's movement. It is as though she had a particular feel for the texture of the encounter that Lewis Carroll had represented in the original text. It is of further interest that she maintains the inverted word order of a question even when it is embedded as a complement: "She was wondering why did the fawn jerk back." She is here using a widespread feature of African American English that can be paralleled to distinctive patterning in West African languages (Hill, 1992).
6. Some parents assume the teacher role—*in loco magistri*, so to speak—and ask their children teacher questions. Frequently their children find these acommunicative intrusions into a normally communicative relationship irritating.
7. Throughout our interviewing, we encountered children who were uncomfortable with recycling only a part of some larger whole. In this instance, there were children who felt that the target response was not a good answer because it did not include *large* as well as *gentle*. African American children who had participated in programs such as Operation Head Start were predisposed to adopt this position since they were trained to provide complete responses to all questions.
8. Many of the 13 mentioned heart attack.
9. A translation of the French expression *style indirect libre.*
10. A similar pattern is reflected in children's performance on the probe in which the passage was removed and the tasks were presented without choices. Among European American children, 61 percent chose *seven* and 72 percent chose *three days;* of African American children, 57 percent chose *seven* and 57 percent chose *three days.* The fact that these figures are 15-20 percent higher than on the actual test reflects the conditions of the probe. Without access to the passage, the children were forced to rely on memory. They obviously needed the passage before them in order to carry out the required calculations.
11. It is ironic that researchers (e.g., Bereiter & Englemann, 1966) have claimed that African American children reflect a language deficit precisely because they are overly prone to anchor language in their own 'here and now.'

12. Influenced by Piaget's notions of egocentrism, some researchers have claimed that children have difficulty in decentering to the 'here and now' of their interlocutors. These claims are, however, generally based on children's performance on artificially constructed tasks. Tanz (1980) has shown that in everyday talk children do manage to decenter to another's 'here and now.' In fact, she points out that children's competence in using anchored language can come only from observing others using it (i.e., children learn to use their own 'here and now' only by decentering to another person's).

13. We initially believed that children would be better able to infer a textually mediated 'here and now' when it is embedded in human interaction. Children's difficulties with this passage, however, have led us to doubt this notion.

14. A boy recently arrived from Haiti provided unexpected commentary on the little girl's age: "She is four years old in Haiti. But in New York she is five years old." He went on to explain that children begin school earlier in Haiti.

15. During the interviewing we discovered a poignant exception to these patterns. One African American girl chose *eight* in responding to (A) and, in explaining her choice, used the word *awful* that ends the passage: "It was awful that she would not go to school till she was eight. She wouldn't learn to read till she was eight." When the interviewer asked her whether that wasn't a bit late for learning to read, she replied: "I don't know, 'cause when I was seven, I couldn't be able to read."

16. In ALICE AND THE FAWN, we pointed out how, in the absence of a comparable specifier, a number of children, particularly those disposed toward a communicative approach, gravitated toward the passage end while responding to the first task.

17. A reader does not, of course, have to accept the mother's interpretation as the only valid one. But given that the daughter does not subsequently challenge the mother's interpretation, it tends to be viewed as normative.

18. There are further complexities involved in processing the temporal information in this passage. Readers who are interested in pursuing this matter can find further discussion in an Addendum, pp. 119–123.

19. Certainly such a reader would find the choice of *three days* odd, for it fails to capture the symbolic dimensions of the little girl's utterance (i.e., equating going to school with reading).

20. In the case of a child speaking with an adult who represents authority, there is a particularly strong reliance on that adult to establish meaning. When the adult is a parent, such reliance is perhaps even more acute: as research in language acquisition demonstrates, early language learning is dependent upon the primary caretakers—often the parents—ascribing socially normative meaning to what the child says.

chapter 4

Gapped Narratives

We are aware that describing only the narratives in this chapter as gapped may be misleading. Any narrative—and certainly the brief kind found in a test unit—contains many different kinds of gaps that the writer expects the reader to fill in. Consider, for example, the various kinds of gaps in BLACK BONNET—the reader doesn't know who Miss Esther is, what her relation is to the old lady, why the old lady is expected, why she doesn't show up, and so on.

Still the narratives presented so far differ from the ones that we are about to present in one fundamental respect: they were taken from some larger whole or, at least, they lead the reader to respond as if they were. Their most salient gaps are best described as external rather than internal; that is to say, they are located at the margins of the narrative rather than within its very fabric. In the case of truncated narratives, it was the ending that was missing for the reader. In the case of excerpted narratives, it was both the beginning and the ending.

The narratives that we now present were not taken from a larger whole; or if they were, they were so substantially rewritten that they seem to have a beginning, a middle, and an end. Achieving this semblance of wholeness has, however, been costly. In order to pack a whole story into 50 words or so, the writer has to get rid of the transitional detail that readers ordinarily depend on as they move from one part of a story to the next.

We have already observed how children, when expanding a truncated or excerpted narrative, often end up with too much of a story—at least for the purposes of test taking. Here we will observe much the opposite. As children work with a gapped narrative, they often end up with too little of a story and so are forced to patch together various bits and pieces in the hope that somehow one will emerge.

HURRICANE

The first gapped passage that we will consider is a narrative about a hurricane:

> The hurricane dumped huge amounts of rain on the island. Its strong winds knocked down trees and blew away houses. The island's streams and rivers began to overflow, flooding the town. Luckily, the mighty storm soon abated.
>
> A. This story says that trees were
>   flooded   strong
>   blown over   blown away
>
> B. In the story, the word "abated" means
>   died down   got worse
>   rained   blew

The content of the passage is summarized in Figure 4.1. This narrative is only 37 words long, but it does manage to convey a sense that it is not part of anything else. In achieving this effect, however, a major gap has been left between sentences 3 and 4. At the end of sentence 3, the discourse has given readers no reason to suspect—other than the visual clue that they are only one brief sentence away from white space—that the storm, and the narrative, too, are almost over. In fact, the use of *the* in *the hurricane* and *the island* has suggested that more specific information will be supplied in due course. In view of this legitimate expectation, the reader is surprised to discover that the six words of sentence 4 conclude the narrative. It is as though the writer, having just launched a story, for some unknown reason interrupted it and then decided to tack on a brief conclusion. The resulting gap is so peculiar that we suspect this passage was written especially for this test unit rather than adapted from existing prose.

In order to get a better sense of how the passage violates a reader's expectations, we gave just the first three sentences to 20 third and

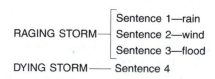

FIGURE 4.1

fourth graders. We then asked them to write one sentence that would fit in with the first three. No one produced a sentence anywhere near the one that ends the passage. Oddly enough, one girl, who is a highly skilled writer, did begin her sentence with the word *luckily*.

> Luckily, the island was almost uninhabited so the few who were there tried hard to survive.

Nearly all the children wrote about how the people tried to escape but were unable to. Generally, the storm overwhelmed them in some way:

> For those who had not already escaped, death was immenent.

> The people tried to run but the wind kept them from moving.

> People tried desperately to get off the island and stay out of the water.

> Many people leaving their houses in deperation and have no where to go.

> People ran or yelled, but most of them dying trying to get away, because there was no where to go.

> Pretty soon no one could see anything, the torrential rain was blining and numbing everyone.

> The people jumped into row boats and attempted to get away but, the wieght the row boat was carrying was too much and many flipped over sending thier passangers to their doom.

Before discussing the two tasks in detail, we would like to point out certain similarities between them. To begin with, both can be characterized as *acommunicative*: using the distinctions introduced in ALICE AND THE FAWN (see pp. 94–95)—*overt/covert* and *focused/unfocused*—we can derive three different forms for each task, as shown in Figure 4.2. The actual form of each task, given in capital letters, uses a formulaic expression containing *story* to make clear that it is acommunicative. Task (A) is also unfocused, since readers discover only in the process of doing it that it calls for defining vocabulary rather than recycling information.

	(A)	(B)
Covert	Trees were _____.	The storm finally _____.
Overt (unfocused)	THIS STORY SAYS THAT TREES WERE _____.	The story says that the storm finally _____.
Overt (focused)	In the story, "knocked down'" means _____.	IN THE STORY, THE WORD "ABATED" MEANS _____.

FIGURE 4.2

In (B), the vocabulary-defining function is made explicit with the formula *the word "abated" means*. The test makers probably expressed the vocabulary-defining intent of these tasks in different ways because they wished to avoid using the same form for two consecutive tasks. We can speculate that (A) was made unfocused and (B) focused because the alternative in each case requires an adjustment to the usual formula. In (A), an exact adherence to the alternative form would produce

*The word "knocked down" means _____.[1]

The readily apparent solutions to this problem are all awkward: *the phrase "knocked down"* or *the words "knocked down"* or just *"knocked down."* In (B), following the alternative form would produce

The story says that the storm _____.

Unless the task makes clear that it is referring to the state of affairs at the end of the passage, three of the four choices—*blew, rained,* and *died down*—would be defensible answers. One solution is to add a word like *finally* to the usual formula, as shown in Figure 4.2; the other is to use the focused formula, which requires no adjustment.

(A) and (B) are also similar in the patterns of response they elicited during the pilot testing. In selecting the target response, the performance of the African American and European American children differed substantially on each task (Table 4.1). This unit provides further evidence that the gap between these two groups generally widens on acommunicative tasks. The gap on (B) is, in fact, greater than any other in our corpus.

Turning now to the distractors, we find that each task has a choice that expresses 'intensity' (Table 4.2). When we present (A) and (B) in greater detail, we will try to account for the appeal that these distractors had for the African American children. It is worth noting that if the target responses and the 'intensity' distractors are combined, the differences between the two groups are nearly evened out (Table 4.3).

TABLE 4.1

	African American	European American
(A) blown over	33%	47%
(B) died down	23%	47%

TABLE 4.2

	African American	European American
(A) strong	27%	14%
(B) got worse	37%	17%

TABLE 4.3

	African American	European American
(A) blown over + strong	61%	60%
(B) died down + got worse	64%	60%

TABLE 4.4

	African American	European American
(A) blown away	27%	28%
(B) blew	25%	19%

TABLE 4.5

	African American	European American
(A) flooded	13%	11%
(B) rained	15%	16%

The responses of children in the two groups were much closer on the remaining two distractors. The 'blowing' distractors were more attractive to both groups, a result that was not surprising to us nor, we suspect, to the test makers (Table 4.4). Finally, the 'water' distractor on each task was the least favored (Table 4.5).

Let us now turn to (A) and examine why children had so much difficulty with it. Fewer than half of the European American children and only a third of the African American children selected the target response. Why weren't the others able to match *blown over* with *knocked down*? There are a number of factors that seem to have contributed to their difficulty.

To begin with, some of the children we interviewed simply did not realize that the task was vocabulary-defining. We came across at least two factors that contributed to this lack of awareness: to begin with, the task does not present, as one child put it, "a hard word" that needs to be defined; indeed, this task violates a basic principle that is generally followed in constructing a vocabulary-defining task: movement from a less familiar word to a more familiar one, as exemplified by the movement from *stroke* to *pet* in ALICE AND THE FAWN. In this task, the movement is from the more familiar *knock down* to the less familiar and more polysemic *blow over*. We suspect that this violation resulted from the test makers' wish to set up a difficult choice between the *blow*-initiated verbs.

Apart from this confusion about the point of the task, some children thought of *knocked down* and *blown over* as simply too different to be considered synonymous. Consider, for example, what one third grader had to say on this subject:

C I would have said *flattened* or something, because *blown over* is not exactly a synonym for *knocked down*. Some people who, you know, aren't really with it wouldn't really get that.

I Why? What's the difference between *knocked down* and *blown over*?

C Well, *blown over* is like, well, it could snap back up, you know, like a clown could be blown over and then just snap back up. But when it is knocked down, it is knocked down.

She certainly has a point in distinguishing these two verbs. From our vantage point, the crucial difference between the two has to do with agency: the prototypical agent for *knock down* is either a person or a hard object, whereas for *blow over* it is simply air. To test this distinction, one of us asked four colleagues to use each verb in a sentence and here's what they wrote:

1) The child was knocked down by his older brother.
   The garbage can was blown over during the night.

2) My mother got mad and knocked me down.
   I was blown over by the strong wind.

3) I knocked down the garbage can as I pulled out of the driveway.
   My hair was all blown over my head as I stepped onto the bus because it was so windy.

4) Riddick Bowe knocked down Evander Holyfield in Round 7.
   I was blown over by the way my girlfriend looked yesterday.

As can be seen, the contrast in agency is consistently reflected in the sentences they wrote (although the final sentence employs a metaphorical use of *blow over*).

Certain children who selected *blown over* were able to forego such semantic niceties and simply view this verb as synonymous with *knocked down*. Here's how one child defended her choice:

> It couldn't be *blown away*, because it says, "Its strong winds knocked down the tree." *Knocked down* is like *blown over*, almost the same thing, just in different words....It says blew away the houses, not the trees.

Another child clearly distinguished *blown over* from *blown away*, when the interviewer asked him to do so:

> *Blown over* means the tree is still there, and *blown away* means the tree is not there anymore.

One other child was able to make the distinction in much the same way:

> *Blow away* means something really goes away with the wind, and *blow over* means something is...still there, but *over*, like *turn over*.

He seemed to have a particularly good feel for the role of *over* in phrasal verbs.

Not all children who selected *blown over* could articulate clearly their reasons for doing so. One child was fairly clear about the meaning of *knocked down* ("bent down something") but quite vague about what *blow over* means: "It means 'blow out, just tumble away', right?" Another child expressed a good deal of exasperation when asked to explain his choice:

I   Why did you say *blown over*?
C   Oh, boy.
I   Well?
C   You see the story? It says that a strong wind knocked down trees and blew away houses. So it blows over trees because if it was knocked down it should say *knocked down*, but there wasn't.
I   Okay, if it said *knocked down* here, you'd say that.
C   Yup.
I   But you said *blown over* because why?
C   Because it's like another way of saying *knocked down*. And something blew over like that.

He then demonstrated what happened to the trees by placing his elbow on the desk with his forearm upright and moving his hand down so that it rested on the desk.

If children do not view the task as vocabulary-defining, they are forced to treat it as some kind of a recycling task, since all three of the distractors—*strong, flooded, blown away*—are actually used in the passage. If children respond to the passage holistically, they can be easily attracted to either *flooded* or *strong*. To begin with, each embodies a theme that is well represented in the passage:

flooded	rain—streams and rivers—overflow—flooding
strong	hurricane—huge amounts—strong winds—knocked down—blew away—mighty storm

Moreover, it is possible to support each of these choices logically. With *flooded*, for example, one might reason that the passage says that towns were flooded, and the towns must have had trees in them, and therefore the trees must have been flooded too. As one child recently arrived from Haiti put it, "The trees were covered by water, too." The interviewer had a strong sense that the word *hurricane* had stimulated him to draw on personal experience in constructing the scene. As for the choice *strong*, one can reason that the trees must have been strong, because strong winds knocked them down but were unable to blow them away like they did the houses. Since most children probably think of a house as stronger than a tree—particularly if they are thinking of a house as an urban apartment building—the fact that the trees hung on and the houses didn't might be taken as an especially dramatic illustration of their strength. Some of the children we interviewed were able to articulate the discrepancy between what happened to the trees and what happened to the houses. As one African American boy put it,

> It should say *blow away*—blow away both the houses and the trees. Houses are bigger than trees.

This child was certainly an alert reader, though this quality worked against him on this task.

After reading the passage, most readers are left with a general impression of the effects of the hurricane, but when they get to (A), few have any memory of exactly what was said about trees. They thus have to go back to the passage and ask: "What happened to the trees anyway?" They will find the relevant information embedded in a compound predicate:

Its strong winds	knocked down trees
	and
	blew away houses.

In using this information to complete the task, one possibility is that wires will become crossed, producing

Its strong winds   blew away trees
                   and
                   knocked down houses.

For children who conceive of houses as stronger than trees, it would be natural to think of them as less likely to be blown away. Since the actions expressed by the two verbs could be sequential, some children may have reformulated the original information much like the following child did:

Its strong winds knocked down and blew away trees and houses.

Even when readers have located the relevant information and separated it accurately from its context, matching it with the task sentence is not straightforward, as shown in Figure 4.3. The shift from active to passive, together with the suppression of the agent of the action, produces a sentence that looks and sounds quite different, even though the meaning is much the same. The shift to passive also makes it hard to use a substitution strategy to validate a particular choice:

Its strong winds blown over trees and blew away houses.

Even those who are able to change the form of *blown over* appropriately will obtain a problematic result:

Its strong winds blew over trees and blew away houses.

This double use of *blow* is so unlikely in this context that it could well cause readers to reject *blown over* as an answer.

Added to these syntactic pitfalls is the previously mentioned difficulty of distinguishing between phrasal verbs that begin with the same word. *Blow* is quite productive in this role. Using *storm* as a subject, here are some of the possibilities:

Intransitive
They expect a storm to *blow in* tonight.
Do you think the storm will *blow out* anytime soon?

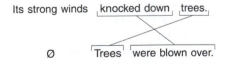

FIGURE 4.3

I hope a storm does not *blow up* after we go to sleep.
The storm will *blow over* before we have to leave.

Transitive
The storm *blew over* my pot of geraniums.
The storm *blew down* the water tower.
The storm *blew off* the shutters.
The storm *blew away* the barn.

Thus we have two senses of *blow over*. The image behind the transitive use is a vertical object that becomes horizontal. The image behind the intransitive use is movement along a horizontal plane, which leads to what is perhaps the most familiar meaning of the verb—"cease to be active" (it was this sense that certain children we interviewed were most familiar with, presumably because of their tendency to think of *over* as meaning "finished").

Blow and *over* also occur together in sentences in which *blow* has a double complement, an object and a prepositional phrase:

The wind *blew* her hat *over* the fence.
The wind *blew* my hair *over* my eyes.
The wind *blew* the balloon *over* the lake.

In the first sentence, the hat ended up beyond the fence; in the second, the hair ended up covering the eyes; in the third, the balloon ended up directly above the lake. Each of these sentences has a briefer form:

Her hat *blew over* the fence.
My hair *blew over* my eyes.
The balloon *blew over* the lake.

These examples demonstrate the semantic principle that high-frequency words are polysemic; that is, they are used in a wide variety of contexts and tend to cover large, diffuse areas of meaning. They are given a precise sense only when used in a particular context. Thus, in the last three examples, shifts in the meaning of *over* are cued by the physical characteristics of the objects it is relating to one another:

hat/fence	➜	'beyond'
hair/eyes	➜	'covering'
balloon/lake	➜	'directly above'

Another characteristic of polysemic vocabulary units is that, when they are encountered out of context, a core meaning seems to take over, and many of the senses they have in particular contexts recede and become

Here are two sentences. Circle the number of the sentence that describes the picture.

1. The hurricane blew over both trees.
2. The hurricane blew away both trees.

FIGURE 4.4

unavailable.[2] Let us exemplify this process by describing two probes that we carried out. In the first, 22 third graders were given the task in Figure 4.4, and 17 of them circled (2), indicating that in a supportive context, pictorial as well as linguistic, they were able to distinguish between *blow over* and *blow away*.

In the second probe, 55 third and fourth graders were asked to use the words *blow over* in a sentence. The results varied greatly. Only 2 supplied sentences in which *blow over* clearly had the meaning of 'cause to be horizontal' required by (1):

> The house blew over.
> The boat got blow over.[3]

A few others wrote sentences in which *over* might have this interpretation:

> The storm blew over the house.
> The storm blow over the ship.

When children are asked to supply a sentence in this way, their first instinct is probably to start with a personal subject such as *I, he,* or *my mother*. Several children combined a personal subject and *blow over* with interesting results:

(1) I blow over the leaves.   I can blow over a feather.
    Blow over that bug.   I will blow over that napkin.
    Blow that ant thats on you.   because it was over here.

(2) I blow over the lamp.   I told my brother to
    I blow over a chair.   blow over the men.
    I will blow over the statue.

In the first group, the reader gets an image of someone causing a light object to move by blowing on it. In the second group, objects are 'caused to be horizontal,' but they are too heavy to be moved by someone's breath. The more appropriate lexical item would appear to be *knock over*. The sentence in which the brother is asked to *blow over the men* might, of course, refer to small figures such as toy soldiers.

It is particularly interesting that some children were so constrained in producing a sentence using *blow over* that they actually used it in place of other phrasal verbs beginning with *blow*:

The boat's engine had a blow over. (blow out?)
I blow over the paper bag. (blow up?)
The wind blow over my hat. (blow off?)
The wind blow over my scarf. (blow away?)
The boy had a big blow over. (blow up? blow out?)
I blow over my door. (blow open???)

In addition, there were sentences representing some of the meanings of *blow over* that we have mentioned.

Blow my hair over my ears.
The wind could blow over the fence.
The storm will blow over in an hour.

And there were a considerable number that remain inexplicable:

I was blow the sky.
That blow over is very windy.
A blow over is the kind of that is blows over the hill.
You blown you over santa?

All in all, this probe turned out to be difficult for these children. Only about a fifth were able to place *blow over* in a context that resulted in a viable sentence.

Let us now turn to an interview in which an African American child chose *blown away* because he was working with a sense of *over* that prevented his matching *blown over* with *knocked down*:

I   Show me in the story where it says *blown away*.
C   OK. *Its strong winds knocked down trees and blew away houses*. It should say *blow away*, blow away houses and trees.

I So you think *blown away?*

C Yeah. No! *Knocked down,* but here it doesn't say *knocked down.*

I No. What about *blown over?*

C I don't think it fits *blown, blown*—I don't think it fits *knocked down.*

I Why not?

C Because *blown over* doesn't mean "knocked down," 'cause if it were knocked down, it just fell on the floor.

I And if it's blown over?

C It blows *over* something.

I What does *knocked down* mean?

C That the trees will fall down.

I OK. What does *blow over* mean?

C It means that the tree flies over something else.

Notice that this child is initially so far from seeing how *blown over* might fit in that he actually suggests that the passage is wrong, that it means to say that both trees and houses were blown away. Further on, the nature of this blockage becomes clear. When *over* is taken out of context, the core meaning of 'above' is what he focuses on. After further discussion with the interviewer, he was able to see how *over* could mean something else in the context of *wind* and *blow* and *trees.*

When a lexical item is used in a text, it has a syntagmatic relationship with other units that are present; that is, it plays a role along with them in forming the meaning of the whole. When a lexical item appears in isolation, as when it constitutes one of the four choices in a test task, it has a paradigmatic relationship with the other three; that is, it is opposed to rather than conjoined with these three (i.e., a syntagm embodies an 'and' relation, a paradigm an 'or' relation). Moreover, each of the choices is related paradigmatically to the part of the passage that is relevant to the task. Breaking up syntagmatic wholes and looking for synonymous relationships among paradigmatic units, as children must do in completing a vocabulary-defining task, puts a special strain on their capacity to process language.[4]

When children deal with phrasal verbs, the situation becomes even more strained. Once a phrasal verb is removed from a syntagmatic relationship, the bond between its two components is loosened, and they begin to be affected by their roles as individual words. And since phrasal verbs like the ones used in this unit as well as the single words that form them are all high-frequency lexical items, the possibilities for polysemous combinations are multiplied, especially when the multiple-choice task itself encourages a certain proliferation. To put this more generally, as long as phrasal verbs operate syntagmatically, children can handle them perfectly well. It is when they are forced to deal with these verbs paradigmatically that they tend to lose their grip on them. In effect, much of their confusion is spawned by the nature of the task itself.[5]

This contrast between syntagmatic ease and paradigmatic vertigo is perhaps another example of a principle that is often followed by sports psychologists. We are most skillful when we can do something holistically and keep it on the margins of awareness; any tendency to be analytic or to turn our full attention on what we are doing is likely to break our natural rhythm and be counterproductive.

We can demonstrate these matters concretely by substituting single words for the choices *blown over* and *blown away*:

Sentence 2:   Its strong winds knocked down trees and displaced homes.

Task (A):   The story says that trees were
flooded   strong
flattened   displaced

Flattened and *displaced* are not entirely satisfactory as substitutes, but perhaps this alternative version does provide a useful perspective on how the presence of phrasal verbs in this task forces children to adopt an analytical approach.

To sum up, the apparent function of (A) is to see whether children can figure out that *knocked down* and *blown over* mean much the same thing. But there is a paradox. Even children who knew the meaning of these verbs were not able to complete the task successfully. In effect, what (A) is really testing is whether children can negotiate the rather complicated syntactic and semantic terrain that we have just traversed.

In turning to (B), we can see that it contrasts sharply with (A): where (A) is perplexing, (B) is transparent. Its vocabulary-defining function is unmistakable. Moreover, it is an especially good example of how a vocabulary-defining task should function on a test of reading comprehension. It meets well the three crucial conditions for such a task:

1) The vocabulary-defining intent is made clear.
2) The word to be defined is unlikely to be known by the test takers.
3) The passage contains a clue that signals what the word means.

As to the first condition, the form of the task makes clear the vocabulary-defining intent. As to the second, we were able to assure ourselves that most young children do not know what the word *abated* means. We gave the task shown in Figure 4.5 to 60 third and fourth graders. Only 8 percent selected *decrease*. Moreover, African American and European American children were virtually indistinguishable in the degree to

What does the word *abate* mean?

1. hit	3. feed	5. help
2. decrease	4. increase	6. hurt

FIGURE 4.5

which they were able to define *abate* correctly. Dale and O'Rourke (1976) do not list this word at the early grade levels, but even at the twelfth-grade level, they report that only 41 percent of students are familiar with the word *abated*.

As to the third condition, the passage does contain a salient cue as to the meaning of *abated*: the connective *luckily* suggests that the storm was no longer as strong as it had been. Hence even test takers who do not know the word *abated* can reliably select *died down*, the only choice that expresses a weakening of the storm.

It was clear that many children were able to use this passage clue effectively in figuring out what *abated* means. Consider, for example, the sharp focus on *luckily* in the following exchanges:

(1)

I How do you know the answer is *died down*?
C *Luckily.* I know the word.

(2)

I Did you know *abated*?
C No. But it says *luckily*; if it *got worse*, it should be *unluckily*.

(3)

I Why do you think *died down*?
C Because it says *Luckily, the mighty storm soon abatted.*
I Okay. Now wait a minute. You could pronounce that better.
C Abated.

One can presume from this child's mispronunciation of the key word that it was unfamiliar to him. One can also presume from his special emphasis on *luckily* that he recognized it as the major clue.

Other children were more explicit about why *luckily* is an effective cue. Here is how one girl defended her choice:

I Why did you choose *died down*?
C Well, it says *luckily*; *luckily* means probably it's good.

This child went on to demonstrate a rather delicate control over how connectives work:

It wouldn't be *got worse*, because it would have said *but*....

The interviewer then asked her if she had ever heard the word *abated* before. She replied:

I've heard it but I wasn't sure what it meant. But the sentence told me what it is.

An African American third grader also focused on the importance of the word *luckily*:

C   Uuhh, I took *died down*.
I   Give me a reason.
C   Because you can't say *luckily*—*luckily*—you—That's it. 'Cause if you're lucky, it won't get worse. It gets—it stops.

His use of the word *stops* suggests a more abrupt ending than *died down* does. It is noteworthy that the two components in this phrasal verb—*die* and *down*—can each be directly associated with 'stopping' (e.g., *He died* and *The computer's down again*). It can also be noted that both these components carry a negative connotation, which may have prevented certain children from associating this phrasal verb with a positive state.

In order for children to utilize *luckily* as a clue, they must hold, at least for the moment, a world view in which it is considered fortunate for a violent and destructive storm to come to an end. When we first analyzed this unit, we wondered whether certain children might subscribe to the opposite world view, one in which observers are lucky when things get worse, because they are then able to experience maximum excitement. Much that occurs on television, in movies, and in videogames would seem to encourage such a stance. We did not, however, find any children who were willing to own up to this view. Whatever their predilections when playing computer games or watching television, children presented themselves as responding to this passage rather chastely.[6]

Nevertheless, a fairly large number of children—particularly the African Americans—did, in fact, select *got worse* during the pilot testing. This attraction is not surprising, given the way in which (B) exploits the gap in this passage. Indeed, children who do not know what *abated* means and who are unable to interpret *luckily* in the expected way will probably not realize that a gap exists.[7] They are more likely to think that the last sentence continues the theme of the first three and so select *got worse* for their answer (as we observed on p. 129, children often sup-plied disaster endings when the final sentence was removed). In the ordinary course of things, it is to be expected that a story will continue to build for a while before there is a turn of events. To use our terms for characterizing narrative, this passage is likely, for children who miss the relevant clues, to seem truncated (i.e., lacking an ending) rather than gapped (i.e., lacking a middle).

When we began our discussion of HURRICANE, we noted that the 'intensity' distractor for each task (i.e., *strong* and *got worse*) was surpris-ingly attractive to African American children during the pilot testing. We have suggested certain aspects of the passage and the tasks that might have led children to select these distractors. We suspect, though, that something further is operating here.

Various bits of evidence have led us to speculate that members of Afri-can American culture are more likely to work with a macroframe—one that might be referred to as 'strength in the face of adversity'—that makes *strong* salient for them in (A). There may be a similar frame oper-ating in (B) that reinforces the choice *got worse*. We might even relate these frames by suggesting that one needs strength in the face of adver-sity because things are, in fact, likely to get worse. In the second part of this volume, we will have further occasion to speculate on the use of comparable macroframes by African American children. These kinds of frames are not easy to document, but we suspect, on the basis of our own experience as readers, that they do play a powerful role in shaping how individuals understand what they read.

CHEE TONG

The second unit that we will consider in this chapter differs markedly from the first. HURRICANE was characterized by one large gap, but the passage below reflects a number of gaps, both large and small.

During the day, Chee Tong traveled around the city with his stove. The boatman took his boat up and down the river, but at night he always tied up at the same place. There they met, and together they ate the evening meal, prepared and cooked by Chee Tong. It was a most satisfactory arrangement—the boatman provided shelter, Chee Tong the meals.

A. What did the two men do together?
   cook   tie up
   go up the river   eat

B. What was the shelter?
   a boat   a house
   a stove   an arrangement

This narrative is fundamentally unlike the ones that we have examined thus far: the events that it describes occur habitually rather than uniquely. As a consequence, the narrative feels a bit more like exposition. It moves, for example, toward an overtly formulated generalization—that Chee Tong and the boatman have *a most satisfactory arrangement*. Moreover, lurking at each point in the story is an unformulated generalization—both Chee Tong and the boatman faithfully follow a diurnal schedule. It is, of course, this fidelity that makes possible the description of their activities from a habitual perspective.

The pervasive gapping in this passage can be approached in a number of ways. To begin with, it is useful to point out how culturally alien its world is. An intelligible rendering of this world would require more textual space than is available in a test unit. Consider, for example, what the first sentence presents. Any reader is likely to wonder who Chee Tong is, why he travels around the city with a stove all day, or, for that matter, what kind of object the word *stove* refers to. A number of children we interviewed were unable to imagine a stove so small that a man could carry it around all day. For them, stove refers only to the familiar object—multiple burners placed on top of an oven—where their food is cooked; it cannot even be extended to, say, the hibachi used on a cookout. Some resolved this problem by picturing Chee Tong as a fairly large man. But making the man bigger is, in many ways, just as difficult as making the stove smaller: the children we interviewed were prone to think of Asian men as small, at least when compared to Western men.

Some of the narratives we have considered—for example, SHOP SIGN, LEAVING HOME, and BLACK BONNET—are distant in time rather than in space, presenting cultural worlds that have largely vanished from the American scene. The children we interviewed in metropolitan New York could generally make at least some connection with these worlds, but Chee Tong was largely inaccessible. It was as if they could find no foothold with which to enter this world.

Much of this difficulty can be traced to the fact that the passage information is not only culturally distant but structured in a potentially confusing way. Consider, for example, the use of *Chee Tong* and *the boatman*. These two nominals are intended to refer to separate persons, as indicated by the use of *they* in sentence 3. But before readers reach this sentence, they may decide that the two refer to a single person. Here is how one adult reader described her reading of this passage:

> I processed the first two sentences as referring to one individual. I pictured a Chinese vendor traveling around an island like Manhattan, by boat, cooking and selling some Chinese version of a fast-food shish-kebab. I was not prepared for *they* in the third sentence. It created a kind of dissonance which wasn't resolved until the fourth and final sentence when the role of each of the story characters was delineated.

In listening to children's oral reading of this passage, we came to suspect that many were, in fact, misframing the first two sentences. In order to find out more about what children make of these sentences, we presented them as a "story opening" to 55 African American and European American children in the third and fourth grades. After the children read the two sentences, we asked them to complete the story. We then evaluated the stories to determine whether the children thought that Chee Tong and the boatman were the same person. As shown in Table 4.6, both groups of children were attracted to the same-person frame,

TABLE 4.6

	African American	European American
one person	13	23
two persons	8	7
unclear	2	2

and the European Americans were attracted even more than the African Americans.

It is interesting to compare the kinds of stories that the two groups of children wrote. The African American children, reflecting the predisposition we observed in their responses to HURRICANE (p. 129), tended to write about various kinds of disaster. Here are some of their story-endings in which a single person is involved:

> Next morning [he] untied boat to go for [a] ride but a storm come and recked the boat but he stayed alive.

> Somebody stold the boat at night. Then he called the poilice. Ofter Dan picked up the phone.

> Everytime he went some place he end in the same place. When he took his stove it gave him bad lock. Everybody uset to think that he was crazy.

> Always hurt his arm because he rowed to long. Kept trying to get another place but he couldnt. Soon caught in rain storm and was scared, and stopped traveling with boat and stove.

And here are some of their endings in which two people are involved:

> One day when he was in his boat he got lost. The boatman saw him and rescue him. Then they went home and never got lost again.

> So it will not get away. The next day the boat was gone. They maad a boat and look for the other

> When he goes some place he come back the same day. His boat sunk with the stove on it. The boatman had to take his boat up and down the river.

> The man who wood always take his boat up and down was not nice and chee tong was always stuck in the house all day he did not like it.

The European American children also included disaster in their endings, but they were more inclined to incorporate fantasy:

> Traveled for hours with stove. Landed on island. Woke up and noticed it was only a dream.

> Then the stove fell off of his hands. And then he started chasing it. And then it sank in the water and he never got it again.

Another common element for the European American children was commerce:

He finally sold his boat and got out of that place.

Chee Tong selling his stove. One woman bought it for $50. Chee Tong went home to relax. His troubles were over.

We then asked 20 adult readers to do the same task: 7 constructed an ending in which Chee Tong and the boatman are the same person, while the other 13 thought two people were involved. Here are a couple of endings that illustrate how adults read the first two sentences as involving a single person:

Chee Tong tried to catch as many fish as he could. He would then cook the fish and sell them as he went up and down the river. He always felt good about his work at the end of the day.

He tied his boat here because it was close to where he lived. In the morning he would untie the boat and go up and down the river again and sell hot food to many people.[8]

A number of factors in the first two sentences encourage readers to think of a single person. To begin with, there is a familiar literary schema in which a person is introduced first by name and then by occupation. Consider the following example from *The Warden* by Anthony Trollope, in which the italicized name and occupation refer to the same person:

Mr. Harding was shown into a comfortable inner sitting-room...and there waited for *Sir Abraham*. Nor was he kept waiting long: in ten or fifteen minutes he heard a clatter of voices speaking quickly in the passage and then *the attorney general* entered.

A single-person interpretation is also prompted by the temporal framing in the first two sentences. *During the day* provides the time frame not only for sentence 1, but for the first half of sentence 2. Then *but at night* provides a contrasting frame for the rest of sentence 2 (Figure 4.6). In effect, there is no temporal separation of sentence 1 from sentence 2 to help the reader establish that Chee Tong and the boatman are different people. To put the matter another way, the time-meshing of sentence 1 with sentence 2 can encourage a person-meshing as well. Moreover, when presented with the two contrasts in rapid succession, readers are more likely to process the one that is overtly marked (i.e., *but* separates 'day' and 'night', whereas 'Chee Tong' and 'the boatman' are not separated by any formal marker). The use of *traveled* to describe Chee Tong's movement with the stove may have also contributed to the notion that he is the boatman pictured as going up and down the river.

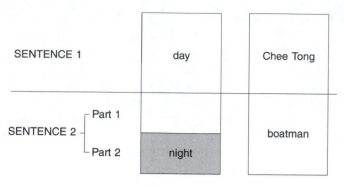

FIGURE 4.6

Certainly *traveled* suggests (1) using an external means of locomotion and (2) covering a good deal of territory.

A single-person interpretation is also supported by what we might describe as an INERTIA PRINCIPLE in text interpretation; that is to say, readers simply assume identity of reference unless they encounter a firm signal to the contrary. One might claim that the first two sentences provide just such a signal—two patterns of movement that presumably call for the reader to establish a separate person for each:

Sentence 1:   ...traveled around the city with his stove
Sentence 2:   ...took his boat up and down the river

Some children, however, viewed these two patterns as complementary aspects of a single movement, the first describing *what* Chee Tong carried—a stove—and the second *how* he carried it—by means of a boat. Such a merger helps, in fact, to solve the problem of picturing Chee Tong as himself transporting the stove. It does, however, raise another problem: how can Chee Tong move around the city in a boat? This problem is not difficult to solve if readers imagine a city with canals. Some children, in fact, claimed that they had seen such a city in movies about China. No child actually mentioned a Chinese city by name, although one did refer to Venice. He told about how he had bought food from a boat vendor there.

One might assume that a reader would eventually overcome any initial confusion, given that the pronoun *they* in sentence 3 provides clear evidence that Chee Tong and the boatman are, in fact, two different people. We did come across one girl who, initially confused, was able to explain how she used this cue:

First I thought the boatman was Chee Tong. But I figured it out after it said that they ate together. It can't be one person eating with himself. So it had to be two people.

We discovered, however, that children of this age are prone, once an interpretive frame is in place, to assimilate all incoming information to it. In this instance, the initial frame of a single person tends to dissolve under the pressure of new information—we encountered only a handful of children who held on to it right to the very end—but the dissolution of this frame, in turn, leads to a general breakdown in comprehension. When children were asked to recall what they had read, most were reduced to silence or, at best, managed only a few halting phrases that did not make much sense.

In spite of this relatively global breakdown, a substantial number of children were still able to select the target responses for the two tasks. In responding to (A), for example, 40 percent of the European American children and 41 percent of the African American children selected *eat*. From a certain perspective, the task is straightforward—it calls for children to recycle what is overtly expressed in the passage:

Sentence 3: together they *ate* the evening meal
Task (A): What did the two men do together? *eat*

Many children, however, had difficulty in understanding sentence 3. It reports a sequence of three activities—the first two involve both men, but the third only Chee Tong.[9] The order in which the activities are reported—the TEXT SEQUENCE—does not match the PREDICATED SEQUENCE—the order in which they occur. The third activity in the text sequence is the second in the predicated sequence, as shown in Figure 4.7.

Sentence 3				
Text Sequence			Predicated Sequence	
Persons	Actions Involved		Persons	Actions Involved
First activity	Chee Tong & boatman	meeting	Chee Tong & boatman	meeting
Second activity	Chee Tong & boatman	eating	Chee Tong	cooking
Third activity	Chee Tong	cooking	Chee Tong & boatman	eating

FIGURE 4.7

This lack of matching arises directly from a sentence structure in which a participial modifier follows a main clause. This kind of sentence is common in modern prose—it was, for example, a hallmark of Hemingway's style—but we suspect that it is rare in the materials that children read. In responding to (A), readers are required to deal directly with this temporal discrepancy. They must identify that what the two men did together was 'eating'—the second activity in the text sequence, but the third in the predicated sequence of events.

The major distractor was not, as might be expected, *cook*, the activity interchanged with *eat*. Both the African American and the European American children were more attracted to *go up the river*, though, as shown in Table 4.7, the difference between the two distractors was negligible in the case of the African American children. It is not easy to explain the greater popularity of *go up the river*. Perhaps one reason can be found in the explanation offered by an 11-year-old African American girl. When defending her choice of *go up the river*, she appealed to discourse structure at large:

> When there is a story, it always has the body part. That's the middle part and I think that this part is more important than the part where they ate.

For her, the story was mainly about two men's experience in a boat, and so she preferred an answer dealing with their movement in water. The fact that they ate together seemed an incidental detail. Upon further questioning, she conceded that the passage did not actually describe their going up the river together. She claimed, however, that they must have, for as she put it:

> If you invite somebody on a boat, you're sure to give him a ride.

We can observe, once again, that a child, working with an incomplete narrative, makes an extended inference that leads away from the detail the task calls for.

Before leaving (A), we might note that many children were confused by the use of *tied up* in sentence 2, even though not many chose the dis-

TABLE 4.7

	African American	European American
cook	27%	20%
go up the river	29%	33%

tractor *tie up* in (A). One child, however, who did choose it, defended his answer by saying that "Chee Tong and the boatman tied their feet together." Upon hearing this, the interviewer was so nonplussed that she was unable to pursue what the child had in mind. Perhaps he had been stimulated by some tale of traditional China—and even more specifically a scene of foot-binding—which he was now bringing to bear on the world of Chee Tong.

In this passage the use of *tie up* without a complement represents a nautical idiom that children are not likely to know. We were curious as to what children would make of the sentence, *At night he always tied up at the same place*, apart from any specific context. So we asked a group of 20 children what this sentence meant to them. Here's a sampling of their responses:

he was doing homework

there were traffic jams all over the city and bridges

He is always tied up in his bedroom. He is doing homework, and he looks tired. His mother is yelling at him too.

I think that he is tieing a horse up at night

It sounds like he is always in the same bed his blankets under his arms and legs twisted around

He's tied at a top of a tree at night

that his parents tie the person to his bed all night.

Smoking, drinking out with another women.

None of the children mentioned a boat.

Let us now turn to (B), a task which, at least on the surface, directs children's attention to sentence 4, just as (A) directs their attention to sentence 3. As already suggested, sentence 4 provides a summary of that which has preceded. Structurally speaking, it is a difficult sentence for young readers to understand. It can perhaps be best described as cataphorically structured. It begins by stating that *it was a most satisfactory arrangement* and then goes on to specify what constituted the arrangement. This specification is, however, gapped in that it consists of two sentences with the verb missing in the second:

(1) the boatman   provided   shelter
(2) Chee Tong   Ø   the meals

The verb in (2) is, of course, to be supplied from (1), but this involves an operation that not all children are able to perform. It was evident from oral reading that a number of children were unable to expand *Chee Tong Ø the meals* to *Chee Tong provided the meals.*

Added to this structural ellipsis is a deeper ellipsis in the information base that underlies sentence 4. (1) and (2) above express two agents— the boatman and Chee Tong—and two contributions—shelter and meals—but they do not express the means through which these contributions are made. Using information from the previous sentence, the reader has to infer that the boatman uses his boat to provide shelter and that Chee Tong uses his stove to provide the meals as shown in the following schema:

PERSON	MEANS	CONTRIBUTION
the boatman	boat	shelter
Chee Tong	stove	meals

The first of the two inferences is the one that (B) calls for, but substantially less than half of the children were able to make it during the pilot testing—only 34 percent of the African American children and 42 percent of the European American children selected *a boat*. The two groups followed the same pattern in their choice of the distractors, as indicated in Table 4.8. The proportion selecting each distractor is slightly higher for the African American children.

The overall pattern suggests that many children may have been floundering on this task. The greater attraction to *an arrangement* and *a stove* may have been due to the fact that they were actually used in the passage. Whenever children are confused by a passage, repetition distractors tend to make a particularly strong showing. *An arrangement* may have also been selected because it is a word that "sounds right" for a test. Children are not sure of its meaning and by virtue of this uncertainty are attracted to it.

Even those who managed to select *a boat* as the target response were generally not able to connect the notion of a boat with shelter. Rather they were forced to rely on a strategy of systematically eliminating the distractors. One boy explained that *a house* was not mentioned in the passage, *a stove* was "not a place to live" (though he did say it could keep

TABLE 4.8

	African American	European American
a stove	24%	20%
a house	14%	13%
an arrangement	28%	24%

"flies and bugs away"), and *an arrangement* was "a promise so it couldn't be a shelter." A girl, who was quite adept at test taking, explained her choice in the following way:

I   Why did you choose a *boat* for question (B)? You told me that you wanted to say *an arrangement.*

C   An arrangement is a word; you can't sleep or, you know, stay in a word.

I   Right, so you know what the word *shelter* means.

C   Right, a shelter is a place. It can't be *a house* because they mentioned nothing of a house. It can't be *a stove* because you can't, you know, sleep in a stove basically, unless you are one of the Chinese Brothers. And the only thing left was *a boat*, and they didn't mention a boat, and the boatman provided shelter and I think the only thing that he could provide was a boat, not a house or anything. So that's why I chose this.

We can see how well she has internalized a basic test-taking principle—stick as closely to the passage as possible.

We would now like to turn to children's difficulty in selecting *a boat*: about 40 percent of children in both groups selected it during the pilot testing. During the interviewing, we came across many children who had difficulty in imagining a boat as a place of shelter. They seemed to lack the notion of a houseboat on which people can live. One child, for example, argued that two men would not be able to cook, eat, and sleep in the same boat. As we increasingly encountered this point of view, we decided to ask children, during the course of an interview, to draw the boat described in the story. Most drew a skeletal picture of a boat that lacked any means of shelter, as illustrated by the two drawings in Figure 4.8. A few did manage to draw some semblance of a boat that could provide shelter, as illustrated by the two drawings in Figure 4.9. The second drawing even includes a stove within the sheltered space.

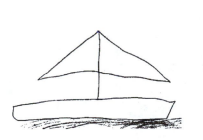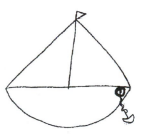

FIGURE 4.8

FIGURE 4.9

Generally speaking, children placed only one person in the boat, though a few placed a second person as well, as shown in Figure 4.10. Although this drawing provides no shelter, it does provide ample means for identifying each person: the boatman, proverbial pipe in mouth, has his hand on the tiller and Chee Tong wears a shirt with a large letter *C* emblazoned on it—the rest of his name is on the boat itself.

While examining children's drawings, we became aware that a higher proportion of those who drew some kind of houseboat managed to select *a boat* in response to (B). In order to test the strength of such a correlation, we decided to ask 55 third and fourth graders to read the passage, do the two tasks, and then draw a picture of the boat in the story. The results of this probe are shown in Table 4.9. Those who drew a boat with shelter were far more likely to choose *a boat* than those who drew one without shelter. These results are quite suggestive, though they must be interpreted with caution. Many children lack drafting skills and so resort to a conventional representation such as those shown in Figure 4.8.

While most children associate the word *boat* with a small, unenclosed structure, we did come across children who were familiar with the concept of a houseboat. During one interview a father asked his third-grade

FIGURE 4.10

TABLE 4.9

	Those Choosing a boat (23)	Those Not Choosing a boat (32)
drawings with shelter	11	4
drawings without shelter	12	28

child why he had associated a boat with shelter. Rather than providing a direct answer, the child went to the bookshelf, brought back one of his favorite books, and opened it to the picture reproduced in Figure 4.11.

Other children reported firsthand experience of a houseboat. One child explained that

> a lot of people live on boats—they have houseboats and sailboats—my grandfather has a houseboat and he keeps it in the garage.

Even children who did not actually use the word *houseboat* were able to express the notion that a boat could provide shelter. One nine-year-old boy, struggling with this idea, came up with a rather odd explanation for his choice of *boat*:

I   Why did you choose *boat*?
C   Because that's what I thought it was. They don't tell you in the story that he has a house. So I said the boat, because you can sit under a boat.

Source: Used by permission of Viking Penguin, a division of Penguin Putman, Inc.

FIGURE 4.11

Realizing that he had used the word *under* in a strange way, he went on to explain: "It may have been a boat that has a room inside it." Clearly this boy had some notion of shelter in mind when he uttered the odd-sounding words, "you can sit under a boat." This unit, perhaps more than any other in our corpus, illustrates how closely children's understanding of a text—and the language they use to talk about it—is linked to the imagery they form of the world that the text evokes. In this sense, it provides firm evidence of children's natural focus on a situation model rather than the text base.

It is surprising that *a house* was not more widely selected, given that it can be readily associated with the word *shelter*. But then this choice presupposes that children know what *shelter* means, and certain children we interviewed seemed not to. In order to understand better third and fourth graders' sense of the word *shelter*, we asked 20 children to use the word in a sentence. Only 2 responded that they did not know the word. Most of the other 18 were able to use the word in an acceptable way, though some of the sentences were a bit strange:

> a preting place to stay
> ah, something to live in
> food, clothes, house
> I have alot of shelter space in my house.
> The Indians took shelter before they attacked.

As illustrated by the last sentence, many associated the word with the threat of violence. Consider, for example, the following sentences that refer to a bomb shelter:

> We will go to see a nuclear shelter.
> He lives near a bombshelter.
> Let's use the bomb shelter as a play for tomorrow.

Many also associated it with a storm:

> When the hurricane came, we ran for shelter.
> The shelter kept them safe from the storm.
> Head for shelter, guys.
> I found shelter in a cave.
> We best get or go to shelter or our hair will get wet.

On the basis of this probe, we concluded that most children at this age do have a fairly good sense of the word *shelter*. We also concluded that children do not tend to associate this word with *house*; only two children even mentioned *house* and neither made it a central point.

During the interviewing, we came across three children who provided an ingenious justification for their choice of *house* in (B). One of these children, when describing his choice of *eat* in (A), referred to how the two men always ate together "in the sailor's house." When the interviewer asked the child what he meant by this expression, he responded, "Oh, that's the boatman's house where they store boats." He went on to describe this house in some detail:

> It's a log cabin and has one stove and they live there and that's where he keeps his boat. It's like a shed where he keeps his boat and they don't have any lights and he lives next to a river.

The interviewer then asked him if this house was mentioned in the passage. He replied, "No," but went on to explain that the reason the boatman "tied up at the same place" each evening was so that he and Chee Tong could stay at his house.

One other child felt a similar need to explain this provocative textual detail. He, too, pointed out how the boatman returned to the same place each night so that he could meet Chee Tong in his house; and he, too, pictured the house with Chee Tong's stove inside:

> It was a small house but quite comfortable where Chee Tong put his stove and cooked, and it was near the harbor where these two men tied the boat up together.

The third child actually drew the picture in Figure 4.12 to illustrate her understanding of the passage. She seems to have used her knowledge of native Americans in representing the alien world referred to in the passage. It is as if she knew that she should avoid the look of her own culture, though Chee Tong's stove does seem a bit like a modern range.

These children managed to supply a plausible answer to a question that the passage leaves unanswered: just why did the boatman tie up at the same place each night? If these children lacked the notion that a boat can provide shelter, they then used the passage to infer a house that could provide the needed shelter. The inference that they made can be viewed as a motivated one, even though it does extend the text base. We here observe the complex way in which children's real-world knowledge interacts with the inferences they make as they struggle to make sense out of a gapped text.

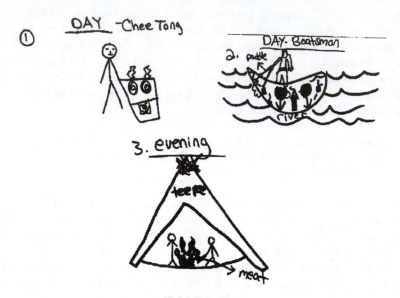

FIGURE 4.12

ADVERTISING TAILOR

We have saved for last the passage that constitutes the most dramatic example of a gapped narrative:

An advertising tailor put a sign on the ballpark fence. The sign announced that he would give away a suit of clothes for each home run. Biff took notice. He began to hammer out a wardrobe at such a terrific pace that the owner of the little shop trembled when he heard the news of the game.

A. Biff "hammered out a wardrobe" by making

a closet	a notice
home runs	suits

B. The tailor was surprised to see how much he had

made	trembled
sold	promised

At first glance, the world that this passage presents might not seem so alien as the one that Chee Tong inhabits. It is, after, all, situated on home soil, and it is even concerned with our national sport, one that many children learn to play at an early age. One might, then, expect young readers to be in a better position to fill in the many gaps in the passage; yet as we interviewed children, we became aware that, for many, this world was even more confusing than Chee Tong's. Among the many questions that it raised for them were the following:

1) What does an advertising tailor do? Why does he want to give away suits for home runs? Is he a baseball fan who wishes to support the local team? Does he see this as a way to improve his business?

2) Who's Biff—a baseball player or the tailor's assistant? What does *hammer out a wardrobe* mean? Did Biff build a closet, make suits, hit home runs, or what?

3) Who is the owner of the shop—the advertising tailor, Biff, or perhaps even the tailor's boss? Why is he trembling when he hears the news of the game? Is he afraid he's going to lose money or is he excited by the team's performance?

Most of these questions revolve around the identity of the characters. This passage, like CHEE TONG, lightly sketches in two people whose relations are difficult for children to work out. In both passages, one person is identified by profession, the other by proper name. The name *Chee Tong*, of course, signals that the character is Chinese. We thought that the name *Biff* might signal that the character is an athlete of some kind, and so we asked 25 third and fourth graders to select from an alphabetized list any word they might associate with the name *Biff*. Here are the numbers who selected the various words (nouns in the left column and adjectives in the right one):

boy (17)	short (15)
man (6)	weak (14)
girl (2)	young (13)
woman (1)	strong (7)
	old (6)
	tall (4)

Our expectations were not borne out. The children tended to think of someone named *Biff* as a young boy who was short and weak rather than tall and strong. This probe does, however, provide further evidence for a point already made—children tend to see the characters in these passages as children rather than adults. When we asked a group of 20 adults to do the same task, their choices accorded more with our expectations. For them, Biff tended to be a man who was tall and strong.

It is not simply the world represented by this passage that is alien to children; a good deal of its language is alien as well. Consider, for example, the peculiar way in which the person's profession is identified. The word *tailor* itself is not all that familiar to children, but when it is preceded by *advertising*, the result is bizarre. As an attributive, *advertising* usually means "specializing in advertising," as in *advertising agency*. It is difficult to think of any natural examples that parallel the use in this unit, in which the phrase is equivalent to "a tailor who advertises." We are thus more likely to think that an advertising attorney is someone who specializes in the legal aspects of advertising rather than someone who promotes his services through TV spots. In order to avoid the awkward phrase *advertising tailor*, the test makers could have used an opening sentence such as the following:

> In order to advertise his business, a tailor decided to put a sign on the ballpark fence.

There were children, however, who were able to make sense out of the phrase, as illustrated by the following exchange:

I   What's an advertising tailor?
C   It's a tailor that wants to make business. If you hit home runs, you went there and got clothes. Then maybe your parents might go there or other people might go there to the shop.

The oddity of the phrase *advertising tailor* is accentuated by the rapidity with which it is abandoned (i.e., the tailor is next mentioned as *the owner of the little shop*). It is not surprising that some children thought another person was being introduced. In order to link the two expressions to a single person, children need the notion of 'self-employed person' (i.e., they have to picture the owner of the shop as doing his own work). During the interviewing, we became aware that many children did not think of a shop owner in this way. As one child in Harlem put it, "He's the guy who comes by for the rent."

By the same token, it would have been more natural to introduce the baseball player with greater specificity. The first two sentences are concerned solely with the tailor's world, and then suddenly three words— *Biff took notice*—plunge the reader into some other world. A mediating phrase such as *one of the star players* would have guided the reader more gently, but test makers, as we have pointed out, often construct a passage to fit with the tasks that they wish to set. In this instance, the capacity of (A) to discriminate among children would be substantially reduced if Biff were overtly identified as a baseball player. We can see, once again, how normative text may be skewed in order to set up a task.

How children sort out the various ways of referring to the characters— *an advertising tailor, Biff, the owner of the little shop*—is fundamental to how they respond to the two tasks. Consider, for example, (A), which requires children to figure out what the expression *hammered out a wardrobe* means. What they think this expression means is related to who they think Biff is. If they picture him as a baseball player, they are then in a position to choose the target response *home runs*. If, however, they think of him as the tailor's assistant, they are likely to choose either *a closet* or *suits*. It is instructive to examine the results of the pilot testing in Table 4.10, which also displays the agent, instrument, and activity entailed by the three choices discussed above. The other distractor, *a notice*, is included in the table, even though it does not neatly entail a particular set of choices for agent, instrument, and activity.

The various entailments represented in Table 4.10 are based on a normative understanding of the passage, but as we discovered during the interviewing, children were able to select the target response for reasons that we had not imagined. One nine-year-old boy, for example, thought that home runs meant that the tailor's assistant was making home deliveries of all the suits the tailor was making:

C   See, the guy would go to your house and let you try them on at your house; and then if you didn't want them when he came....

I   (interrupting in amazement) That's what a home run's about here?

C   Yeah.

TABLE 4.10

	Agent	Instrument	Activity	African American	European American
		Target Response			
home runs	a baseball player	a baseball bat	hitting home runs	35	38
		Distractors			
suits	the tailor's assistant	a sewing machine	making clothes	21	22
a closet	the tailor's assistant	a hammer	making furniture	11	16
a notice	Ø	Ø	Ø	29	28

In presenting this test unit to graduate students who come from countries where baseball is not played, we discovered that a number of them came up with a similar interpretation. A student from Nigeria pointed out that an expression like *milk run* can be used to talk about home deliveries.

As indicated by the results of the pilot testing, children selected a choice—either *suits* or *a closet*—that fits with Biff being viewed as the tailor's assistant about as often as they selected the target response *home runs*. In evaluating these results, it is important to bear in mind that not all the children who chose *suits* or *a closet* necessarily thought that Biff was the tailor's assistant. Some children were so confused by the passage that they had no clear idea who Biff was. Moreover, some were attracted to one of the two choices, and having selected it, were forced, for consistency's sake, to view Biff as the tailor's assistant. Consider, for example, what one girl who chose *suits* said:

> Well, the tailor promised all these suits...and his apprentice—or little assistant or whatever—decided that he would start making a lot of suits because he wanted them to give away a lot—or something like that...and then the tailor was surprised—or trembling—when he heard how many suits he had made because he didn't plan to give away that many.

She seems to have ignored the equation, suit = home run, and so operated solely in the tailor's world. For her, Biff had to be the "tailor's apprentice or little assistant" (she later admitted to utter ignorance of baseball). We may thus conclude that children's responses to (A) could be the cause as well as the result of their decision about Biff's identity. In such instances, passage response and task response are best viewed as reciprocally related.

Before we consider children's approach to *hammered out a wardrobe*, let us first consider their understanding—or lack of it—of the two lexical items that this predicate contains. The collocation of *hammered out* and *wardrobe*—in the secondary senses used here—is, to put it mildly, unusual. This may be the sole instance in the world of English prose that the two have ended up together. The items themselves, moreover, are likely to be unfamiliar. The verb *hammer out* is not listed in Dale and O'Rourke's *Living Vocabulary* (1976). *Wardrobe* is listed but not until the sixth-grade level, and at this point children's knowledge of its meanings is represented as

all one's clothes	86%
a place to put clothes	85%

In one interview conducted with a 10-year-old girl and her 13-year-old brother, the two children ended up arguing about which of these two meanings was intended in this test unit. The argument is difficult to reproduce because the children kept interrupting each other, but let us pick it up at a point where the older brother is attempting to convince his sister that Biff needed to build a closet where he could put all the suits he was winning:

BR I'm not saying that the tailor hammered out a wardrobe; I'm saying Biff built a wardrobe with his hammer—hammer is a tool.

SI I don't think so, because why would he make a wardrobe when he's playing baseball?

BR Because every home run he makes, he gets a suit; he knows he's going to make a lot of home runs so he knows he needs another wardrobe or he's not going to have enough room for all those suits he's going to win from the tailor.

SI I don't understand it now; you're confusing me.

BR Let me tell it a lot straight from the finish...

SI Then quit dilly dallying.

BR It doesn't matter if I dilly dally; you just keep interrupting me. See, I meant like Biff hammered out a wardrobe by making home runs. He hammered out a wardrobe because he was making home runs. See, I don't really know how to put this.

SI (makes exasperated noises) I think it is—no, I think it's *home runs*, not *a closet*.

BR I'm not saying *a closet*.

SI You said a wardrobe, though. You said he built a wardrobe.

BR I meant like a wardrobe that you keep your clothes in.

SI   I know, a closet, something like that...

BR Because it says a wardrobe. It's like a dresser where you keep, like, your clothing; I have a wardrobe.

The interviewer, apparently having noticed the brother's use of *wardrobe* in both senses, intervenes and asks the girl what she thinks a wardrobe is:

SI   Oh, wait—a wardrobe is not where you put the clothes—it is the clothes.

BR I'm waitingggggg.

SI   Be quiet. See, he hammered out a wardrobe; he, like, ah, kept hitting home run after home run; he got suit after suit till it formed the whole wardrobe.

As the interview continues, the children finally stop fighting with each other and turn on a common enemy:

SI   I hate these questions; they're being vague.

BR Yeah, who wrote this?

SI   Why do we have to take it? It sucks.

Sensing their frustration, the interviewer intervenes:

I   So you're getting angry—you don't like them, huh?

SI   No, I don't want to do this anymore.

BR They are not so good. I mean they didn't have all the things they needed to have.

In order to get a clearer picture of how third and fourth graders understand *wardrobe* and *hammer out*, we gave the tasks shown in Figure 4.13 to 55 of them. The children's responses to the first task are displayed in Table 4.11.[10] As we expected, it was the more concrete meaning—a piece of furniture—that children in metropolitan New York drew on when dealing with *wardrobe* apart from any specific context.[11]

---

1. What is a wardrobe?

2. Use the words *hammer out* in a sentence.

FIGURE 4.13

TABLE 4.11

	A Place to Store Clothing	A Collection of Clothing	Other
3rd grade	19	0	9
4th grade	22	4	1

In dealing with the second task, a surprising number of the 55 children—10 to be exact—ignored the word *out* and simply used *hammer* as a noun to refer to a physical object:

A hammer is usuaful.
I used the hammer to hang up my picture.
I used a hammer and a nail to hang up the picture.
I use a hammer to put the nail on the wall.

Two children who used *hammer* as a noun did try to include *out*:

A hammer out is a tool.
He needed a hammer out side.

Even among the children who used the lexical item as a verb, the majority (87 percent) imagined an activity in which an actual hammer is used; and most of them—25 out of 35—drew on the familiar combination of *hammer* and *nail*:

I hammered out a nail.
He hamerout the naile.
Did you hammer out the nail yet?
I hammered out the nail on the wall.

Children's use of this combination may have been motivated by more than just the frequency with which *hammer* and *nail* occur together. Some children apparently felt the need to justify the presence of the word *out* in *hammer out*. One child, in fact, included the phrase *out of the wall* to make explicit the direction in which the nail was being hammered:

He hammered out the nail out of the wall.

The child managed to convey the image of a nail being removed, though he could have done so more easily by using a verb such as *pull out*. It is, in fact, not easy to construct a plausible scenario for the phrase *hammer out a nail.* Presumably it might be used if one person were asking another to remove a nail that was sticking through a thin board (i.e., by hammering the nail out from the 'point end' rather than from the 'head end').

A handful of children did manage a somewhat figurative use of the verb *hammer out* (i.e., one in which a physical hammer is not necessarily present). Consider, for example, the following sentences:

> I hammered his faced out.
> Say like if I want to hammer you out.
> We can hammer out our way from the store.

The use of a physical hammer is not, strictly speaking, ruled out by any of these sentences, but the more likely instrument would be a fist. There were two sentences, however, that activate a domain in which the use of an actual hammer has no role:

> You use hammer out for base words.
> Don't use the word hammer because dad will get mad.

Some African American children apparently had access to rather interesting uses of the expression *hammer out.* As one child who had recently moved to New York City put it,

> If you live in New York, you can hear *hammer out* many times, because it's a gangster's word.[12]

None of the children's figurative uses of *hammer out* expresses the notion 'constructing a framework' that is basic to adult usage. We asked 30 adults to use this verb and the majority supplied an abstract complement, as in

> The lawyers hammered out the divorce agreement.
> I hammered out an outline for my paper.

Given the nature of these complements, the verb conveys a notion of reaching, by means of sustained verbal activity, a functional closure that will allow matters to move forward. We may thus conclude that normative use of *hammer out* in the adult world is figurative rather than nonfigurative (i.e., it does not involve a physical hammer).

Clearly, the use of *hammer out* in the passage does not parallel the examples we have just considered. In the first place, its complement *wardrobe*—unlike *agreement, outline,* or *plan*—does not refer to a verbal domain. Moreover, this use does not, strictly speaking, convey the idea of constructing a framework that allows further work to proceed. In other ways, however, it does resemble the normative examples. It does, for example, manage to convey a notion of closure, for *wardrobe* describes a collection of clothing which, in some sense, can be viewed as complete;[13] and then, too, it fits within the figurative pattern since the use of a physical hammer is not entailed in constructing a wardrobe made up of clothes.

In order to understand what *hammered out a wardrobe* means, readers must take account of what the tailor had promised (i.e., a suit = a home run). Hence they are to understand that Biff was really hammering out home runs rather than suits; the linking of *hammer out* and *home runs*, given baseball idiom, is not unusual (this idiom exploits the analogy between the swinging of a hammer and the swinging of a bat).[14] Figure 4.14 illustrates the underlying relations in this predicate. As the arrows indicate, *hammer out* cannot readily be joined with *suits*. Unlike plural *home runs*, it does not activate the image of a hammer-like object; and unlike singular *wardrobe*, it does not activate the notion of closure. Yet it is *suits* that connects *home runs* and *wardrobe*. In effect, the verb can collocate more readily with the end points of the chain than with the mediating link itself.

The relations that we have just identified are, in fact, only a portion of a larger network which, ideally, a reader works out when responding to (A). Given the complexity of these relations, we display them from an information-processing perspective in Figure 4.15. We use the terms TEXT-DEPENDENT, LANGUAGE-DEPENDENT, and READER-DEPENDENT to identify the primary information source for each relation. The topmost relation in the diagram, 'home run = suit,' can be described as text-dependent in that (1) it does not hold beyond the text under consideration, and (2) it cannot be inferred by the reader from other relations. By way of contrast, a relation such as 'wardrobe = suits' is

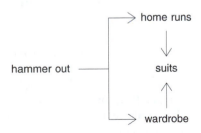

FIGURE 4.14

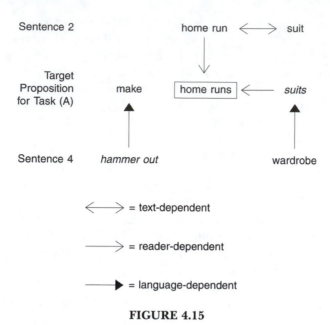

FIGURE 4.15

described as language-dependent in that it does, in fact, hold beyond the text. In effect, the words *wardrobe* and *suits* function within the same lexical set, so their relation can be viewed as fundamentally anchored in language itself.[15]

The relations described as reader-dependent are both anchored in the target response itself. Neither is directly given by the text nor does either constitute a meaning-relation within a language system. Rather each relation represents an inference that readers have to make if they are to integrate text-dependent and language-dependent information. In fact, one arrow runs from the text-dependent portion of the network, the other from the language-dependent portion. This convergence of the two arrows graphically illustrates how readers must chunk disparate bits of information if they are to arrive at the target response. As one adult reader vividly put it,

> I had the distinct sense of a number of things clicking into place when I selected *home runs* as the right answer.

Within the network, the relation 'hammer out = make' is identified as language-dependent. This labeling is not altogether satisfying, for *hammer out* and *make* are not parallel in the same way as are, say, *wardrobe* and *suits*; and yet these two verbs can be included in the same lexical set.

Make is the more general of the two; that is to say, it can collocate with a wider range of complements. Note, for example, the wide range that is illustrated by the four choices provided in (A): *a notice, a closet, suits, home runs*. It is ironic that *home runs*, the target response, is the one that fits least well with this verb. To someone who knows baseball, *making a home run* sounds very odd.

We were not surprised to find that when boys discussed this task, they often used *hit* with *home runs*. Consider, for example, the following excerpts from interviews:

> They are going to need a lot of clothing because a lot of home runs would be hit during the game.
>
> *Hammer* means hit a home run.
>
> *Hammer out* means hit the ball as hard as he could and hit a home run.

A few boys were so troubled by this lack of fit that they apparently rejected the target response. As one 10-year-old boy put it,

> That's stupid. Nobody would ever say *make a home run*.

For most boys, however, the inherent elasticity of the verb *make* allowed them to accommodate this odd usage.

By way of contrast, girls were more prone to talk about *making home runs*:

> So I was thinking about Biff...how many *home runs* Biff had made.
>
> You know he *made* a lot of *home runs* for the upcoming game.
>
> Oh, you mean because he kept *making home runs*.
>
> So someone heard of the many *home runs* he was *making*.

One girl even used *do* with the target response *home runs*:

> Well, he hadn't made any clothes yet because he didn't know how many *home runs* a person was going to do.

These responses provide evidence, once again, of children—in this case, certain girls—benefiting from a lack of relevant real-world knowledge (see ALICE AND THE FAWN, p. 92).

From a broader perspective, girls' lesser knowledge of baseball probably did more harm than good, for it meant that they had less access to certain cues. When they attempted to explain what *hammer out* means in the passage, they often became confused, making vague references to the hammer-and-nail scenario we discussed earlier:

> *Hammer out* means—let me think—he put it up on the wall.

One girl did manage to suggest that *hammered out a home run* should have been used in the passage:

> Instead of saying *he hammered out a wardrobe*, [it should] say he *hammered out a home run*, and then it wouldn't be confusing.

Even she, however, has not quite mastered the idiom, for she uses *hammer out* with singular *home run*.[16]

In discussing her frustration at not knowing the expression *hammer out*, one 10-year-old girl summed up well the frustration that many children experienced in responding to this unit:

> C   I didn't know what hammering out a wardrobe means—*hammer* sounds sort of like making something very quickly, like sewing and everything. And *hammer*, I never heard of that term, you know, because in baseball you would say "hitting out a wardrobe" or something like that....So I don't know anything about baseball, so how should anybody know that? Nobody teaches what *to hammer out a wardrobe* means.
>
> I   Yes, I find that very hard to understand, too.
>
> C   They can't do that to kids. How are kids supposed to know that?

In closing our discussion of (A), we would like to present what one nine-year-old African American child volunteered during an interview. An ardent baseball fan, he began, with no apparent provocation, to mimic how a baseball announcer might describe Biff at bat:

> Biff was up to bat and the first pitch came and he swung and missed. The second pitch came and he swung and missed; the third pitch came and was a ball; the fourth pitch came and was a ball; the fifth pitch came and was a ball. And the fourth pitch—the sixth pitch—came and he swung as hard as he could and he hit—he hit it either over the fence or hit it over everybody's heads. He ran and, well, he got it all on errors. Maybe lots of home runs are on errors—at least in our league they are.

Incidentally, he was able to do this task—and the next one as well—with apparent ease.

Before leaving (A), we should note that the distractor *a notice* was selected relatively frequently during the pilot testing: nearly 30 percent of both the European American and African American children selected it. We were somewhat surprised by this result, since as we noted in Table 4.10, the choice of *a notice*, unlike the other three, does not entail an integrated view of agent, instrument, and activity within the passage. The fact that the word *notice* occurs at the major gap in the passage—the shift from what the tailor did to Biff's response—seems to have made it a prime target for misinterpretation. During the interviewing, we discovered that a number of children made some kind of association between *sign* and *notice*:

I   Why did you choose *a notice*?
C   Well, it says, "An advertising tailor put up a sign on the ballpark." A sign is like a notice. You can't put a closet up or a home run or suits. He put up a notice to tell the people what he was going to do.

Other children provided vague explanations for their choice of *a notice*. One child, for example, said:

Biff was a baseball player who made the tailor notice him.

Let us now move on to (B), one of the most difficult tasks in our corpus of test material. In all our interviewing, we came across only one third grader who was able to articulate clearly what the test makers presumably had in mind in constructing this task. Here is how she explained her response:

I think it's *promise*....He probably thought to himself: "I'm in such deep trouble because I told him he could get a new suit for every home run but I never expected this many."

The results of the pilot testing are given in Table 4.12. African American and European American children selected the choices in similar proportions and were least attracted to the target response *promised*.

TABLE 4.12

	African American	European American
made	39%	37%
trembled	18%	24%
sold	26%	26%
promised	17%	13%

Many of the difficulties that we discussed in connection with (A) are also present in (B). For example, children are, once again, led astray by assuming that Biff is the tailor's assistant. Two new problems, however, emerge:

1) To whom does the word *he* in the task stem refer?
2) How is the word *promised*, one of the four choices, to be understood?

When we began to interview children, we discovered that a number of them, especially African Americans—thought that *Biff* was the antecedent of *he*.[17] So we decided to present the two tasks with the passage removed to third and fourth graders—17 African American and 17 European American—and then ask them whom *he* refers to. The results are shown in Table 4.13. The results were so unexpected that we decided to give the same task to 30 adults. Their patterns of response, shown in Table 4.14, were similar to the children's.

We were puzzled by these results, having assumed that test takers, at least adult ones, understand that the language of a task tends to be self-contained—and so the antecedent for any pronominal is included in the same task. In interviewing children, however, we discovered that some of them worked with an opposing perspective—for them, language should be interpreted as linking the two tasks:

Given the first question, it is natural for me to assume that *he* refers to Biff because the second question follows the first question.

I was relating (B) to (A) so I was thinking about Biff—how many home runs Biff had made.

Such a point of view helped us to make sense out of the pilot test results: the most frequent choices—*made* and *sold*—make sense if *he* refers to Biff, while the least frequent choices—*trembled* and *promised*—make sense only if *he* refers to the tailor. As we progressed with the interviewing, we began to discover why children link *he* with *Biff*. As one child put it succinctly,

TABLE 4.13

	African American	European American
Biff	11	8
tailor	6	8
unclear	0	1

TABLE 4.14

	African American	European American
Biff	7	8
tailor	5	8
unclear	2	0

It had to be Biff because the tailor was surprised.

Another child expressed the same point in explaining his rejection of *trembled* and *promised*:

> *Trembled* doesn't make sense because the tailor would not be surprised to see how much he trembled. *Promised* doesn't make sense either because he would not be surprised by what he did.

These children—and apparently many others—worked with a notion that might be roughly stated as follows: within narrative, characters are represented as surprised by what others do rather than by what they themselves do. As one child put it, "The tailor can't be surprised of his own promise because he made it."[18]

There is, however, a further reason for linking *he* with *Biff* that was articulated by one student.[19] He pointed out how the passage itself has already focused on the tailor's surprise at what Biff did:

> It is more natural to think of *he* as referring to Biff because in the prose passage at the top, the tailor was surprised on account of Biff, or something that Biff did.

In effect, the passage has predisposed the reader to associate the tailor's surprise with what Biff did, and so it is only natural that this association will carry over to the task.

What is particularly disturbing about this lack of fit between passage and task is that it is more a matter of clumsy wording than of actual substance. The student went on to point out that the tailor knew what he had offered and so, in the strict sense, should not be surprised by what he had said he would do:

> To take *he* as the tailor doesn't make sense because he was fully aware of what he had promised. He wrote it and put it on the fence.

In effect, the tailor is not really surprised by his promise—to use the wording of the task—but rather by Biff's extraordinary response to it.

Once readers have linked *he* to Biff, they are not in a position to select the target response. Rather they must choose between *made* and *sold*; and the choice between these two is, in turn, constrained by whether they view Biff as a baseball player or the tailor's assistant. If they view Biff as a player, they can choose only *made*, in which case the unspecified grammatical object of *made* must be a mass noun like *hitting* [*of home runs*] or *clothing* (the latter describing the reward for the former). If, however, they view Biff as the tailor's assistant, they can select either *made* or *sold*, in which case the unspecified grammatical object could be only a mass noun like *clothing* (referring to the actual suits made or sold by the assistant).

We were surprised that more than a quarter of the students selected *sold* during the pilot testing. As was the case with *a notice* in (A), this choice seems to reflect an inability to cope with the gapped passage. A confused reader might be forced to resort to merely associating words— *tailor*, the grammatical subject of (B), goes best with the verb *sold*. Consider, for example, what one child said who chose *sold*:

I   Who's Biff?
C   It could be the one that works for the owner of the shop.
I   What does he do?
C   He sells.

By way of contrast, *made* is a motivated choice, once a reader has decided that the *he* in (B) goes with Biff. As already suggested, this choice allows a reader to view Biff as either a baseball player or the tailor's assistant. The major block to choosing *made* comes from the presence of the modifier *how much* in (B). As already pointed out, its unspecified grammatical subject must be a mass noun. Readers, however, prefer to supply one of the count nouns—*home runs* or *suits*—actually present in the passage. A number of children who selected *made* were aware of this tension between the two kinds of noun, but managed to deal with it ingeniously. Consider, for example, the response of the student we have just quoted:

If it [the task] was referring to either *home runs* or *suits*, then it would have to be *how many*. So the tailor was surprised to see *how much* of a wardrobe Biff had made.

On the other hand, some children rejected *made* simply because they could not fit together *how many* and *home run*. One girl, who was initially attracted to *made*, finally decided against it:

Well, it makes no sense then....If you are talking about *he* as Biff, it would be "how many he had made" instead of *much*. So since it is *much*, it must be *promised*.

In effect, this lack of grammatical fit helps the girl to back into the choice of *promised*.

Let us now turn to the other major difficulty that children experienced with this task, using the word *promise* to describe what the tailor did. The notion of promise for many children was limited to the domain of face-to-face interaction (presumably this is where they hear the word most frequently). As one child put it, "A promise is like something that your mommy and daddy do." Another child made a similar point in response to the interviewer's question:

I   Why wouldn't you have used the word *promise?*
C   Because a promise is—like—more direct.

For her, a promise was a direct commitment from one person to another and so she was unable to absorb the more generic notion of 'promise' called for by the task (i.e., one that encompasses a public commitment as well as a personal one).

Some children searched for another word to use in place of *promise*. As one girl put it,

> *Promise* didn't really sound right. I couldn't put anything else—I sounded out the most likely answer. *The tailor was surprised to see how much he had given away* would have been better.

Other children were able to come up with alternative words. One girl suggested *gave*:

C   Well, *gave* came to my mind. I looked to see how much he had gave, you know. I was going to check to see how much he had gave, because he gave a lot of clothes. But I didn't find it.
I   But you couldn't find *gave* here.
C   No, so I just settled for *trembled*.

A boy suggested that the word *offered* would have been better. When the interviewer asked why he preferred this word, he replied:

> It just isn't—*promise* sounds more like—I don't know—not like a business deal really. A promise would be more—like—I promise not to tell somebody or something. *Offer* has more to do with a deal than *promise*....A promise sounds more like—I mean you're really a bastardly person if you

break a promise. And an offer—if you break that, you might be a lousy businessman. If you break a promise, you really mentally wound someone.

He ended up by saying that the word *pledged* would have been the best choice of all.

One African American girl had trouble reconciling *promise* with the fact that the tailor was giving away the suits:

I   What if the answer is *promised*?
C   *Promised*?
I   Does that make sense?
C   Not really.
I   How come?
C   Because it says he was giving away suits. He didn't promise them. He was giving them away.

There were other children who reproduced criticisms of advertising commonly heard in adult talk:

You know how a lot of advertisements, they say—like—how great the thing is. Most advertisements always say how great everything is and, you know, most of them, how good their product is. They often tell a lot of lies.
All advertisers lie so that in an ad they can't really be considered to have promised anything. Promising means that you really will do something; advertisers shouldn't be assumed to be making promises.

One child went so far as to characterize the tailor's posting of the sign as a bribe. She claimed that, for her, the word *promise* could be used only to describe what "one person says to somebody he knows well."

In view of all these comments, we asked 24 third and fourth graders to evaluate whether certain sentences use *promise* in an acceptable way. As shown in Figure 4.16, the number of children accepting a given sentence is placed in parentheses next to it. More than twice as many children preferred the interpersonal context to the commercial one. This

---

Homer promised his mother that he would be back by 5:00. (20)
The ad for the sneakers promises to improve your game. (9)
This movie promises to be exciting. (4)
The weather promises to be good today. (3)

FIGURE 4.16

result suggests that children's prototypical understanding of *promise* is strongly connected to the interpersonal domain (Rosch, 1977).

In closing the discussion of this unit, we would like to point out a difficulty with (B) that completely escaped our notice until we talked with a nine-year-old boy who knew by heart all the Yankees' batting averages. He did not view the tailor's posting of the sign as business advertising. Rather he assumed the tailor made the offer as a baseball fan because "he wanted that team to win and be able to give out suits." This child selected *trembled* as the response to (B), because it describes well the excited state of a baseball fan as he listens to a game.[20] We can observe here the child responding to a question that the passage raises but fails to answer—just what motivated the tailor to post the sign? The child's inference that the tailor was a baseball fan can be viewed as invited by the passage, since it presents him as choosing an unusual—and potentially risky—way to advertise his business.[21]

We can observe, once again, how a gapped narrative leads children to fill in missing information which then confuses them as they deal with a highly constrained task. In effect, a gapped passage, by its very nature, encourages children to expand the story, and it is not uncommon that such an expansion follows lines not envisioned by the test makers. They constructed a task that assumes the use of *trembled* in the passage will be interpreted as indicating that the tailor was afraid that he would have to give away too many suits. This perspective is captured in the *New Yorker* cartoon shown in Figure 4.17, which was apparently based on an actual sign at Ebbets Field in Brooklyn. One third-grade girl managed to capture this same humor by pointing out, "The tailor only promised a suit of clothes, not a whole wardrobe."

Source: ©*The New Yorker* Collection 1938 George Price from cartoonbank.com. All Rights Reserved.

FIGURE 4.17

NOTES

1. We here use an asterisk, following the convention of linguists, to indicate an ill-formed sentence.

2. We have often observed this process when discussing the English personal pronouns. Native speakers often resist the idea that *they* is used to refer to objects as well as people. Yet they use it in just this way dozens of times a day: "Where are the *forks*? *They*'re in the top drawer." The core meaning of *they* is strongly associated with animate entities. When this pronoun occurs in isolation, its core meaning is so pervasive that it is difficult to conceive of it as also being used in connection with inanimate entities, even though this second use is ubiquitous.

3. Most of the children were so intent on having *blow over* present in letter as well as spirit in their sentences that they neglected to use *blew* or *blown* where required.

4. Children's performance on word-association tasks indicate that they tend to draw on syntagmatic relations in their early years. As they grow older, they increasingly draw on paradigmatic ones.

5. Phrasal verbs began to be a noticeable part of the lexicon almost 500 years ago (Martin, 1987). Since then their number has increased rapidly, becoming a virtual torrent in the twentieth century, especially in American English. This unruly area of the lexicon has been subjected to a good deal of linguistic investigation, but so far no simple principles have been found that account for their use. We still feel they are awkward—not when we are using them, nothing could be more natural—but when we are forced to think about them. This lack of ease in dealing with these verbs is manifested in several ways. They were not taken account of in commercial dictionaries until the 1950s, and even now coverage remains fragmentary. Indeed, dictionaries designed for those learning English often are more comprehensive in this area, because they have a mission to explicate what is commonly thought of as idiomatic. Phrasal verbs are generally thought of as prime examples of idioms; and in some quarters their use is even considered to be slangy—style manuals can still be found that advise writers to replace phrasal verbs with single words drawn from Latinate stock.

6. One child did mention how hard it was to talk about luck when the storm had "already messed things up so bad." We would like to make one further point with respect to the use of *luckily*. We thought about doing a probe in which children would respond to a version of the passage in which this word would be replaced by a more neutral one. We were not able, however, to come up with a replacement as easily as we expected to. For example, a simple connective like *but* somehow sounded too blunt. This limitation itself provides further evidence that the textual gap is so substantial that it is not easily negotiated.

7. A fourth-grade girl identified another possible clue to the gap. Although she didn't know the meaning of *abated* and missed the cue provided by *luckily*, she still managed to get the right answer. She said that the presence of

mighty before *storm* in the final sentence made her think that the storm was first described as especially bad so that there would be a more vivid contrast when it was later described as getting better. She claimed that writers "like to set things up this way." After reflecting upon what she said, we think that she is probably right—that the word *mighty* does, in fact, contain a subtle clue of this kind.

8. While teaching English in the People's Republic of China, one of us gave this same task to 18 students at Nanjing University. It is interesting that their performance was the inverse of adults' performance in this country: 12 of them thought Chee Tong and the boatman were a single person, whereas 6 thought that two people were involved. The fact that this passage activates a Chinese cultural context did not seem to help them in reading it. Indeed, a couple of them pointed out that it seemed like a Western representation of a Chinese world. They pointed out, for example, that the name sounded more like a Western caricature than an authentic Chinese name.

9. For economy's sake, we will consider preparation and cooking of the evening meal to constitute a single activity.

10. Most responses classified as Other mentioned something to be worn on the body: *a boot, a kind of gown, something to put on, something you wear under your clothes, something like to cover yourself.* Two responses, however, had no apparent connection to a clothing domain: *a cart* and *something that is in a lease.*

11. This more concrete meaning would, however, be relatively unknown to children in certain parts of the country (e.g., the Midwest). We question the wisdom of including on a nationwide test any word that has markedly variant patterns of usage in different parts of the country. Dialect lexicography is sufficiently advanced that test makers are in a position to avoid such words.

12. An African American member of the research team informed us that he has often heard the word *hammer*—but not *hammer out*—used to describe sexual activity.

13. The word *out* often conveys the notion of closure in phrasal verbs (e.g., *I'm all tired out*). If *away* is used in place of *out* in a *hammer*-initiated phrasal verb, the notion of closure is not conveyed. For example, after the sentence *The lawyers hammered away at the divorce agreement,* one expects to hear a *but* that will introduce the fact that closure was not actually reached.

14. It would perhaps be more accurate to say that the linking of *hammer* with singular *home run* is not unusual (e.g., *Sosa has just hammered his 60th home run of the season*). The linking of *hammer out* with plural *home runs* would be less usual simply because of the constraints on the two-word verb that we identified ealier, namely, the repeating of some action to achieve a goal (e.g., *During September Mark McGuire hammered out home runs at an even faster pace than Babe Ruth had.*) *Hammer out* may be used occasionally with singular *home run*, given that the ball actually does go out of the playing field. In this sense, a home run, compared to, say, a single or a double, does represent a kind of closure.

15. Some text-dependency is, of course, at work in that the passage mentions a suit of clothes rather than a piece of furniture. In this sense, a text always

narrows the range of what individual words can mean, but the reader is, of course, the one who must activate these narrowed meanings.

16. Note how boys tend to use *hammer* rather than *hammer out*: "*Hammer* is hit...in baseball;" and "When you hit a ball, you usually call that *hammering* it*." One boy switched from *hammer out* to *hammer* and went on to associate the word with the man who hit more home runs than any other baseball player in history: "To *hammer out* a wardrobe, to *hammer*, the word is associated with hammering Hank Aaron of baseball." This boy was obviously a baseball fan—Hank Aaron's nickname was "the hammer."

17. We were amused to discover that the girl, whom we earlier identified as in a gifted class, actually used the word *antecedent* during the interview: "The pronoun *he* didn't really have an antecedent."

18. One might like to argue that, even apart from the specific domain of promising, people are surprised by their own actions. All of us have a great deal of evidence that we do, in fact, surprise ourselves by what we do. But we take such surprises as belonging more to untold worlds of interior life than to the told worlds of human experience that we read about—but then writers such as Proust surprise us by making known these untold worlds.

19. We use the word *student* rather than *child* since the person interviewed was in high school. One member of the research team interviewed four students at the high school level in order to contrast their responses to this unit with children's. Among other things, she wanted to find out whether older students would be better able to understand the word *promised* in the way that (B) calls for.

20. This child was also bothered by the use of the verb *see* in the task stem (i.e., *The tailor was surprised to see....*) He pointed out that the tailor "didn't even watch the game" so it was "weird to talk about his seeing."

21. We were interested to learn that this child, despite his abysmal performance on reading tests, went on to become a nationally ranked chess player at the junior level. The skill that made him an expert chess player—the capacity to envision large consequences of small detail—is vital in any real understanding of text but is often counterproductive in a testing situation.

Part III

Testing Reader Flexibility

In Part II we described different ways in which the narrative passages used on standardized tests of reading comprehension are incomplete. We began by pointing out that, given the brevity required by the test format, incompleteness is inevitable. We went on to distinguish various kinds of incompleteness and classified narrative passages as *truncated, excerpted, or gapped*. The main concern of our discussion was to show how children tend to fill in an incomplete narrative and then use this fuller version when responding to a task. We discussed several tasks in which the incompleteness of the narrative stimulated constructive processes that worked against selecting the target response.

In Part III we will consider certain kinds of cognitive demands that test units make on readers. We will be mainly concerned with three kinds of units that are well-represented in our corpus and that occur frequently on the tests we have examined:

1) units that lead readers to construct one frame and then to abandon it as further information is presented that requires the construction of a different frame;
2) units that require readers to move back and forth between the two poles of multiple pairs of lexical oppositions such as *hot/cold, wet/dry*, and *dark/light*; and

3) units that shift from a highly evocative passage to tasks that are decidedly analytic.

As a convenient shorthand, we will refer to these three kinds of units as FRAME UNITS, POLARITY UNITS, and REGISTER UNITS.

The cognitive abilities required by these three kinds of units are quite different, but the units do have something in common. They can all be seen as attempts to test flexibility in reading. The idea that a reader should be flexible is hard to fault. A reader should obviously be able, when the situation calls for it, to shift frames in order to accommodate incoming information, to adapt the general notions conveyed by lexical polarities to a specific context, to shift from an imaginative register to one that is straightforward. It should be remembered, however, that in real-world reading such cognitive flexibility, by its very nature, functions over an expanse of text; and there is no reason to think that flexibility can be adequately demonstrated in the reading of one brief paragraph. Indeed, our interviewing has led us to believe that the cognitive abilities required by frame, polarity, and register units are quite different from those that underlie flexible reading in the real world.

In Part II all the units, by definition, included narrative passages. In Part III, however, most of the passages are expository. The differences between narration and exposition will become significant when we consider incompleteness in the passages, especially the kind of incompleteness that we have referred to as a *gap*. The gaps that we will observe in the expository passages are comparable to those noted in Part II, but because of the differing norms for narrative and expository prose, they do not have the same effect. Writers of narration aim to be arresting and evocative, and one of the techniques for attaining these effects is ellipsis, not saying everything at once, but leaving some things for the reader to figure out. The communicative assumptions that writers of exposition make are quite different. They, too, wish to be interesting, even provocative, but their chief obligation is to be as clear and as readable as their skill and subject matter will allow. Thus, while gaps are, to a certain extent, expected in narration, in exposition they are likely to be regarded as violations of communicative norms.

chapter 5

Shifting Frames

A s we pointed out in Part II, readers are often led to construct a frame that they are later forced to abandon. A particularly vivid example of this can be found in CHEE TONG (pp. 145–146), where many readers initially thought of Chee Tong and the boatman as a single person. Indeed, such a misframing is not surprising when readers encounter a gapped narrative, for they lack the crucial detail that they need to establish the appropriate frame.

In this chapter we deal with three passages—the first expository, the second descriptive, and the third narrative—which lead readers to establish an initial frame that they are then to repudiate as they deal with new information. Each of these passages is followed by a task that includes a distractor based on the initial frame. In responding to such a task, we will show that children are prone to select this distractor because of a developmental predisposition that Piaget describes as SYN-CRETISM; namely, once children establish an interpretive frame, they tend to use it to assimilate new information even though it may not readily fit. We will have numerous occasions to observe children assimilating new details in quite ingenious ways. Such ingenuity can be a valuable resource in reading—indeed, in thinking at large—but it leads to unfortunate results on reading tests, at least as they are presently constituted.

MINNESOTA

We will begin with a frame unit based on an expository passage:

> So much flour and so many dairy products come from Minnesota that it is often called the Bread and Butter State. It is also called the Gopher State because of all the gophers that live in the prairies. The name of the state comes from the Indian words meaning "sky-tinted water."
>
> A. This story is mainly about Minnesota's
>   products   prairies
>   names   history
>
> B. When the Indians said "Minnesota," they were talking about
>   gophers   water
>   a state   bread

This passage consists of only three sentences: each of the first two explains a different name for the state of Minnesota; the final sentence accounts for the name *Minnesota* itself. It is significant that there is no sentence providing a general statement of what the paragraph is about; in effect, there is nothing that functions as a topic sentence. In this respect, the paragraph deviates from what might be called the CANONICAL PARAGRAPH in English, which can be characterized as follows:

> A paragraph usually begins with a topic sentence that expresses the main idea of the paragraph. The succeeding sentences support or develop this main idea.

In detailed treatments of the paragraph, the *usually* in the above characterization is enlarged upon to include a good many variations and exceptions. In simpler treatments, such as are found in materials designed to improve reading comprehension, the *usually* tends to get transformed into *almost always*. There is convincing evidence, however, that the topic sentence, insofar as it is intended as an explanation of how writers actually write, has been overemphasized to the point of distortion. In a study of a large corpus of contemporary expository prose, Braddock (1974) found that only about 13 percent of the paragraphs began with what might be described as a topic sentence. Evidently, the appropriate word for the frequency of the canonical paragraph is *occasionally* rather than *usually*.[1]

The first sentence of this passage does look very much like a topic sentence. As readers proceed through the rest of the paragraph, they discover that the expectations raised by this sentence are not, in fact, satisfied. In order to investigate these expectations further, we presented the initial sentence to a group of adult readers, telling them that it was the first sentence in a paragraph. We then asked what they thought the paragraph was likely to be about. Out of 45 responses, only 2 people mentioned *names*: one thought that the paragraph might be about the names of different states, and the other guessed that it was about Minnesota's nicknames. Of the remaining respondents, about two-thirds thought that the paragraph would be about Minnesota's agriculture or its products; the other third suggested that the paragraph was likely to be about Minnesota as a whole. Having established 'names' as much less important than 'products' in the first sentence, we wondered how salient it was for readers of the passage as a whole. To find out, we gave the passage to 40 children and 40 adults and asked them what it was mainly about. Without prompting from multiple choices, only about a third of the children mentioned *names* in their responses; and among the adults, only about two-thirds mentioned *names*.

The focus on 'products' does not come merely from the fact that they are mentioned in the initial sentence of the passage. It comes as well from the unusual way in which information is structured in this sentence. The sentence begins by stating a variable—flour and dairy products—and goes on to state what happens when the production of that variable reaches a critical point—the producing area gets a nickname that refers to the products. It is unusual to find this syntactic construction in reading material at the third-grade level. We suspect that it resulted from adapting the original passage, which may have opened with something like "Minnesota is called the Bread and Butter State because it produces a great deal of flour and dairy products." This shifting of *flour and dairy products* to initial position strengthens the readers' sense that 'products' is the topic of this paragraph (linguists, in fact, refer to such syntactic shifting as TOPICALIZATION).

During the pilot testing, 46 percent of the European American children and 30 percent of the African American children chose *products* for (A). Evidently, the former were more influenced by the initial sentence of the passage, presumably because they were more susceptible to the notion of a canonical paragraph. As one ten-year-old child of academically inclined parents put it, "the main topic does start with the first sentence." She was briskly confident of her choice of *products* until the interviewer—who happened to be a solicitous father—could not resist suggesting:

I   I think you've done it too quickly. Think about the alternatives. Which...

C   (interrupts) *Names.*
I   Why?
C   Because it says it's often called the Bread and Butter State and it is
     also called the Gopher State and it's called Minnesota and stuff.

The ease with which she could cite from memory extended chunks of the passage—all appropriately concerned with Minnesota's names—was quite striking. It seems clear that her initial choice had been driven by a school-based notion of how a paragraph ought to work.

Other European American children whom we interviewed were more stubborn about holding onto *products.* Consider, for example, the following exchange with a nine-year-old boy who had just completed the third grade (he had quickly chosen *products,* but as the interview progressed, had gradually become aware of the fact that every sentence in the passage deals with a name for Minnesota):

I   Then you think the answer might be *names?*
C   Yeah. Yeah, you could say that.

He hesitated and then spoke quietly:

C   Yeah...but *products* is better.
I   Why is it better than *names?*
C   Because they really said more about *products* than they did about
     names.
I   Are you sure?
C   Not too sure.
I   What are the products they talk about?
C   Flour and dairy products, bread and butter.[2]
I   So all the flour things and all the dairy things. So that's one sentence
     about products. How many sentences about names?
C   Three.
I   So what do you think it's mainly about?
C   *Products.*

It is difficult to know just why he was determined to hold on to *products.* At this point the interviewer, showing signs of fatigue, moved on to the second task.

We can, however, make an observation similar to the one we made when discussing SHOP SIGN, where it was clear that a number of children had resisted the notion that a story could be mainly about only a shop sign. They felt that all the talk about the sign was just to get the story underway and that the real story was about something much more important, say, the candy shop itself (see p. 46). It may be that this child had a similar feeling about 'names' in relation to 'products.' Even with limited experience of expository prose, children presumably have developed a sense that names are the kind of subject matter used to get a piece of writing on its way. In prose that deals with a geographical region such as a state, an etymological explanation of a name is often only incidental, providing a bit of local color at the outset. The writer then moves on to the real subject matter, which, in the case of a state, might very well be its products or even its history. If names were to be the central subject, the writer would probably indicate this by a general statement like

> We can learn a great deal about the state of Minnesota from its many names.

But notice that even with this sentence a reader might justifiably consider the attention to names to be only a means of fulfilling a more basic purpose—giving information about Minnesota. To focus on names unambiguously, a writer might wish to write something like

> The state of Minnesota has been given many names.

One can even imagine this sentence introducing only a relatively short stretch of prose that would eventually yield to broader concerns. The point we wish to make can be stated quite simply—names is not a very likely subject for a "story" about a state.

In the preceding sentence, *story* has been placed in quotation marks to call attention to the fact that it is the word actually used in the task stem. It may well be that the presence of this word—whose potentially powerful effects were discussed in SHOP SIGN (pp. 45–46)—also contributed to children's choice of *products*. In the case of a truncated passage—and this passage, given its exclusive attention to names, can be viewed as one—the word *story* may lead children to establish a more extended text that they think the passage is initiating.

Certain children experienced another source of difficulty in choosing *names*: they had an unduly restricted notion of this term. They seemed to think that only the last sentence of the passage dealt with the real name of Minnesota, the first two sentences being concerned with, as they put it, "nicknames." It is as if they were afflicted with a mild case of nominalism, distinguishing between what the state is called—Bread and Butter State or Gopher State—and what it really is—Minnesota. We will encounter further evidence of such nominalism when we consider how children responded to (B).

Some children were attracted to the choice *history*. They seemed to view the attention to Minnesota's names, particularly the Indian etymology, as a way of getting a history of the state underway. Here is how one child explained his choice of *history:*

> C   Well, a lot of the dairy products and the food and stuff come from Minnesota, and I'm sure they had them there a long time. And the gophers lived there a long time too, I'm sure. And [looking back at the passage] right, the Indians—they lived there a long time. So it's about the history of Minnesota and everything about it.
> I   Were there any other responses that you thought about?
> C   Yes, it was, let me see, oh yes, *names.* But then I thought it was about the history of names. The names *Bread and Butter State, Gopher State,* but *history* made more sense.

At this point the child begins to have certain doubts about his choice:

> Well, maybe, no; do you mean *history* is wrong?

Before the interviewer could respond, the child blurted out:

> Sure, it's *names.* That's it—*Bread and Butter State, Gopher State.*

We were often struck by how rapidly children could shift to the appropriate frame, once the one with which they started was called into question. From one perspective, such shifting is the mark of a good reader, which is one reason Feuerstein (1977), in his model of dynamic assessment, documents whether children can make such shifts.

Before leaving (A), we should note that children were not especially attracted to the distractor *prairies.* According to Dale and O'Rourke (1976), this word is unfamiliar to young children. During the interviewing, however, we discovered that many children were familiar with it because of the book and the television series *Little House on the Prairie.* Here's how one girl struggled with this name when she was asked whether she knew the word:

> Prairies...prairies are open spaces...uh...with grass and a lot of wide spaces....I only heard of....What's that...a house on the prairie...but I didn't...the story, that story, the house on the prairie.

Let us now turn to (B) and begin by observing that if children are to respond appropriately, they need to draw on a good deal of historical knowledge: for example, that the people living in this country before the Europeans came were called *Indians* and that these people did not speak English. We might well question whether third graders can be expected to possess this knowledge. During the interviewing, we came across a good deal of confusion about these matters. Consider, for example, the following exchange that took place just after the child had read the test unit:

I   The word *Minnesota*, does it mean anything?
C It's a state. I'm not sure, but I think the teacher told me about Minnesota.
I   Yeah, it's a state. Is it an English word?
C Nope, it comes from another country. Somewhere else.
I   Where?
C From Indians.
I   Where do Indians live?
C In India.
I   And where else?
C Well...like...
I   Do you know who Columbus was?
C The teacher taught me that last year. We did centimeters and stuff like that.
I   He discovered America.
C Oh, yeah.
I   And who lived in America before Columbus came here?
C I don't know. Native Americans.
I   Indians.
C Oh yeah, they are also called Indians.

It is not surprising that this girl was confused in responding to the task.

This task was difficult for children during the pilot testing—only 26 percent of the African American children and 28 percent of the European American children selected the target response *water*. There was no one distractor that was especially attractive. The one most frequently selected by both the African American children (34 percent) and the European American children (31 percent) was *gophers*. It is difficult to understand why nearly a third of the children selected this word, but its relatively strong showing seems to be related to the fact that many children, unsure of its meaning, understood it as referring to some kind of a product. Hence the children who chose *products* on (A) were especially prone to choose *gophers* on (B).

During the interviews, a number of children associated the word with something edible such as poultry or livestock. One child even spoke about "gophers grazing on the prairies." Another child, who was initially attracted to *gophers* but then decided to reject it, even made 'edibility' the criterion for determining whether gophers can be considered a product:

I   Would you say gophers is a product?
C   Not unless the Indians ate gophers.

The word *gophers* was frequently mispronounced during the inter-views: several children pronounced it as *golfers*, and one of these chil-dren even justified his choice of *products* for (A) by identifying tourism as one of Minnesota's "main products." Obviously for many children there was a strong interaction between the two tasks: having established prod-ucts as a general frame in responding to (A), they then thought of gophers as a specific kind of product, whether something edible or oth-erwise, when responding to (B).[3]

One other distractor—*a state*—was misleading to certain children dur-ing the interviews, even though it was not all that attractive during the pilot testing (22 percent African American and 25 percent European American). Some of these children were simply ahistorical in their think-ing, assuming that Minnesota was a state even for the Indians. One child, for example, said, "It [the passage] means like when Indians say 'Minnesota,' they are talking about the state."

Other children who selected *a state* had a more sophisticated approach. Certain of them would waffle between *water* and *a state*, as illustrated by a delicately structured exchange between a mother and a daughter (note how easily they manage to jointly construct a sentence):

I   You were attracted to *a state*, but then you changed it to *water*. Maybe you should tell me...
C   ...what brought me to *state*?
I   Yes, and then to *water*.
C   The name of the state [heavily emphasized] comes from the Indian words *sky-tinted water*. I didn't realize sky-tinted water...I thought that this was something else, just a name; I didn't realize the answer was about words. I thought they were talking about a state, not water.
I   But why did you choose *water* then?
C   *Sky-tinted water.*

She uttered her last words with such heavy emphasis that it was clear that she understood the metalinguistic intent of the task.

This attraction to both *water* and *a state* was evidenced by a nine-year-old African American boy who was an especially gifted reader:

C   I think it's *water* but it may be *a state* (he had marked *water* on his answer sheet).
I   Why do you say that?
C   Because they were mainly naming this state when they said *Minnesota*. They weren't really talking about water.

I   Who?
C   The Indians.
I   Then what were they talking about?
C   A state.
I   Really? Where does it say that?
C   Oh, it doesn't say it in here (pointing to the passage).
I   What does it say?
C   It says, "The name of the state comes from the Indian words meaning 'sky-tinted water.'"

He then goes on to read aloud the task, repeating all the choices again. He ends by saying quietly, "I had said *water*." The interviewer continues to question him:

I   Do you still think it's *water*?
C   No.
I   Why?
C   Because they're not talking about water. There's no mention of just water.
I   There isn't?
C   Except for the name which that name came from.

This child is obviously struggling with a subject that is difficult to talk about. He seemed to feel that, even for the Indians, it was the name for something that might be called their own state (e.g., the sacred place where their ancestors had lived).

There is good reason to suspect that he may have been right. In the first place, the expression itself has a mythic ring to it, one that might have been used to refer to a geographical expanse that included many lakes (i.e., "the land of the sky-tinted water"). Moreover, the very fact that these Indian words came to be the name of a state suggests that they may have already been used in reference to the land. There is a good deal of historical evidence that those who settle a particular territory often refer to it by whatever name the indigenous population uses. From this perspective, it is not unreasonable to infer that the Indians may have been actually talking about their own kind of state (i.e., the sacred land they had inherited from their ancestors).

It is evident from the foregoing discussion that children confront particularly vexing problems in attempting to understand that the name of the state Minnesota comes from Indian words that refer to water of a particular hue. To begin with, children have to think of the word *Minnesota*, which is for them an ordinary name in English—much like *John*, *Paul*, *New York*, or *Ohio*—as constituting the phrase *minne-sota* in an Indian language (the inserted hyphen reveals the morphemic structure of the Sioux language). Moreover, they have to think of *sky-tinted water* as a way of translating into English what the Indians said rather than as what they actually said. It is at this point that the metalinguistic process seems to break down, for the phrase *sky-tinted water* is so unusual that it comes to be associated with what the Indians said in their own language. A number of the children we interviewed evidently thought that what the Indians actually said was *sky-tinted water*—an expression that sounds exotic—rather than *Minnesota*—which, to their ears, sounds like an ordinary English word.

To illustrate how these confusions work, let us consider an interview with a child who initially selected *grasshoppers* as a response to (B). When reading the passage, he pronounced *Gopher State* as "Grasshopper State" and *gophers* as "grasshoppers," and when responding to (B), he once again pronounced *gophers* as "grasshoppers." In general, this child did not have serious decoding problems, but he did have a tendency to read too quickly and would occasionally make such an error. Having once made an error, he would tend to repeat it if not corrected. In this instance the interviewer did not correct the error immediately, but he did re-read the passage at one point in the interview, and from then on the child pronounced *gophers* correctly without any overt recognition of the change he had made.

After a good deal of discussion with the interviewer, the child did manage to select *water*, but certain confusions still remained, as evidenced by the following exchange:

I   What's the Indian name for the state?
C   *Sky-tinted water*—so they were talking about water.
I   What's the Indian name for the state? *Sky-tinted water* is English; what's the Indian?
C   I don't know. I don't know—I only know one Indian word.

At this point the interviewer attempted to shift the child's attention to the larger text structure in an effort to resolve the confusion:

I   There are three names here. Why's it called the *Bread and Butter State*?
C   Because of that dairy—the dairy products?
I   Why's it called the *Gopher State*?
C   I don't know. They don't even say. Because of all the gophers that live in the prairies.
I   Yeah, so it's called the *Gopher State* because there are lots of gophers.
C   Yeah, that live in the prairies.
I   So why's it called *Minnesota*?
C   Because of—uh—water.
I   So what do the Indians call it?

C (with assurance) *Sky-tinted water.*
I But those are English words.
C (with exasperation) I don't know what the Indians called it.
I The Indians don't know English.
C Yes, they do.
I Not these Indians.
C The American Indians do.
I Okay.

The interviewer, sensing that the confusion is well-entrenched, decided to explain directly to the child:

Minnesota is an Indian name and in the Indian language *min-ne-so-ta* means "sky-tinted water," so that's what they mean. The name of the state—Minnesota—comes from the Indian words meaning "sky-tinted water."

The child, at last, seemed to understand the metalinguistic problem and exclaimed:

So Minnesota should really be called *sky-tinted water.*

The interviewer responded:

If they translated the words instead of using the Indian words—

The child interrupted with a series of high-pitched and impatient exclamations:

Yeah, yeah, yeah, yeah. Instead of using the Indian words, they could use *sky-tinted water.*

Encouraged by his success in dealing with this problem, the child decided to establish just who these Indians were, and the following exchange ensued:

C But is this from the Indians from India or the American Indians?
I Well, what do you think?
C Indians from India.
I Where's Minnesota?
C In America, but it's gotta be the Indians because the Indians in America know—uh—English.

Here we can observe an anachronistic dimension in the child's thinking that might have contributed to his earlier difficulty. This failure to think historically is of particular interest in light of the subsequent exchange, for it becomes clear, as the interviewer pressed the child to work with a historical perspective, that he did have potentially relevant information:

I   Did they know English when Columbus got off the boat?
C   Yes, they did. No, they didn't. But they knew it when Columbus—
I   Did Columbus know English?
C   Yeah, he was the one who taught it to them. If Columbus hadn't been there, we would've never known any English.
I   Was Columbus an Englishman?
C   Yes.
I   Where was he born?
C   He was born in Genoa.
I   Where's Genoa?
C   In *Italia*.
I   Okay, and where did Columbus—
C   So he was Italian.
I   And where did Columbus go after he was in Italy?
C   He went to—uh—Spain—and then he went to the New World.
I   Did he ever go to England?
C   Nope, he never set a foot in England.
I   Well, we don't really know. He might've, but I've never heard of it if he did.

The child, feeling himself trapped, countered with

But he did know English.

At this point a long exchange took place in which the child stubbornly defended his original position that Columbus did, in fact, know English and even taught it to the American Indians. In listening to this exchange, one recognizes the familiar human propensity to defend, even in the face of overwhelming odds, some position that has been staked out. It is not altogether clear just why the child held on so tenaciously. Perhaps he was simply engaged in a power struggle with the interviewer, who happened to be his father.

What is important to observe is that at various points in the interview the child does display relevant knowledge but is unable to bring it to bear on the task at hand. This illustrates a point that is often overlooked when the relations of real-world knowledge to reading are discussed: namely, that successful reading depends upon children not only possessing relevant real-world knowledge but also being able to apply that knowledge in appropriate ways.

We have dealt with this interview at some length because it illustrates how children of this age can be quite ingenious in their use of oral skills and yet not be in a position to deal with the tasks that are set for them on reading tests. This child, for example, did not select either of the target responses: in (A) he chose *products* rather than *names*, and in (B) he selected *gophers*, which he initially pronounced as "grasshoppers," rather than *water*. Even when he changed his response to *water*, he was still not able to say what the Indian name was. To the very end he held on to the notion that American Indians were able to speak English. We suspect that he may well have been operating with a certain assumption nourished by books and movies that American Indians—and, for that matter, just about everyone else—can speak English. It is not always easy for a child to appreciate that the English coming out of an actor's mouth is there just so that an English-speaking audience can understand. Clearly this test unit forces children to deal with metalinguistic issues that most of them are not ready to handle.

JAYS AND CROWS

Let us consider a second unit in which readers are led to construct one frame, but then are required to abandon it and replace it with another:

It was the season of jays and crows. Their harsh voices pierced the silent air. From everywhere in the woods came the hollow drilling of woodpeckers and the dropping of acorns. Small creatures moved about the floor of the woods noisily. In the dry, crackling ocean of leaves the running squirrel sounded like a man, the hopping sparrow like a dog.

A.   This story is mainly about
birds   voices
sounds   trees

B.   The story says that the air was
harsh   cold
silent   clear

This passage, like many others on reading tests at this level, deals with the natural world. Some of these passages are expository, evidently drawn from the natural science curriculum. Others such as this one provide imaginative descriptions of nature that seem to have been extracted from a larger narrative.

This passage appears to be the initial paragraph in a story, but it does not actually initiate the story line, as does, say, SHOP SIGN, in which the focus on the sign does not preclude mention of Mrs. Doyle, the shop owner who promises to play a significant role in the events to follow. Rather, this opening scene of noisy, busy nature serves as a backdrop. Soon—perhaps in the next paragraph—the real story will begin: Mother Bear and her cubs will enter the scene, or perhaps even Prince Albrecht and his huntsmen. Thus, when children are asked in (A) to decide what *this story is mainly about*, they haven't really been given a story but only the expectation of one.

For someone who sees this passage as—to use the categories of Part II—a truncated narrative, the main point will be that the story to come takes place, or at least begins, in some wooded area in the fall. As is often the case in imaginative writing, background information is presented through an accumulation of detail rather than a summary statement. All the passage details cumulatively establish the woods as the scene of the events to come.

If this passage is viewed as establishing a setting for imminent narrative, none of the alternatives in (A) is likely to be satisfying. No choice that refers to time or place is offered; rather the choices simply recycle passage details that might help the reader to infer this information. In an attempt to discover what interpretive frames children might develop without the influence of multiple-choice tasks, we presented this passage to 20 fourth graders and asked them to tell what it is about. The children's written answers refer to five themes that they find in the passage: the season, sounds, birds, animals, nature. Of the 11 children who mentioned a single theme, 3 mentioned a season (2 summer, 1 spring), 4 mentioned either specific kinds of birds or birds in general, 2 mentioned animals, and 2 mentioned nature; 4 children gave answers that combined two of these themes. The 8 children who mentioned sounds combined this theme with one or two of the others:

> It's about seasons. Little animals wondering and the sound of acorns dropping to the ground.

> how jays and crows sing and wood pecker eats

> sounds from all kinds of birds

> About jay, crow and other animals making different noises

> It is about forest and the sound and the animals.

> About the sounds of animals

> All the sounds of spring are coming back

> The sound of the fall in the woods

Clearly these children's conceptions of what the passage is about are too rich to be expressed in a single word. A similar kind of richness emerged during the interviewing when children were asked to describe what they had just read. One girl, for example, said, "It is about the state of the forest—the sounds and who is in it—small animals, jays, crows, squirrels, humans, or dogs."

What happens when children bring such a rich conception to a task like (A) and are forced to funnel their thoughts into a single word? To take an individual example, notice the last phrase in the list of responses above. Given the level of generalization that the writer has chosen, it would be hard to improve upon it as a statement of what the passage is about. This child has managed to capture three major themes in one elegant phrase and would, no doubt, be uncomfortable if asked to single out any one of them. If he were confronted with the actual choices for (A), he would probably choose *sounds* since *fall* and *woods* are not included (notice how his singular use of *sound*, appropriately modified, better captures the mood of the passage than does the plural *sounds*).[4]

Given that none of the choices is satisfactory, what, then, do readers do when they are confronted with them? Clearly it is *birds* and *sounds* that compete for their attention. During the pilot testing, as shown in Table 5.1, *birds* was the clear winner for both African American and European American children (for the latter group *birds* won by a margin of 2 to 1). Clearly the initial sentence led many children to set up a 'bird'-frame that they did not manage to give up.[5]

In attempting to account for children's preference for *birds*, we can begin by reiterating a point made in MINNESOTA (p. 187). Just as 'products' is more likely than 'names' to be a subject of expository prose, so 'birds' is more likely than 'sounds' to be a subject of descriptive prose; and presumably even at a fairly early age, readers develop some sense of the degree to which prose is likely to be concerned with one kind of subject matter as opposed to another.

It is also useful to compare this passage to SHOP SIGN, where children were also asked to decide what the story is mainly about. When discussing that task, we claimed that *a sign* was the target response because the information it conveyed was more prominent and more pervasive than any other within the passage (see pp. 49–50). We can apply these same criteria to the present passage. In applying the criterion of prominence, we find, as already suggested, it favors *birds*. The initial sentence—*It was the season of jays and crows*—seems to focus clearly on birds. Some children, in fact, trotted out the familiar notion of topic sentence in explaining their choice of *birds*. A child in a bilingual program in Chinatown explained,

> It tells you this passage is about the season of jays and crows just on the first sentence.

He went on to make more explicit his thinking about a topic sentence:

C   In English it's called *the topic sentence*. This topic is what the whole paragraph talks about. It's like the topic of my report. Everything should be related to this topic.

TABLE 5.1

	African American	European American
birds	52%	43%
sounds	26%	30%

I   How do you know this?
C   I learned it from school. We have to do a lot of exercises. My teacher gives us all the sentences in a paragraph except a topic sentence and we have to figure it out.
I   Do you think this rule always works?
C   Yes.
I   How about for this story?
C   Yes, the first sentence tells you that the paragraph talks about birds.
I   Are only birds mentioned in the story?

By this point, the child seems to sense that the interviewer has some other agenda and asks if the passage can be read again. The interviewer agrees, and after a second reading, the child responds to the earlier question:

Not really. It talks a lot about sounds. There are two sentences about small creatures but the story is mostly about birds.

This exchange illustrates well a point that we made when discussing MINNESOTA (see pp. 184–185). Children can be led astray by the school-based notion that every paragraph has an initial topic sentence; this assumption is particularly unwarranted here since the passage is descriptive rather than expository.

It is not only that the theme of 'birds' is prominent—it is pervasive as well, since some kind of bird is mentioned in all five sentences. The first two sentences are about jays and crows; the third sentence then introduces a third kind of bird—the woodpecker. The fourth sentence appears to be only about *small creatures...on the floor of the woods*, but we discover in the final sentence that among these creatures is a *hopping sparrow*. The distribution of 'birds' in the passage is represented in Figure 5.1.

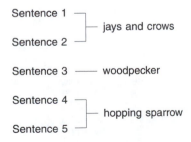

FIGURE 5.1

It is easy for a young reader to have the feeling that birds are everywhere. As one child put it in explaining her choice of *birds*, "Because there are a lot of birds in the story." Some of this feeling, no doubt, comes from the fact that children find 'birds' to be a much more accessible concept than 'sounds.' To begin with, a bird is an entity that they can experience through all the sensory channels: It can be seen, touched, smelled, and tasted as well as heard, whereas a sound can only be heard. In addition, a bird is an entity whose form persists over time, whereas a sound has no comparably permanent form—it is fleeting and momentary. Furthermore, a sound tends to be thought of as existing only by virtue of our perceptual experience, and so we have traditionally posed such conundrums as "Does a tree falling in the forest make any noise if no one is there to hear it?" In contrast, we think of a bird as existing independently of our perception, and hence do not think to pose a question such as "Is a bird really in the forest if no one is there to see it?"

These differences between the concepts 'birds' and 'sounds' seem to be related to the typical ways in which the two are represented in language structure. Consider, for example, the two diagrams in Figure 5.2, which show the various ways in which these concepts are manifested in

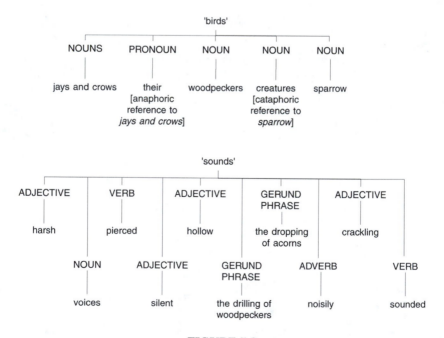

FIGURE 5.2

the passage under consideration.[6] All the references to birds are expressed by nominals—a single pronoun and nouns referring to four different species of birds—*jays, crows, woodpeckers,* and *the sparrow.* Just as the general category of 'birds' is quite familiar to children, so these more specific categories are familiar as well. Moreover, they can be easily grouped together to support the general category.[7] By way of contrast, the references to 'sounds' form a diverse set of linguistic units—adjectival, adverbial, and verbal as well as nominal—and it is difficult to group them.

Comparing the two diagrams makes clear that 'birds' is a more easily retrievable concept for children. It also makes clear, however, that 'sounds' is, in fact, much more pervasive within the passage. Operating only from the crude perspective of counting up the words or phrases in each diagram, we discover that 'sounds' wins out by a score of 10 to 5. Some children who chose the answer *sounds* had a rough feel for this kind of calculation. Consider, for example, the following exchange:

I   Why did you pick *sounds?*
C   Because it says—umm—"harsh voices pierced through the silent air" and then it says "moved noiselessly" and it says what they sounded like and things like that.

She uttered her final phrase "things like that" in an offhand manner, as if she could go on *ad nauseum* citing bits of the passage that would support *sounds.* Other children were more patient in spelling out these bits:

I   You chose *sounds.* Why?
C   It didn't say it was about birds. It only said, "It was the season of jays and crows." There was nothing about birds the whole time.

She then reads from the passage and stresses heavily every word that has to do with sounds. Having done this, she concedes that some of the sounds have to do with birds:

It's all kinds of sounds. It's not only about birds; it's mostly about sounds, not birds.

One nine-year-old boy was able to go through the passage and pick out all ten of the words and phrases that have to do with sounds.

'Cause it says that "their harsh voices pierced the silent air"; and also "the hollow drilling of woodpeckers," "the dropping of acorns, small creatures moving about the floor of the woods noisily," and "the dry crackling of leaves, the running squirrel sounded like a man, the hopping sparrow like a dog." It's about sounds.

He was able to perform this hunt-and-find operation with great dispatch.

The foregoing discussion raises the intriguing question of the degree to which a successful reading of this passage, at least as measured by children's responses to (A), depends on their capacity for sensate imagination. Presumably, readers differ as to how much and how vividly they can experience sight and sound as they read. Children who can, in some sense, hear the various sounds represented in the passage while reading might be in a better position to select *sounds* as a response to (A). We do not, however, know any reliable way of investigating the auditory sensations that children experience while reading.

Despite such limitations, one graduate student specializing in education for the hearing impaired did present this unit to 20 deaf children in the fourth grade. Fifteen of them selected *sounds*, reflecting their particular sensitivity to language that deals with the domain in which they experience sensory deprivation. Such compensatory responses are well documented for those who have some kind of sensory deficit.

Hitherto, our comparison of 'sounds' and 'birds' as conceptual themes in the passage has been merely descriptive. We borrowed two criteria from SHOP SIGN to determine which of the two is more prominent and more pervasive at the surface level of the passage. We can also borrow the notion of hierarchical relations used there (see pp. 48–49) to make a further comparison at the level of rhetorical structure. We can begin such a comparison by noting that neither of the two candidates for the top of the hierarchy—'birds' or 'sounds'—is actually used in the passage, though they are, of course, provided as choices in (A).

Let us first consider how readers might build a hierarchy with 'birds' at the top. After reading the first two sentences, they might establish the kind of hierarchy shown in Figure 5.3. After the third sentence, they could extend such a hierarchy to include woodpeckers, as shown in Figure 5.4. They would, however, have difficulty in accommodating *the dropping of acorns* mentioned there. Moreover, as they move on to the fourth sentence, they would, no doubt, wonder how to place *small crea-*

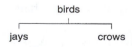

FIGURE 5.3

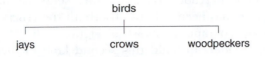

FIGURE 5.4

tures within this hierarchy; and by the time they reach the final sentence and discover that one of the small creatures is a squirrel, their original hierarchy would clearly not be able to account for everything in the passage.

Hence they could try out a new hierarchy with 'sounds' at the top. After the first two sentences, their hierarchy would be fairly simple, perhaps resembling the one shown in Figure 5.5. As they reach the third sentence, it would, however, gain the kind of complexity represented in

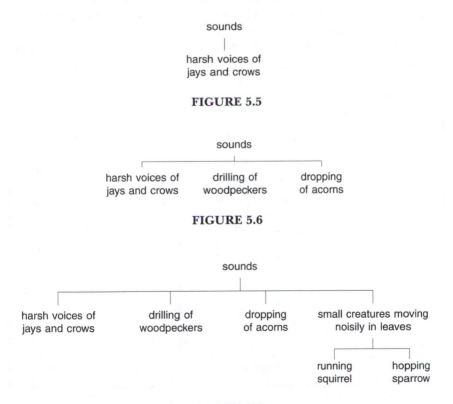

FIGURE 5.5

FIGURE 5.6

FIGURE 5.7

Figure 5.6. By the time readers reach the final sentence, they would find that their hierarchy has been able to absorb all the crucial bits of information the passage contains, as shown in Figure 5.7.

It is easier for readers to build this second kind of hierarchy if they know that jays and crows are noisy birds. During the interviewing we found little evidence of such knowledge, so we decided to conduct the probe shown in Figure 5.8 with 28 third graders: 17 of the children did put crows in the noisy box but only 7 put jays there; by way of contrast, 26 put woodpeckers in the noisy box. These results suggest that many children do not readily think of jays as particularly noisy, which makes it more difficult for them to subordinate 'birds' to 'sounds.'

Apart from such gaps in knowledge, the process of subordinating one concept to another within an actual text is a demanding task, one not easily carried out by children of this age. They are prone to rely on more superficial cues such as saliency ('birds' is more salient than 'sounds') or temporal sequencing ('birds' comes before 'sounds') in developing a conceptual hierarchy, if they develop one at all. They obviously do not experience the same need as adult readers to organize concepts hierarchically while reading.

In terms of sequencing, it should be noted that the passage builds toward an ever greater concern with 'sounds.' It culminates in a sentence

---

Here is a list of birds:

| robins | jays | pigeons | woodpeckers | sparrows | parrots |
| crows | eagles | canaries | blackbirds | hawks | starlings |

Put the birds that make a lot of noise in the noisy box. Put the birds that don't make a lot of noise in the quiet box. If you are not sure whether the birds are noisy or quiet, put them in the not sure box.

NOISY	QUIET	NOT SURE

FIGURE 5.8

that presents this concern with considerable rhetorical flourish, stating that, *in a dry, crackling ocean of leaves*, a squirrel *sounded like a man*, a sparrow *like a dog*. Three figures of speech are tightly packed together: the metaphor *ocean* and the final pair of similes express the ways in which silent nature magnifies the crackling of leaves. Furthermore, this figurative language can itself be viewed as a signal, at least for adult readers, that 'sounds' is what the passage is mainly about, for figurative language is often used to highlight thematic concerns.

Having highlighted various features of the passage that support the choice of *sounds*, we would like to end by reporting a probe conducted by a graduate student who had the intuition that the word *sounds* is not readily associated with what animate beings emit. She asked 20 colleagues to write down what the word *sound* brought to mind. Only 3 mentioned an animate being or a sound associated with an animate being. The others wrote down words such as *siren* or phrases such as *honking horns*. As shown by these examples, the choices tended to reflect what people typically hear in an urban environment. Certainly, the venue of this probe influenced these results but they are still suggestive: the word *sounds* may not be readily associated with auditory sensations stimulated by an animate being.

Let us now turn to (B), which is, from a purely formal perspective, one of the most straightforward tasks in our corpus. To begin with, it is a recycling task that is overtly signaled by the initial formula *The story says*. Moreover, the information to be recycled can be easily located in the passage. It occurs in a simple nominal group—*the silent air*—located in the second sentence; and, a reader, in extracting *silent* from this group, does not have to worry about leaving behind any unused information (see, for example, ALICE AND THE FAWN, where the reader has to extract only *gentle* from *its large, gentle eyes*).

Given the directness of this task, why didn't more children select *silent* during the pilot testing (only 31 percent of the African American and 36 percent of the European American children managed to do so)? Perhaps this question can be best answered in the words of two African American children:

It can't be silent with so much noise.
Sounds and *silent* just don't go together.

The second child, having picked *sounds* in (A), felt uncomfortable with the choice *silent* in (B). Rather she chose *harsh,* explaining that since *harsh voices pierced the silent air*, the air itself had to be harsh. This child displayed a similar kind of thinking on other units: when dealing with HURRICANE, for example, she claimed that the trees had to be *strong* because they weren't blown away like the houses. In effect, this child tended to be concerned with how things end up rather than with how they are. This dynamic orientation to reading tended to lead her away from the target response.

A similar kind of dynamism was evidenced in the responses of other children. One African American boy said that "the air couldn't remain silent because of all that noise in the woods." The interviewer then asked:

I   But couldn't it be *silent* based on this sentence? (pointing to *Their harsh voices pierced the silent air.*)
C   No, 'cause they pierced it.

Another African American boy who chose *harsh* wanted to know whether the question was concerned with "before their harsh voice pierced the silent air or not." The interviewer asked why he wanted to know that and he responded:

'Cause if the harsh voices pierced the silent air, the air is not silent anymore.

Even children who selected the target response *silent* recognized a legitimate reason for choosing *harsh*. When the interviewer asked one child if he had been attracted to any other choices, he answered,

It might be *harsh* because if *harsh voices pierced the air*, it became harsh.

All these children can be viewed as using cause-and-effect reasoning to make an invited inference, but one that is unacceptable on a test of reading comprehension. When we come to the next chapter, we provide further evidence of this dynamic framing on the part of African American children; and in the concluding chapter we provide a more extended discussion that draws together various kinds of evidence for such framing on their part.

WHITE CIRCLES

As an experiment, we suggest that you read just the first sentence of the following passage and then pause to consider what frame it suggests to you:

> As she rolled to a stop in the center of the business district, she quickly was surrounded by townspeople.

Now consider the passage as it is actually written. After you read the first sentence again, notice what happens to your original frame as you read the succeeding sentences:

As she rolled to a stop in the center of the business district, she quickly was surrounded by townspeople. They were surprised when a woman stood up in the cockpit. When she raised her goggles they were even more surprised. She had been flying into the sun all day and her face was sunburned a bright red except for white circles around her eyes where her goggles had protected her. She blinked out at the assembled population of Hobbs like a boiled owl.

A.   She came into town by
    airplane   car
    motorcycle   parachute

B.   The people were surprised by her
    owl   blinking
    goggles   white circles

When we asked a group of third-grade children to read only the first sentence and then complete the story that it initiates, they came up with a number of frames, but the dominant one was that of a young girl on roller skates or roller blades. Here is what one child wrote who used that frame:

> First, they asked for her name and telephone number. Then, they took her into the city hall. There, she found out that she had just set a record as the rolling champion of the world! She was given medals, prizes and compiments for her fine work. Finally, she got into her car and drove home.

We have thus far in this chapter considered two passages in which the initial sentence is misleading if it is interpreted as providing orientation for what is to follow. In each instance, readers are led to construct what can be described as a DISCOURSE FRAME (i.e., a general frame of what the passage is about). As they accumulate further bits of information, they need to abandon this frame and replace it with one that is less probable in the kind of text they are dealing with.

The present passage, however, does not begin with a general sentence orienting readers to what follows. It does, however, begin with a sentence that leads readers to construct a frame that they must later repudiate if they are to respond appropriately to (A). Such a frame can be described as a CONTENT FRAME in contrast to the discourse frame in the previous passages.

In contrast to JAYS AND CROWS, which we characterized as truncated, this passage is best viewed as excerpted—it presents an isolated scene that is not situated in a larger context. The first sentence presents some woman, referred to only as *she*, entering an unidentified urban area.[8] After reading only this sentence, most adult readers agree on two points: (1) that the woman arrives in some kind of a wheeled vehicle, and (2) that her arrival is, in some sense, noteworthy.

As to the first point, adults—unlike the children who picture a little girl on skates—work with a less literal interpretation of the verb *rolled*. From a purely pragmatic perspective, the subject that precedes this verb is more likely to be a wheeled vehicle than a person (e.g., *the car rolled to a stop* rather than *she rolled to a stop*). In this passage, the naming of a specific vehicle was probably avoided in order to make possible the first task (i.e., if existing prose was edited to produce this passage, we suspect that *she* was substituted for *the plane* in the first sentence).[9]

As to the specific kind of vehicle involved, adult readers tend to think of it as a car, given that the woman arrives in the center of a business district.[10] They are less likely to picture a woman as entering such an area in a truck or on a motorcycle. They are also less likely to imagine the woman on a train, even though railroads do run to the center of business districts; and certainly not a single adult—or child for that matter—who responded to our probe imagined the woman as entering the business district in an airplane.

The second point—that her entry is noteworthy—could, in principle, have been related to the woman entering the business district in an unusual way. Adult readers, however, did not make such an invited inference. Rather they tended to view the woman as some kind of celebrity entering the city on a special occasion. In effect, they construct a frame that might be characterized as 'celebrity arrival.'

This frame works for the first sentence, but it begins to disintegrate when readers come to the second and discover that the townspeople *were surprised when a woman stood up in the cockpit.* This sentence provides two bits of information that do not fit well with the initial frame. First, if the person who entered the business district were a celebrity, the townspeople would have known in advance who it was; hence the fact that this person was a woman would not have been surprising. Second—and more importantly—the fact that the vehicle has a cockpit does not fit with the initial frame.

For adult readers the cue provided by *cockpit* is crucial to constructing the 'airplane'-frame, but children seem to make less use of it. During the interviewing we came across only one child who was able to make explicit the connection between the word *cockpit* and the choice *airplane*:

I   You chose *airplane*. Why?
C   Well, *when a woman stood up in the cockpit*...a cockpit, a cockpit is in a plane. That gives it away.

We might note that not only is her grandfather a pilot but she herself frequently flies back and forth to Europe.

In order to get a better sense of children's knowledge of this word, we gave 150 children in a suburban school the task shown in Figure 5.9. These children were roughly balanced in age (third grade versus fourth grade), ethnocultural identity (African American versus European American), and gender. When the children's responses were considered together, a relatively small proportion—37 percent—selected *in an airplane*. Surprisingly, children at the two grade levels differed only negligibly, but when gender and ethnocultural identity were considered, the differences were quite marked: *in an airplane* was selected by (1) 25 percent of the girls, 54 percent of the boys, and (2) 24 percent of the African Americans and 56 percent of the European Americans. There were also substantial gender differences among the African American children—girls 15 percent and boys 37 percent.

During the interviewing we discovered that girls, in particular, were confused by the use of the word *cockpit* in this passage. Some tried to devise a special meaning for the word that would accord with their emerging understanding of the passage. One girl, a quite skilled reader, found two little words within the bigger one and defined it as "a large

---

Where can you find a cockpit?

| 1. in a car | 3. near a racetrack | 5. in a henhouse |
| 2. on a farm | 4. in a train | 6. in an airplane |

FIGURE 5.9

pit where cocks fight." In responding to (A), she selected *parachute*, since it allowed her to picture the woman as vertically descending into such a pit.

Other children found still another way to deal with the word *cockpit*. They pictured a special kind of vehicle in which the driver sits in an enclosed glass bubble, like something that they might see in a comic book or a film. Others thought of a less extreme way of reconciling *cockpit* with the concept 'land-vehicle.' The woman might have entered the town in a racing-car with a glass bubble on top; and since women are not ordinarily racing-car drivers, the townspeople would obviously have been surprised.

Once a racing-car has been imagined, children are able to assimilate the other cues—*goggles* and *flying*—that would ordinarily be regarded as leading to the target response *airplane*. In fact, they seemed to associate *goggles* with a racing-car driver more than with an airplane pilot. For them, an airplane pilot is the tall man in a spiffy uniform who sits at the controls of a 747.

Having managed to assimilate *goggles*, children who pictured a racing-car had to then deal with the verb *flying* in the next sentence:

She had been *flying* into the sun all day.

This cue is perhaps more difficult to assimilate than *goggles*; yet once a racing-car has been imagined, a metaphorical interpretation of *flying* is possible. Certainly the verb is used in everyday speech to describe the movement of an ordinary car at high speed:

After getting stuck in the traffic jam, I was really *flying* once I got on the freeway.

A figurative use is even more motivated when describing the movement of a racing-car:

He was *flying* around the track at an unbelievable speed when his rear tire blew out.

One child even used this kind of a schema to justify his choice of *motorcycle*. Figure 5.10 shows the drawing he made for this passage.

To summarize the foregoing discussion, children are able to provide a plausible interpretation of the passage by imagining the woman in a racing-car, or even a motorcycle; and this interpretation has the additional advantage that it does not require readers to imagine an airplane entering the business district. In order to imagine such a scene, they would

FIGURE 5.10

have to think of the early days of aviation—of famous women like Amelia Earhart or Beryl Markham. But young children have little sense of such women pilots. We asked 30 third-graders to identify Amelia Earhart and not a single one could. None of them could identify Charles Lindbergh either, and only one knew who the Wright brothers were.

During the interviewing, we did come across two boys who managed to infer that the incident described in the passage happened some time ago. As one of them put it,

> It was a very old one [plane]. 'Cause she was wearing goggles.

Having pushed the plane back in time, he was then able to scale it down to the right size:

> It [plane] has to be a very small one, because she's rolling into a town.

The other boy also had a sense that the plane was small:

> I   What kind of airplane is this?
> C   With propellers.
> I   For how many people?
> C   For one, maybe two.

He was also able to assimilate the fact that the woman was wearing goggles to an earlier era of aviation. When discussing the effects of the goggles, he came up with a simile, which, to our ear, was far superior to the one in the passage (i.e., *like a boiled owl*): "She looked like a giant panda."

In contrast to these two boys, most of the children we interviewed had the same difficulty we talked about in BLACK BONNET, namely, taking hold of textual cues that signal a bygone world. It led one ten-year-old boy to mutter in exasperation:

What kind of a plane can you get sunburned in?

The results of the pilot testing, shown in Table 5.2, suggest that African American children—who were evenly divided between *airplane* and *car*, with a third of them choosing each—experience even more difficulty in retrieving such a world.

A number of children in both groups selected *parachute*, the other choice associated with *airplane*: 23 percent of the African American children and 17 percent of the European American children. For some children this choice was a way of resolving a contradiction. The passage seemed to be about an airplane, and yet they could not picture an object of such magnitude—a jetliner was the only kind of airplane they seemed to know about—as actually entering the center of an urban area. As one child put it,

> An airplane can't go in the business district. It can't go where a lot of stores and people are.[11]

A parachute, however, could be used to enter a town's center. Moreover, such a stylish entry would certainly lead the townspeople to gather around, keeping alive the theme of 'surprise' as well as that of 'airplane.' One child even related an arrival by parachute to the use of the verb *rolled* in the opening sentence; he pictured the woman pilot, once she had landed, rolling over and over.

The choice of *parachute* can also be made to fit with the fact that her face was sunburned. A Japanese graduate student explained such a choice in the following way:

> I selected *parachute* for question (A), by guessing from the sentence in the middle: *She had been flying into the sun all day and her face was sunburned a bright red*....The word *flying* hints either airplane or parachute. And then I thought that, in order to get sunburned, she must have been exposed to the air.

In closing this discussion of (A), we would like to show a picture drawn by a Latino boy who selected *parachute* (Figure 5.11). His picture man-

TABLE 5.2

	African American	European American
airplane	33%	47%
car	33%	26%

FIGURE 5.11

ages to put together a lot of different elements: for example, the plane appears to be a modern jetliner, yet it appears to have an open cockpit. The woman appears to still be "flying into the sun;" yet she may well be ready to descend toward the buildings that apparently constitute "the center of the business district." What is most striking is that the parachute is represented as wings, giving the picture a kind of whimsy that can be found in Saint-Exupery's *Le Petit Prince*.

(B) was even more difficult for children than (A)—during the pilot testing only 25 percent of both the African American and European American children selected the target response *white circles*. The reasons for this difficulty are of a quite different order from those we have been discussing. With (B), it does not really matter whether readers picture the woman as having entered the town by airplane or car, or, for that matter, by parachute or motorcycle. Rather, the difficulty arises largely from the way in which the task itself is constructed. To begin with, if children select the target response *white circles*, they produce a sentence which, as one child put it, "really sounds weird":

The people were surprised by her *white circles*.

When one boy was told what the answer was, he reacted in disgust:

Oh no. It's *white circles*? Yuk, that's stupid. That doesn't even fit. Is that really right?

Even children who selected *white circles* were bothered by the way in which it completed the sentence. One child justified her choice of *white circles* by laboriously working through her reasons for rejecting the other responses. She ended by pointing out that she didn't like "the way *white circles* sounds." One child who did manage to choose *white circles* was so confused that he thought these words actually referred to the strange-looking goggles that the woman was wearing.

The children are certainly right when they say that the target proposition for (B) does not sound like English. There are firm constraints on the use of personal possessives like *his* or *hers*. Just as we can't say *her bags* when we mean *the bags under her eyes*, so we cannot use *her white circles* as an equivalent to *the white circles around her eyes*. To produce something acceptable, we would have to provide something fuller, perhaps a sentence such as

> The people were surprised when they saw the white circles around her eyes.

But this would violate the test format in that the target response would be much longer than the three distractors.

Before continuing with this test unit, we can turn to another unit from our corpus—HUNG BRIDGES—in which selecting the target response produces an ill-formed sentence:

> Suspension bridges are hung from towers by strong cables. Golden Gate Bridge in San Francisco is one of the world's longest suspension bridges. The world's smallest such bridge may be in the Boston Public Garden. No great ocean liners sail under Tiny Bridge, but Swan Boats do.

> A. These bridges are
>   towers   long
>   small   hung

> B. Where is Tiny Bridge?
>   in London   in San Francisco
>   at Golden Gate   in Boston

Selecting the target response for (A) results in a target proposition that would be very difficult to interpret if it were considered in isolation:

> These bridges are *hung*.

Again, a crucial modifying phrase—*from towers*—has been omitted in order to have choices that are equally brief. It was, no doubt, assumed that the modifying phrase would be carried over from the passage. If so, it was an assumption that many children did not share. As with the previous unit, the children we interviewed tended to complain about how the sentence sounded. During the pilot testing, only 22 percent of the African American children and 31 percent of the European American children selected *hung*.

The problem of an ill-formed target proposition occurs with some frequency in testing. As we have suggested, it results from the constraints that test makers work with. They must provide four relevant choices, all of similar length, that can function as the final element of the same stem. These pressures can lead to a target proposition that works only if a reader supplies certain passage material that has been elided. Unfortunately, children who are particularly sensitive to language are those who are most likely to reject such a sentence.

Returning now to (B) in WHITE CIRCLES, we can consider one other feature that confused a number of the children we interviewed. The task stem is initiated by the words *The people were surprised*. Using a frequently recommended technique, these children went back to the passage to see whether they could locate these words—or at least a close approximation to them. If they were successful in their search, they could be fairly certain that the task was merely requiring them to recycle material. In this instance, the children were able to find what they were looking for. The second sentence begins in almost the same way as the task itself does. The only difference is that its first word is *they*, but it is clear that this pronoun refers back to *the townspeople*:

Sentence 2:   They [the townspeople] were surprised....

Task (B):   The people were surprised _____.

Apparently all the children had to do to answer (A) was to bring down the information in the second part of sentence 2, namely, that the pilot turned out to be a woman: *They were surprised when a woman stood up in the cockpit*.[12]

As the children made a tour of the choices in (B), they discovered that none of them, in fact, matches what is in sentence 2. Rather all the choices have to do with what comes later in the passage. Two of them— *goggles* and *white circles*—have to do with information provided by the next two sentences—that the townspeople *were even more surprised* to discover, when she raised her goggles, that she had *white circles around her eyes* (the rest of her face was described as *sunburned a bright red*). The other two choices—*owl* and *blinking*—have to do with what is reported in the final sentence—that *she blinked out* at the people *like a boiled owl*. In effect, none of the choices has to do with the two events that would seem to be the most surprising to the townspeople: a plane landing in town and the pilot turning out to be a woman. Rather the choices have to do only with the last surprise mentioned in the passage—that the woman had white circles around her eyes because she had been wearing goggles in the sun. We can use the display in Figure 5.12 to capture the hierarchical relations among these surprising events. In effect, it is the first surprise that makes possible the second and the second that makes possible the third.

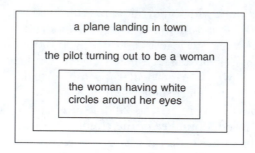

FIGURE 5.12

In order to obtain evidence that the word *surprised* in (B) leads children to a more holistic interpretation, we asked 20 third graders to provide their own answers to the question *Why were the townspeople surprised?* They all wrote down something connected with either the plane landing in town or the pilot turning out to be a woman (some managed to combine these two). Two children also mentioned the goggles that caused the woman to look like a boiled owl.

During the pilot testing, it was *goggles* that was the most popular choice for both the African American (31 percent) and the European American (45 percent) children. A focus on *goggles* was also evidenced in children's retelling of what they had read. Notice, for example, how in a retelling by an African American girl the goggles creep up into the second sentence:

Um, this lady, she came to a business district. She rolled off into the sun and she had goggles to protect her eyes.

This early placement seems motivated—the woman is wearing goggles because she is "rolling off" into the sun. Her retelling ends with a return to the goggles:

Everybody was surprised of her face because her skin was red and around her eyes it was red where the goggles were.

It's hard to interpret what she means here. She may have the right idea but not be able to express it, or she may even think that it is the goggles themselves that are causing the redness.

When interviewing children, we discovered that many seemed to back into choosing *goggles*. They were usually able to dismiss *owl* and *blinking* rather quickly, though some were attracted by the odd language in the final sentence. If they then decided that *white circles* didn't sound right, they were left with no choice but *goggles*. When explaining this choice, they would often report two facts together: (1) the woman raising her goggles, and (2) the townspeople discovering that she had white circles beneath them. It was as if the goggles, as the cause of the white circles, were somehow more basic. In defending this choice, however, certain children drifted back to the earlier surprise of the townspeople. Consider, for example, the following exchange between a mother and her daughter in which the latter insists on distinguishing carefully between *surprised* and *more surprised*:

C   I put *goggles*.
I   Read it over again.
C   *White circles*. No, 'cause that's even *more surprised* so that's later. They were *surprised* when they saw the woman in the cockpit. Then later they were *more surprised*, right?
I   Look again.

She does and recycles once more what she has just said. When her mother tells her that *white circles* is the right answer, she becomes indignant. Somehow she had worked out a frame much like the following one in her mind:

townspeople surprised   ➜   woman wearing goggles
townspeople more surprised   ➜   woman with raised goggles (hence white circles around her eyes)

She felt that the task should match the passage more closely. If the task used the word *surprised*, then it should match up with where *surprised* was used in the passage. Certainly she has a point, given the frequency of tasks that recycle exact words on reading tests.

One other child who chose *goggles* focused on the earlier surprise as well:

I   Why did you say people were surprised by her goggles?
C   Well, first of all, they were surprised at seeing her in the airplane and then they said that they were even more surprised seeing her lift up the goggles.
I   Why were they surprised?
C   I think because she was a lady. Is that right?
I   Yes, but they were surprised for a second reason. What happened when she raised her goggles?
C   She looked like a boiled owl.
I   Mmm.
C   Is that why they were surprised?

I   Don't you think you'd be surprised to look at somebody who looked like a boiled owl?

C   I guess.

I   Right. That's the reason they were surprised. [she then reads the task stem] *They were surprised by her* [she laughs loudly] *white circles.* Why did you choose that?

C   Because it was the mark left from her goggles.

I   Right.

C   And it was the white circles that made her look like an owl.

When the interviewer handed in a transcript of this exchange, he appended this note at the bottom:

The word *goggles* was being made to serve as a code word summarizing an event.[13]

In ending our discussion of (B), we would like to report briefly on an interview that one of us conducted with a principal of an elementary school. Over the years this man has maintained an interest in standardized testing and was eager to describe how he responded to the various test units in our corpus. Here is what he had to say about (B):

There isn't any good answer to that question because that isn't the sort of question that anyone would normally ask anyway. The fact is that people were surprised about the whole thing—anyone would be. A lady lands in a plane in the middle of town, and you're not going to care about the particulars.

He expressed a similar concern in responding to other units: for example, SHOP SIGN, where children were forced to deal with a small mystery rather than the larger one. As a school administrator, he was especially bothered at forcing children of this age to forsake a more holistic understanding of the passage for the sake of a relatively trivial detail.

NOTES

1. Whether writers should use the canonical paragraph more frequently is another matter, one that those concerned with improving writing might consider. Those concerned with improving reading must deal with how something is written rather than with how it ought to be written. A more promising approach to the paragraph can be found in Rodgers (1966).

2. His pronunciation of these juxtaposed phrases suggests that he had made the connections between flour and bread, dairy products and butter. Judging from their oral reading, not all children were able to make these connections.

3. We observed a similar kind of interaction between tasks among graduate students who are not native speakers of English: for example, one Chinese woman, having selected *products* for (A), justified her choice of *gophers* for (B) by describing it as a "specialized computer product." Apparently she had in mind the software program called *gofer*.

4. We presented the passage and this task without choices to a group of adults attending a lecture on reading tests. Two-thirds of the 22 native speakers in the group thought that the passage was about 'sounds.' The fact that so many were able to get the target response even when the choices were not given may be explained by the nature of the occasion and the fact that most of the respondents were reading teachers. It is interesting that of the 9 non-native speakers in the group, only one gave *sounds* as an answer.

5. Associated with this initial 'bird'-frame is a 'season'-frame that also has to shift for many readers as they move through the passage. We asked 20 adults to read only the initial sentence and then write down what time of year they thought was being described. Only 7 thought it was autumn; 9 voted for spring and 4 for summer. As the passage unfolds, there are many cues that the season was, in fact, autumn: woodpeckers preparing winter homes, acorns falling to the ground, and lots of dry and crackling leaves.

6. In listing words and phrases that suggest 'sounds,' we have been as inclusive as possible. Perhaps some justifications are in order. In isolation, a word like *pierced* would not ordinarily suggest 'sounds,' but the related word *piercing* is frequently used in two senses that refer to 'sounds': "loud" and "shrill." *Silent* has been included because it has the semantic feature [-sound]; or to put it another way, one cannot refer to the absence of sound without necessarily bringing up the concept 'sound.'

7. One member of the research team had a five-year-old child who knew how to read. When the child read this unit, he felt quite sure that birds was the right answer to (A). Here's how he defended his choice:

I You picked *birds*?
C Mmhmm. Because *woodpecker* and *jays and crows*. So it's right.

He had no trouble at all recalling the names of three of the four birds mentioned in the passage.

8. We use the term *urban area* deliberately in order to avoid either *town* or *city* (see LEAVING HOME, pp. 62–63). One child was particularly bothered by the use of *townspeople* in this passage:

C I have something to ask.
I Sure, what is it?
C If this is a business district, how could there be townspeople? It's the city, not a town.

9. Assuming such a substitution did take place, it was confusing to some of the children we interviewed. Two of them, for example, felt that the word *she* referred to the airplane itself (having heard *she* used with a ship, perhaps they decided to extend it to a plane).

10. A number of readers pictured the car as a convertible (with the woman standing up inside it), although some imagined the woman as driving the vehicle (the fact that she is used as the subject of *rolled* motivates a reader to place the woman behind the steering wheel).

11. Just as the plane she imagined was too big, so the urban area—with all its stores and people—was probably too big as well. This child, having grown up in Manhattan, probably had something like the Wall Street area in mind.

12. A number of children—girls as well as boys—commented on how strange it was that the pilot was a woman. One ten-year-old boy even blurted out: "Women are just too scared to fly planes." As educators, we were, at times, tempted to resist certain kinds of response, but, as researchers, we held ourselves in check since we wanted children to be free to report the full range of their responses to the test material.

13. When discussing SHOP SIGN, we pointed out that a thing—the sign—was made to stand in for a larger event—the opening of a candy store. For this child, the goggles, as the interviewer points out, seem to function in a similar way.

chapter 6

Resolving Polarities

I n this chapter we present five units which, on the surface, vary considerably in the demands that they make. They all, however, reflect basic properties that we can use to identify a polarity unit: the passage includes multiple pairs of lexical oppositions, which are then used in structuring at least one of the tasks. In research on testing over the years, we have been struck by the prominent role that lexical oppositions play in structuring tasks: they are, for example, at the heart of a major genre of vocabulary testing in which the test taker is expected to select the opposite of a given lexical item. On reading tests, this prominent role is evidenced in the way that multiple-choice tasks are constructed. Anyone who has attempted to develop such tasks knows how difficult it can be to come up with a set of choices which formally resemble each other and yet provide sufficient contrasts in meaning. An appealing way of handling this difficulty is to construct a set of choices around lexical oppositions. As will be shown in this chapter, test makers, working with two pairs of lexical oppositions, can generate four choices by systematically permutating the members of each pair. If we use A and B to represent the two pairs and + and − to represent the two poles of an opposition, we can represent the four choices in the following way:

A+ and B+   A- and B+
A+ and B-   A- and B-

Such paradigmatic generativity is attractive to test makers, but it can be quite confusing to children. In HURRICANE, we described such confusion with the term *paradigmatic vertigo* (see pp. 139–140).

It is not surprising that children experience difficulty in handling lexical oppositions within multiple-choice tasks. Even in the best of circumstances, adult language users are prone to reverse lexical oppositions, as evidenced by their tendency in everyday communication to say one word when they mean its opposite. In fact, this phenomenon is so common-place that listeners generally don't bother to correct the speaker: they simply use the context to plug in the opposite and allow the speaker to proceed. These reversals are so frequent and yet so easily managed that they provide compelling evidence for what we know on other grounds: that the poles of a lexical opposition are neurolinguistically connected. Another way of demonstrating such connectivity is through semantic analysis, which has demonstrated that the poles of a lexical opposition are more alike than different. As Cruse puts it, "opposites typically differ along only one dimension of meaning: in respect of all other features they are identical" (1986, p. 197). Hence, *big* and *small* share features such as [+material quality] and [+size] and differ only in that *big* repre-sents relative abundance and *small* relative absence of whatever quality is under consideration.

Beyond this reversing of lexical oppositions in everyday communica-tion is another kind of reversing that can be thought of as more princi-pled. This latter kind constitutes an increasingly important area of linguistic research that throws new light on deeper aspects of language structure. We can exemplify a more principled reversal of lexical opposi-tions by considering a familiar problem: the resetting of our clocks each spring and fall as we move between standard time and daylight saving time. As many of us can attest, we are often confused as to whether to set our clocks at an earlier point or a later one, and our way of talking about this problem does little to dispel the confusion; if anything, it often makes matters worse. Consider, for example, our reliance on words such as *forward* and *back* to indicate the direction of the change:

Please be sure to set your clock back before you go to bed tonight.

In hearing the word *back*, some people think of an earlier time, others of a later time, and still others are uncertain: they are able to envisage both possibilities and so when, say, midnight comes, they do not know whether to move the clock hands to 11 or to 1.

Because of the confusion engendered by such expressions, attempts have been made to standardize the use of the terms *forward* and *back*. In the mnemonic *Spring forward and fall back*, the word *forward* indicates movement to a later time and *back* to an earlier time; and in published information about resetting clocks, these terms are generally used in this way as well. Despite these efforts at standardization, the opposing use still creeps in. We have a friend who continues to say, "Spring back and fall forward," even though he has been often told that he is reversing the phrase; and in a brochure put out by a telephone company to aid its customers in resetting their clocks, we discovered a slip in the use of the term *back* in the final sentence. Throughout the brochure, *back* had been used to indicate movement to an earlier time, but in its final use it indicated later time.

Even if individuals do not reverse the terms *forward* and *back* when resetting their clocks, they are still likely to be confused as to whether they have gained or lost an hour. This confusion has to do with predictable associations across pairs of opposing terms. Consider, for example, pairs such as *big/small* and *strong/weak*: everyone would agree that *big* goes with *strong*, because each is associated with the positive pole of some scale; correspondingly, *small* goes with *weak*, because each is associated with the negative pole.

Such associations are quite common and they control our thinking—and thus our understanding of language—much more than we are ordinarily aware of. If we have used *forward* when resetting a clock to indicate a change to a later time, we are prone to think that we have gained an hour, given our ready association of 'moving forward' with 'gaining' (i.e., both are associated with a positive pole). This association is misleading, however, for when we set our clocks forward from midnight to 1 in the morning, we skip over that hour, a loss clearly registered in our bodies if we awake the next morning at our accustomed time to begin the day with an hour's less sleep.

We can now turn to the question of why *forward* and *back* are so easily reversed in temporal expressions. The more standard interpretation is that *forward* signals a later time and *back* an earlier time. This interpretation can be understood from two perspectives: drawing upon the terms introduced in LEARNING TO READ (pp. 109–110), we can describe these two perspectives as *anchored (deictic)* and *unanchored (non-deictic)*. Just as human beings use these two perspectives in interpreting spatial expressions, so they use them with temporal expressions, even though the unanchored perspective may not be justified: from a scientific vantage point, time cannot be viewed as possessing any inherent orientation. Nevertheless, language users, in their ordinary use of language, use an unanchored perspective and ascribe such orientation to time. Working with a spatial template, they can view time, much like their own bodies, as oriented toward the future, and so any movement to an earlier point, as shown in Figure 6.1, is expressed by the term *back* (and any movement to a later point would be expressed by the term *forward*).

Even if language users do not ascribe an inherent orientation to time, they can still think of *back* as referring to an earlier point. They can construct, as shown in Figure 6.2, a temporal field that is oriented, along with themselves, toward a further point, in which case any movement

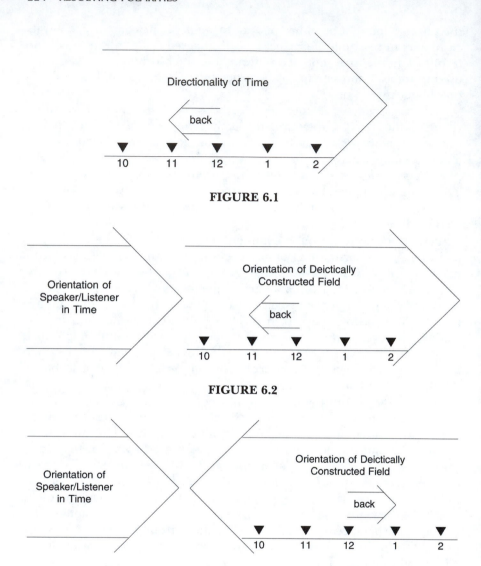

FIGURE 6.1

FIGURE 6.2

FIGURE 6.3

contrary to this orientation would be represented as *back* (and any move-ment congruent with this orientation would be represented as *forward*). Such an anchored perspective can be described as IN TANDEM, since both language users and the constructed field are oriented toward a fur-ther point. In effect, both anchored (in tandem) and unanchored per-spectives can be used to understand *back* as referring to an earlier point.

Yet there is a considerable tendency, as already indicated, for *back* to be interpreted in the opposite way—as representing movement from an earlier point to a later one. Such an interpretation can also be viewed as anchored, but in this instance the language users, as illustrated in Figure 6.3, construct a temporal field oriented toward rather than away from themselves. Such an interpretation can be described as MIRROR IMAGE in contrast to *in tandem*.[1]

Why do language users, when deictically constructing a temporal field, make use of mirror imagery when the use of in-tandem imagery would be congruent with their view of time as having an inherent orientation toward the future? In responding to this question, we can return to our discussion of the human tendency to use a spatial template in representing time and, for that matter, many other phenomena.[2] The tendency to spatialize temporal phenomena is reflected not only in the use of spatial terms such as *back* but also in the imagery used to interpret these terms. Language users in Western cultures tend to use mirror imagery and construct a spatial field oriented toward themselves when they describe the relation between two objects with terms such as *front* or *back* (see Figure 6.4). Given this tendency to spatialize temporal phenomena, it is not surprising that language users can be drawn to mirror imagery when describing the movement between standard time and daylight saving time. Indeed, in this situation such spatialization is often stimulated by the presence of a material object (i.e., the hands of a clock can spatially represent the temporal movement).

It is of particular interest that the use of mirror imagery seems to occur more frequently with *back* than with *forward*. We can identify at least two factors that may account for this. To begin with, the word *back*, as illustrated in Figure 6.5, participates in two sets of lexical oppositions, one with *front* and the other with *forward*. And just as *back* participates in

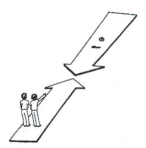

"Hey, there's my pen in front of the ball."

FIGURE 6.4

two sets of lexical oppositions, so *forward,* as shown in Figure 6.6, partic-ipates in two sets as well. Whereas *forward/back* is used to signal a dynamic mode of experience, *forward/backward* is used to signal move-ment with respect to normative directionality (e.g., *In order to get out of the snow, I rocked the car forward and backward*).

In general, the lexical opposition *front/back* is used to describe spatial phenomena, the opposition *forward/back* to describe temporal phenom-ena. Or to state the matter more precisely, these two kinds of lexical opposition, as shown in Figure 6.7, are associated with two kinds of expe-riential modes, STATIC and DYNAMIC, which are, in turn, associated with the two kinds of deictic imagery we have been discussing. Hence the term *front* is strongly marked for a static mode associated with mirror imagery, the term *forward* for a dynamic mode associated with in-tandem imagery. The term *back,* however, is more neutral and can, in principle, be used to represent either mode and its concomitant imagery.

Apart from this formal factor is a pragmatic one that probably has even more weight. A basic use of *forward* and *back* in the temporal domain is with reference to rescheduling. Given that human affairs ordi-narily run behind schedule,[3] when events and meetings are rescheduled, they tend to be moved to a later time. If *forward* is used to express this postponement, then we can draw on the standard interpretation and in-tandem imagery. But if *back* is used to express postponement, then

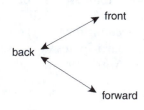

FIGURE 6.5

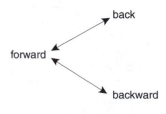

FIGURE 6.6

Lexical Opposition	Experiential Mode	Interpretive Imagery
front/back	static	mirror
forward/back	dynamic	in-tandem

FIGURE 6.7

we are forced, in processing the expression, to use the more spatialized interpretation associated with mirror imagery.

When language users need to move an event or meeting to an earlier time, they run a greater risk of confusion and so are more likely to introduce other cues that will make their meaning clear. Consider, for example, the following sentence, excerpted from a faculty memorandum:

> In order to accommodate earlier discussion of the budget, we shall be bringing the next scheduled faculty meeting forward by one week.

Here *forward* is used to signal movement to an earlier date and thus runs counter to the pragmatic expectation of postponement. This unexpected movement is signaled by two cues: (1) the use of the term *earlier* itself, and (2) the use of *bringing*, a verb that signals orientation toward the earlier point in time at which the language user and his audience are located. This kind of supporting detail should not be viewed as redundant, but rather as providing what the writer needed to counter the pragmatic assumption of postponement.

If we consider the domain of spatial and temporal polarities from a transcultural perspective, it becomes even more complicated. A body of research has accumulated that shows a greater use of in-tandem imagery with reference to spatial phenomena among speakers of languages in different parts of the world: for example, speakers of Hausa and Djerma in West Africa (Abubakar, 1985; Hill, 1974, 1975a, 1975b; Isma'il, 1979) and speakers of Chinese and Mongolian in East Asia (Hill, 1991a, 1991b; Ho, 1997; Wei, 1996) use such imagery in describing the relation between the two objects shown in Figure 6.4. Rather than using a word for 'front' to describe the relation between a nearer object and a further one, they use a word for 'back,' *baya* in Hausa and *ho* in Chinese.[4]

This greater use of in-tandem imagery has also been documented among African American and Chinese American speakers of English (Ji, 1998; McKenna & Hill, 1997). These transcultural differences are of particular interest since they interact in complex ways with variables of age, gender, and socioeconomic class (e.g., African American students are even more likely to use in-tandem imagery if they are male, younger, and from a lower socioeconomic class).

We do not have space to explore this research any further, but it is important to observe that it has opened up even greater complexity in the domain of spatial and temporal polarities. Indeed, if we examine the use of such polarities in transcultural communication, we often find a discontinuity between what one language user expresses and what another understands. We will have occasion to examine such transcultural discontinuities as we present African American children interacting with the test units in this chapter.

In concluding this introduction, we would like to suggest that lexical oppositions, given all the complexities surrounding their use, might be best viewed as placeholders: that is to say, they signal a polarity, but just how it is to be understood ultimately depends upon the context of language use. It is for this reason that writers need to provide supporting detail when they make use of lexical oppositions. In the test units that we present in this chapter, this kind of supporting detail is largely absent. Multiple pairs of lexical oppositions are packed into a short stretch of prose, and little detail is provided to specify how they are to be understood.

BACTERIA

This unit is based on a passage which reflects, at least on the surface, conventional characteristics of expository prose. Indeed, it is an example of what we earlier described as the *canonical paragraph* (see MINNESOTA, p. 184).

From the earliest times, people have found ways to keep food from spoiling. The ancient Egyptians kept grain in dry, cool storehouses. They added salt to fish and meat or dried them in the sun. For centuries people have also kept meat from spoiling by smoking it. All of these methods kill bacteria that cause rotting.

A. Which will keep meat from spoiling?
    water   grain
    bacteria   salt

B. Bacteria grow best when food is
    smoked   dry
    warm and damp   cool and dry

The passage begins with a topic sentence, which states the main idea that human beings have known ways to preserve food from the earliest times. The next three sentences support this proposition by citing specific examples. The passage ends with a summary sentence that tells why the previously mentioned methods are effective.

As for the supporting sentences, the first two contain no indication that they are examples of *ways to keep food from spoiling*. As is often the case, the writer simply assumes the reader will use a principle of contiguity to infer this connection. Such an assumption is warranted for adult readers and even for many child readers who have internalized an appropriate textual schema. As one of them put it, "It is just natural to connect these sentences back to the first sentence." We did, however, come across children who were unable to make this connection—at least they were unable to answer a direct question about what the ancient Egyptians did to keep food from spoiling. Some of these children could make the connection with the third supporting sentence, which makes the relationship with the topic sentence explicit by repeating the words *keep...from spoiling*.

The first two supporting sentences (sentences 2 and 3) differ from the third one (sentence 4) in another way that can be confusing. The movement from a definite time frame to an indefinite one is signaled by two contrasts: (1) *The ancient Egyptians* versus *For centuries people*, and (2) past tense versus present perfect tense. Given these contrasts, how is the reader to interpret the use of *also* in sentence 4? Are the methods of preservation mentioned in sentences 2 and 3 still used? Are the ancient Egyptians included in *people*, or was preservation by smoking unknown to them? Careful readers might further wonder what they should infer from the fact that there is both meat and fish in sentence 3 but only meat in sentence 4. Is smoking somehow inappropriate for preserving fish?

The diagram in Figure 6.8 represents one way of looking at the structure of this passage, a way that focuses on what children are asked to do in the two tasks that follow. The three areas into which the diagram is divided—initial sentence, middle sentences, and final sentence—reflect the basic structure of the passage.

The initial sentence is divided into its basic parts. The nominals—*people, ways, food, spoiling*—are placed in brackets. The words that relate the nominals to each other—*found, keep,* and *from*—are boxed. The "is unequal to" symbol ($\neq$) is used before and after *from* to indicate that it is an *adversative;* that is, it marks a basic disjunction in the passage between the concepts of 'food' and 'preservation' and the concept of 'spoiling.' In addition, since the passage presents 'food' and 'preservation' as desirable, the elements representing these concepts are preceded by a plus

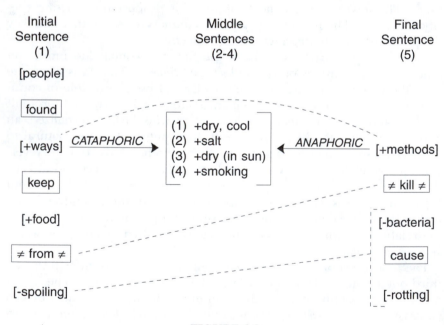

FIGURE 6.8

sign. Correspondingly, since 'spoiling' is presented as undesirable, the elements representing it are preceded by a minus sign.

The word *ways* functions cataphorically to tie the initial sentence to the middle sentences. In other words, *ways* presupposes information that follows. What is presupposed is expressed in the middle sentences, namely, four techniques for preserving food. These techniques are represented in the diagram by the significant component(s) of each one: (1) dry, cool, (2) salt, (3) dry in sun, and (4) smoking. Thus, *ways* may be viewed as a placeholder in the initial sentence for material subsequently expressed in the middle sentences.

The diagramming of the final sentence starts with another placeholder—*methods*—which presupposes the same material in the middle sentences as was presupposed by *ways*, only this time the relationship is anaphoric. *Methods* is related to *bacteria* by the word *kill*, which is adversative. *Bacteria*, in turn, is related to *rotting* by the word *because*. As in the initial sentence, the elements on either side of the adversative are given opposing signs.

Presented in this way, the initial and final sentences can be seen to have similarities in structure that are not readily apparent in their surface form:

1) Both sentences contain a general word which refers to the material in the middle sentences: *ways, methods*.
2) Both sentences contain an adversative: *from, kill*.
3) Both sentences are divided into plus and minus sections: *ways, food, methods* versus *spoiling, bacteria, rotting*.

In Figure 6.8, these similarities are indicated with dotted lines.

Many of the children we interviewed found this test unit as a whole difficult to handle. Their attempts to summarize what they read were usually quite confused, and a number complained openly about both the passage and the tasks. Consider, for example, the following exchange that took place with a child who had been complaining at some length about this unit:

I   What was hard about it?
C   'Cause it didn't exactly say what the questions are. In a lot of stories they ask a question and it will be turned around, but it will be kind of like an answer. It'll be a statement but it'll have the question in it.
I   In the passage?
C   Right, but this doesn't exactly have that.
I   So what do you have to do to get the answer to the question?
C   Well, usually I just read it over again, think about it, and then pick the answers.

Before discussing the tasks individually, we would like to comment on ways in which they are similar. First, the target response for each task can be arrived at by searching the middle sentences of the passage. In the case of (A), all children have to do is find something associated with food preservation—salt—and then recycle it. In the case of (B), the search is more complex: since the passage does not directly discuss what contributes to the growth of bacteria, they must set up a frame in which they can oppose one of the choices to one of the ways of preserving food mentioned in the passage. In other words, they must figure out that the target response *warm and damp* is a polar opposite of *dry, cool* in sentence 2.

A second similarity has to do with the fact that each task can be answered on passage-independent grounds. In order to learn more about children's capacity to respond without the passage, we administered the two tasks in isolation to 30 children: 20 of them were able to answer (A) correctly and 12 were able to answer (B).

In general, children's use of real-world knowledge on reading tests is poorly understood. Certainly a test unit in which children can choose the target response without having read the passage is defective, for they are able to get credit for possessing skills that they have not, in fact, demonstrated. Test makers do strive to use unfamiliar material, but given their goal of using passages that are typical of the kinds of reading that children do in school, they can hardly succeed in neutralizing the effects of real-world knowledge. Such neutralization is particularly difficult with a passage like BACTERIA, which deals with generic knowledge, with concepts and principles rather than individual facts. Even for those who have never thought about what causes and prevents food spoilage, a reading of the passage is bound to activate certain frames—coolness might be associated with refrigeration, for example, or drying in the sun with TV commericals for raisins—and these frames could affect children's path toward a response in unpredictable ways. It is paradoxical that we should seek to neutralize the effects of real-world knowledge in testing reading comprehension, and at the same time advise readers that their comprehension can be increased—that is, they will achieve critical reading—if they maximize the number of connections they make between a text and their existing knowledge and experience.

Let us now consider (A) as an individual task. The most systematic way of responding to this task is to take each of the choices and search the *ways* and *methods* of food preservation given in the passage for information that will either agree or disagree with it. Since (A) asks for something that will *keep meat from spoiling*, the search will be for attributes that are on the desirable side in the passage, that is, those marked with a plus in Figure 6.8.

TABLE 6.1

	African American	European American
water	23%	16%
grain	16%	19%
bacteria	28%	20%
salt	33%	34%

Before we examine the various choices, let us first take a look at the results of the pilot testing in Table 6.1. As is often the case on tasks involving polarities, a substantially higher proportion of the European American children selected the target response. We will work through each of the choices, beginning with the least popular, and see what inferences are necessary to validate or disqualify it.

Grain can be easily disqualified because it is one of the foods needing protection from spoiling, not a way of preventing spoiling. In the interviewing we came across one child who chose *grain* because she read the sentence that contains this word in an unexpected way. She interpreted it as paralleling the clause that directly follows it, as shown in Figure 6.9. Thus, for this child, grain was something put in the storehouses to keep whatever was there from spoiling.

The second least favored choice—*water*—is not mentioned in the passage, but it can be disqualified in the following way. 'Dryness' is an attribute of two of the four methods of preservation given. Since it has a plus value in the passage, anything that expresses its opposite—'wetness'—must be regarded as having a minus value with regard to food preservation. *Water* expresses 'wetness,' so it must be disqualified as having the wrong polarity; it is on the undesirable side in the passage, and the target response must be on the desirable side.

As indicated by the pilot testing, African American children were somewhat more attracted to *water*, and during the interviewing we came across two children, originally from the rural south, who defended this choice on the basis of their real-world experience. As one of them put it, "My grandmother used to put food in pots of cold water." Indeed, one

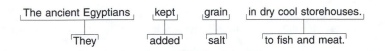

FIGURE 6.9

of us did exactly the same thing when we once spent a summer in a Hausa village in West Africa—the traditional clay pots were designed to keep both water and food cool.

As for the most popular distractor *bacteria*, it can be disqualified in a relatively straightforward way: the passage directly states that they cause spoiling, and in this task the reader is searching for something that prevents spoiling. The relative attractiveness of *bacteria* during the pilot testing can be traced to a number of factors. First, as we pointed out in SHOP SIGN, children are often attracted to a word that they do not know, particularly if it seems to play a key role; here *bacteria* is used not only in the passage but also in (B). Moreover, the particular use of *bacteria* in (B)—the fact that it is conjoined with *grow best*—led certain children to reverse its valence from negative to positive. Presumably some of those children brought this reversed valence to bear on their response to (A).[5] Finally, some children had difficulty in chunking together *keep* and *from* in the stem of (A). They focused on the meaning of *keep* in isolation, which would, of course, lead them to select *bacteria*. As one child put it, "Bacteria is what keeps meat spoiling."

As for the target response *salt*, it can be directly validated by any reader who realizes that the middle sentences of the passage are concerned with ways to prevent spoiling. In effect, it is the only choice in (A) that can be found in the middle column of Figure 6.8. The step-by-step route to the target response outlined here is, of course, only theoretical. It has more to do with the test makers' point of view—how the test unit is constructed and how the target response might be justified—than with the actual processes of test takers. In particular, it makes two assumptions that may be unwarranted:

1) that children have sufficiently developed reading skills to make sense out of the passage; and
2) that children have little or no knowledge of food preservation that can replace or supplement their understanding of the passage.

To gauge the justification for the second assumption, we administered the task in Figure 6.10 to 20 third graders. The numbers in paren-

---

Which of the following keeps food from spoiling?

1. keeping it dry (3)	3. smoking it (1)	5. keeping it cool (20)
2. keeping it warm (2)	4. putting salt on it (2)	6. keeping it wet (6)

FIGURE 6.10

theses indicate how many children chose each item. As can be seen, only a few underlined the specialized techniques discussed in the passage— drying, salting, smoking. All of them, however, underlined *keeping it cool*, reflecting the ubiquitous presence of the refrigerator in American culture. It is interesting that *keeping it wet* made a stronger showing than the answers based on the specialized techniques.[6]

During the interviewing, we did come across a few children who were able to use prior knowledge to select the target response. In fact, it was even used by a first grader who wanted to take the mock test after she observed her mother interviewing older children. Here is how this obviously gifted child justified her choice:

> Salt is a way, salting is a way of smoke, I mean, from spoiling it, wrapping up is one, smoking is one. There's a lot of ways to keep meat from spoiling, but in this section (pointing to the choices) there's *water, grain, bacteria,* and *salt.* And *salt* is one of them. That's the only one in this section. So it must be *salt.*

Notice how she begins with a catalog of methods (including one based on real-world knowledge), shifts to the choices, and ends with a simple matching operation.

As for third graders, one child justified his choice of *salt* by explaining that "Grandma always put salt in the fish and dried them in the sun." It's interesting that he includes two of the methods—drying as well as salting—mentioned in the passage. A more complicated use of real-world knowledge can be found in a joint interview with two step-brothers in the fourth grade, both of whom had selected *salt* for (A):

I   Now how did you go about getting that answer?

C1   I saw it on a film—we had the film on people going across the seas—the Pilgrims—on the seas—and how they had to keep their meat—they preserved it in salt—so I just—I remembered that—

C2   Well, I just knew—

I   You just knew that it was *salt.* Okay.

C2   I just knew.

I   So you didn't even have to go back—

C2   That's why all the explorers went out—because they needed salt and spices to keep the meat good, because—

C1   The Roman soldiers got paid—

I   So you really didn't have to even go back to the passage here.

C1&2   Naah.

I   Just something you know.

C1&2   Yeah.

Both boys maintained that their answers came from general knowledge rather than from their reading of the passage, but this claim should not be taken entirely at face value. For one thing, they were both good readers and would probably have selected the target response even if they hadn't been able to make use of knowledge gained from their social studies class. A more important consideration is that they had, in fact, read the passage. Once readers have negotiated a text, activating high-speed and automatic responses that are largely out of consciousness, their evaluation of what part of their understanding came from the text and what part from prior knowledge can only be suggestive. Still another consideration is that there were two interviewees, and as they talked with each other, the interview began to take on some of the characteristics of ordinary conversation. As has been often observed, conversational norms as to what is relevant to a matter at hand are looser and more inclusive than the norms usually associated with comprehending a written text. Thus, the interview itself rather than the passage may well have stimulated the wide-ranging historical references to the Pilgrims, medieval trade with the East, and how Roman soldiers got paid.[7]

Let us now turn to (B), which, despite the surface similarities that were identified, is more difficult than (A). During the pilot testing, only half as many children were able to select the target response for (B) as were able to select it for (A). As shown in Table 6.2, the target response *warm and damp* was, taking the two groups together, the least favored choice (a particularly small proportion of the African American children selected it).

How can the radical divergence in children's performance on (A) and (B) be accounted for? We have already suggested one major cause: rather than simply recycling information about food preservation from the middle sentences, children must set up an opposition between such information and one of the four choices in (B). As shown in Figure 6.11, they must extract *cool* and *dry*, which are associated with preservation, and oppose them to *warm* and *damp*, which are associated with spoilage. This operation is demanding for young children and it is not surprising

TABLE 6.2

	African American	European American
smoked	34%	30%
dry	19%	20%
warm and damp	15%	23%
cool and dry	32%	27%

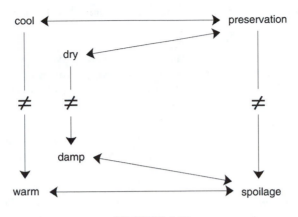

FIGURE 6.11

that many are unable to do it, particularly given a number of confusing features in the passage and task.

Before delineating these features, we would first like to provide evidence from the interviews that certain children were able not only to do this operation but to describe how they did it. At times, the descriptions were indirect, as children struggled to articulate how they set up the opposition. Notice in the following example how the child hesitates, and even makes a false step, before actually articulating the word *opposite*:

> So the, um...um, dry, the um...um, opposite, in the section (pointing to the choices) in the word *opposite* in their descriptions is *warm and damp* instead of *cool and dry*, so it must be that.

Some children were, however, able to focus sharply on the opposition. Here, for example, is how one child justified his response:

> I thought that here it says *Egyptians kept grain in dry, cool storehouses*. So I just tried to find the opposite to *dry and cool*.

Another child made a similar response, actually spelling out the terms of the opposition:

> 'Cause it says *in cool storehouses* and they dried it, and...so the opposite is *warm and damp*.

One child, after describing the opposition she worked out, ended with a general bit of advice:

You have to see what they do in one sentence and then think of the opposite.

She was a test-wise child who also pointed out that all three of the distractors—*dry*, *cool and dry*, and *smoked*—are represented in the passage as favoring food preservation and so the target response can be selected by a process of elimination—an example of the backing-into-the-answer strategy (see p. 238).

Another child, who was initially attracted to *cool and dry*, described her shifting to the target response in rather sophisticated terms:

> First, I picked *cool and dry*, but then I said, "No, this paragraph is about ways to keep food from rotting and all the methods they did." It says, "The ancient Egyptians kept grain in dry, cool storehouses." That tells you that that is where they keep it to keep it from rotting and bacteria goes where it rots. So it had to be the opposite *warm and damp*.

We can here observe a young child talking her way through an operation that she initially failed to focus on.

A rather puzzling exchange occurred with a child who was one of the least promising comprehenders we talked to. While most children were able to go through 22 units in about 20 minutes, at the end of an hour he had only managed to complete 7. His reading aloud of the passages was painfully slow and he resisted talking about the material or how he had handled it, though he was willing to talk about almost anything else. Yet he got most of the answers right, including *warm and damp*.

I   Okay, now does it say that in the passage?
C   No.
I   How did you figure that out?
C   I guessed it.
I   I don't believe that you guessed it. It's the answer that you were expected to get.
C   Because the opposite of smoke and dryness—that's what it says.

This child was presumably associating 'smoke' with 'cool/cold' in some way: perhaps he was thinking of dry ice, breath in cold weather, or even the cool air that one finds in a smokehouse.

We can now turn to other features that may have complicated the operation that (B) calls for. Some of these features have to do with the passage and others with the task itself. As for the passage features, we will focus on the final sentence, which provides the basis for (B). There are several aspects of this sentence that make it more difficult than the initial sentence, which was the basis for (A). To begin with, in our analysis of the structure of the passage, we referred to the final sentence as a summary sentence. It is, however, a summary sentence of a special kind; for while it provides closure for what has gone before, it does so by bringing up a new aspect of the subject—causation. If this passage were followed by more text, readers would ordinarily expect it to expand on causation in some way. Perhaps a succeeding paragraph would begin with something like "Bacteria are tiny living things that. . . ." Such a paragraph would probably continue by describing how bacteria cause spoilage and end up with a statement of the information that is called for in (B), namely, that bacteria flourish in the presence of heat and moisture. Thus, we might say that (B), rather than recycling information from the passage, anticipates what, given our ordinary expectations of text, would eventually be stated in an explicit way. The fact that this task requires children, in a certain sense, to extend the passage may have prevented some of them, especially those who have internalized the parsimonious principles of test taking, from responding appropriately.

A second difficulty with the final sentence is the presence of the word *bacteria*. When 30 fourth graders were asked to define this word, almost half of them left the page blank. Most of those who managed to write something defined it as "germs," or less frequently as "disease." Only one child seemed to know that the meaning was broader than this; he described bacteria as "a living think inside bodys." This sense of bacteria as "living" was also evidenced in certain of the interviews. One child, for example, said:

> Bacteria likes warmness and damp and they crawl around more. This helps them to eat more, like, they have water to drink too—like damp is for the bacteria to crawl faster.

Another difficulty with the word *bacteria* is its form. As illustrated by the preceding response, the child first treats the word as singular (i.e., she uses the verb *likes*) but then shifts to the plural pronoun *they*). Both the passage and the task treat it as plural (using *cause* and *grow* rather than *causes* and *grows*), yet it does not end in -*s*, and children are almost certainly unfamiliar with its singular form *bacterium*. About one-third of the children who gave us definitions of *bacteria* construed it as singular, going counter to a context in which it was clearly marked as plural. It may well be that *bacteria* is among the first Latinate plurals that children come across.

Still another difficult aspect of the final sentence is that it verges on being ill-formed. If we take the relative clause as explaining *bacteria*, it should be non-restrictive:

> All of these methods kill bacteria, which cause rotting.

On the other hand, if this clause is taken as restrictive, as dividing bacteria into two groups—those that cause food to rot and those that don't—the sentence would, according to the usual rules of English, contain a definite article:

> All of these methods kill the bacteria that cause rotting.

Let us now turn to certain confusions in the task itself. A more straightforward way of initiating (B) would be with words such as "Food spoils fastest when it is. . . ." With such a stem, children would understand more easily that they are to look for attributes opposed to the ones associated with food preservation in the passage, whereas in (A) they had sought attributes congruent with the passage. To put it another way, they would be in a better position to understand that the two tasks reverse a basic polarity: the target response for (A) is [+food preservation], while for (B) it is [−food preservation]. We should note that the mere fact that (A) involves the positive and (B) the negative may have also contributed to children's greater difficulty with the latter. There is psycholinguistic evidence (Lyons, 1977) that, all other things being equal, the negative is more difficult to handle than the positive.

As already suggested, one effect of the peculiar wording in (B) is that it makes bacteria and their activities sound positive (*grow* and *best* are heavily weighted toward the favorable side in the subjective lexicon). It is likely that an actual discussion of food preservation would include phrasing such as *bacteria multiply most rapidly* rather than *bacteria grow best*. If our analysis of the passage into desirable and undesirable elements separated from each other by adversatives is on the right track, this presentation of something from the undesirable side in favorable terms can be disorienting. We might even think of it as reversing the polarity of the passage, changing minuses to pluses and pluses to minuses. Perhaps the confusion that this shift may cause can be better conveyed by an analogous sentence in another problematic area. How might readers react, for example, to a discussion of the perils of smoking that contained the following assertion?

> Lung cancer grows best when you smoke non-filtered cigarettes.

We have already suggested several characteristics of the stem in (B) and its relationship to the passage that are likely to cause children difficulty. We would now like to point out additional difficulties that are associated with the choices. Fundamental to these difficulties is the fact that three of the four choices involve the oppositions *cool/warm* and *dry/damp*, which we will refer to as the *temperature scale* and the *humidity scale*, respectively. Moreover, two of the responses—*warm and damp* and *cool and dry*—involve pairing one member from each of the two scales.

Following up on our conviction that polarities are inherently difficult to process, we investigated which associations of temperature terms and humidity terms children find most natural. Independent of any context, 92 percent of the 45 children we asked thought that *warm and dry* "sounds better" than *warm and damp*; and 80 percent were more comfortable with *cool and damp* than with *cool and dry*.[8] It is hard to know how much it matters that these preferred sequences are the opposite of those used in the choices for (B). As we have observed on a number of occasions (e.g., WHITE CIRCLES), children often depend upon whether something "sounds right" when they are deciding on a response to a task.

The fact that *cool and dry* was favored somewhat more than *warm and damp* during the pilot testing may have been due to the fact that these words can be found in the passage, though in a different sequence—*dry, cool storehouses*. It is possible that children who tried to work out the opposite of *dry, cool* became confused and settled for simply reversing the sequence. In a very real sense, *cool and dry* does represent the opposite of *dry and cool*.

In order to get a clearer sense of whether children prefer a particular sequencing of these terms, we presented both sequences to 25 children and asked them which one "sounds more natural." About three-quarters of them preferred *cool and dry*, the order that was used in the task. Research by Cooper and Ross (1975) suggests that orderings of this kind often become stable at a relatively early age and that they provide evidence for deeper principles of information-processing. Hence, any reversal of a preferred sequence may become an additional source of confusion for young readers.

Another difficulty in choosing a response for (B) is the permeability of the dividing line that the passage establishes between 'warm,' 'damp,' 'bacteria,' and 'rotting,' on the one hand, and 'dry,' 'cool,' and 'preservation,' on the other. This was pointed out to us by one of the children. After she had heard an explanation of why *warm and damp* was the target response, she pointed to *dry in the sun* in the passage and asked,

Why would the Egyptians have put their food in the sun if they didn't want it to get warm?

Once we gained this insight, we could see that *smoking*, another of the methods of preservation, presents a similar problem. Everyone, including third- and fourth-grade children, has experienced the necessary relationship between smoke and the intense kind of warmth called fire.

Smoked was, in fact, the most attractive choice during the pilot testing. It is difficult to say why this should be so. It may be significant that three of the simplest test-taking strategies all lead to *smoked*: (1) it can be found in the passage; (2) it contrasts with the other three choices, all of which contain temperature or humidity terms; (3) its meaning, at least in this passage, is mysterious. With respect to this last strategy, *smoking* is a familiar word that is used to refer to something relatively unfamiliar to many children. According to Dale and O'Rourke (1976), *smoke* is known to 94 percent of fourth graders in the meaning "to puff tobacco"; on the other hand, the meaning "to preserve with fumes" is not widely known until high school. During the interviewing, we came across one child who managed to put these two notions together. Figure 6.12 shows the drawing he made in order to make sense of the passage (the child explained that the object at the top of the drawing is a "large slab of meat").

In order to find out how children would handle *smoking* in the context of food preservation, we asked 35 fourth graders, *How would you smoke meat or fish?* The responses of many children indicated that they had a fairly accurate idea:

> with a stick and put the meat on the stick and turn it around
> hang it up and put a fire under it
> when the meat absorbs the smoke from the fire
> you cook it in smoke
> put it in a smokehouse

Other answers ranged from the unhelpfully general to the extraordinarily ingenious:

> it is from the market
> with fire

FIGURE 6.12

by a fire
put it on a grill
burn it and smoke it
make it very hot and it will smoke
people open it up and put smoke in it
you would put fish in pan and keep it over a fire
light it and put it in your mouth
you smash up the meat or fish, put it in the pipe and light it

We were particularly intrigued by the last two responses. When analyzing this unit during the early stages of our research, one of us had appended the following question, as a tired stab at humor, to various speculations about how children might deal with the notion of 'smoking':

Will some children imagine a frankfurter lit like a cigar or a pipe filled with chopped chicken liver?

Throughout the course of our research, we were amazed at the tenacity with which some children hold on to the prototypical meaning of a word, even though it may force them into bizarre conceptions of the world they are reading about.

RAISINS

We turn now to another unit that manipulates polar terms from the temperature and humidity scales.

Raisins are made from sweet varieties of grapes. The ripe fruit is usually placed on trays right in the vineyard. There, it dries in the sun. Drying may take several weeks.

A.   Raisins are made from grapes that have a lot of
water   varieties
skin   sugar

B.   What kind of climate is best for making raisins?
warm and dry   warm and wet
cool and dry   cool and wet

At the level of coherence, this passage readily divides into two parts. The first sentence tells what kind of grapes are used for making raisins, while the remaining three sentences describe the procedure for making them. This bipartite structure is reinforced at the level of cohesion, as shown in Figure 6.13. The first sentence introduces the word *grapes*, while the second shifts to *the ripe fruit*, which is then recycled by grammatical mechanisms in the final two sentences. If the first task is viewed as a continuation of the text, we can observe a shift back to *grapes*. During the interviewing, we came across children who were confused by this shifting from 'plural' to 'singular' and then back again to 'plural.' One child, who was quite a skilled reader, thought that "any kind of fruit"— not just grapes—was being referred to.

Although the passage is divided into two parts, they are not related in an explicit manner. That is left up to the reader. For an experienced reader, this connection will be automatic, since the passage embodies a familiar discourse frame that we can call PROCESS DESCRIPTION. Working within this frame, a reader views the first part of the passage as describ-

	Cohesive Chain	Kind of Cohesion
Sentence 1	grapes	
Sentence 2	the ripe fuit	Lexical (superordinate)
Sentence 3	it	Reference
Sentence 4	Ø	Ellipsis

FIGURE 6.13

ing raw material, the second as describing a procedure for transforming this raw material. As shown in Figure 6.14, the two parts are easily related under the general theme "how raisins are made," or to use a phrasing common at the elementary school level, "where raisins come from." This bipartite structure is reflected in the tasks as well: (A) is based on the first part and (B) on the second.

When we asked 20 third graders to identify the source of raisins, only 9 responded with *grapes*. On the other hand, during the interviewing we did encounter a few children who were quite knowledgeable. One child even volunteered to make a picture about "how we get raisins." She pointed out that "we didn't get the whole story." It's as if she viewed the passage, to use a term from Part II, as truncated. Figure 6.15 shows her drawing, which included a final stage which she described as "packed raisins" (presumably she meant "packaged raisins"). As can be seen, these "packed raisins" are labeled as "sunned raisins" (perhaps she had the brand *Sunmaid* in mind).

We will discuss task (B) first, since it is the one that deals with polarities, our major focus throughout this chapter. In order to respond to this task, a reader must decide, on the basis of the information given in the passage, which climate is best for making raisins. All four of the choices consist of a temperature term followed by a humidity term. Given this fixed ordering, all possible combinations of the terms *cool/ warm* and *wet/dry* are realized, as can be seen in Figure 6.16. As indicated by the arrows, each term on the horizontal axis—*cool* and *warm*—is combined with each term on the vertical axis—*wet* and *dry*—to produce four pairs of terms: *cool and wet, cool and dry, warm and wet, warm and dry.*

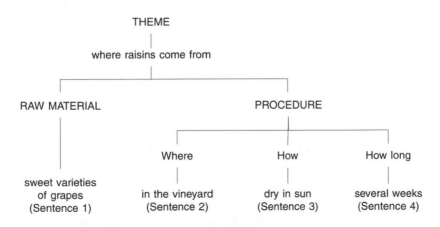

FIGURE 6.14

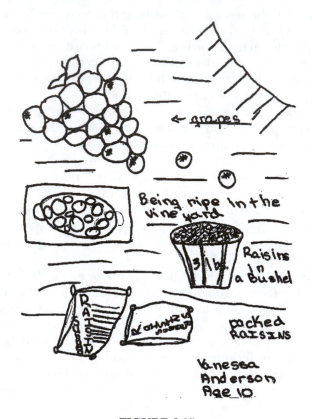

FIGURE 6.15

We anticipated that children would have difficulty handling multiple pairings of opposing terms from two different scales. But such was not the case. In fact, (B) was one of the easiest tasks in our corpus. During the pilot testing, 57 percent of the African American children and 61 percent of the European American children selected the target response *warm and dry*; each of the three distractors was chosen by about 15 percent of the children within both groups. The ease with which children did this task can be traced, at least partly, to two factors:

1) All four of the choices reflect the preferred ordering of temperature term followed by humidity term.
2) The target response pairs *warm* with *dry*, which, as we pointed out in BACTERIA (p. 241), is a more natural pairing than *warm* and *wet*.

Moreover, children's real-world experience readily supports a schema in which temperature increase is associated with faster evaporation, as,

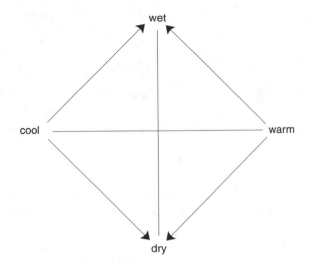

wet

cool

warm

dry

FIGURE 6.16

for example, in drying clothes. Hence, in responding to (B), they were able to draw on the textual cue *dries in the sun*. During the interviews, a number of children focused on this information in describing their response to (B). Here is how one child defended his choice:

> Because it takes a lot of sun, so it would be *warm and dry*. It needs a lot of sun so it won't be wet.

Here is an exchange with a child who began by stating that this task might have been "tricky":

> I   Did you know about raisins?
> C   Oh, yeah—and I'll tell you why I found out the *warm and dry*. That one might've been tricky for some people, but I can show you how.
> I   Yeah, go ahead. Tell me why.

She then gave a step-by-step exposition of her reasoning:

> Well, in (B) it says, "What kind of climate is best for raisin making?" I chose *warm and dry*. The reason I chose *warm and dry* is because the next-to-last sentence says, "There it dries in the sun." *Dry* means it has to be dry out, and the sun is also equal to *warm* or *hot* or whatever—whatever synonym it is.[9]

Rather than engaging in such laborious reasoning, one child, who showed a propensity for rather dry wit, defended his choice of *warm and dry* as though it were altogether obvious:

I   How did you know that [a warm and dry climate is best]?
C   Well, they wouldn't say "dries in the sun" to mean "wet."

The interviewer laughed before concurring:

Yeah, I guess *dry* doesn't mean *wet*, does it?

The child, obviously pleased, could not resist recycling his bit of irony:

Well, it doesn't mean gets wet in the sun.

We should note that the polarity demands of this task led certain children to make a misleading statement about weather. One child, for example, reasoned that

if the climate was wet, then the sun wouldn't come out. It doesn't rain where there is sun.

Presumably he meant to say that when it is raining, the sun doesn't come out. But the rainbow is a vivid reminder that even this statement is not reliable. This child's misleading statement is symptomatic of a larger human problem associated with the use of polarities: their mere presence often leads us to oversimplify the phenomena that we are dealing with; or to use a common phrase that itself incorporates a polarity, they lead us to see things in "black and white."

When we were putting together the 22 units that comprised our mock-test for children, it occurred to us that RAISINS deals with food preservation, that, in fact, it is an example of the "drying in the sun" method that is mentioned in BACTERIA. We decided to place it immediately after BACTERIA in order to see whether there would be any carry-over from one passage to the other. More specifically, we wondered whether the association that is set up between *warm* and *damp* in BACTERIA would cause children any problem in associating *warm* with *dry* in this unit. During the interviews, only one child mentioned the similarity between these two units. Perhaps children did not think of raisin-making as a form of preservation. Probably more important was the fact that BACTERIA was so difficult that most children were not able to establish a relationship between *warm* and *damp*. It is now clear that we should have placed RAISINS—the easier unit—first, and then looked for evidence that children made use of the relationship established in RAISINS when they subsequently had trouble in understanding BACTERIA (this from-easier-to-harder paradigm is usually followed by those who construct tests and interview schedules).

Although we found no evidence of carryover from BACTERIA to RAISINS, we were surprised to discover another carryover—from RAISINS to the following unit on the mock-exam, SHOP SIGN. In our discussion of SHOP SIGN, we pointed out that many children pronounced *sundries* as "sun-dries." One child even pointed out that "sun-dries" are like the raisins "in the story we just read." It is not surprising that leakage from one unit to another occurs when children are forced, as they are by a reading test, to move rapidly from one bit of text to another. Whenever children cannot make sense of a particular passage, they naturally search for further information that can be brought to bear on the problem at hand. We have given many examples of how children bring in elements of their experience to solve such a problem. Another source of information, especially for inexperienced test takers, is the test material they have just completed. In fact, we came across a few children who did not seem to understand that every unit is to be considered apart from the other ones.

Just as we can observe interaction between test units, so we can see interaction between tasks within a unit (see ADVERTISING TAILOR, pp. 172–174, for discussion of a particular kind of interaction that was misleading to children). In RAISINS, certain children, especially African Americans, who selected the distractor *water* in (A) and the distractor *warm and wet* in (B), followed an ingenious line of reasoning. Using the fact that the drying took a long time (i.e., three weeks), they reasoned, for (A), that the grapes must have had a lot of water in them; and, for (B), that the climate must have had a certain dampness. With respect to (A), one African American girl expressed this thinking succinctly:

It has to be *water* because of all that drying in the sun.

Another African American girl spelled out the same kind of reasoning in even greater detail:

It was *water*, 'cause here it says, "Drying may take several weeks." So if they have to dry a long time, they must be moist.

With respect to (B), an African American boy provided an elaborate explanation for his choice of *warm and wet*:

Look, first I didn't understand so much so I picked *warm and dry* because of this (points to *dries* in text). But then when I read it more I think— uhm—*warm and wet*, because here it says, *There, it dries in the sun. Drying may take several weeks.* Weeks. I think weeks are very long, so I don't think *dry* is very good.

A nine-year-old African American girl provided a particularly interesting justification of the same choice:

When you grow something, you got to have it wet. And warm, the story says the sun, so I used *warm.*

After making this statement, she immediately became aware that she had confused raisins with grapes and exclaimed in frustration:

I blew it. Raisins don't grow at all. They come from grapes.

Her confusion is not all that surprising when one considers that the place where the grapes are grown is likely to be the place where they are dried in the sun. From a financial point of view, it would not make sense to transport grapes to a special place for drying. Hence her initial reasoning about the best climate for "grow[ing] something" is probably justified; but as we have often observed, such reasoning, though crucial to real-world reading, is counterproductive on a reading test.

Upon encountering these responses, we were reminded of the children who, in responding to HURRICANE, reasoned that the trees must have been strong because they were able to withstand the strong wind (p. 134). In both units, children use a textual cue—and in each instance it is a salient one—to make an invited inference. Yet in each instance this textually grounded inference leads them away from the target response. What is of particular interest to us is that both of the inferences involve a polarization between crucial bits of information in the passage. In HURRICANE the trees are opposed to the wind with respect to strength; and it is the trees that win out since they are not blown away. Here the opposition is, as it were, between the polar opposites 'wet' and 'dry,' and it is 'dry' that wins out because of both the sun's heat and the inexorable passage of time. In the conclusions, we will have more to say about such active polarizing, especially as it affects the performance of African American children on reading tests.

Let us now turn to (A), which turned out to be a considerably more difficult task than (B). During the pilot testing, both groups of children were much more attracted to the distractor *varieties* than the target response *sugar,* as shown in Table 6.3. We will first discuss children's difficulty in selecting *sugar* and then the reasons for their attraction to *varieties.*

In order to select *sugar,* children must understand, as shown in Figure 6.17, that the words following *Raisins are made from* in both sentence 1

TABLE 6.3

	African American	European American
varieties	47%	62%
sugar	18%	14%

and the target proposition for (A) have the same referent (i.e., that they are different ways of talking about the same thing). Some of the children we interviewed were able to make this connection. Consider, for example, the following exchange:

C   Oh. I think it might have been *sugar*, because they were *sweet varieties*.
I   What is it that makes grapes sweet?
C   Sugar.

In defending her choice, another child slowly read the first sentence aloud, placing special emphasis on the word *sweet*. She then drew on familiar territory in connecting up *sweet* and *sugar*:

Sweet would refer to something that tastes like candy. In candy is sugar.

One boy managed to connect the two words, but then went on to make the following claim:

Because sugar—sugar is in all—all grapes.

This statement is, of course, true, but it does not reflect the contrastive use of *sweet* in the passage (i.e., that raisins are made from particular varieties of grapes which, when compared to other varieties, can be characterized as *sweet*). We find evidence, once again, of a child selecting

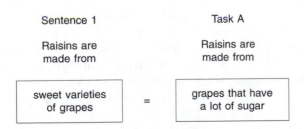

FIGURE 6.17

a target response without properly understanding the relevant portion of the passage.

One child who was a sophisticated test taker pointed out that "it was a very tough choice between *varieties* and *sugar*." In order to decide between them, she used each to complete the stem. After using *varieties* in this way, she said:

> That's not a very good sentence, and since it is a test, you have to have good sentences.

She then tried out *sugar*, and as she was completing the sentence, she suddenly became aware of the connection between *sugar* and *sweet* and exclaimed:

> Sweet is almost the same as sugar.

It was the active use of *sugar* that stimulated her to connect it with *sweet*.

Most of the children we interviewed, however, had difficulty in making connections between *sweet* and *sugar*. There seem to have been a number of factors that contributed to this difficulty. To begin with, there is a metalinguistic problem: children had to align disparate linguistic categories, an adjective and a nominal. Some children were explicit about their resistance to this operation. Consider, for example, the response of a child who was told that her choice of *varieties* was not the right one:

C   Then what? Don't tell me I have to go back to *sugar* because of *sweet*?
I   That's right.
C   But that's not logical. *Sweet* is an adjective—you mostly think it's not that important. You think more of *sweet varieties*. Raisins are made of "sweet of grapes"? That doesn't make sense—*varieties of grapes*, see?

She actually constructs an aberrant nominal group—"sweet of grapes"—to demonstrate that an adjective cannot be made to function in place of a noun. There is also evidence that she is bothered by the fact that *sweet*, despite its low profile in the passage, plays such an important role in (A). She does have a point—the passage, after all, does not directly state that the grapes themselves are sweet, only that the varieties are.[10]

For other children, it was a restricted conception of 'sugar' that impeded their selecting the target response to (A). A number of children were amazed to discover that *sugar* was, in fact, the right answer. As one child put it, "How can you get sugar into grapes?" For him, sugar was apparently the white, crunchy stuff that is sprinkled over breakfast cereals or stirred into beverages. In order to get a sense of whether children think of sugar as belonging to fruit, we presented a list of foods to 20 children and asked them to circle "each food that contains sugar" (the number who circled each food is placed in parentheses):

cake (20)   hamburgers (2)
candy (20)   banana (2)
raisins (5)   lettuce (1)
apples (4)

This probe suggests that children lack a generic understanding of the word *sugar*, that it is a substance present in natural products as well as refined ones. The results of this probe are not surprising when one considers how often grownups admonish children to eat fruit in order to avoid the negative effects of sugar. In particular, raisins are often advertised as a "healthy snack" that children should eat in place of candy. It was interesting to observe that one child who did have a generic understanding of the word *sugar* was bothered by the passage precisely because it ignored the distinction between 'natural' and 'refined':

> I wasn't sure about the first question. Because *sugar* could be natural or— uh—refined sugar. So I put *sugar* because it said *sweet*. But, I mean, it could be natural sugar—they should've said natural or refined sugar.[11]

In matching up *sweet* and *sugar*, it is not simply children's restricted understanding of *sugar* that can create problems. An overly broad understanding of *sweet* can interfere as well. Even when it refers to taste, *sweet* is not always connected with sugar: butter is sweet when it has no salt in it, and milk is sweet when it hasn't turned sour.[12] Here is what one child said when he was asked what *sweet* means:

C   Tastier.
I   How do things get sweet? If you had some food that wasn't sweet enough, what would you do?
C   Add salt or something like that.

This child's notion of 'sweet' is surprising, but it is not difficult to see how he arrived at it. From all the contexts in which he has encountered the word, he has presumably generalized that it refers to a taste that is good in some way rather than one that is specifically associated with sugar or honey. When food doesn't taste quite right, a common solution is to put salt on it. This is likely to give it a good taste, or, from this child's point of view, a sweet one.[13]

In considering the connection between "being sweet" and "containing sugar," we can note certain trends in the culture that tend to break down this relationship. Sugar has gained a bad reputation: it contributes to tooth decay, it encourages obesity, and it may be implicated in a host of other ills. Yet it is hard to do without sweetness. Nonsugar sweeteners make it possible to solve this problem, to have sweetness without sugar, and food products that taste sweet are widely advertised as being *sugar-free* or having *no sugar*. A related development is the concern about products that contain *hidden sugar*. These products don't taste sweet, yet contain a surprising amount of sugar. Consumer worries about hidden sugar are allayed with such slogans as *all natural* or *no sugar added*. Given all these indeterminacies around the words *sweet* and *sugar*, it is not surprising that children experienced a good deal of difficulty in matching them up. It appears that they had concepts of 'sweet' (too general) and 'sugar' (too specific) that were not sophisticated enough to establish the necessary relationship between the two.

As already mentioned, most children ended up selecting *varieties*. In explaining their attraction, we can begin by observing that this choice can be readily distinguished from the other three—*water, sugar, skin*—all of which are concrete nouns. This formal difference, no doubt, enticed children, particularly since *varieties* is a word that sounds "learned." One girl, in fact, explained her choice of this word purely in terms of her reasons for rejecting the other three (i.e., she seemed to be using a backing-into-the-answer strategy):

> I chose *varieties* because they'd be dumb to pick watery grapes if they're going to dry them. That'd be really dumb. And it can't be *skin*, because...can you find the word *skin* any place? And it can't be *sugar*, 'cause I know there's no sugar in raisins.

She apparently felt no need to justify *varieties*—it was just the word left over after she got rid of the other three.

There were children, however, who more actively justified their choice of *varieties*, as exemplified by the following exchange:

> I   Why did you choose *varieties*?
> C   Because it is more directly connected to the grapes than *sugar*.
> I   So did you also think *sugar* is possible?
> C   Yes, I did, but though *sugar* has a similar meaning to *sweet*, I think *variety* [the child slips to the singular form] is an answer because it is more directly connected to the grapes.

This child repeats the phrase *more directly connected*, but the interviewer does not pursue what the child had in mind. We suspect that he was influenced by the particular syntactic role of *varieties*: it functions as the head noun of the phrase in which *grapes* is found, whereas *sweet* functions only as a modifer of that head.

There were also children who selected *varieties* because they viewed this task as simply recycling passage information, as the following exchange illustrates:

I   Why did you choose *varieties*?
C   Because *varieties* is mentioned in the passage.
I   Didn't you think of any other choice?
C   I thought *sugar* could be because it has a similar meaning to *sweet*. But it is not directly mentioned, so I canceled it out. I just tried to find the same words mentioned in the passage.

Although this child was aware of the connection between *sweet* and *sugar*, he falls back on a familiar strategy in making his choice.

The selection of *varieties*, of course, results in a sentence that is not, strictly speaking grammatical:

*Raisins are made from grapes that have a lot of *varieties*.

During our interviewing, we came across children who were able to articulate their frustration with this sentence. We have already discussed a child who actively chose *sugar* because when she tried to complete the stem with *varieties*, the sentence that resulted was not "very good, and since it is a test, you have to have good sentences." We were intrigued by the following exchange with another girl who could be relied on to reject any choice that was odd-sounding:

C   *Varieties* doesn't make sense.
I   Why not?
C   Because it just doesn't sound like it would make sense; you would say, "Raisins are made from a variety of grapes."

She here demonstrates her metalinguistic awareness by using an appropriate syntactic form of the deviant distractor proposition as a means of rejecting it:

*Raisins are made from grapes   →   Raisins are made from
  that have a lot of *varieties*.   a variety of grapes.

Most children did not, however, mention any problem with this sentence. It was generally accepted by those who used their sense of syntactic deviancy as a tactic in making choices for other units.

It appears, then, that we are dealing with a rather delicate syntactic constraint that most children of this age have not properly mastered. It is not easy to specify its exact nature, but we might notice the following parallels:

The seeds of grapes are numerous.	The varieties of grapes are numerous.
Grapes' seeds are numerous.	*Grapes' varieties are numerous.
Grapes have numerous seeds.	*Grapes have numerous varieties.
Grapes have a lot of seeds.	*Grapes have a lot of varieties.[14]

The reason that *varieties* cannot go through the possessive transformations (phrasal genitive, attributive genitive, *have* genitive) in the same way that *seeds* can is that the underlying relationship between *grapes* and *varieties* is existential:

There are a lot of varieties of grapes.

It is, of course, impossible to relate *grapes* and *seeds* existentially:

*There are a lot of seeds of grapes.

Interacting with this syntactic problem is confusion about what the word *varieties* means. By the fourth grade, children tend to be familiar with this word, and yet they do not have a precise feel for its range of use. We came across a number of children who knew that *varieties* meant "kinds" but still felt this word was the best answer:

I   Why did you choose *varieties*?
C   Well, it made sense—*a lot of varieties*—you don't just have one kind of raisin. There are those yellow ones and those big ones with seeds that grandmommy gets.

There was a particularly interesting exchange around *varieties* with a nine-year-old boy of rather firm opinions:

I   Why *varieties*?
C   It says it.
I   Where?
C   *Raisins are made from sweet varieties of grapes.*
I   What does *varieties* mean?
C   Kinds.

At this point the interviewer tries to get the child to substitute *kinds* for *varieties* within the task:

Do grapes have lots of *kinds*? Does that sound all right to you?

He doggedly returns to his original assertion:

C   It says it. It just says it. I did it from the story because it says that *raisins are made from sweet varieties of grapes.*
I   What does that sentence mean?
C   Different kinds of grapes.
I   All right. What kinds in particular?
C   Sweet ones.
I   So what would sweet grapes have?
C   Sugar.
I   Does that answer sound right to you?
C   Yeah, and *varieties* makes sense to me also. I was just following the story.

Even after this child was led to *sugar,* he was not willing to let go of his initial choice. It is as if his teacher had drilled into him to focus only on what the passage says.

Other children seemed to confuse different senses of the word *varieties*: "kind," "assortment," and "diversity." These senses are so closely related that it was often difficult to tell whether a particular child didn't know all these senses or was just unable to decide which one was suitable in this context. Here is what one child said when asked what the word *varieties* means:

C   It means different kinds.
I   And why did you choose the word *varieties*?
C   Because I thought that raisins could be made out of—like every kind of grape.

She was apparently thinking of *variety* as "assortment" rather than "kind."

We came across another girl who seemed to operate with the notion of *variety* as "diversity":

I   Okay. What are varieties?
C   A lot of mixtures.
I   Could you say that all grapes have varieties?
C   No.
I   Why not?
C   Because all grapes don't have all kinds of mixtures.
I   I don't really know what you mean by mixtures of grapes.
C   They don't have a lot of things added into the grapes.
I   I see. So varieties are things that are in the grapes?
C   Mmhmm.

I   Now if you had a bunch of grapes, would they all be the same or would they....

C   Sometimes they'd be different.

This girl seems to be working with two notions: (1) that *varieties* refers to the mixture of ingredients inside a grape, and (2) that the grapes used for raisin-making are those with a sufficient number of internal ingredients.

We discovered one other child who seemed to think of *varieties* as ingredients that are actually put into the grapes:

Varieties are something to put in grapes or something like vitamins or something.

This boy's repeated use of *something* perhaps indicates just how material his conception may have been. He may even have thought that varieties are something injected into grapes in order to turn them into raisins. Certainly children now grow up in a world where technology is used to do just this sort of thing.

HARD LEAD

In this unit readers are required to work with three sets of lexical oppositions—*hard/soft, thick/thin,* and *dark/light.* It is important to observe, at
the outset, that *hard, thin,* and *light* are all members of other common
lexical oppositions, as illustrated in Figure 6.18. Bennett (1976) has
suggested that a term involved in more than one opposition is more
difficult to process than one involved in a single pairing. As children
read the passage and think about (A), they may expend a good deal of
energy in maintaining focus on the oppositions that are relevant to this
context.

Near the top of most pencils there is a symbol, usually a letter or
number. It tells you whether the pencil lead is soft or hard. If you
want your writing to be thick and dark, you select a pencil with a
soft lead.

A. You choose a hard lead to make lines that are
    thick   red
    hard   light

B. The letters or numbers near the tops of pencils are
    useless   dates
    symbols   lead

Let us first examine the structure of this expository passage. Its "main
idea"—that pencils are marked in some way to indicate whether they
have hard or soft lead—is spread across the first two sentences. The first
sentence states that pencils are marked with *a symbol, usually a letter or
number;* it is only in the second sentence that readers find out what the
symbol stands for. In effect, readers are required to chunk together the
first two sentences in order to come up with the main idea. By this time,
they have only one sentence left to read, and it deals with the relation-

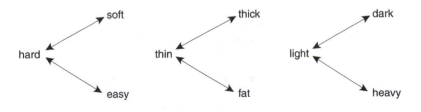

FIGURE 6.18

ship between pencil lead and the physical characteristics of writing. But it does this in only a partial way. It tells only of the kind of writing that results from using soft lead. The piece of contrasting information—the kind that results from hard lead—is saved, as it were, for (A). The fact that this task forces readers to take the reasoning in the passage one step further may encourage them to do the same with other incomplete passages; as already pointed out (see ALICE AND THE FAWN, p. 91), such an expansion can introduce information that leads away from the target response.

Its failure to provide closure is not the only problem associated with the third sentence. Both the *if*-clause and the *then*-clause[15] in this conditional sentence contain a good deal of internal complexity. The *if*-clause, for example, is composed of two underlying clauses: (1) *you want your writing,* and (2) *your writing to be thick and dark.* Moreover, the coupled terms *thick and dark* must be associated with the single term *soft* in the *then*-clause. This association is especially difficult because it works against the conventional association of *thick* and *dark* with *hard.* This is a point that we will shortly take up in greater detail.

There is a further difficulty in sentence 3 that is even more fundamental. The result of a certain action has been expressed in the *if*-clause, whereas the action itself is expressed in the *then*-clause, as illustrated in Figure 6.19. This reversal is made possible by placing the result of the action under the scope of *you want* in the *if*-clause (i.e., if you want a certain result, there is a certain condition that you must observe). The more

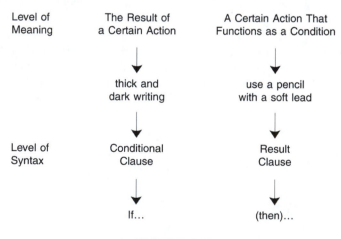

FIGURE 6.19

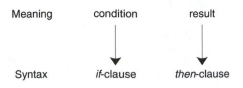

FIGURE 6.20

conventional association of 'condition' with an *if*-clause and 'result' with a *then*-clause is illustrated by a sentence like

If you use a pencil with soft lead, you will get thick and dark writing.

As shown in Figure 6.20, this version of the sentence is easier to read than the one in the passage, given the iconic relation between its meaning and syntax.

The difficulty of extracting information from sentence 3 is compounded by the form of (A), which follows the conventional order. This task, which is not overtly conditional, begins with the 'condition'—*you choose a hard lead*—and ends with the 'result'—*to make lines that are light* (since *to make* can be expanded to *in order to make*, the second part of the sentence would ordinarily be described as expressing 'purpose'). In effect, (A) reverses the order of information in sentence 3, as illustrated in Figure 6.21. This diagram uncovers a number of discrepancies

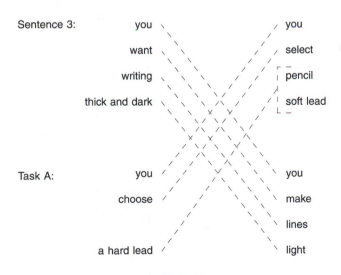

FIGURE 6.21

between the two versions that are potentially confusing: (A) uses the phrase *a hard lead* rather than *a pencil with hard lead*. There is also the rather strange use of *make lines* in (A), an expression more associated with drawing than writing.[16] The shift from *writing* in sentence 3 was necessary because it is not possible to use *thin and light* in describing writing, at least not to refer to its physical characteristics. For example, the first of the following phrases strikes our ear as much more natural than the second:

> If you want your writing to be thick and dark
> If you want your writing to be thin and light

This contrast demonstrates how lexically opposed categories can function asymmetrically in actual language use.[17]

There is a further difficulty in (A). Given the information in sentence 3, readers anticipate an answer opposing both *thick* and *dark;* yet each of the choices in this task consists of a single word. Figure 6.22 represents the strategy that leads to the selection of the target response. The solid arrow shows the relationship between 'lead' and 'writing' that is set up in the passage. The dotted arrows indicate the relationships that readers are led to infer in (A), causing them to anticipate the target response *thin and light.* If they scan the four choices, however, they discover that such a choice is not available and so are forced to settle for the partial response *light* (for similar tasks, see ALICE AND THE FAWN and CHEE TONG).

During the pilot testing, only 29 percent of the African American children and 34 percent of the European American children selected *light.* The partial nature of the target response certainly contributes to the difficulty of this task, but perhaps an even greater problem is the conventional associations among these polarities that we alluded to earlier. Apart from any specific context, *soft* tends to be associated with *thin and light* and *hard* with *thick and dark.* It is as though all the former are somehow 'less' and all the latter somehow 'more.' The broken-line arrows in

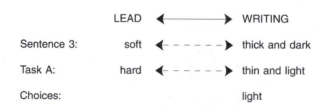

FIGURE 6.22

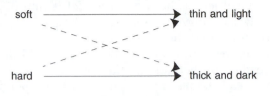

FIGURE 6.23

Figure 6.23 indicate the reversal of conventional associations that readers need to make when they are dealing with the relationship between pencil lead and the physical characteristics of the writing it produces.

In order to ascertain children's knowledge of these matters, we presented two tasks to 25 third graders who had not been exposed to this test unit. First, we asked them what they knew about numbers on pencils. Seventeen knew that the numbers had something to do with the lead. Their answers were distributed as follows:

the kind of lead (3)
how hard or soft the pencil is (4)
how dark or light the pencil is (10)

The other 8 thought the numbers had to do with such matters as

the quality of the lead (5)
the amount of lead (1)
what company made the pencil (1)
whether the pencil can be used on a test (1)[18]

We next asked the children about different kinds of pencil lead. When we asked them what kind of line they thought hard lead makes, 15 circled *thick* and 10 circled *thin*. When we asked them what kind of line soft lead makes, 17 circled *light* and 8 circled *dark*. So well over half of the children made the conventional associations among these polarized terms rather than making the necessary reversal. We were not surprised by this result, given how strong these conventional associations are. In this instance, these associations were probably strengthened by what children actually do to vary what kind of lines they make on a page. If they press hard on a pencil, they can obtain lines that are thicker and darker; and, of course, if they press only softly, the lines will be thinner and lighter.

The reversal of the conventional associations is much easier for readers to handle if they understand the physical processes that motivate it. If pencil lead is soft, more of it rubs off on the page, leaving thicker and darker writing. But if lead is hard, then less of it rubs off, leaving lines that are, relatively speaking, thin and light. The passage, of course, provides no hint of this explanation, so if readers are to grasp it, they must work it out on their own. In principle, children could bring such knowledge to their reading of the passage, but when we asked 30 third graders who had not read the passage why soft lead in a pencil makes dark lines, we discovered that none of them could provide an appropriate explanation.[19] Moreover, during the interviewing none of the children who had read the passage provided an appropriate explanation either, although one child did manage to say that if you "press hard, you get dark writing."[20]

This failure was particularly disconcerting in the case of the children who managed to choose the target response *light*. Consider, for example, the following exchange with a child who was precocious in his use of language:

I   So why did you pick *light*?
C   Because it says, *If you want your writing to be thick and dark, you select a pencil with a soft lead*; and this is hard lead so it's got to be the opposite.

Given the sophistication of his response, the interviewer went on to ask why it is that hard lead makes a light line. This highly verbal child was reduced to saying that "the story didn't talk about that." Anxious to move on to the next task, he showed no curiosity about the connection between hard lead and light lines.

This child's response demonstrates that there can be a sharp separation between (1) manipulating verbal symbols, and (2) gaining knowledge about the world referred to by those symbols. Many of the activities associated with formal schooling encourage this separation, but our methods of testing especially do, since they require students to move rapidly if they are to succeed. Once children have worked out the oppositions represented in Figure 6.23, they are forced to go on to the next test unit without pausing to wonder why pencils with hard lead make light lines. We think that it is fruitful to distinguish between two levels of comprehension, which we can characterize as SYMBOL-MANIPULATING and KNOWLEDGE-BUILDING. We choose this latter term deliberately, for we suspect that children are not likely to remember the information presented in this unit very long. If the unit had, however, enabled them to work out why hard lead makes light lines, they might have added to their stock of permanent knowledge.

Another unit in our corpus illustrates well how a child can arrive at the target response through purely verbal associations that sidestep the real concerns of a passage:

Animals would destroy cactus plants if it were not for their forbidding spines. A plant experimenter, Luther Burbank, produced a spineless variety of prickly-pear cactus. But cattle and other animals devoured it so rapidly that the spineless cactus did not have a chance to survive long in nature.

A.   Burbank's new plant did not live long in nature because it
   was too weak   needed water
   had no seeds   was eaten up

B.   Burbank's plant had no
   juice   taste
   spines   fruit

As indicated by Figure 6.24, the target response for (B) can be arrived at by establishing certain relationships between the stem and sentence 2 in the passage. If children perceive certain parallels between (B) and sentence 2, they can select the target response by merely associating *spineless* and *no spines*. This strategy enables them to get the right answer without comprehending any of the ecological processes that unify the content of the passage and make it potentially knowledge-building. They might not realize that spines are prickles; they could conceivably even think of the spines as "backbones" and still be able to do (B) successfully.

As they stand, the passages in HARD LEAD and BURBANK'S CACTUS lack anything that would encourage any actual knowledge-building. In the real world, writers who address a subject like this are primarily concerned with informing their readers, with helping them make sense out of their environment. Thus, they would take account of the cognitive traps that make this material hard to understand. They would be especially careful to supply additional information to help anchor slippery relationships. In the case of HARD LEAD, they might explain the physical characteristics that underlie the relationship of hard lead to light lines, or they might make clear that the hard/soft contrast is not an either-or

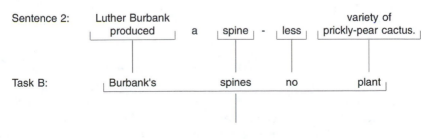

FIGURE 6.24

but a continuum. They would certainly want to enable their readers to use their new knowledge—or the newly reorganized bits of previous knowledge and experience—by explaining at least the most common system used to express degrees of hardness or softness. And they would seek to concretize all this information by explaining what tasks the different kinds of lead are most appropriate for.

There is a further problem with respect to the lexically opposed pairs in HARD LEAD. Even if one understands that hard lead goes with light writing—whatever that is—and that the numbers on pencils indicate the degree of hardness, there is still the problem of whether a numerical increase indicates greater hardness or softness. In one class of graduate students—mostly reading teachers—half thought that a #1 pencil was harder than a #2 and the other half thought that it was softer.[21] Clearly, anyone who could come up with an effective mnemonic in this area—something along the lines of *Thirty Days Hath September*—would earn lasting gratitude.

As we have sought to demonstrate, one of the reasons this unit seems unnatural is that it neglects, seemingly perversely, numerous opportunities for being helpfully explanatory. Another reason for its unnaturalness is the odd way in which it addresses the reader:

> If you want your writing to be thick and dark, you select a pencil with a soft lead.

How are readers to take this? The writer has assumed a good deal: that readers have noticed the difference between light and dark writing; that they are concerned about whether their own writing looks light or dark; that they have knowledge enabling them to produce light or dark writing according to their wish. In fact, this writer goes so far as to tell readers what they customarily do in a particular situation.

Perhaps the *you* in the passage is meant to be indefinite. We can test this possibility by using another way of expressing an indefinite actor:

> If people want their writing to be thick and dark, they select a pencil with a soft lead.

This version is better in that it doesn't necessarily include the reader in its assertions, but there is still the implicit assumption that people are generally knowledgeable about these matters, and many readers will realize that this is not the case. As we have seen, a more accurate assessment of the situation is that people do not know very much about pencils and lead, that, indeed, they are confused, and that they need information and guidance. Perhaps the most usual way of expressing the advisor/advisee relationship between writer and reader utilizes the word *should*:

> If you want your writing to be thick and dark, you *should* select a pencil with a soft lead.

And similarly for (A):

> You *should* choose a hard lead to make lines that are light.

The gap between what would normally be written in this situation—if you want a certain result, then you *should* do thus—and the way the passage is actually written provides another example of how difficult it is to write something for a school task without inadvertently producing aberrant prose. The connections between language and its functional context are so various, and operate on so many different levels, that it is inordinately difficult to shape words for a school function and at the same time provide real-world camouflage. As we have pointed out, the alternative of adapting existing language for a school purpose is also problematical, but perhaps it more often achieves a satisfactory result.

Let us now turn to (B), which, though not dealing with lexical oppositions, is interesting in other ways. This task is based on the first sentence of the passage and is evidently meant to be a vocabulary task: do the children know something about how the word *symbols* is used? The most straightforward way to ascertain this would be a target proposition like *letters and numbers are symbols*. In other words, as illustrated in Figure 6.25, the class of 'letters and numbers' is included in the larger class of 'symbols.'

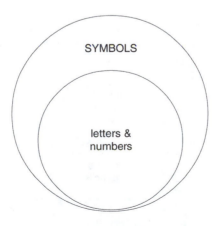

SYMBOLS

letters & numbers

FIGURE 6.25

Such a target proposition would not, however, be sufficiently dependent upon the passage. It would make sense apart from the passage, and it could be answered on the basis of general vocabulary knowledge. This is perhaps why the target proposition used in this task—*The letters and numbers near the tops of pencils are symbols*—includes extra material from the passage. As shown in Figure 6.26, the target proposition sets up relations among three different classes: the class of 'letters and numbers on pencils' is included in the larger class 'letters and numbers,' which, in turn, is part of the class 'symbols.'

That *near the tops of pencils*[22] has been included to satisfy a requirement of the test format is not likely to occur to readers. For them, a more likely interpretation will be that some letters and numbers, specifically those that appear on pencils, are symbols, while other letters and numbers are not, as illustrated in Figure 6.27.

For readers who don't have any idea of how the word *symbols* is used, the fact that this interpretation is not accurate will present no problem, and they are likely to select the target response. Those who do have some prior knowledge of how this word is used are likely to think further. The most likely direction for them to go is to restrict the scope of 'symbols' so that it matches the restriction placed on 'letters and numbers.' Thinking along this line might produce an interpretation like the following:

> The letters or numbers near the tops of pencils are symbols that indicate the kind of lead a pencil contains.

This proposition sets up a single class which can be described in either of two ways:

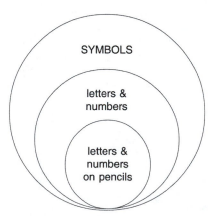

FIGURE 6.26

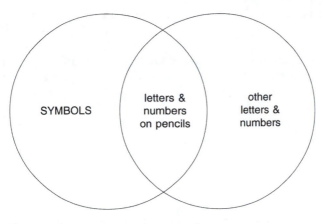

FIGURE 6.27

1) letters and numbers on pencils, or
2) symbols that indicate the kind of lead a pencil contains.

Hence this interpretation can be represented by an image much simpler than the ones previously used, as illustrated in Figure 6.28.

Readers who have come this far may well begin to consider the choice *lead* as having some merits. Choosing *lead* would produce a proposition like

The letters or numbers near the tops of pencils are *lead*.

This is not precisely stated; it would be more accurate to say that

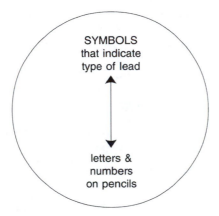

FIGURE 6.28

The letters and numbers near the tops of pencils represent the type of lead.

It should be remembered, however, that such an all-purpose use of the verb *be* is frequent in speech and by no means unknown in writing. Consider, for example, the following:

What's this little number here mean?
That's the lead. It tells you whether the pencil is hard or soft.

So readers who have come this far are faced with the choice between two dissonant propositions:

The letters or numbers near the tops of pencils are *symbols*.
The letters or numbers near the tops of pencils are *lead*.

Taken out of context in this way, the first seems preferable. But one can certainly sympathize with those who pick the second. After all, using information from the passage to flesh out a target proposition so that it sounds reasonable is just what is required in various units that we have discussed (see WHITE CIRCLES, pp. 213–214).

At this point, it is interesting to observe how these considerations match up with the results from the pilot testing shown in Table 6.4. As can be seen, *symbols* was favored by both groups, though not to the same degree. For each group approximately half as many chose *lead* as chose *symbols*. There is a remarkable divergence between the two groups on *useless*; proportionately, it was selected by four times as many African American children as European American children.

How can we account for this divergence? Certainly some of the children who selected *useless* must have known they were picking an odd answer, but somehow they couldn't resist it. It's funny; it's irreverent; and for those who have been struggling with this unit, it is, no doubt, God's truth. On a more general level, *useless* represents a chance to talk

TABLE 6.4

	African American	European American
useless	35%	9%
dates	8%	9%
symbols	38%	56%
lead	19%	26%

back to the test, to say what one really feels. We cannot readily say just why the African American children were so much more attracted by this opportunity. One possibility is that they, as already suggested, are especially attracted to responses that are communicative, that do not merely recycle the content of the passage. Not many of the African American children we interviewed actually chose *useless*, but some of them did find it tantalizing and laughed at its communicative possibilities. It perhaps goes without saying that test makers should avoid distractors that encourage children to go beyond the usual confines of the test situation.

ICEBERG

In the polarity units that have been presented so far, the opposing categories have been explicitly named, if not in the passage, at least in one of the tasks. There are other units in which only one member of a set of opposing categories is referred to, and the reader is left to work with both parts of the opposition in order to respond to the tasks successfully. We will consider two of these units, beginning with one that is concerned with a natural phenomenon.

An iceberg is a large chunk of frozen fresh water that floats in the sea. Most of the iceberg is below the surface. Just the top part is visible.

A.   Icebergs are made mostly of
sea water   fresh water
salt   rock

B.   Most of the iceberg is
hidden   visible
surface   top

This is the shortest passage in our corpus. It consists of three brief sentences that total only 29 words. Each of the first two sentences contains information about an iceberg that runs counter to common-sense assumptions that children generally hold:

Sentence 1:   An iceberg is made up of *fresh water*.
Sentence 2:   Most of an iceberg is *below the surface* of the water.

To confirm that children tend to hold contrary opinions—namely, (1) that an iceberg consists of sea water, and (2) that most of it is above the surface—we presented the task in Figure 6.29 to 20 third graders (the

---

Circle the number of each statement that is true.

1. An iceberg can be found in the Arctic Ocean. (13/19)
2. An iceberg can be found in the Indian Ocean. (2/2)
3. An iceberg is made of fresh water. (4/2)
4. An iceberg is made of frozen salt water. (12/15)
5. Most of an iceberg is above water. (12/10)

FIGURE 6.29

first number in the parentheses following each statement indicates the number of children who underlined it). Twelve children underlined statements 4 and 5, which are false, while only 4 underlined statement 3, which is true.

We then gave the same task to 20 graduate students (the second number in the parentheses following each statement indicates the number of adults who underlined it). Like the children, these adults tended to think that an iceberg is made of salt water, but unlike the children, all 20 were aware that most of an iceberg is below water.

In constructing the prose used in the passage, the writer did not take account of the fact that what it conveys runs counter to the opinions that children are likely to hold. In effect, there is no use of the rhetorical strategy *you may think such-and-such, but, in fact...*, which is so common in nature writing for children. The rhetoric of this passage is much like its subject matter—only the tip of the information it deals with is visible.

The actual language of the passage is highly elliptical as well: it forces the reader to activate a number of semantic polarities, but, for most of them, only one of the two poles is actually named. This characteristic is illustrated in Figure 6.30, in which the following conventions are used to represent various kinds of polarities within the unit:

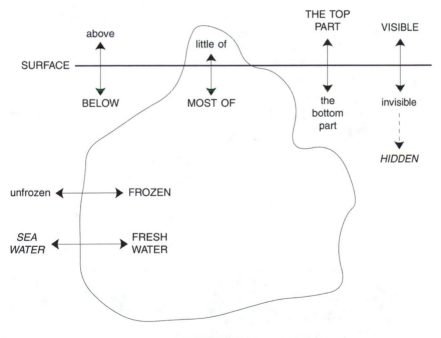

FIGURE 6.30

1) Those referred to in the passage are in capital letters.
2) Those referred to only in the tasks are in italic capital letters.
3) Those that the reader must infer are in small letters.

The reader is required to infer one of the poles in 5 of the 6 polarities. In this sense, this unit contrasts sharply with the three that we have already considered in this chapter.

During the pilot testing, as shown in Table 6.5, slightly more than half of the children in both groups selected the target response *fresh water* for (A). Its major competitor, *sea water*, attracted a substantial proportion of the remaining children in both groups.

On the surface, (A) appears to be a straightforward task requiring the reader only to recycle information in the first sentence:

Sentence 1:   An iceberg is a large chunk of frozen fresh water...
Task (A):   Icebergs are made mostly of *fresh water*.

In comparing the two versions, we can see that they are not altogether equivalent. First, the passage presents the fresh water as *frozen* (i.e., the iceberg is made of *ice*), while the target proposition speaks only of fresh water. Second, the passage states that an iceberg is frozen fresh water, while the target proposition says that it is *mostly* fresh water, implying that it also contains other ingredients. Children who are anxious about "trick questions" sometimes fasten on discrepancies such as these. For example, one child who picked *sea water* equated *mostly* in (A) with *most of the iceberg* in the second sentence in the passage. When the interviewer asked him why he had made this connection, his explanation became quite confused. We will not here reproduce his rather lengthy explanation, but it seemed to be based on three points:

1) The part of an iceberg above water is made of fresh water.
2) The other part, the larger part that can't be seen, is made of sea water.
3) Therefore, an iceberg is made mostly of sea water.

TABLE 6.5

	African American	European American
fresh water	53%	58%
sea water	40%	31%

In order to prevent such a confusion and achieve a better fit between passage and task, the task stem might be recast as follows:

Icebergs are made from _____.

The substitution of *from* for *of* makes clear that an essential process—namely, freezing—intervenes between water and its presence in an iceberg.

It should also be noted that since the fresh water is located in the sea, it can be legitimately described as *sea water*. In fact, one child explained that she chose this answer because it was "obvious" that the water was "fresh." Thinking that the test maker had set up a trick question, she characterized the water in terms of its location rather than its state. The interviewer was sympathetic and immediately responded:

You're right. It's part and parcel of the sea.

Another variation between the target proposition for (A) and its source in the passage is the way in which each indicates that its subject is generic rather than particular: the passage refers to *an iceberg*, while (A) refers to *icebergs*. In between these two generic references, however, is a non-generic one. *Most of the iceberg* in the second sentence of the passage necessarily refers to a particular iceberg. This unmotivated shift, which is repeated in (B), substantially weakens the coherence of this test unit.

Two of the oppositions in this unit are relevant to (A):[23]

FROZEN ↔ unfrozen
FRESH WATER ↔ *SEA WATER*

From one point of view, answering (A) is simply a mechanical operation, one requiring neither previous knowledge nor even any knowledge gained from the passage. As a practical matter, however, it is probably necessary to have the framework suggested by the above oppositions in order to see that recycling is, in fact, what the task called for. In other words, to complete this task easily, children need to have the real-world knowledge that will allow them to make sense out of the two oppositions listed previously. Most of the children we interviewed possessed such knowledge for the first opposition. In effect, they knew that water and ice are different forms of the same substance.

With respect to the second opposition, however, many children lacked the requisite knowledge. In the first place, none of the children showed any evidence of understanding how icebergs are formed (with such understanding, they could, of course, explain where the fresh water comes from). Moreover, there were a number of children who were apparently confused by what the words *fresh water* mean. They seemed to think of it as paralleling *fresh vegetables* or *fresh milk*. One child, using this analogy, was confused about how the water could be described as fresh and frozen at the same time: for her, the vegetables that her mother brings home from the store are either in one state or the other. Another child even thought that "all that ice," as he put it, had managed "to keep the water fresh"; for him, fresh water and sea water were not necessarily opposed. During the interviewing one child even used the expression "fresh sea water," suggesting that, for him, the relevant opposition was *fresh sea water* versus *stale sea water*. Another child, who began with this confusion, managed to come to an appropriate understanding upon rereading the passage.

I   What does *fresh water* mean?
C   It's new.
I   Like what?
C   Like fresh fruit. New water. Is it clean water?

He then decided to reread the passage, and after a moment's reflection, he said:

It's water that is not sea water. River water? It is the water without salt in it.[24]

Let us now turn to (B) and examine the proportions of children who selected the two most favored choices during the pilot testing (Table 6.6). Children in both groups were rather evenly divided between the target response *hidden* and the distractor *visible*, which was slightly favored by each group. The rest of the children were divided between *top* and *surface*, with the African American children preferring the former and the European American children the latter.

In strictly informational terms, four of the six semantic oppositions represented in Figure 6.30 are relevant to (B): two of them are mentioned in sentence 2 and two in sentence 3. In order to make any head-

TABLE 6.6

	African American	European American
hidden	32%	35%
visible	37%	38%

Kind of Information	First Part (Sentence 2)	Second Part (Sentence 3)
Proportion	MOST OF	
Location	BELOW ──┐	
	≠	
Orientation	└──▶ TOP	
Sensory status		VISIBLE

FIGURE 6.31

way in responding to (B), children must realize that these sentences divide the iceberg into two parts, the first referring to its upper part and the second to its lower, as shown in Figure 6.31.

To proceed beyond this point, children must infer from the partial opposition between *below* and *top* that the two parts of the iceberg are being presented in opposing terms. Once they make this inference, they can then fill in the holes in Figure 6.31, producing something like what is shown in Figure 6.32.

Having constructed this larger field, children are then in a position to evaluate the choices in (B). None of them can be found in the first-part column above. *Hidden*, however, expresses sensory status, and is a synonym for *invisible*, one of the words in the first-part column. In order to align all these oppositions accurately, children must realize that the dividing line between the two parts of the iceberg is the surface of the sea and, furthermore, that the part under the surface is not visible.

In addition to working with these multiple oppositions, children must negotiate two structural ellipses that require them to retrieve information across sentence boundaries:

1) *Below the surface* in sentence 2 can be expanded to *below the surface of the sea* by retrieving information in sentence 1.
2) *Just the top part* in sentence 3 can be expanded to *Just the top part of the iceberg* by retrieving information in sentence 2.

These ellipses may appear inconsequential, but they can be confusing to inexperienced readers. The first one seems to have been particularly confusing to the children we interviewed. Rather than expanding *below*

Kind of Information	First Part (Sentence 2)	Second Part (Sentence 3)
Proportion	MOST OF ⟶	little of
Location	BELOW ⟶	above
Orientation	bottom ⟶	TOP
Sensory status	invisible ⟶	VISIBLE
	↓	
	HIDDEN	

FIGURE 6.32

the surface to *below the surface of the sea,* some children expanded it to *below the surface of the iceberg* itself. Consider, for example, what one child had to say:

I   What surface are they talking about?
C   The iceberg's.

This interpretation appears strangely involuted, but it is important to bear in mind that the passage focuses so exclusively on an iceberg that some children apparently did not realize that there was anything else that could have a surface. Moreover, the rather odd sentence *Most of the iceberg is below its own surface* does make a certain kind of sense. It could, for example, mean that "most of the iceberg is contained within itself," a proposition which could then be equated with the target proposition in (B), namely, that *most of the iceberg is hidden* (the difference between the two would, of course, lie in what is doing the hiding—the surface of the sea or the surface of the iceberg). It was not clear from the interviewing whether any children actually made such an interpretation. But some of them who understood *surface* in sentence 2 as the iceberg's own did, in fact, pick *surface* in (B). Such a choice leads to another strange-sounding sentence: *Most of the iceberg is surface.*

To our way of thinking, an ill-formed distractor proposition is just as inadvisable as an ill-formed target proposition (see WHITE CIRCLES). In this instance, such a proposition, given the crucial role of *surface*, may have been particularly confusing to children. Consider, for example, how one child struggled to make sense of this proposition:

> Because if it [the answer to (B)] was *surface*, you could say a submarine is *surfaced*, and it's on top of the water. If an iceberg was *surfaced*, you probably would see this 60-foot thing on top of the water.

Apparently, the ill-formed distractor proposition led this child to treat the word *surface* as a verb.[25]

During the interviewing we turned up other odd bits of blockage on this task. There was one girl, for example, who was convinced that if the larger part of a floating body was under the water, it would necessarily keep sinking down and eventually disappear. When she drew a picture of the iceberg in the water, she made sure that most of it was above the water. She also pointed out that "the story said *float*," a word that she took to mean "on top of the water."

A number of children we interviewed seemed to have been misled by the word *float* in much the same way. Following up on the probe we reported earlier, we asked a class of 25 fourth graders to draw a picture of an iceberg: 19 drew only the part above water; among the remaining 6, 4 made that part larger than the part below, and only 2 made the part below larger. We then asked two more classes to draw a picture of an iceberg, but this time we added, *Be sure to include the part that is under the water.* Out of 39 children, 16 drew the two parts about the same size; 15 made the top part larger; and only 8 made the part under the water larger.

During the interviewing, we attempted to explore whether children knew something like the Titanic story that they could use to infer that an iceberg is mostly under water. One father, for example, asked his daughter what the expression *tip of the iceberg* means. Her answer was not very clear, so he asked her to draw a picture. She drew something that looked like 'Bald Mountain,' explaining that the tip was "the white part at the top" (this drawing is presented in Figure 6.33).

Since we had confirmed that adults tend to be aware that most of an iceberg is below the water, we decided to investigate whether older children were aware of this fact. We asked 24 eighth graders to draw a picture of an iceberg. Twenty made drawings that showed more of the iceberg below the water surface. We then asked them to specify numerically how much of the iceberg was below the surface: 17 gave answers that were two-thirds or more, and 4 were even able to give the actual proportion (i.e., eight-ninths). We then asked them where they had gotten their information. Here are some of the things they wrote down:

FIGURE 6.33

read about it	saw a show
Trivia book	saw a movie on the Titanic
Orca [a movie about a whale]	did a report last year
Scott Mabry told me about it	

As to the other elliptical expression in the passage—*the top part*—children generally had no difficulty in understanding that it refers to the iceberg. They were, however, less certain about just which part of the iceberg is the top. In principle, they should oppose *the top part* to *below the surface* in the preceding sentence and interpret it as "that part which is above the surface of the sea." But since the preceding information is itself elliptical, they often became confused and came up with other interpretations. Here are the four interpretations we encountered during our interviews:

1) the very tip of the iceberg,
2) the part above the water,
3) the top half of the part that is visible,
4) the top half of the entire iceberg.

These four possibilities are represented in Figure 6.34. Some children apparently interpreted *top* as referring to the entire surface of the iceberg. One child may have had this in mind when she defended her choice of the distractor *visible:*

C   It says, *Just the top part is visible.*
I   And that tells you that most of it is visible?
C   Yeah, 'cause it says that the top, and like most of the top could be visible. The top's like the whole thing.

The foregoing analysis suggests that this unit, given its extreme brevity, should have been particularly difficult; and yet it is important to

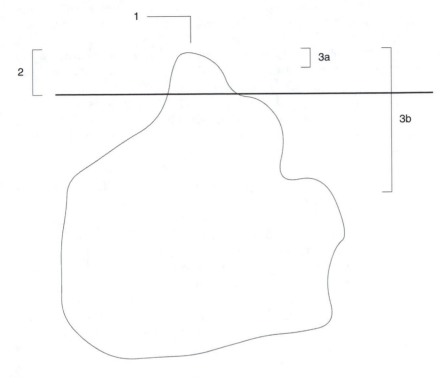

FIGURE 6.34

bear in mind that children, at least with respect to the first task, were relatively successful during the pilot testing. This success seems to be at least partly due to the fact that children were able to fall back on their real-world knowledge. During the interviewing, a number of children referred to their reliance on such knowledge. One girl, for example, even claimed:

> Well, I didn't have to read the paragraph for this one because there was an article in my *Cricket* magazine about it.

Two boys who were not native speakers of English chose the target response entirely on the basis of real-world knowledge. We can say this with some confidence because the interviewing demonstrated that they did not know the meaning of either *visible* or *surface*. The source of their reading power was a recent viewing of the movie *Raise the Titanic!* One of these boys also mentioned that his father had told him "all about icebergs." It was evidently a subject of great interest to him. According to the interviewer,

I couldn't have held him back if I had wanted to. He went wild and started drawing sharks in the water and really became involved in the situation.

The drawing he made after reading this brief unit is displayed in Figure 6.35. Notice the detail he has provided for an iceberg that was presented only generically: not just one iceberg, but two, with considerable emphasis on their bulk under water; the Titanic with a fissure running from top to bottom; and even a benign-looking shark. It is as if he has used the bit of text to activate a rich world that he carries inside himself.

One striking feature of polarity units is the way in which they combine a high cognitive load with limited textual space. The oppositions that they contain and the kinds of inferences that they require are not unusual in themselves, but in the texts we encounter in our everyday world, we would expect to find them distributed over a much larger expanse. Iceberg provides a remarkable example of this compression. In just 29 words it implies six sets of opposing terms, and all of these oppositions must, in principle, be activated in order to complete the tasks successfully. If one knows something about icebergs, these various oppositions can be readily worked into a larger frame. In fact, someone who already has this frame in mind has difficulty even imagining the problems that this unit poses to readers who do not have it. In our analysis, we have tried to give some sense of these problems by detailing the various connections that this unit requires a reader to make.

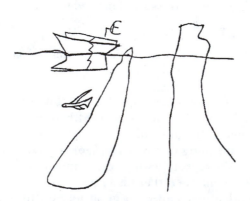

FIGURE 6.35

GEORGE WASHINGTON BRIDGE

We now turn to another unit that forces the reader to work with opposing categories that are not overtly realized.

The George Washington Bridge, completed in 1931, spans the Hudson River between New York and New Jersey. The plan for the bridge called for stone coverings over the two towers. But the steel structure itself was beautiful, so the towers stayed as they were.

A. In this story, "called for" means
   picked up   telephoned
   realized   required

B. The finished towers are made of
   stone   steel over stone
   steel   stone over steel

At first glance, this passage appears to be easier to understand than ICEBERG. It, too, consists of three sentences, but they are more fully developed, and the relations between them are more explicit. Sentence 1 provides spatial and temporal information as an orienting frame for this bit of narrative about the construction of the George Washington Bridge. Sentence 2 tells what materials were supposed to be used in constructing the towers, and sentence 3 provides the reason for a departure from this plan. On the surface, the relationship between sentences 2 and 3 seems to be effectively rendered. The *but* at the beginning of sentence 3 signals that some information in this sentence will contrast with what has gone before. This contrast is primarily embodied in lexical material: *stone* describes the covering that was planned, and *steel* the structure that was actually built.

Despite this overtly signaled contrast, most children seemed to lack a larger framework that would support an appropriate understanding of the passage. In order to build this framework, they have to work with two further contrasts:

1) the contrast between 'plan' and 'execution'; and
2) the contrast between 'structure' and 'ornament.'

We can use these underlying contrasts to create a four-cell matrix, which can then be filled in with *stone* and *steel*—the words that carry the overt contrast (Figure 6.36). As indicated by the solid arrows, the plan for the steel structure was executed, but the one for the ornamental stone covering was not. The reason is given in sentence 3: once the steel

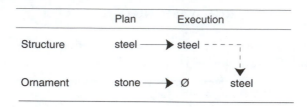

	Plan	Execution
Structure	steel ⟶ steel	
Ornament	stone ⟶ ∅	steel

FIGURE 6.36

structure was in place, it was considered beautiful and so the stone was not added. The dotted arrow in the diagram indicates that steel has taken over the ornamental function. It is worth noting that the contrast between 'plan' and 'execution' is more overtly realized than the one between 'structure' and 'ornament,' with the former signaled by the *but*-relation between sentence 2 and sentence 3. The latter contrast is merely suggested by the word *covering* and by the reference to an esthetic criterion, and apparently many children did not make use of these cues. A number of the children we interviewed thought of the stone as integral to the support system of the bridge; we will shortly describe how this affected their response to (B).

Before we consider children's responses to the tasks, we would like to present a revised version of the passage written by a child who was in a class for the gifted. Both at school and at home she had been encouraged to do a great deal of reading and writing on her own. After reading the passage, she said that it was not clear and asked if she could write a new version. Here is what she wrote:

> The George Washington Bridge was completed in 1931. It went over the Hudson River, going from New York to New Jersey. According to the instructions, the plan was to cover the towers in stone but they looked good in steel so they were left the way they were.

In shortening the passage, she has eliminated certain sources of confusion, such as *the steel structure itself*. She has also used a more active style: for example, *the plan was to cover the towers in stone* in place of *the plan for the bridge called for stone coverings over the two towers*.

As is common with a polarity unit, one task deals with passage content and the other with vocabulary. (A) exemplifies a typical pattern for a vocabulary-defining task: a more frequent sense of a vocabulary item is given in one or more distractors, while the target response represents a less familiar sense that fits with the passage. In this task, two distractors—*picked up* and *telephoned*—were included that are more familiar than *required*, the target response.

Many of the children we interviewed scoffed at these distractors, particularly *telephoned*. One child, for example, said,

> It's really ridiculous to say *telephoned*.

This dismissal of the distractors, however, did not prevent a number of children from complaining about having to choose *required*. One child suggested that *wanted* should have been used in place of *required*:

> Well, when you plan, you want something. So maybe *wanted*. When I want something, I don't always get it.

Apparently for this girl, *required*, unlike *wanted*, meant that the bridge planners would necessarily get their stone covering.

A similar kind of uneasiness about *required* is conveyed in the following exchange with a child:

C   In this story, *called for* means—well, I don't think *required* is a very good word, but it was the closest to the one that I think would fit.

I   What's that?

C   The planner of the bridge *asked for* [the italicized words are pronounced with heavy stress] stone coverings over the two towers.

I   Uh-huh.

C   Because *required* is not a good word. Because they could change plans. Because, well, it is sort of like a command—that's the final thing. This is what's going to happen.

I   And what would happen if you didn't include the stone covering?

C   Well, I don't know. Plans would get all messed up. They would have to change the plans or something, or somebody would sue somebody, and there would be a big problem....*Required* isn't a really good word because a lot of architects change their plans in mid-building.[26]

As we turn to (B), we can begin by observing that, as in RAISINS, all four choices manipulate contrasting words. In this case, the construction materials, *stone* and *steel*, are first presented alone and then combined in opposing ways (*stone over steel* and *steel over stone*). The results of the pilot testing are shown in Table 6.7. A greater proportion of the African American children selected the target response on this task. Moreover, the European American children were more attracted to the distractors that contain pairs of terms. It will be useful to discuss the inherent complexities of this task before we attempt to make sense of these results.

TABLE 6.7

	African American	European American
stone	35%	26%
steel over stone	8%	17%
steel	38%	30%
stone over steel	19%	27%

During the interviewing, we discovered three major gaps in children's understanding of the passage that led to confusion on this task:

1) a failure to understand that the steel structure is to be associated with the two towers;
2) a failure to understand which part of the bridge the word *towers* refers to; and
3) a failure to understand that (B) is concerned with the towers as 'executed' rather than as 'planned.'

Any one of these failures is sufficient to disorient children, but the cumulative weight of the three can lead to so much confusion that their response becomes largely a matter of guesswork. Let us take a closer look at each of the three gaps.

In order to link *the steel structure* with *the two towers*, readers need to establish the lexical chain that is displayed in Figure 6.37. This linkage is difficult to work out on either formal or functional grounds. From a purely formal perspective, the shift from singular to plural seems to have weakened the link for many children. How can *towers* be a single structure? We may further note that repeating *towers* in sentence 3 may have alleviated the need for linking *towers* and *structure*.

From a functional perspective, it is not clear what *the steel structure* refers to—the entire bridge, the suspended horizontal span, or only the

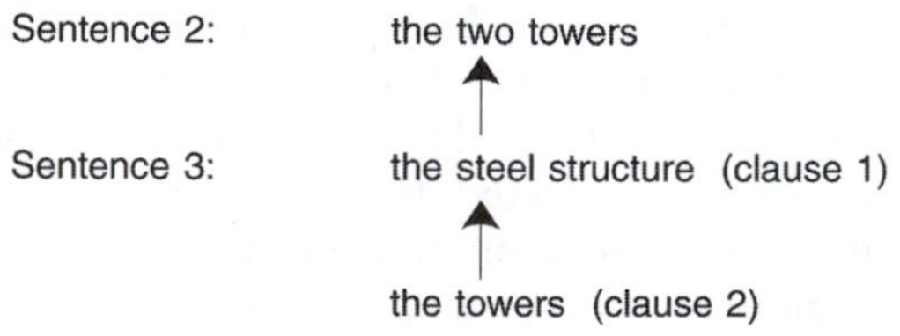

Sentence 2:   the two towers
                            ↑

Sentence 3:   the steel structure (clause 1)
                            ↑

                       the towers (clause 2)

FIGURE 6.37

two towers. Readers cannot, strictly speaking, decide purely on the basis of the passage. If they do use their real-world knowledge, they are likely to think of the steel structure as constituting the entire bridge. If the towers are perceived as part of the bridge, such indeterminacy need not in itself be confusing, yet we have found that it often is. The very fact that a bit of information floats can give children the sense that they are failing to understand something that they should; and this sense can lead them to doubt whether they have understood even that which seems to be clear. In effect, a single indeterminacy can cause an entire text to wobble.

Let us now consider the second gap in children's understanding— their failure to identify which parts of the bridge *two towers* refers to. This failure is understandable, given that (1) *tower* is a word that can represent a number of different entities, and (2) it is not a word frequently used in connection with a bridge. To find out how children might handle these problems, we carried out a number of different probes. We began by asking 30 fourth graders in a suburban school what they think of when they hear the word *tower*. Nearly all of them mentioned some kind of building, many making reference to the World Trade Center in lower Manhattan, which is often referred to as the "Twin Towers." In describing the characteristics of a tower, most used the modifier *tall*, some used *big*, and a few used *round* or *circular*. Moreover, a number of children characterized it as a high place, using expressions like

> look out place
> a tall gall
> a thing that sort of sticks up alone
> something on top of a building

We also asked 30 fourth graders in a Manhattan school to draw a picture of the George Washington Bridge. Before examining their pictures, it will be useful to take a look at a photograph of the bridge (see Figure 6.38). Four features of the bridge are particularly relevant:

1) the presence of two towers,
2) a criss-crossing pattern in the towers,
3) multiple cables that hang vertically, and
4) the two levels of roadway.

As we examine the children's drawings, we will see that these features are often well represented; the first drawing in Figure 6.39, for example, includes all four features.

Source: Used by permission of the Port Authority of NY & NJ.

FIGURE 6.38

After the children had completed their drawings, we asked them "to draw a circle around the part(s) that could be called a tower." Many of the children were reluctant to complete this second step: they claimed that they didn't think of any part of the bridge as a tower. Some claimed that bridges cannot have towers, since towers are really, as it was vari-

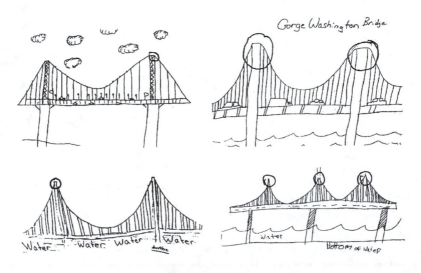

FIGURE 6.39

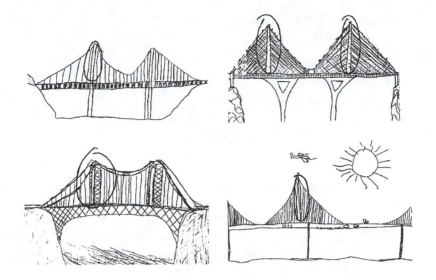

FIGURE 6.40

ously put, "monuments," "tall buildings," or "places to store water." Nevertheless, 25 children did eventually circle a part of the bridge that they had drawn:

> 11 children circled the very top of the bridge (for examples of "bird's-nest" towers, see Figure 6.39).

> 8 children circled a structure rising from the roadway (for examples of "flagpole" towers, see Figure 6.40).

> Only 2 children circled the structure that is, in fact, the tower, one that rises from the river bed up past the roadway (for these drawings of the "real" towers, see Figure 6.41).

FIGURE 6.41

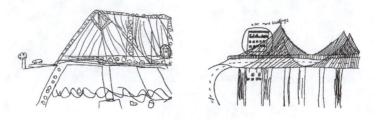

FIGURE 6.42

We should also note that certain children, apparently unable to regard any part of their drawing as a tower, inserted a tower-like shape into their drawing and then circled it (for examples of "stuck-in" towers, see Figure 6.42). As we observed in connection with the use of *smoked* in BACTERIA, the prototypical meaning of a word can exercise considerable power over children.

While giving a lecture on reading tests at a major university in the People's Republic of China, one of us asked 40 students to make a drawing of the bridge they imagined while reading this test unit. Nearly half of them included towers that protected access to the bridges (for examples, see Figure 6.43). Their responses provide a particularly vivid example of the power of culture in reading: historically, the use of bridges in China—and, for that matter, in many parts of the world—was controlled by sentries who stood guard in towers.

We also asked a group of 30 adults in Manhattan to draw a picture of the George Washington Bridge and then respond to two questions:

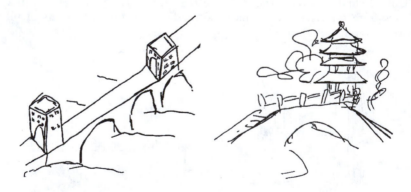

FIGURE 6.43

1) What is the name of the support structures for the bridge?
2) How many of these support structures are there?

The adults' drawings were generally far less detailed than the children's. Figure 6.44 provides an example of just how underdeveloped certain adult drawings were. Several adults were embarrassed by their drawings, making comments like the following:

> I don't know what it looks like. I drive by it on the West Side Highway twice a day to and from work.

> I drive by it every day and have no idea.

For the drawings that these two people made, see Figure 6.45.

We can think of a couple of factors that might account for the greater detail in the children's drawings. For one thing, they practice drawing more. Moreover, they appear to observe the world more closely; or to put the matter another way, they may have more access to their direct visual experience of the world, perhaps partly due to the fact that they depend less on print for getting information.

As for the adult responses to the two questions, only one person used the word *tower* in response to the first one. It turned out that he had once taken a course in bridge design (see Figure 6.46 for his drawing). In responding to the second question, only 6 were aware that the George Washington Bridge has two support structures. Many claimed

FIGURE 6.44

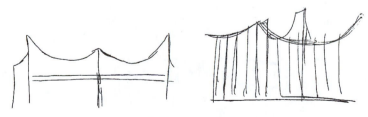

FIGURE 6.45

that the bridge has 6 or even more of these structures (see Figure 6.47 for the drawing of someone who claimed that it has 12).

In presenting our research in an American university setting, we once asked the audience to respond to this unit and then draw a picture of the bridge, both as planned and as executed. Among the members of the audience was a Chinese student who was pursuing a doctorate in linguistics. Figure 6.48 shows the drawing he handed in of the bridge as planned. It was as if esthetic concerns led him to picture the stones, like beads on a necklace, strung along the top of the suspension cables supported by the towers. It may be that this placement was also motivated by a sense that *over* primarily signifies a "higher location."

Let us now turn to the third gap in children's understanding of the passage that created confusion in their responses to (B): their failure to understand that this task is concerned with the towers as executed rather than as planned. In order to understand this failure, we need to examine more closely the temporal framing of the passage. The initial sentence is set in the present (*The George Washington Bridge...spans...*), leading the reader to think of the bridge as it is today. The rest of the passage, however, uses only the simple past tense, even though at least three points can be distinguished in a temporal sequence (see Figure 6.49). This formal leveling of temporal sequence in sentences 2 and 3 may have led children to blur the distinction between plan and execution.[27]

Two features in the task stem itself may also have contributed to such a blurring: (1) the use of *finished* to modify *towers*, and (2) the use of present tense. As to the first feature, the use of *finished* is, of course,

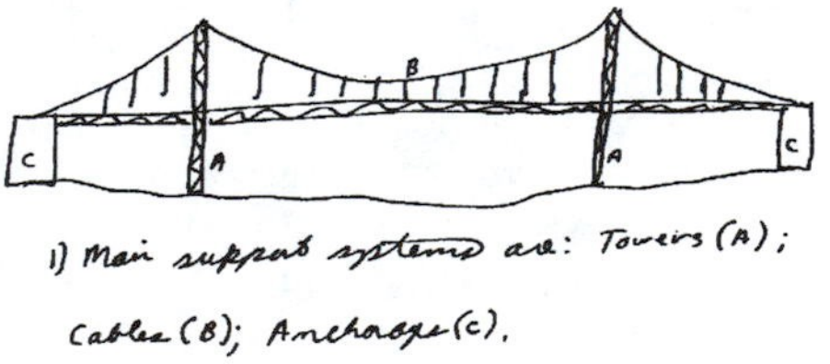

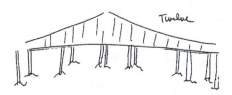

1) Main support systems are: Towers (A);
   Cables (B); Anchorage (c).

FIGURE 6.46

FIGURE 6.47

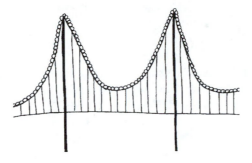

FIGURE 6.48

intended to identify the towers as they were actually constructed (i.e., made only of steel). From the vantage point of the plan, however, the towers can be viewed as still unfinished. In a finished state, the towers would have consisted of stone over steel. As to the second feature, the use of present tense in this task is, no doubt, motivated by the fact that, even today, the towers consist only of steel.[28] Such tense marking, however, can be interpreted as neutral, allowing a reader to supply whatever temporal frame is motivated by other discourse features—and clearly some readers, interpreting the modifier *finished* as explained above, supplied the 'plan' frame. If this task is to maintain present tense, it might be clearer if *finished* were removed, perhaps by rewriting the task as follows:

As they now stand, the towers are made of _____.

Another solution would be to shift from present tense to past tense. In this case, the task could be rewritten as

When the towers were built, they were made of _____.[29]

	Verb	Temporal Points in a Sequence	
Sentence 2	called for	$time_1$	prior to bridge construction
Sentence 3			
Clause 1	were	$time_2$	immediately after bridge construction
Clause 2	stayed	$time_3$	subsequent state after bridge construction

FIGURE 6.49

This latter rewriting would provide greater consistency with other content-oriented tasks that follow a narrative passage written in the past tense. As we pointed out in LEAVING HOME, readers can become confused when a task shifts to present tense.

We have deliberately refrained from discussing how children's real-world knowledge may have affected their response to (B). Most of the children we interviewed lived in metropolitan New York and so could be presumed to have some idea about how the bridge actually looks. During the interviewing a number of children did talk about how such knowledge affected their responses. One interesting discussion involved two boys who were slightly older (one was in the fourth grade, the other in the fifth). The interviewer began by asking them how they got the answer *steel*:

> C1 Well, I drive over the bridge every other weekend.
> I Imagine kids in Omaha, Nebraska, who have never been on the George Washington Bridge. They might get a question like this, too. You think they'd be able to answer it?
> C2 No. They'd be—they wouldn't know.
> C1 Yeah, it says it in the paragraph.

At this point, the two boys began to argue about whether Omaha kids would be able to answer (B) purely on the basis of the passage (they were both talking at once and so what they said was difficult to transcribe). Finally, the interviewer broke in with the following question:

> I You don't think they could get the answer from what's here?
> C2 No.

C1 began to concede some ground, admitting that the passage does lack details and so may be difficult for the child lacking real-world knowledge:

> C1 You should put in more, like you should say: They were putting stone over the steel skeleton on the bridge first.

C2 was not prepared to make a similar concession. He persisted with his point:

> C2 But if we were going to answer the question—say they [the kids in Omaha] have the Scarlet Red Bridge, or something like that. How would we answer? We don't know anything about it.
> C1 Yeah, we have to answer about the Golden Gate Bridge.[30]

The interviewer decided to recycle the question of real-world knowledge:

> So you think you really have to know the bridge to answer the...

C1 seemed to know where the question was going and so, once again, made the point that the passage lacks detail:

> Yeah, but you should really put in more details.

He then analyzed the passage, showing how difficult it is to extract the needed information. He concluded with the following remark:

> So it would be a fat chance. If somebody doesn't notice that, they wouldn't get it right.

Having heard, at last, C1's concession, C2 returned to his initial point:

> It's a New Yorker's test.

C1 then countered for a final time:

> Well, New York Stater's.

We have quoted at length from this interview because C1 effectively establishes a point that we have emphasized throughout our analysis of polarity units: a passage involving multiple sets of polarities needs a good deal of supporting detail if readers are to be in a position to handle these polarities.

Although we concur with C1's evaluation, we believe that C2's insistence on the importance of real-world knowledge can be misleading. We would like to cite three cases where such knowledge either had no effect or actually led children in the wrong direction. One child chose *stone over steel*, even though he can see the George Washington Bridge when he leans out his bedroom window. He seemed indifferent about whether his response fit with his real-world knowledge. His real concern was that his response encompass as much information in the passage as possible: he felt a strong need to choose an answer that included *stone* and *steel*, simply because, as he put it, "both of them were talked about in the story." On his responses to other tasks, he showed the same inclination to account for as much passage information as possible. A number of children seemed to select a compound target response for much the same reason.

Once they were caught up with working through the opposition between *stone* and *steel*, they felt that their answer had to include both words.

One child chose *steel over stone*, even though she passes the bridge frequently and knows that it is made of steel. She explained that only its "outer covering" is made of steel and that underneath is "solid stone," adding that towers are always made of stone so that they will be strong. In the schema constructed by this girl, the builders had planned to add even more stone to hide the steel covering and to make the bridge even stronger. But since the steel turned out to be beautiful, they decided not to. We might note that this interpretation is not actually contradicted by any of the passage information. Moreover, it is congruent with the familiar notion that a tower is an object made of stone. When we asked 30 fourth graders to describe what a tower is made of, nearly two-thirds responded with *stone* or a stone-like material such as *bricks* or *concrete*.

Another child was actively misled by her real-world knowledge. Each day she rides to and from school on the Henry Hudson Parkway in Manhattan. At the point where she passes underneath the George Washington Bridge, massive stone bulwarking undergirds the approach to the bridge. As she looks up, she can see the steel of the bridge looming above this stone. It is apparently this image that she had in mind when she selected *steel over stone* (i.e., steel supported by a stone base). Having to manipulate the choices *steel over stone* and *stone over steel* may have encouraged her to bypass the sense of *over* as "covering" and use the sense "higher in vertical space."[31]

In closing our discussion of GEORGE WASHINGTON BRIDGE, we would like to make an observation that applies to all the polarity units. In discussing these units, we have frequently resorted to graphics, and we have noticed that children who do well on such units often have the same inclination. Making a sketch helps them align the various bits of information that are necessary for completing these tasks. We would recommend that test makers allow children to make drawings on scrap paper. In principle, children should be allowed to make use of any comprehension strategy that does not violate the integrity of the test. To our way of thinking, the testing of reading comprehension gains in validity as it allows—indeed, encourages—children to use strategies that are important to them in their ordinary reading.

NOTES

1. In presenting deictic perspectives, we have assumed a prototypical communicative setting: that is to say, one in which language users are located at the same spatiotemporal point. But just as language users are often at different

points in space, so they are often at different points in time, especially now that electronic technologies are used to facilitate communication around the world. As a consequence, language users are increasingly forced to adjust to an interlocutor's different temporal location, just as they have always made such adjustments to a different spatial location. Such adjustments add even further indeterminacy to the deictic use of language, a point that we will not pursue here, since discussions of resetting a clock ordinarily take place between language users who share the same temporal location.

2. Many linguists (e.g., Lakoff & Johnson, 1980; Lyons, 1977) adopt what is called the LOCALIST HYPOTHESIS, in which space is viewed as basic to all domains of linguistic representation. Consider, for example, the domain of communication. In describing activity within this domain, human beings are prone to draw on a conduit metaphor and thus use expressions such as "I was able to get *through* to her."

3. We can observe here what we earlier described: the use of a spatial template to represent temporal phenomena. The term *behind* is ordinarily used to describe the relations between objects in a field when a further one is obscured by a nearer one (i.e., mirror imagery is used to construct such a static field). The temporal use of *behind*, however, corresponds more closely to a less common use of the term with respect to spatial phenomena, one in which it is used to describe the relation between two entities in motion (e.g., a person running behind, say, a bus in the hope that (s)he might overtake it).

4. We should note that this cross-language research is ultimately anchored in human anatomy: orientational terms can be compared across languages by virtue of a common reference to the human body. We should also note that this research has uncovered conditions in which speakers of any language can shift between mirror imagery and in-tandem imagery in representing spatial as well as temporal phenomena (see Hill, 1992, for further discussion).

5. For evidence that children draw on a later task in responding to an earlier one, see HURRICANE (p. 143).

6. Older readers do possess more specialized knowledge about food preservation. Here is how 20 graduate students responded to the same task:

keeping it dry (16)	putting salt on it (20)
keeping it warm (0)	keeping it cool (20)
smoking it (20)	keeping it wet (1)

7. We concede that an interview can be a powerful stimulant to invention even when only one child is present.

8. Climatic conditions may influence these pairings considerably. If we were to test a similar group of children in, say, Arizona rather than New York, the results might well be different.

9. During the interviewing, we came across one child who insisted on distinguishing 'warm' from 'hot.' For her, the word *warm* did not indicate a sufficiently high temperature to ensure that the grapes would actually be dried.

10. We noticed that as children initially read the passage, they did not pronounce the word *sweet* with contrastive stress. Only after they had struggled with the task did some of the children begin to use such stress.

11. In ADVERTISING TAILOR, we discovered a comparable impediment to children's choosing the target response *promise*. Some children, using this word only in an interpersonal domain, lacked the generic conception that would have enabled them to apply it to a commerical transaction. These two test units provide compelling evidence that children tend to focus on the prototypical sense of a word (Rosch, 1977) and often are not able to deal effectively with more peripheral senses.

12. *Sweet* is used to describe other kinds of sensation as well: air can smell sweet, music can sound sweet, children can look sweet, and things like success can even feel sweet.

13. Research in idiosemantics turns up numerous discontinuities of this sort. Words that are used to talk about sounds, smells, tastes, and feelings are especially likely to develop such idiosyncratic meanings, since they don't occur frequently enough in contexts that support precise, mutually verifiable discriminations. By way of contrast, our experience usually does enable us to achieve fairly uniform meanings for words that refer to visual concepts. It is of interest that a number of languages, particularly in West Africa, set up an opposition between a word for visual sensation and a word that covers all other kinds of sensation. In Hausa, a language spoken primarily in northern Nigeria, the greater stability of the visual is captured in the saying, *Gani ya kori ji* "Seeing drives out all other sensation" (i.e., hearing, tasting, smelling, touching).

14. It is possible to devise a situation in which *have* and *a lot of varieties* can be combined, as in the following exchange:

    "Where's the best place to buy grapes?"
    "Oh, the fruit stands on Broadway have a lot of varieties."

    Such a possibility may have contributed to children's sense that the distractor proposition was, in fact, acceptable.

15. The word *then* does not actually appear in the surface of this sentence. We use it as a convenient way of referring to the apodasis of a conditional sentence, just as the word *if* has been used to refer to the protasis.

16. In a personal communication, Kenneth Goodman has suggested that a draftsman would be more concerned with making thin, light lines than thick, dark ones. Hence, in his judgment, it would have been more natural to use *thin and light* rather than *thick and dark* in the passage (this point assumes, of course, that the *you* it addresses is concerned with drawing).

17. In linguistic theory such asymmetries have generally been accounted for by categorizing semantically opposed terms as MARKED or UNMARKED. In general, the unmarked term has a wider pattern of distribution. Thus, in the following sentences we are much more likely to use the unmarked terms *thick* and *dark* than the marked terms *thin* and *light*:

How *thick* is that board over there?
How *dark* is your new suit?

In fact, *thin* and *light* would only be used in cases where the entities being talked about are, in some way, presupposed to be thin or light.

18. We asked 20 African American third graders the same question and only one knew that the numbers indicated how hard the lead was. We also asked them if they knew what number of pencil to use on a test, and all but one provided the answer #2. In fact, many children, during the interviews, associated pencil numbers with taking tests. Although they knew that a #2 pencil was needed for a test, that knowledge unfortunately provided no help in responding to (A); if anything, it was misleading. Consider, for example, how one child described a #2 pencil: "Well, your #2 pencil is supposed to be the darkest pencil, and it doesn't have the softest lead. It has the hardest lead, and it comes out really dark and thick." It turns out that she thought a #2 pencil was used for tests precisely because (1) its lead is hard (so it won't break easily), and (2) it makes dark lines (so they can be read easily).

19. We gave the same task to 20 graduate students and only 12 of them provided a clear answer. We suspect that a certain polarization between *soft* and *dark* makes this question difficult even for adults. In this regard, Howard Gardner's (1991) theory about the persistence of certain primordial conceptions into adulthood may be relevant.

20. Certain children could come up with an explanation if they were provided an appropriate stimulus. We discovered that spreading butter on toast was a particularly good stimulus. Working with this familiar situation, a number of children were able to connect *hard* with *thin* and *soft* with *thick*.

21. For those of you who are wondering which group was right, a #1 pencil has softer lead and thus makes thicker and darker lines. The even split among the graduate students is a dramatic reminder of the degree to which our knowledge can blur when we are forced to manipulate different pairs of lexical oppositions.

22. *Top* is not a particularly apt word to describe either end of a pencil: for the lead-end, the word *tip* is more frequently used. Moreover, the use of *top* presents a polarity problem of its own, for it is not at all clear just which end it refers to. We asked 30 fourth graders to apply the word *top* to one end of a pencil and here is what they did:

lead-end	22
eraser-end	8

Hence the majority of the children did not agree with the use of *top* in the passage: for them, it refers to the end where the action is rather than the end that just happens to be at a higher point during the act of writing. In fact, one child who was interviewed about this passage said: "At first I thought the word *top* meant this end (pointing to the tip). I tried to find the symbol here. But then I thought it would be gone when we sharpen the pencil." To avoid such confusions, speakers of English might do well to avail themselves of the expressions *pencil mouth* and *pencil butt* used in Pidgin English in West Africa. We can recognize here a particularly subtle manifestation of the familiar conflict between deictic and nondeictic uses of language discussed in the introduction to this chapter (pp. 223–228).

23. We here maintain the three ways of representing polarities that were used in Figure 6.27.

24. Children's difficulty in making sense of *fresh* is not surprising if one considers how unusual the use of the word is in this context. In many languages, the primary opposition is between 'salt water' and 'sweet water' (e.g., in Turkish the terms are *tuzlu* and *tatli*, respectively).

25. One of the other choices in (B) also results in an ill-formed proposition: *Most of the iceberg is top.*

26. Incidentally, this is the same girl who was unhappy with *knocked down* as a synonym for *blown over* in HURRICANE. She had become something of a specialist in lexical semantics.

27. *Stayed* (sentence 3, clause 2) suggests a certain volition that could have been avoided if a verb like *remained* had been used (i.e., the towers *remained* as they were).

28. It may have also been motivated by the use of present tense in (A), for, as we have frequently observed, there is a tendency for the two tasks in a unit to be formally aligned.

29. Both of these solutions require a longer task stem, but they are still shorter than others in our corpus (for a particularly long task stem, see LEARNING TO READ).

30. This is apparently a reference to HUNG BRIDGES.

31. One adult we interviewed interpreted *over* in this way. In defending his choice of *steel over stone*, he said, "Stone is used as foundation, and *over* that foundation the steel bridge is built."

chapter 7

Changing Registers

I n all three chapters of Part III the test units require some kind of
basic shift in the reader's stance. In this final chapter, however, the
units to be considered differ in one fundamental respect from those
in the previous two: the shifting that they call for is not motivated by the
passage itself, but by its relations to the tasks that follow. The passage is
written in one register—an imaginative, even evocative one—and the
tasks are written in another—one that is best described as simple and
matter-of-fact. In order to negotiate these units successfully, children
must know how to shift from one register to another.

Considered broadly, such shifting is inevitable in a test unit and, for
that matter, in any school activity that moves from a sample of language
to tasks that deal with that sample. Students are required to move, as it
were, from language-in-use to language-about-language. Such movement is, of course, a fundamental aspect of school discourse—it is
present not only in tests and textbooks but also in a good deal of
teacher talk.[1] We often assume that children, early on, become aware of
this boundary and learn how to negotiate it. On the basis of our interviewing, we suspect that this awareness is poorly developed in many children. We encountered a number of children who seemed to process the
passage and tasks as though they were continuous.

In Part II we observed numerous examples of style carryover in children's responses to a task. In dealing with ALICE AND THE FAWN, a number
of children selected a distractor because it led to a proposition more con-
sonant with the imaginative style of the writing.[2] In attempting to understand such responses, we should remind ourselves that a compelling theory
of reader response, one that can be traced to antiquity, holds that writing
style and reading style cannot be separated, that our interpretive stance as
readers is necessarily determined by the stylistic texture of what we read.

Let us take a moment to characterize the two passages that will be discussed in this chapter. One is written in a narrative-descriptive mode:

> Far back in the deep woods, the limbs of a large tree stretched gray among the green cedars. Once that tree, too, had been green, but now the leaves were gone, and the tree was dead. Low, near the ground, a black hole opened into the hollow trunk of the tree. Inside the hole a mother bear and her two babies lay on a nest of grass and leaves.

The other is written in an expository mode:

> The first time a mother alligator hears her babies she cannot see them. Their little grunts are coming from a pile of mud and old leaves. That is where the mother alligator laid her eggs many weeks ago.

Both passages, however, present a nature scene in an anthropomorphized style: each uses what might be called a 'mother-and-babies' frame to present the nonhuman.

This style is common among writers who present the natural sciences to children. It is as though they intend not only to inform children about nature but to inspire them to view it as related to their own lives. We will not consider here the advisability of encouraging children to think of a creature like an alligator as filled with "mother love," although we once heard of a child who lost an arm trying to pet a baby alligator.[3]

There is one other reason for our reserving these two units for the final chapter. Each contains a task whose target response was inaccessible to virtually all children at these grade levels, and it is clear that in each instance the style of the passage plays a crucial role in leading children toward a communicative distractor and away from an acommunicative target response. Hence we will be concerned with showing how various stylistic features work together to create an interpretive frame that this distractor strongly reinforces. In both cases, however, this frame is incongruent with some local detail in the passage. In effect, the reader is forced to choose between holistic pattern and local detail in formulating a response, and it will be our claim that the stylistic texture of these passages strongly encourages the holistic response.

GREEN CEDARS

We will first consider the unit that contains the narrative-descriptive passage:

> Far back in the deep woods, the limbs of a large tree stretched gray among the green cedars. Once that tree, too, had been green, but now the leaves were gone, and the tree was dead. Low, near the ground, a black hole opened into the hollow trunk of the tree. Inside the hole a mother bear and her two babies lay on a nest of grass and leaves.
>
> A. The green trees were
>
>   gone   dying
>
>   cedars   hollow
>
> B. Where was the nest?
>
>   inside a tree   on a dead limb
>
>   in a cave   on a green tree

This passage parallels JAYS AND CROWS in that each describes a nature scene that holds the promise of a story to come. The promise is even stronger, however, in GREEN CEDARS, which begins with a long-range shot of a dead tree among green cedars and ends with a close-range shot of a mother bear and two babies nesting in the tree.

We asked 23 children what they thought the passage was mainly about and left them free to respond as they wished. We were curious to see whether they would write something connected to the trees, the bears, or some combination of the two: 15 of the children wrote about the trees, 3 about the bears, and 4 managed to write about both. Combining the two was difficult, since 'trees' and 'bears' were not woven together throughout the passage, as were 'birds' and 'sounds,' the competing themes in JAYS AND CROWS. One of the children who combined the two themes wrote the following:

> A tree gave its life for a mother bear and cubs.

This child may well be onto something. The passage does have a mythic quality: first, the dying of the tree and, then, the discovery of new life within it.

We also asked these children what they thought "the rest of the story would be about" and provided them with three choices. Here is how they responded:

what the bears do (16)   how trees die (5)   how bears make nests (2)

During the interviewing, when children were asked to tell about what they had just read, they tended to focus on the bears. But most had trouble in moving from the tree-part of the story to the bear-part. As one child put it:

> I can't get it. At the beginning it's talking about trees, but at the end it's talking about bears.

Another child attempting to make this shift had a couple of false starts before adopting a 'you' frame:

> There was a tree which was alive with green leaves, which was green. It was a great cedar and one day the leaves began to fall down and there were no leaves and the tree was dead and finally there was a—it was a hollow tree—and you could see a bear and two baby bears lying on the grass inside the tree and there's a nest in there.

Both tasks in this test unit call for the recycling of relatively unimportant information from the passage. (A) requires that the green trees surrounding the tree in focus—the dead tree—be identified as *cedars*, whereas (B) requires that the bear nest be identified as *inside a tree*. In both instances, readers are required to engage in a hunt-and-find operation, an activity which goes against the grain of the imaginative register of the passage. In effect, the passage invites readers to open out onto a larger scene, but the tasks force them to close in on local detail.

This search for low-level detail is particularly difficult to conduct in the case of (A), for readers have good reason, as we will show, to reject the target response, even if they do manage to locate it. In fact, *cedars* was the least attractive choice during the pilot testing. About a seventh of both the African American and European American children selected *cedars*, about a fifth *gone*, and about a third selected each of the other two distractors, *dying* and *hollow*.

The stem of (A) consists of only four words. In selecting the target response, readers need only to locate in the initial sentence the nominal in which *green* modifies *cedars*, and then use this overtly expressed modification to formulate a response. This operation seems to be easy, and yet few children managed to carry it out. Even the children who selected *cedars* tended to provide other reasons for their choice. One child, for example, said that he chose it because all the other choices—*gone*, *dying*, *hollow*—were about "brown trees." Presumably what he had in mind was the dead tree.

In accounting for the difficulty of the task, we should first point out that surprisingly few children seem to know what a cedar is. When we asked 24 children to describe a cedar, only 6 identified it as a tree; 4 said that it was wood and 14 said they didn't know. When we asked 20 African American children in a Harlem school to draw a picture of a cedar, none drew a tree. We suspect that this lack of vocabulary knowledge plays an important role in children's difficulty with (A).

But even if children know the word *cedars*, the task is still difficult. It is important to recall that other tasks in which information had to be retrieved from a single nominal were also difficult for children (see ALICE AND THE FAWN and JAYS AND CROWS). When engaged in this kind of retrieval, children apparently view the modifying information as so trivial that they cannot accept it as constituting the point of the task. Moreover, selecting *cedars* results in a sentence that is not only trivial but, on pragmatic grounds, peculiar. Given that trees are prototypically green, it is strange to use this color to identify a particular group of them. It's a bit like saying, "The birds that fly are robins." In responding to the sentence *The green trees were cedars*, one child made the claim that "it doesn't sound like English."[4] She made a similar claim when dealing with the target proposition *The people were surprised by her white circles* (see WHITE CIRCLES, p. 213).

It can be argued that the target proposition in (A) is motivated on pragmatic grounds if the reader assumes that the dead (i.e., nongreen) tree is not a cedar (i.e., the green trees are being identified as cedars so that they might be contrasted to a nongreen tree that is not a cedar). The passage does, in fact, provide information that supports this assumption. The second sentence states that the tree's *leaves were gone*; and, of course, a cedar is ordinarily thought of as having needles rather than leaves.

Most of the children we interviewed, however, thought that the dead tree was a cedar. When we asked them why they thought so, they focused on the passage information that *once that tree, too, had been green*. In addition, some claimed that the trees must have been cedars since they were growing together. No child we interviewed called attention to the word *leaves* as a reason for thinking that the dead tree was not a cedar. In fact, one child justified his choice of *dying* by referring to *leaves*:

I wrote *dying* because they were writing all that stuff about the leaves falling off. That also could have been just the effects of fall. I wasn't sure.[5]

The word *leaves* can, of course, be used generically to refer to any greenish growth on a tree. In the survey already mentioned, the 6 children who knew that a cedar was a tree were asked what was on the top part.

All 6 used the word *leaves* in their answer. When buying a Christmas tree in Manhattan, we have discovered that Christmas-tree vendors tend to use *leaves* in this way as well.

We asked 15 children to make a drawing of the scene they envisioned while reading this test unit. Some of their drawings suggest that they viewed the dead tree as a different kind of tree from the surrounding cedars (see, for example, the drawing in Figure 7.1). This difference may, of course, be attributed simply to the child's wish to contrast the dead tree with the living ones.

There is one other problem with the target proposition: the form of this proposition tends to call for an exclusive interpretation; that is to say, all the green trees were cedars. In imagining the scene described by the passage, readers are likely to picture an extended forest—the passage opens with the expression *far back in the deep woods.* Hence children might well imagine a forest with different kinds of green trees and so, working with the exclusive interpretation, experience dissonance in choosing *cedars.*

All the distractors, as noted earlier, were more attractive than *cedars* during the pilot testing. As for *hollow,* its appeal seems to be related to two factors. To begin with, as the only choice connected to the bear-part of the passage, it allows children to achieve a semblance of integration between the two parts. But an apparently even more important factor is the form of the task. A sentence that begins with a nominal plus the verb *to be* is more likely to be completed by an adjective than by a verb or a noun. In order to confirm this greater frequency, we asked 30 third graders to complete the sentence *The people were* _____. Over three-quarters placed an adjective in the blank (this high proportion was

FIGURE 7.1

also evidenced when the children responded to sentences in which *bears*, *cars*, *trees*, and *houses* were substituted for *people*). The other one-fourth filled in the blank with a verb form; no child filled in this sentence frame with either a nominal or an adverbial.

The selection of *dying*, the other most popular distractor, is congruent with the active role for readers that the stylistic texture of the passage calls for. A number of stylistic features work together to encourage such an active role. Consider, for example, the opening sentence: it pictures a tree whose limbs *stretched gray among the green cedars*. The tree is not overtly identified as dead. The reader can, however, infer death from the contrast between *gray* and *green*, an inference which is, in fact, confirmed in the second sentence. In order to see if children use the initial cue *gray* to infer death, we presented 25 children with only the first sentence and asked them what they knew about the tree with gray limbs. Only 8 of them said that it was dead. We should note, however, that all 25 were urban children for whom a green/gray polarity may not be operative in symbolizing life and death in trees. Not only do such children generally have less experience with trees, but urban conditions can considerably dull the green of living trees.

The initial sentence also provides detail that can lead a reader to imagine a scene of infection, one in which the gray tree is actively spreading death to its green neighbors. The dead tree is pictured as penetrating the space of the living ones (i.e., its limbs are described as *among the green cedars*). More particularly, the verb *stretched* provides a sense of 'active penetration': it is almost as if the tree is acting with volition. Such penetration was captured in certain drawings that children made, such as the one in Figure 7.2 (see also the drawing in Figure 7.1).

FIGURE 7.2

As can be seen, the hole in the tree is placed quite near the ground, presumably so that heavy animals such as bears will be able to crawl in.

The second sentence provides further detail to support the notion that the green trees are infected with death. The stark use of *too* provides the haunting sense that the dead tree had once belonged to the community of the living but is now cut off; and the contrast between *once/now* and *had been/was* suggests that time itself destroys the living, and so the green trees, too, must one day die.

A formal aspect of the distractor proposition, *The green trees were dying*, also fits with this interpretive frame. The verb *die* carries past progressive marking (i.e., *were...dying*), but there is no specification of a larger temporal frame in which to interpret this marking.[6] In the absence of such a frame, a past progressive verb is apt to suggest a process so gradual that it cannot be readily marked off in time:

> We finally became aware that the river bottom *was shifting*.

Hence *the green trees were dying* has a particular resonance in describing ongoing processes of nature which, having touched one green tree, will inexorably touch the others as well.[7]

Given all these stylistic features, we were not surprised to discover that a number of children we interviewed pictured a congested forest scene in which contagion was spreading from the dead tree to the other trees. As one child put it, "The green trees were right around the big tree that was dead." Certain children were quite eloquent in expressing the inference that the green trees will one day be dead. As one child put it, "Once one tree dies, they're all going to." Another child expressed the same sentiment with even greater brevity: "The green trees will die, too." For these children, it seems clear that contagion was in the air. At the end of some interviews, we asked children if they had ever heard of Dutch elm disease and discovered that quite a number of them had. One even began to discuss the effects of acid rain on trees.

This sense of contagion was also evidenced in the commentary that children made on their drawings. Consider, for example, what one child said about the drawing shown in Figure 7.3. In discussing this picture, the child gave the feeling that death is everywhere: the leaves on the ground "had fallen from the dead tree, home of the nest of the bears" and the dead tree was enclosed by other trees "in a forest of dead trees." The child drew everything in this forest with black crayons. Later when she discovered that the target response to (A) was *cedars*, she went back and colored in the surrounding trees with green. It is also worth observing that she drew these trees much smaller, thus emphasizing the centrality of the tree with the bears.

FIGURE 7.3

To sum up, the distractor proposition *The green trees were dying* provides poignant commentary on a forest scene in which one dead tree is viewed as emblematic of the fate of its neighbors. Indeed, we find this commentary more fitting than that provided by the target proposition, *The green trees were cedars*. The former fits the register of the passage, whereas the latter merely provides information about a detail that has no interpretive import.

A graduate student specializing in children's literature conducted an interesting probe on this unit. Working with the notion that children are accustomed to reading illustrated books, he gave this passage to 12 children along with a picture that showed the limbs of the dead tree actively penetrating the surrounding trees (see Figure 7.4). Under

FIGURE 7.4

these conditions, half of the children selected *dying*. In defending this choice, the children tended to focus on a sense of contagion. As one child put it, "Pollution can kill trees. There it says *gray trees* and gray is polluted. First there's one polluted tree, then others. The gray tree kills other trees." One child even spoke of "mud flowing down to the other trees."

This probe raises an intriguing question about reading tests. Since children often read illustrated books, they are accustomed to using pictures as well as words in constructing meaning. Is it thus appropriate to assess their reading comprehension on words alone? This question becomes even more important in a computer age in which graphics play an increasingly important role. We will return to this question in the concluding chapter.

Before leaving (A), let us consider the remaining distractor *gone*, which was less frequently chosen than *dying*. But it, too, is able to express, though with considerably less finesse, a similar interpretive frame. From a temporal perspective, *gone* is an inaccurate choice; and yet the finality of this verb provides a peculiar heightening of the feeling that the green trees are doomed to die. One African American child who chose *gone* orally read the stem of (A) as *The green tree was* rather than *The green trees were*. When questioned, he seemed to take (A) as a comment on the dead tree, the one that had once been green.

It is tempting to relate this confusion between singular and plural to dialect interference. Even in a deep creole, however, it is unusual for the plural marker to be phonologically neutralized in a monosyllabic, vowel-final word like *tree*. It may be that the plural -*s* was simply not noticed, and that the boy speaks a dialect in which *was* and *were* are grammatically interchangeable. Whatever the case may have been, this incident did remind us of the potential interference that speakers of a nonstandard dialect can encounter as they read material written in a standard dialect.

Let us now turn to (B), a task that also requires readers to retrieve relatively insignificant information from the passage. In this instance, however, the words that constitute the target response cannot be found in the passage. In order to arrive at *inside a tree*, readers need to combine information in the final two sentences. In effect, they have to carry over the phrase *of the tree* from sentence 3 to sentence 4, as shown in Figure 7.5. Then they must then carry out two additional steps: (1) delete the words *the hole of*, and (2) change the article *the* to *a* before tree. These steps should not be difficult for any child who can appropriately integrate the information in the two sentences.

The most difficult aspect of this task is that it forces children to work against various kinds of real-world knowledge that they possess. To begin with, children do not readily think of a nest as a place where bears live, as indicated by the results of the probe shown in Figure 7.6. This probe was administered to 20 children and the number selecting each response is shown in parentheses. During the interviewing, we did come across one child with a more general view of the word *nest*. A student in a class for the gifted, she suggested that *nest* could refer to

> the home of lots of animals. It necessarily does not need to be comprised of just twigs but can include leaves and grass like that of the bears.

We administered the same probe to 10 adults and discovered that 6 of them selected *bears*. We then asked them to describe where bears build their homes, and a number of them used words that can be found in the passage: 4 of them wrote *trees*, 3 wrote *caves*, and 2 wrote *woods*. We were somewhat puzzled by this difference in the adult and child responses and can think of no ready explanation for it.

Since children think of a nest as a place where birds and squirrels live, they view it (1) as too small for three bears and (2) located high in a tree. The two drawings in Figure 7.7 contain nests that are high off the ground. While being interviewed, the African American girl who produced the drawing in Figure 7.7(a) realized that her initial placement of the nest did not fit with the passage:

C   It says *laid on a nest of grass and leaves*. I thought you gotta make the nest up here [pointing to where she had drawn the nest], but the nest gonna be on the ground [pointing to the ground].

I   Why did you think you had to make the nest up here?

C   I forgot. I thought they was talking about birds.[8]

(3)   ... a black hole opened into the hollow trunk of the tree

(4)   Inside the hole [of the tree], a mother bear ...

FIGURE 7.5

Which of the following build nests?

1. ducks (20)	3. bears (1)	5. alligators (0)
2. squirrels (16)	4. goldfish (0)	6. bees (0)

FIGURE 7.6

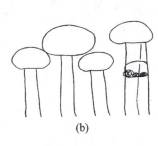

(a)   (b)

FIGURE 7.7

At this point she and the interviewer burst into laughter, mutually recog-
nizing the formidable powers of the word *nest*. She did not necessarily
mean that she had misread *bears* as *birds*—only that the word *nest* had
led her to picture the kind of place where birds live.

Some children were troubled by the fact that bears would have difficulty climbing up to where a nest should be and so pictured the dead
tree as lying on the ground. When one interviewer asked a child to draw
a picture of the scene, the following exchange ensued:

C   Is the tree lying?
I   What do you think?
C   It's not said, I guess. But the tree is dead; it could be lying.
I   You may draw following your imagination.

The child then drew the picture shown in Figure 7.8. It is interesting
that the nest is still placed far from the base of the tree.

Many children were bothered by the discrepancies in size between
what the passage seemed to require and their ordinary experience. Not

FIGURE 7.8

only are nests typically too small to accommodate three bears, but ordinary trees are too small as well. If children are to select the target response, they must envision a tree large enough to hold the bears. Here is how one girl defended her choice of the target response:

> Well, there are very, very, very big trees like the one they are talking about. Trees can get very large and when there is a hole, it goes upwards and downwards. The hole, it stretches all the way. And they [the bears] are usually sleeping very close or on one another, so they do have enough room.

Notice how this child drew on one of the passage words—*stretch*—in trying to convey an image of a tree large enough to hold the bears.

There were some children who chose *in a cave* because they were apparently unable to imagine any tree large enough to hold a bear family in its hollow trunk. As one child put it,

> Three bears can't fit inside a tree so they must have been in a cave or something.

It was as if these children were blocked from absorbing information not congruent with their real-world knowledge (see Kimmel & MacGinitie, 1981, for a discussion of such interferences).

There were other children, however, who seemed to have selected *in a cave* because they were using *cave* metaphorically in order to account for the sheer magnitude of the tree. The imaginative texture of the writing may encourage such a figurative extension of *cave*. One Japanese graduate student selected *in a cave* for just such a reason. As she put it,

> *cave* conveys the image of a dark, warm, and safe living space for the mother bear and her babies. I thought about *inside a tree,* but a dead tree doesn't fit the image of protecting the bears.

She goes on to point out that in Japanese children's literature

> animals are described as very human-like and are often used to convey warmth and maternal love for children. Safety, dependency and security are the first things to be taught to children in Japan.

In closing our discussion of this unit, we would like to describe the response of a child who is an avid reader of science, particularly things astronomical. When he first glanced down at the passage, his eye was caught by the phrase *a black hole*. He immediately exclaimed:

> There's something weird about this story. It says *a black hole*. Do you know
> what a black hole is?

When the interviewer answered "No," he launched into a fairly technical
explanation about what astronomers think might cause a black hole in
space. It is, of course, difficult to say how this initial reaction might have
colored his reading of the passage. He did select the distractor *dying* for
(A), defending this choice with the simple words: "It's talking about all
the trees dying." We couldn't help wondering whether this budding sci-
entist had some intuition that the trees, like everything else, would ultimately disappear into a black hole.

MOTHER ALLIGATOR

We turn now to the other unit in which the passage deals with the natural world. In this case, the writer seems to have an expository goal in mind—to convey certain information about alligator reproduction. The style, however, contains elements usually associated with fictional narrative.

> The first time a mother alligator hears her babies she cannot see them. Their little grunts are coming from a pile of mud and old leaves. That is where the mother alligator laid her eggs many weeks ago.
>
> A. Alligators lay their eggs in
> mud   the night
> water   the winter
>
> B. The "little grunts" in the story are
> old leaves   baby alligators
> eggs   noises

The passage is brief, consisting of only three sentences, each of which is, in turn, relatively short. The first provides a generic description of an alligator's initial experience of its offspring: it can hear them but cannot see them. The sentences that follow provide supporting detail; and yet the level of this detail seems to sever these sentences from the initial one. It is difficult for readers to retain the generic conception of an alligator while processing details such as *pile of mud and old leaves* and *where the mother alligator laid her eggs many weeks ago*. It is as if such detail carries readers into the world of a particular alligator.

The passage also reflects an anthropomorphized style of describing the alligator and its offspring (e.g., the use of *mother alligator* and *babies*). We have already noted that such style is commonly used when children's authors describe animals in their natural habitat; and it is, of course, common for such authors, in another genre of children's books, to displace animals to a human habitat where they take on human ways of living. We can mention here *Alligator Baby*, in which human parents carry home by mistake an alligator baby, but eventually the alligator parents discover this mistake and come to the human home, a human baby in hand, in pursuit of their own baby.

While browsing in the university collection of children's literature, one of us came across *What Is That Alligator Saying?*, a small book that teaches children about the range of ways in which different animals communicate. As we looked through its pages, we discovered, word for word, the passage used in this test unit. The paragraph that was excerpted is preceded by a paragraph that describes how grunting is the basic form of communication between baby alligators and their mother. It is followed by a paragraph that describes the mother alligator, upon hearing her newborn babies, digging them out of the mud and old leaves with her snout.

We have pointed out that in many test units an easy task is paired with a hard one. This pattern is more conspicuous in MOTHER ALLIGATOR than in any other unit in our corpus. If we judge by the proportion of children who selected the target response during the pilot testing, this unit contains both the hardest and the easiest among the 44 tasks that we have considered. Table 7.1 shows the percentage of children who selected the target responses *mud* in (A) and *noises* in (B).

How can we account for such a striking divergence in the performance of both groups of children? On the surface, these tasks parallel the ones in ALICE AND THE FAWN. In both units, (A) calls for recycling information, (B) for defining a word; and as already pointed out, children did poorly on both tasks in ALICE AND THE FAWN, where an acommunicative target response is juxtaposed with a communicative distractor that is congruent with the imaginative world that many readers constructed from the passage.

When we examine the tasks more closely, it is not surprising that they are not parallel to those in ALICE AND THE FAWN. In the case of (B), the imaginative quality of the passage is crucial to children's responses, but in the case of (A) it seems to have had little effect. In accounting for this difference, it is important to observe that (A), unlike (B), includes no distractor highly congruent with the imaginative world constructed from the passage. In fact, the failure of children to select the target response seems to have been more related to their discomfort with its partial nature than with the inherent attraction of any other choice. The passage identifies *mud and old leaves* as the place where an alligator lays its eggs, whereas (A) includes only *mud* as a choice. Certain children called attention to this discrepancy. Here is how one boy defended his rejection of *mud*:

> Because right here [pointing to the choices] it doesn't say anything about leaves.

TABLE 7.1

	African American	European American
Task (A)	64%	78%
Task (B)	3%	4%

We can observe, once again, how formal constraints affect task construction—*mud and old leaves* would have been considered, at least when compared to the other choices, as too long.

We might note that the attraction of *water*, the most widely selected distractor in (A), seems to be partially motivated by children's thinking of an alligator as a 'water creature.' One girl claimed that an alligator lays its eggs while swimming, and so they are really laid in the water. She drew the picture shown in Figure 7.9, which she describes as "the alligator eggs floating down through the water." This child was unable to conceive of the alligator as "getting its eggs out" while its body was lying flat against the mud.

We came across other difficulties that children experienced in visualizing the scene. How does an alligator manage to lay eggs at all? And even if it does lay them, how does it get them under a pile of mud and old leaves? And why does it put them there? In order to hatch its eggs, doesn't it have to sit on them the way a hen does? We can see, once again, how a conflict between real-world knowledge, even when it is poorly developed, and passage information leads to probing questions, the very kind that are critical if reading is to become a knowledge-building activity, but which, in the context of a reading test, only lead children to flounder on what should have been an easy task.

Before leaving (A), we would like to note that one child selected the distractor *the night* as a means of explaining the fact that the mother alligator couldn't see her babies. He didn't seem to worry that (A) is concerned with her laying eggs rather than the hatching of her babies. Another child who was Arabic-speaking chose *the night* because she felt that "having babies is something that shouldn't be seen." This child also

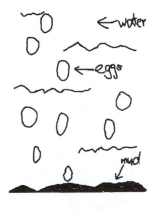

FIGURE 7.9

described the mother alligator as making a nest for her babies. She seemed to have in mind the scene in GREEN CEDARS where the mother bear builds a nest for her babies in the hollow tree; if she did, then we can view this as a further example of unit leakage.

If (A) is so easy, why then is (B) so difficult? Before addressing this question, we should point out that during the pilot testing not only did the fewest number of children select its target response, but the largest number selected one of the distractors: 49% of the African American children and 63% of the European American children selected *baby alligators*. Moreover, this task is difficult for adults as well as for children. It is, in fact, the only task in our corpus for which the majority of adults do not choose the target response. When giving talks at various universities, we have often asked members of the audience to respond to this test unit. Ordinarily, more than half of the adults select *baby alligators* and the proportion often runs as high as two-thirds. In one controlled study of 60 graduate students, only a third selected *noises*, while the other two-thirds selected *baby alligators*; and even many students who selected *noises* claimed that they would have preferred to choose *baby alligators*. When asked to explain why they chose *noises*, they generally focused on the way in which *their* precedes *little grunts* in the second sentence of the passage:

> *Their little grunts* are coming from a pile of mud and old leaves.

Here is how one student commented on this sentence:

> Unfortunately, the word *their* refers to a plural subject and the mother alligator is singular. Cohesion blocks imagination.

It is clear from the initial *unfortunately* and the final sentence, which was carefully underlined, that this student was pulled in opposing directions by the task and was not altogether happy about the direction he had to take. Another student made a similar comment:

> *Little grunts* is bound by the referent of *their* and so cannot refer to *baby alligators*.

She went on to point out that if *little grunts* were taken as referring to *baby alligators*, the sentence, if expanded, would read as

> The baby alligators' baby alligators were coming from a pile of mud and old leaves.

Another student speculated that if *mother alligator* had been plural in the first sentence, he would have chosen *baby alligators* (i.e., *their* would have been interpreted as referring to *mother alligators* and *little grunts* to the baby alligators themselves).[9]

The importance of the phrase *their little grunts* for adult readers who select *noises* was further confirmed in a probe conducted with 10 graduate students. These students were initially presented with the passage for 45 seconds. The passage was then removed, and the students were asked to respond to the tasks and to write down what they remembered of the passage. Within the written recalls, six of the students who selected *noises* included *their little grunts* as the subject of the second sentence; none of the students who selected *baby alligators* included this phrase.

It would be difficult to fault the way in which adult readers use the phrase *their little grunts* to select *noises*. Such use is what the test makers anticipated when they constructed the task. As one of them indicated during an interview, the quotation marks around *little grunts* signal to readers that they "should return to the point where this phrase is used in the passage." Once there, they are then in a position to carry out the operation described above. But most readers—adults as well as children—do not handle the task in this way. Why do they fail to do what the test makers anticipated a skilled reader should do? The passage is, after all, brief—it consists of only 38 words—so it is not difficult to locate *little grunts* and then carry out the bit of logical reasoning that produces the tautological phrase *The little grunts' little grunts*.

This question is not easy to answer, for it has to do with a range of subtle features that cause *baby alligators* and *little grunts* to run together in the reader's mind. Some of them have to do with the passage structure, others with the task structure, and still others with the structure of human thought itself. As to the passage structure, it is important to bear in mind just what its central point is: the mother alligator's restricted experience of her babies, which leads her, contrary to most readers' expectations, to experience them only as auditory sensations. The baby alligators are, for her, only the little grunts they make; and so the reader, identifying with the mother alligator's point of view, equates *baby alligators* and *little grunts*. As one child put it,

> The mother doesn't hear noises—she hears her babies.

Another child captured this same point when she was asked to write down what she had just read. Her response was to first write a brief summary and then draw a picture (see Figure 7.10). This child captures the central point of the passage in her initial sentence (note the crossed out *see*, which represents the normative experience) and then reinforces it in

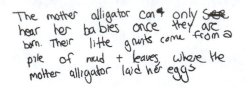

FIGURE 7.10

the drawing, in which the mother is represented as thinking "If only I could see my babies!!!"

It is useful to examine the stylistic texture of the passage to determine how readers are led to adopt the mother alligator's point of view. To begin with, her experience, as already suggested, is consistently anthropomorphized. Fundamental to this style is the use of nouns such as *mother* and *babies* and the accompanying pronouns *she* and *they*. It is instructive to examine the original passage alongside a version in which these markers have been removed:

The first time a mother alligator hears her babies, she cannot see them. Their little grunts are coming from a pile of mud and old leaves. That is where the mother alligator laid her eggs many weeks ago.	The first time an alligator hears its offspring, it cannot see them. Their little grunts are coming from a pile of mud and old leaves. That is where the alligator laid its eggs many weeks ago.

In the version on the right, the alligators and the babies come off as less anthropomorphized.

It is not only certain nouns and pronouns that stimulate a reader's identification with the mother alligator's experience. A temporal expression such as *many weeks ago*, as compared to, say, *many weeks earlier*, presupposes a personal center; and, perhaps to a lesser degree, *the first time* does as well; or to use the language first introduced in LEARNING TO READ, these temporal expressions are deictically anchored—and it is, of course, the mother alligator's 'now' in which they are anchored. In addition, the verbs *hear* and *see* tend to presuppose a personal center, even though we concede that a substitute for these verbs is not easy to find.

Added to this larger gestalt of features are powerful features at the local point where the crucial phrase *Their little grunts* occurs:

1) the use of *little* within this phrase; and
2) the use of *are coming* immediately after it.

In its prototypical use, the modifier *little* refers to an entity that possesses 'bodily extension,' and hence the reader tends to think of the creatures—the baby alligators—that are emitting the grunts. In addition, the verb *come* tends to be associated with agents that can move under their own volition; hence it too, tends to support the association of *grunts* with the baby alligators. When one child discovered that the target response was *noises*, she responded indignantly:

How could...how could sounds...sounds come? They cannot walk or anything.

We should note that the use of progressive aspect with *come* strengthens the association with agents that can move under their own volition. During the interviewing, a number of children used the progressive form of *come* to describe the babies coming out of the pile of mud and old leaves. Here, for example, is how one child justified his choice of *baby alligators*:

So *baby alligators* meant that the babies were coming up from a mud pile and the mother alligator can't see them.

Another child, in fact, made this connection explicit:

Their little grunts are coming from a pile of mud means the baby alligators are coming from the mud.

It is interesting to observe that the use of *come* without progressive aspect considerably dampens this effect:

Their little grunts *come* from a pile of mud and old leaves.

To confirm the powerful effect of the features we have described, we administered the probe in Figure 7.11 to 30 children. All of the children filled in the blank with a word that refers to an entity with bodily extension that can move under its own volition. The most popular choice was *animals* (11 children chose this word). We suspect that if *the* had been used in place of *their*, children would have tended to select creatures like snakes or worms that crawl out from under a pile of leaves.

To sum up, the passage provides not only local features that counteract the effect of *their* before *little grunts*, but also a larger gestalt of features that signal human identification with the mother alligator. These features work together so that *little grunts* and *baby alligators* can become virtually indistinguishable in a reader's mind.

It is not simply the passage that stimulates such identification: the task stem does as well, particularly through its use of quotation marks around *little grunts*. Quotation marks are, of course, used in written language for different reasons: for example, they could have been used, as the test makers claim, merely to indicate that *little grunts* is being recycled from the passage. However, quotation marks are not used for this purpose in any task in our corpus. Rather, they are used to indicate that certain words have a special status. In ADVERTISING TAILOR, for example, the phrase *hammered out a wardrobe* is enclosed in quotation marks to indicate that it is used figuratively in the passage. Extrapolating from this use, we might assume that they have the same function here. If we search the passage for evidence to support this assumption, we are led to the thematic focus on how the mother alligator equates the little grunts with her babies.

Another effect of the quotation marks is that it makes *little grunts* seem like a familiar name, particularly given the frequency of *little* as a component in such naming within children's literature. It is obvious that children have had a good deal of exposure to names like Little Bo Peep, Little Lulu, Chicken Little, and L'il Abner. The quotation marks also highlight the parallelism between *little grunts* and *baby alligators*. Each begins with a modifier signifying 'diminutive.' As one child put it,

> The reason I was attracted by *baby alligators* was that *little* and *baby* are often used in place of each other.

Please fill in the blank with one word.

Their little _____ are coming from a pile of mud and old leaves.

FIGURE 7.11

He went on to give the example of *little ducklings* and *baby ducklings*.

Even if the use of quotation marks does not lead to the effects that we have noted, it does signal that the words *little* and *grunts* are to be taken as a unit, and processing them in this way makes it more difficult to select *noises*. From a pragmatic point of view, it is more natural to think of grunts rather than little grunts as a kind of 'noise,' since conceptual classification usually involves a stripping away of extraneous information. Preserving such information is particularly confusing in this instance because *little*, as already indicated, modifies *grunts* in a peculiar way. Although *little* prototypically refers to an entity that possesses 'bodily extension,' it can be used in semantic domains where such extension is lacking. Consider, for example, the domain of 'sounds.' It appears that *little* is extended to this domain almost by default: no other modifier is readily available to signify diminutive status for 'sounds.' But notice the effects of this extension in an utterance like

> Hear those little squeaks coming from the kitchen? The mice must be at it again.

Little indicates diminutive status with respect not merely to the sounds (i.e., the squeaks) but also the creatures emitting those sounds (i.e., the mice). It is as though *little* retains something of its central function even as it takes on a more peripheral one. Such retention is not accidental but rather reflects a basic property of language, one that helps us to resolve the paradox that we initially posed: how can a reader take *little grunts* as referring to both the baby alligators as well as the sounds that they make?

In order to get a clearer sense of how the phrase *little grunts* works, we asked 20 adults to write down whatever they associated with it. Here are the kinds of things they wrote down:

> 11 responses had to do with people or animals (e.g., elves, puny brats, small pigs, hungry pigs, unhappy midgets);

> 5 responses had to do with sounds (3 included the word *sounds* and 2 the word *noises*); and

> 4 responses had to do with private activities (e.g., going to the bathroom, the end of sexual intercourse).

To return to the matter of the task stem, we would suggest that both quotation marks and the modifier *little* be removed if *noises* is intended as the target response. This would reduce the stem to the following:

> The grunts in the story are _____ .

Even this form of the stem is likely to favor *baby alligators*. The premodifier *the* and the postmodifier *in the story* work together to focus attention on what *grunts* refers to in the passage, and so the reader can still be pulled toward *baby alligators*. If the initial *the* is removed altogether and *in the story* takes its place, the attraction to *baby alligators* is further reduced:

> In the story, grunts are _____ .

This is the ordinary position within tasks for the formulaic expression *in the story*, and it is not clear why it has been placed after the head noun in this task.

Ideally, the expression *in the story* should be totally removed since, even in initial position, it can encourage the reader to imagine how the mother alligator experiences the little grunts. Hence the stem could be ultimately stripped down to

> Grunts are _____ .

In this form, the task, at last, has become independent of the passage. The metalinguistic status of the task is now transparent, and so it would make sense to remove it altogether from MOTHER ALLIGATOR and present it as part of a vocabulary test. In this way, the confusion would be avoided that so often results from including a vocabulary-defining task on a test of reading comprehension.[10]

It might be useful at this point to summarize all the features in the task that stimulate the choice of *baby alligators*. Figure 7.12 presents a flow chart in which these features, one by one, are stripped away until the metalinguistic function of the task is, at last, transparent.

It is not simply that crucial aspects of passage structure and task structure lend support to the choice of *baby alligators*—there are certain structural aspects of human thinking that support this choice as well. There is a natural tendency for us to associate a sound with whatever emits it: a siren with a fire engine, loud roaring overhead with a jet plane, night-time crying with a hungry baby. This tendency helps to explain our extreme discomfort when we hear sounds—all those creaks and cracks in the night—that we cannot attribute to a physical source. It also helps to explain why so many readers experience no discomfort at all in running together *baby alligators* and *little grunts*: the alligators and the sounds they emit can be thought of as one, particularly since that is the

Original:	The "little grunts" in the story are _____.
Remove quotation marks:	The little grunts in the story are _____.
Remove *little:*	The grunts in the story are _____.
Shift *in the story:*	In the story, the grunts are _____.
Remove *the:*	In the story, grunts are _____.
Remove *in the story:*	Grunts are _____.

FIGURE 7.12

way the mother alligator, at least as she is represented in the passage, experiences them.

Having examined readers' attraction to *baby alligators*, we would now like to examine their rejection of *noises*. To begin with, many children thought that identifying grunts as noises was too easy. Consider, for example, this simple exchange between an interviewer and a child:

I   What do you think little grunts are?
C   *Noises,* but *baby alligators* is right.

The word *noises* was uttered with such disdain that the effect was "any fool knows that a grunt is a kind of noise, so clearly noises cannot be the answer." Another boy reflected much the same attitude:

I   What's your answer to (B)?
C   *Baby alligators.* It says *she cannot see them. Their little grunts* mean the alligators, the little alligators.[11]
I   Little grunts is the same as baby alligators?
C   No. *Their* means—their little grunts came from the babies.
I   The little grunts came from the babies, right?
C   Yes.
I   But they're not really the babies?
C   The little grunts in the story are *noises.* I made a mistake. That's too easy. Anybody knows what *noises* means.

At this point, he became upset and refused to talk any further about this test unit.

The reactions of these children provide support for a point made by Aronowitz (1984): if children think of a particular word as familiar, it may be difficult for them to deal with a task that calls for this word to be defined—or, in this instance, exemplified. This seems to be particularly the case for children who adopt a communicative orientation to text. It is for this reason that in the conclusions we recommend that test makers reconsider the way in which they use vocabulary-defining tasks on reading tests.

Fillmore (1982) has made a related point with respect to vocabulary-defining tasks: namely, that the definition that they call for is often not exact. To illustrate this point, he provides the following example from the Stanford Achievement Test:

> To seek is to _____ .
>   find   see
>   settle   search

The target response is *search*, but as Fillmore points out, it differs substantially from *seek*. We can say, for example, *He sought his fortune* or *He searched his room*, but not **He searched his fortune* or **He sought his room*. The careful reader might well reject *search* on these grounds, particularly since selecting *find* would result in, as Fillmore puts it, "a meaningful, if not particularly wise, proverb: to seek is to find" (1982, p. 26). We can observe, once again, the conflict between the communicative and acommunicative that is so fundamental to test taking.

The adults who wrote about their response to this task gave various reasons for feeling that *noises* was not an appropriate word for categorizing *little grunts*. One pointed out that it lacked specificity:

> I was going to choose *noises*, but then decided *baby alligators* was more specific.

Another pointed out that it lacked thematicity:

> *Baby alligators* was tempting. I've been trained to focus on what's most important in a passage. Noises are not important to me. Baby alligators are.

Another adult combined these two reasons in a more extended statement:

> Since grunts literally are noises, I thought that perhaps *noises* was the answer. On the other hand, since noises was never mentioned in the selection, I decided that the phrase *little alligators* [notice once again the mixing of the two crucial phrases] was the only thing in the text that *grunts*

referred to. By *noises* I assumed the questioner means something more general than baby alligator sounds and that *baby alligators* were better because that answer located the source of the noise more specifically.

The children we interviewed were also concerned about a lack of specificity in selecting *noises*. Consider the following exchange with an African American boy who clearly had the word *specific* in mind in the following exchange:

  C   *Baby alligators* was the best answer.
  I   Why do you say that?
  C   'Cause it was *noises*, but if you want to be more 'pecific, you have to say *baby alligators*.

A similar point was brought up by another child who prided herself on being an expert reader:

  C   And the little grunts in the story were baby alligators because it says the mother alligator heard her babies but could not see them, the little grunts. They were grunt babies.[12]
  I   Ummm. And why couldn't the answer be anything else?
  C   Well, it certainly couldn't be *eggs*—very unusual for eggs to make grunts. But they could have been *noises*.
  I   Why didn't you choose *noises*?
  C   Well, *baby alligators* were much more to the point.
  I   If someone wished to choose *noises*, could you say they were wrong?
  C   Well, I would think that they didn't read very well.
  I   Well, what if the person said that the grunting sound isn't a baby alligator?

The child now becomes aware that *noises* is, in fact, the target response and mouths the word in an almost pouting manner. Having absorbed this blow to her pride, she quickly counters:

Okay, they [the grunts] are, but they are also baby alligators. That's more to the point because it didn't say anything about noises.

This child did not initially consider *noises* and then consciously reject it, as did the adults who are quoted above. When she does, however, formulate her reasons against selecting *noises*, they are very much like those of the adults: she considers it to be lacking in specificity (i.e., *baby alligators* is, as she put it, "more to the point") and thematicity (i.e., the passage "didn't say anything about noises").

This child also came up with an ingenious argument to counter the notion that *their* necessarily refers to the baby alligators. As she observed, *their* could refer to the mother rather than the babies, since, as she put it, "the story is really talking about all mother alligators, not just one." When she made this observation, we were forced to concede that she had a point: clearly the semantic force of *a mother alligator* is generic.[13]

There is psycholinguistic evidence to show that readers tend to process a generic noun as plural, even though its form is singular. We did not administer a probe to determine whether children tend to process *a mother alligator* in the opening sentence as singular or plural. We did, however, administer a probe to 20 children in which the passage was altered so that *the baby alligators'* was substituted for *their* in sentence 2. Even with this more explicit version, all the children except one still chose *baby alligators*. Apparently the larger gestalt of features that support this choice overwhelm the local detail, even when it is more palpable, that blocks it.

To sum up, all the readers we have presented above—child and adult—evoke, in some form or another, the principle of 'lack of exact fit' to reject *noises*. Such a use of this principle is ironic since the test makers had intended that it be used to reject *baby alligators* rather than *noises*. It is also ironic that test makers rely on a principle of substitutability, even though its use can be misleading on other test units. Consider, for example, a unit that we refer to as NERVOUS HORSE.

> Her horse was a little nervous, so she let it trot along slowly. Suddenly, something in the bushes rustled. The horse broke into a canter, then into a full gallop. She held on tightly, talking quietly to try to calm it.

> A.   Which pace is the slowest?
>   a canter   a rustle
>   a gallop   a trot

> B.   In the story, "broke into" means
>   robbed   ran into
>   started   tamed

If *started*, the target response for (B), is substituted for *broke into*, an ill-formed sentence results:

> *The horse started a canter, then a full gallop.

By replacing *a* with *to*, one can, of course, achieve a structurally acceptable sentence:

> The horse started to canter, then to gallop.

But even this sentence would reflect a certain semantic discontinuity with the original one. The verb *broke into* introduces an activity that functions in a contrastive relation with a preceding one (i.e., the horse was already trotting when it began to canter, and it was already cantering when it started to gallop). But the use of *started* does not necessarily carry this presupposition (i.e., you can start up an activity from scratch). As a consequence, when *started* is substituted for *broke into*, the notion is not preserved that the horse was doing something else before it began to canter.

Once we shift the principle of substitutability from structural to semantic grounds, we can make an additional argument against the use of *noises* in place of *little grunts* in MOTHER ALLIGATOR. Given the stylistic texture of the passage, readers are forced to identify with the mother alligator's point of view, and, as we have suggested, she does not experience the little grunts as noises, but rather as her own baby alligators. A number of children were visibly upset when they discovered that *noises* was the "right answer." They seemed to feel that it was insulting to the mother alligator to use such a word in describing the sounds that her babies made. As one girl put it,

> The baby alligators weren't making noises. They were just calling for their mother.

From her vantage point, the word *noises* was too harsh in representing how the babies sounded to the mother alligator's loving ear. She went on to claim that the word "sounds, at least, wouldn't sound so bad." Of course this girl has not been a mother who is forced to wake up at night when her baby cries.

It is interesting that one child, while defending his choice of *noises*, slipped inadvertently into using *sounds* in its place:

I   So why did you choose *noises*?
C   I thought it is either *baby alligators* or *noises*. But it is *noises*.
I   Why?
C   It says that the mother alligator cannot see the babies. I don't know the meaning of *grunts*, and I thought it is *voices* or *sounds*, as they come from under that mud. The mother alligator heard the sounds.
I   Who is making sounds?
C   Baby alligators. The mother alligator could not see her babies. So the answer should not be the babies, but the sounds they are making.

He then goes on to explain why he was attracted by *baby alligators*:

The reason I wanted to choose *baby alligators* was that *little* and *babies* are used in the same way, like *little ducklings* and *baby ducklings*.

Apparently the two crucial phrases, *little grunts* and *baby alligators*, had run together in his mind as well.

We can think of an additional reason why *sounds* is semantically preferable to *noises* as a description of *grunts* within the passage: the word *noise*, much more than *sound*, tends to be used to describe an unspecified auditory perception, something whose source is amorphous and cannot easily be identified. In describing the book from which the passage is excerpted, we pointed out how the mother alligator, upon hearing the grunts, knew that it was her babies and went straight to the pile of mud and old leaves in order to dig them out. We suspect that all the subtle features we have described were at play in the discomfort that so many test takers felt with the choice *noises*.

When one of us ran into one of the children we had interviewed nearly a year and a half later, she reminisced about her experience and began to talk about "mother crocodile." She mentioned the babies who, as she put it, "were blind at birth but opened their eyes once they began to move about." This transfer of an inability to see from mother to babies was presumably a further example of leakage from one unit to another. One of the practice units on the mock-test that she had taken began with the following sentence:

Kittens are blind at birth but once their eyes are open they begin to go adventuring.

As we continued to talk, it became apparent that other units had run together in her memory as well. Having worked intensively with many children, we have come to view such leakage as an inevitable consequence of their working through a sequence of short incomplete passages under time pressure. The incompleteness, we suspect, encourages the leakage, for it is only human nature to try to bring together disparate bits of text that do not stand well on their own. To borrow a phrase from the linguist Michael Halliday, human beings are, in their very essence, "text-making creatures."

NOTES

1. In teacher talk, this movement may be, at times, difficult to discern, particularly if it is not overtly signaled. In oral discourse, we have no standardized

device for indicating this movement, as we do in written discourse (i.e., leaving a blank space between the language sample and tasks). We do, of course, possess an ample repertoire of paraverbal and nonverbal resources for marking this movement.

2. We should note that children develop sensitivity to stylistic matters at an early age. Research by Georgia Green (1983) suggests that children, even at the age of 5 or 6, show a considerable capacity for distinguishing different styles of writing.

3. There are writers such as Loren Eiseley and Annie Dillard who use an imaginative style in presenting the natural world to adults. An anthropomorphizing quality can be detected here as well, but its effects tend to be different. These writers are generally committed to the idea that poetry and science are ultimately indissoluble, and so they use one as a means to the other.

4. Some of the awkwardness of (A) would have been alleviated if it had been prefaced with the formulaic expression—*The story says that*—sometimes used to introduce a recycling task.

5. This response may reflect some leakage from JAYS AND CROWS, in which *the dry, crackling ocean of leaves* is used in describing the nature scene.

6. It is common for such a frame to be specified when a past progressive verb is used (e.g., *The fog was coming in while we rowed across the lake*).

7. From a biological point of view, it is, of course, accurate to describe any living thing as *dying*, though such a description does not accord with our everyday way of thinking.

8. Notice that she uses *was* with *they*. She also used this verb when reading (A): *The green trees was cedars.*

9. There were also international students among the adults who responded to this unit. Their responses are not included in the tally reported previously, but it is interesting that those who selected *noises* tended to provide the same reason for their choice. One Japanese student wrote the following:

> First I thought it might be *baby alligators*. Then I reconsidered the words *their* and *grunts*. When we use *their* in this sentence, it means *baby alligators*. So I decided to circle *noises*.

10. Strictly speaking, this task is not vocabulary-defining, but concept-categorizing. If it were to be a vocabulary-defining task, it would take the following form:

> The word *grunts* means _____.

Such a stem would, of course, preclude the choice of *noises* as the target response since it would be considered too general.

11. Notice the mixing of the two crucial phrases, *little* from *little grunts* and *alligator* from *baby alligators*.

12. Here is a further example of the merging of *little grunts* and *baby alligators*. The merging of these two phrases leads more predictably to the phrase *baby grunts*, which was used by one child in the following sentence: "She can't really see them, her baby grunts." It is interesting that when *grunt* precedes

babies, we can almost hear the word *runt* lurking in it. We suspect that the association between *grunt* and *runt* was strong for many children—and adults too—and may have strengthened their attraction to *baby alligators* in ways that are virtually impossible to detect.

13. This girl loved to analyze test units and became adept at identifying various problems. We were dismayed to discover that the following year she began to have difficulties with standardized tests. Her teacher observed that she would choose, almost as a matter of principle, a distractor and then defend it passionately. We hope that her participation in our research has not diminished her ability to perform well on reading tests. If it has, our only defense is that it has made her a more critical reader.

Part IV

Conclusions

We have traversed a good deal of territory in examining how children interact with test units designed to assess reading comprehension. We have dealt with 22 units, the number children must work through on a typical reading test. For an experienced reader, 22 units of this kind do not seem intimidating: each of them consists of only three or four sentences whose total number of words rarely reaches 50. But as our analyses have shown, there can be a substantial distance between words and the world they represent. In fact, the magnitude of that distance often has an inverse relation to the number of words, since the more sparse the text, the more work children have to do in constructing a coherent world.

In the case of experienced readers, this work is largely automated and easily goes unnoticed; in the case of children, such work can be burdensome. As they work through 22 worlds, each quite different from the other, they are often overwhelmed by the welter of detail they encounter. There are the various worlds of nature, ranging from icebergs to cedar forests to mother alligators; and there are the various worlds of human affairs—the public ones that deal with food preservation or bridge construction and the more personal ones that tell of a train trip or a young girl's anxiety about learning to read. Children must enter and leave each of these worlds rapidly if they are to complete all the tasks in the allotted time. After they absorb the considerable detail of one world, they must abandon it—and abandon it thoroughly—or else they risk contaminating the worlds they have yet to enter.

In presenting these multiple worlds, our strategy has been to bring an individual unit into focus and conduct a comprehensive discourse analysis that deals not only with its textual problems (e.g., the passage presents an incomplete world) but children's ways of handling such problems (e.g., in fleshing out the passage, they end up with an enriched world of meaning that misleads them as they work with the tasks). Having worked through each test unit in this way, we now turn to five issues that have emerged as central to our study:

1) passage-task configurations
2) inferencing
3) real-world knowledge
4) metalinguistic demands
5) task structure

After considering these issues, we will turn our attention to the policy implications of this study.

chapter 8

Implications of the Study

A common way of thinking about reading test material is that the passage represents the material to be comprehended and the tasks are simply there to make sure that comprehension has taken place. To our way of thinking, the text to be comprehended is constituted by both the passage and the tasks. There are at least two ways in which multiple-choice tasks contribute to the difficulty of processing a test unit. First, since test takers are not in a position to know in advance which choice will lead to the target proposition, they are forced, at least in principle, to generate multiple sentences by trying out each choice. In the units in our corpus, working through the two tasks potentially leads to producing eight sentences, which represent a considerable amount of textual space in relation to the three or four sentences that constitute the typical passage. The fact that task propositions are generated in the child's mind rather than written out on the page may well add to their weight within the larger text structure.

Second, as has been demonstrated repeatedly in this book, each of these task propositions has the potential for initiating interpretations that did not occur during the initial reading of the passage. Thus, as test takers look for the task sentence that can be best integrated with the passage, they may be led down paths that take them far beyond the norms of everyday reading comprehension—and far beyond the simple model in which a task is seen as validating or invalidating an interpretation that has already been arrived at.

PASSAGE-TASK CONFIGURATIONS

In this study we have delineated different ways in which children establish a larger textual world in which the passage and one or more tasks are integrated as they search for the target response. In describing such integration, we use the term PASSAGE-TASK CONFIGURATION and present here three such configurations in which children were led to select a particular distractor on one or more of the tasks. We describe these configurations as the COMMUNICATIVE CONFIGURATION, FRAME CONFIGURATION, and POLARITY CONFIGURATION.

Communicative Configuration

At various points in our study, we have focused on a fundamental tension between two orientations that we describe as *communicative* and *acommunicative*. In using these terms, we are calling attention to the various ways in which testing practices suspend the communicative norms that govern everyday language use (see pp. 93–94 for further discussion). In applying these terms to test units, we have delineated a configuration in which a communicative passage is followed by a task that combines an acommunicative target response with one or more communicative distractors.

Before examining units that represent this configuration, we would like to consider how the tension between communicative and acommunicative arises from particular constraints that test makers work with. The passages themselves tend to be communicatively oriented, since test makers generally select material originally written for a real-world context or construct material that they feel is similar to real-world texts.

With respect to the tasks, the acommunicative orientation of the target response comes largely from the constraint on test makers to supply an answer that can be clearly defended. As a consequence, they are forced to avoid a constructivist approach to reading comprehension—even if they might prefer it on theoretical grounds—and devise a target response that depends only on information in the text base, as opposed to the situation model that readers construct. The communicative orientation of the distractors comes largely from the pressure on test makers to construct a task that can pull its own weight; that is to say, unless a certain proportion of test takers chooses one or more distractors, a task does not have sufficient discriminatory power to be useful on a test. To insure such power, test makers are led to construct distractors that are genuinely attractive; and the most attractive distractor is one that results from an inference that the passage invites readers to make. Thus, in the communicative configuration, the target response comes from the text base, whereas at least one of the distractors is related to a situation model that some readers are likely to construct.

In illustrating a communicative configuration, we can begin with MOTHER ALLIGATOR. The passage in this unit is centrally concerned with the fact that a mother alligator is unable to see her babies at birth, since they are hatched from eggs that she has buried. As a consequence, she initially experiences her babies only by the "little grunts" they make at birth.

When children come to (B), they discover a task with the stem *In the story the "little grunts" are* _____; and when they come to the choices for (B), they discover *baby alligators*, a choice that parallels the words placed in quotation marks in the stem. By setting up the equation *baby alligators = little grunts*, children are able to capture the central point of the passage—namely, that a mother alligator, since she cannot see her babies when they are born, experiences them only by the sounds they make. Once the passage information has been accommodated to the communicative distractor, test takers are then in a position to select that distractor as the target response.

There is, however, one detail that cannot be readily assimilated to the equation *little grunts = baby alligators*: namely, *little grunts*, as used in the passage, is modified by *their*, which refers to the baby alligators. If little grunts are thus identified as the baby alligators, the result is the tautologous phrase *baby alligators' baby alligators*. To avoid such an illogicality, test takers should select *noises* as the target response. Many children resist making this choice because it does not fit with their sense of what the passage is really about.

The textual configuration that we have just described is represented in Figure 8.1. Within this figure, the overall drift of the passage, which leads to the communicative distractor, is represented by dark shading, while the detail in the passage that supports the acommunicative target response is represented by lighter shading.

Let us now consider ALICE AND THE FAWN, a unit that invites children not simply to interpret the passage holistically but to expand it in some way. This unit readily invites expansion, since it was drawn from imaginative literature with virtually no editorial adjustments. Moreover, this unit contains the two most common types of acommunicative task: (1) one that recycles relatively unimportant information from the passage, and (2) one that merely defines a word from the passage. At the same time, each task presents a communicative distractor that leads children to expand the excerpted narrative they must work with. In the case of the recycling task in (A), the distractor *frightened* encourages children to imagine how the fawn "really looked," particularly since the passage ends by describing the fawn as *moving back* when Alice tries to touch it

COMMUNICATIVE
PASSAGE

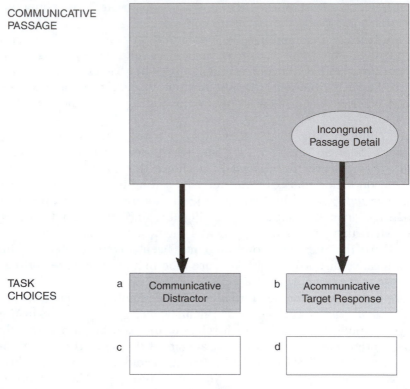

FIGURE 8.1

(i.e., the children are left with an image of a skittish animal in retreat). In the case of the vocabulary-defining task in (B), the distractor *help it* leads children to imagine what Alice was "really trying to do" in reaching out to the fawn. In either case, the communicative distractor stimulates the kinds of constructive responses that teachers encourage children to make when reading imaginative literature.

In dealing with the two tasks, however, children are expected to suppress such responses. To begin with, each of the distractors leads to a proposition that does not fit exactly with certain information in the passage. In considering *frightened* as a response to (A), children should, in principle, be aware of the explicit statement that the fawn did not seem at all frightened (as we pointed out, however, the modality inherent in *seem* can lead children to select *frightened*). In considering *help it* as a response to (B), they should be aware that the passage does not actually indicate that the fawn was in need of assistance. Any inference that Alice was helping the fawn is thus not directly motivated by the passage.

For both tasks an acommunicative target response is available that fits neatly with a passage detail. For (A), the test taker should select *gentle* since the fawn's eyes are described as *large* and *gentle* in the first sentence. For (B), the test taker should select *pet it*, since *pet* parallels *stroke*, at least as it is used in the passage. In effect, the test taker is expected to know that both tasks call for an acommunicative target response, even though this intent is not indicated in the surface wording of either.

Frame Configuration

When dealing with the frame configuration, the reader is confronted with (1) a passage that moves from an initial frame to an alternative one, and (2) a mainly-about task in which a distractor fits with the initial frame, while the target response fits with the one that follows (see Figure 8.2).

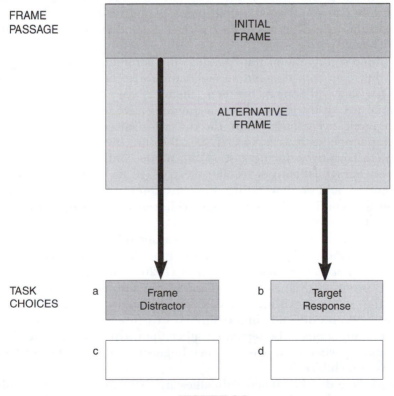

FIGURE 8.2

To illustrate how a test unit embodies the frame configuration, we can examine JAYS AND CROWS, a unit whose opening words are *It was the season of jays and crows*. On the basis of these words, certain children, particularly those who accept conventional school wisdom about how best to structure a paragraph, assume that the passage will be mainly concerned with birds. As the passage develops, these children are faced with information that should, in principle, lead them to alter their initial framing from 'birds' to 'sounds.' It is these two choices—the frame distractor *birds* and the target response *sounds*—that children must distinguish when they respond to the mainly-about task that follows the passage.

It is generally assumed that a mainly-about task is fundamentally oriented to content, and using our categories, it would be classified as *communicative*. From our vantage point, however, it is more oriented to structure and thus better classified as *acommunicative* (or, more specifically, as *metalinguistic*, a point to which we will return), since it requires children to focus on how the text organizes what it conveys. In our discussion of JAYS AND CROWS, we presented a detailed scheme of the textual organization that justifies the selection of *sounds* rather than *birds* (see p. 200); as we indicated at that point, young readers who focus on meaning cannot be expected to have access, even at an intuitive level, to such a scheme.

The frame configuration thus parallels the communicative configuration in that they both demand an acommunicative orientation to reading. The key difference between them is in the role of the communicative distractor within an acommunicative task. In the case of the communicative configuration, the distractor encourages children to take the passage, as it were, too far (i.e., they are invited to expand an incomplete narrative). In the case of the frame configuration, the distractor encourages them not to take the passage far enough (i.e., they are invited to hold on to what they first encounter). Or to put it another way, the first configuration encourages children to be imaginative, the second to be cautious.

In our research we uncovered various reasons for children's susceptibility to a frame configuration. Perhaps most fundamental are those related to developmental issues. As Piaget (1926) points out, young children are prone to what he calls *syncretism*: the accommodation of new information to a pre-existing frame. Compounding this syncretistic tendency is children's difficulty in focusing on structure: their basic orientation in reading tends to be semantic rather than structural, a point that we will amplify when we discuss the metalinguistic demands that reading tests make on children.

Beyond these developmental difficulties are those that have to do with what children are taught in school. A frame configuration can be especially misleading to children who follow the commonly heard admonition to begin with the tasks and then scan the passage in order to find information that would justify particular choices. For children who adopt this strategy, the initial part of the passage often carries undue weight and so they are led to select the distractor that matches the initial frame that they should, in fact, abandon. By the same token, a frame configuration can be misleading to children who work with the notion that a paragraph is initiated by a topic sentence. During the pilot testing the usual gap between African American and European American children was diminished when they were responding to a mainly-about task within a frame configuration. In fact, the European American children were even more attracted to the frame distractor for two such tasks. One plausible interpretation of these results is that the European American children were more susceptible to the misleading notion that a paragraph is initiated by a topic sentence (see pp. 185–186 for discussion). Due to the limited nature of the pilot testing, these results can be only suggestive, but they are sufficiently intriguing to warrant a more detailed investigation of test units based on a frame configuration.

Polarity Configuration

Within the polarity configuration, the reader is confronted with (1) a passage built around multiple lexical polarities, and (2) a task that includes choices embodying various values for these polarities. Such a configuration is illustrated in Figure 8.3: $\pm X$ and $\pm Y$ represent lexical polarities in the passage that can be realized in varying ways; beneath them are the four possible combinations of these two polarities. The arrows show how each of these can be the basis of one of the choices.

Figure 8.3 represents the polarity configuration in full flower, with each of the possible combinations realized as a choice. More typical is a unit in which two or three choices are based on polarities. The only unit in our corpus in which all the choices for a task are based on polarities is RAISINS. In order to answer (B), a task that requires children to describe the best climate for making raisins, children must select among four choices, all of which combine a temperature term with a humidity term. Using $\pm X$ to represent temperature and $\pm Y$ to represent humidity, we can describe the four choices in the following way:

warm and dry $[+X, -Y]$ cool and dry $[-X, -Y]$
warm and wet $[+X, +Y]$ cool and wet $[-X, +Y]$

The target response is *warm and dry* $(+X, -Y)$, since the passage indicates that raisins are made by spreading grapes to dry in the sun. Dur-

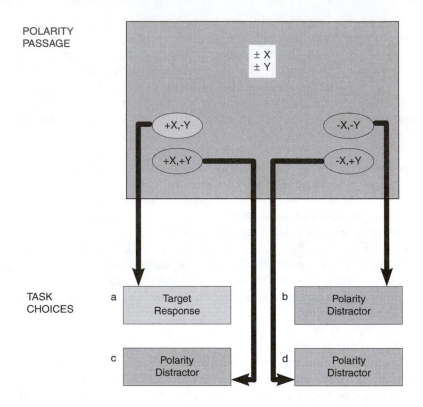

POLARITY
PASSAGE

TASK
CHOICES

FIGURE 8.3

ing the interviewing, certain children experienced difficulty in processing these four choices together. Certainly, children who easily handle a phrase such as *warm and dry* in ordinary prose can become confused when it is placed alongside *warm and wet*, *cold and wet*, and *cold and dry* within a test question. It is as if they experience a paradigmatic vertigo that prevents them from focusing successfully on any single choice.

In characterizing children's difficulties with polarity units, we can introduce the terms WIRE-CROSSING and GAP-JUMPING to describe two major sources of confusion. Although these sources can be clearly differentiated, they both can be traced to the fact that the poles within a lexical opposition are more similar than is commonly realized. Typically, they share a bundle of semantic features and differ by only one feature.

In the case of a wire-crossing response, children inadvertently replace one lexical pole with its opposite: for example, they can slip, in responding to (B) in RAISINS, from a negative pole such as *dry* to the opposing pole *wet*. Such slippage results in the phrase *warm and wet*, in which both poles are positive. The fact that wire-crossing responses often lead to a consistent valence—two positives or two negatives—suggests that they derive from psycholinguistic processes.

In the case of a gap-jumping response, the movement from one lexical pole to the other is not so much a matter of inadvertent slippage. It is rather that textual information, no matter how slight, may provoke children to shift from one pole to the other. In responding to RAISINS, certain children used the phrase *several weeks* to move from the lexical pole *dry*, which was well-established in the text, to the opposing pole *wet*, which was not explicitly named. These children reasoned that the climate had to be wet since it took several weeks for the grapes to dry. We should note that both wire-crossing and gap-jumping responses readily support the choice of the distractor *warm and wet*.

With respect to gap-jumping, we noticed that certain African American children were prone to make such a response not only to a polarity unit, but to other units as well. In responding to (A) in HURRICANE, a task that was designed to elicit a synonym for *knocked down*, certain African American children selected *strong*, reasoning that the trees had to have strength, since they were merely *knocked down*, unlike the houses which were *blown away*. When discussing this unit, we speculated that these children may have been working off a macroframe that could be described as 'strength in the face of adversity.' It is as if they set up a polarized relation between strength and adversity, or, to return to our current metaphor, they jumped from a textually established pole (i.e., adversity) to an opposing one based on an invited inference (i.e., strength).

A similar kind of response was made by certain African American children to (B) in JAYS AND CROWS, a task designed to recycle information (*silent air* ➔ *air is silent*). Working with the passage sentence that *harsh voices pierced the silent air*, they reasoned that the air could no longer be described as *silent*, since it had been pierced and had thus become harsh like the voices. In effect, these children displayed a certain dynamism in their response: if a particular entity is presented in one state but then is acted upon, that entity is best described in a new state to which the action leads.

If such dynamic responses are indeed more common among African American children, we suspect that they may reflect deeper processes of acculturation that can be quite difficult to document. In thinking about how best to characterize these processes, we would like to return to the research on spatial and temporal polarities (Hill, 1991) presented initially in LEARNING TO READ (pp. 109–111) and then in the introduction to polarity units (pp. 223–228). As briefly indicated, this research has uncovered ways in which African Americans tend to differ from European Americans in using lexical polarities such as *front/back:* for example, African Americans are more prone to interpret these terms non-deictically (i.e., anchoring them in an external point of reference); and even when they interpret these terms deictically (i.e., anchoring them in their own point of view), they make greater use of in-tandem imagery (i.e., viewing the external point of reference as oriented away from their own location in space).

In a semiotically oriented presentation of this research, Hill (1998) has suggested that such differences may simply represent the proverbial tip of an iceberg. In effect, African Americans—and, indeed, individuals from many other cultural traditions in different parts of the world who respond in a similar way—may be working off a system of information-processing that, in contrast to the one dominant in European cultural traditions, can be viewed as more projective. In effect, such individuals, rather than operating from a static vantage point, tend to project to external points of reference in describing spatial and temporal relations; and even when these individuals do work from their own point of view, they construct a deictic field as if they were themselves projected into it (i.e., their own front/back is congruent with that ascribed to the reference object).

If African Americans do make greater use of this system of information processing, then what we are here describing as a gap-jumping response may reflect this system: that is to say, rather than working from a textually established pole, readers can project to an opposing one, if information is provided that allows such projection to take place. In the case of JAYS AND CROWS, the information that allows projection from 'silence' to 'sound' is directly represented in the text. In the case of the other units, however, readers project from a textually established pole to an opposing one that is not overtly identified but which can be plausibly inferred: in RAISINS they project from 'dryness' to 'wetness' and in HURRICANE from 'adversity' to 'strength.' In all these instances, we can observe an active stance toward textual information—which obviously runs counter to the more static orientation that testing calls for—that leads a reader to project from one pole to its opposite.

In discussing such differences, we must be careful not to draw an overly sharp distinction between what individuals in different ethnocultural groups do. The research on spatial and temporal polarities has revealed a good deal of heterogeneity among both African Americans and European Americans. When this heterogeneity is more closely examined with respect to other variables—for example, age, gender, and socioeconomic class—it can be viewed as highly structured (Herzog, Weinreich, & Labov, 1968).

By the same token, the research we here report has uncovered European American as well as African American children using a textually established point to infer its opposite. We suspect that our research would have also yielded structured heterogeneity if it had been based experimentally on variables such as those listed above. As pointed out in Chapter 1, we view individual identity in modern society as complex: not only does it reflect various influences associated with age, gender, socioeconomic class, and ethnocultural group, but each of these variables is itself complex. If we consider, for example, only the ethnocultural variable, we can observe that individual identity is often comprised of different ethnocultural influences. It is for this reason that we characterize individual identity as transcultural.

We do not have space to explore this line of inquiry any further, but we would like to make one further point. Since African Americans, when operating within their own ethnocultural tradition, handle basic lexical polarities such as *front/back* and *before/after* in a different way, they may be particularly susceptible to any testing material built around lexical polarities. It is as if they are forced to continuously call into question the basic framework they use in handling such polarities, which, as we have shown, can be difficult even for children whose ethnocultural framework is more congruent with the test makers'. Such questioning can be particularly detrimental when students are responding to standardized tests that are expressly designed to reward those who respond rapidly. This speededness works against students from ethnoculturally diverse backgrounds, since they generally work with a more varied sociolinguistic repertoire and thus require more time when dealing with standard English.

Before leaving polarity units, we would like to make a final point: these test units tend to encourage a superficial mode of reading that we characterize as *symbol-manipulating* (as opposed to the mode we characterize as *knowledge-building*). We introduced these terms in connection with HARD LEAD, a unit that deals with the symbols stamped on pencils. We used the first term in describing how certain children were quite adept at manipulating the polarities involved in responding successfully to (B), a task that requires them to identify the kind of writing that results from the use of a pencil with hard lead. In order to identify the target response, children need to align three pairs of lexical polarities in the following way:

LEAD		WRITING
soft	→	thick and dark
hard	→	thin and light
		(only *light* is set up as the target response)

As we pointed out, many children had difficulty in aligning the polarities in this way because they must actively resist a normative alignment in which the positive terms and the negative terms are grouped separately:

hard, thick, dark   [+X, +Y, +Z]
soft, thin, light   [– X, –Y, –Z]

The children who avoided this normative alignment were generally able to respond appropriately; they were not, however, able to explain why hard lead results in writing that can be described as *light* (i.e., hard lead does not rub off on the page as easily as soft lead does). When we asked one boy who had quickly aligned the polarities to provide an explanation, he responded somewhat curtly that "the story didn't talk about that"; he was obviously impatient to move on to the next task. This child was, in fact, a skilled test taker and had wisely learned not to be distracted by the content of the various worlds he must move through rapidly.

We do not wish to undervalue the strategic intelligence this child displayed: there was an elegance in the way that he selected relevant bits of information and aligned them in an appropriate way. What is unfortunate is the way that the testing situation encouraged him to avoid any real curiosity about the deeper meaning of what he was reading. As has often been observed, testing exercises a powerful influence on curriculum and instruction and thus encourages an unduly narrow focus on what we are here describing as symbol manipulation.

INFERENCING

In describing three major kinds of configuration in our corpus of test material, we have dealt with a range of inferences that these configurations lead children to make; and, as we have seen, these inferences, in turn, can lead children to select a distractor. As we consider the domain of inferencing more systematically, we would like to focus as well on inferences that lead to the choice of a target response. We will use the framework introduced in Chapter 1 to categorize the various kinds of inferences—those leading to a target response as well as to a distractor—that are on display in the preceding section. We will be largely concerned with inferences that can be described as *motivated* or *invited*, since both kinds of inferences constitute a relatively normative response in real-world reading. In Chapter 1, we pointed out that

1) a motivated inference can be associated with a *motivated situation model* (i.e., in constructing such a model, the reader makes inferences that are directly motivated by the text base); and

2) an invited inference can be associated with an *invited situation model* (i.e., in constructing such a model, the reader makes inferences which, though not directly motivated by the text base, are stimulated by it).

As already indicated, it can be difficult to distinguish between these two kinds of inferences, especially when they involve the use of real-world knowledge. We will mention only briefly our other two categories of inference, *automated* and *extended* (see pp. 9–11 for discussion of these categories).

Motivated Inferencing

Let us begin our consideration of motivated inferences by focusing on those that lead to the target response. In presenting the polarity configuration, we focused on a mainly-about task that calls for readers to conduct a structural analysis of the text base in order to select the target response. In responding to JAYS AND CROWS, for example, readers, once they have analyzed information in the text base, are then in a position to infer that sounds are both more pervasive and prominent than birds. In effect, such an inference is motivated by structural properties in the text base.

In certain instances, readers are faced with a problematical choice between this kind of motivated inference leading to a target response and an invited inference that leads to a distractor. To illustrate such a choice, we can return to the mainly-about task in SHOP SIGN, where readers can infer that the sign is the most pervasive and prominent bit of information in the text base. Since that base represents, however, only a truncated narrative, the use of the word *story* in the task stem invites readers to infer that the new shop that the sign is advertising, or even the shop owner Mrs. Doyle herself, is more likely to be the true subject of the emerging story.

The tension between these opposing kinds of inference introduces a further level at which readers must carry out inferencing. In effect, they must make what can be described as a META-INFERENCE about what the real point of the task is. It is such meta-inferencing that is particularly crucial in a reader's response to a multiple-choice task; yet this higher level of inferencing is virtually ignored in test makers' description of what their tasks call for. In general, they use a simple dichotomy between *literal* and *inferential* to describe only what readers must do to select the target response. In effect, they ignore the various kinds of inferences that lead to distractors as well as the higher level of meta-inferencing that readers must engage in when deciding between the various choices on a given task.

Let us now turn to inferences leading to a distractor and determine which of them can be classified as motivated. In the most strict terms, the only inference that can be classified in this way is the one that readers make when responding to MOTHER ALLIGATOR: namely, that the baby alligators can be viewed as *little grunts*. In discussing this inference, we presented two ways in which it is motivated by the text base:

1) The text base is organized around the notion that the mother alligator can only experience her babies by the sounds that they make.
2) The passage is written in a style that encourages the reader to connect *baby alligators* and *little grunts* holistically.

In introducing our categories of inferences in Chapter 1, we identified one other inference as motivated, which is also associated with a distractor. When readers respond to ALICE AND THE FAWN, they can use two bits of information in the text base to infer that the fawn is frightened:

1) It [the fawn] didn't seem at all frightened (the very denial implies that it actually was).
2) It [the fawn] moved back a little (the fact that this action occurs at the end of the passage gives it added weight).

Although these bits of information do motivate the inference that the fawn was frightened, children must suppress this inference when responding to the task that sets up *frightened* as a distractor. The point of the task is not whether the fawn was frightened, but rather how the fawn's eyes looked (in the opening sentence the fawn's eyes are described as *gentle*). Many children, however, failed to maintain this distinction between the state of the fawn and how its eyes looked and thus selected *frightened* in response to this task (certainly the eyes of a fawn can be readily associated with its emotional state).

We should note that for many children this inference was motivated not only by the text base but also by their real-world knowledge that the fawn is an animal that is easily frightened. We will discuss such subtle interaction between text base and real-world knowledge as we move on to consider invited inferences.

Invited Inferencing

We can begin by listing the inferences in the preceding section which led to distractors and which can be categorized as *invited*.

1) Since Alice was petting the fawn and speaking gently to it, she was try-ing to help it. (ALICE AND THE FAWN)
2) Since the grapes took several weeks to dry, the climate was wet. (RAISINS)
3) Since the trees were only blown over (unlike the houses which were blown away), they were strong. (HURRICANE)
4) Since the harsh voices pierced the silent air, the air ceased to be silent. (JAYS AND CROWS)

None of these inferences is directly motivated by information in the text base; yet in each instance information is available that invites readers to make the inference. In most kinds of real-world reading, such invita-tions are taken up with relative impunity. Indeed, much of the skill of reading lies in keeping such invited inferences in play until certain information either confirms them or forces them to go away. As we have seen, the test passages under consideration are so sparsely developed that they seldom provide the needed information that forces children to suppress the various inferences that they put in play: for example, chil-dren are not informed what Alice did when the fawn moved back so they are not really in a position to know whether she was, in fact, trying to help it.

We may thus conclude that invited inferences, which are, in many ways, the lifeblood of real-world reading, have to be systematically sup-pressed when children are handling test material. Unfortunately, such inferences are often stimulated by a distractor on a multiple-choice task. Hence we can think of them as being doubly invited: they are first put into play by a sparsely developed passage but then again by a distractor on a multiple-choice task. If we focus, however, on the actual dynamics of test taking, it is the distractor that often issues the invitation to chil-dren, and once they have taken it up, they return to the passage in order to seek confirmation.[1]

If we were to consider our entire corpus of testing material, we would find a number of distractors that issue such an invitation. As such exam-ples multiply, we come across certain inferences that are difficult to clas-sify. Just as certain inferences hover between motivated and invited, so others hover between invited and extended. To take just one example, certain children, in responding to (A) in GREEN CEDARS, inferred that the green trees were dying. From a certain vantage point, this inference can be viewed as extended, since the passage makes no direct mention of any death or disease with respect to the green cedars. Yet as we pointed out in our analysis, this passage is written in a highly evocative style that calls for an imaginative response. If readers do respond to this

style, they can readily use two bits of information to ground their inference that the green trees were dying:

1) The passage is built around a dead tree that is described as once itself
   having been green.
2) This dead tree possesses gray limbs that are described as stretching
   gray among the green cedars.

Given these bits of information, it is not difficult for readers to infer that
the live trees are being infected by the dead one. Such an inference is
grounded not just in the text but in the reader's real-world knowledge
as well. In effect, the inference depends upon what might be called an
'infection' schema (i.e., the knowledge that one living organism can
transmit disease and death to another).

Of course test makers take the position that when test takers are
selecting a target response, they should suppress any inference based on
real-world knowledge. But this position is inconsistent with what readers must do in responding to (A) in CHEE TONG, a unit in which two
men—a food vendor and a boatman—are portrayed as meeting each
night in order to exchange food and shelter. Readers can select the target response only if they use their real-world knowledge of a houseboat
to infer that the shelter was a boat. Certain children who lacked this
knowledge were forced to turn to the text base and make the invited
inference that the boatman *always ties up at the same place* so that he and
the food vendor could seek shelter in a small house near the dock.
Although this inference is not, strictly speaking, motivated by the text
base, it is more grounded in that base than is the one that leads to the
target response.

In closing this section, we would like to observe that readers are probably most secure in making an inference when it is grounded not only in
the text base but also in their real-world knowledge. Indeed, when there
is sufficient congruence between the two, readers have difficulty even
being aware that they are making use of their real-world knowledge. Let
us now turn to the next section where we further explore the complex
ways in which real-world knowledge enter into reading.

REAL-WORLD KNOWLEDGE

In developing tests of reading comprehension, test makers attempt to
select material and construct tasks in which the role of real-world knowledge is minimized. They reason that if readers can answer a task without
having read the passage, they receive credit for a skill that they have

not, in fact, demonstrated. This policy is laudable but difficult to implement. The goal of minimizing real-world knowledge is in conflict with the goal of using material typical of the kinds of reading that children do—it is difficult to find representative material that is at the same time unfamiliar.

Even when test makers do come up with unfamiliar material, children are still forced to use whatever real-world knowledge they have to make sense out of it. This is not at all surprising, since as reading theorists (e.g., Goodman, 1986; Smith, 1994) have often pointed out, real-world knowledge is fundamental to reading comprehension, or, for that matter, to any act of comprehension. Such a claim can be made painfully clear to most adult readers by simply asking them to pick up a research report on, say, the evolution of lichen in polar climates. Only those few who possess the relevant knowledge are in a position to make much sense of it; and if any lay reader does manage to make some headway, it will be through a strategic use of real-world knowledge whose relevance may not be immediately apparent.

Misleading Effects

In our own research, we often observed children drawing on whatever knowledge they could to make sense out of the brief passages they were confronted with. Indeed, the brevity of the passages, when coupled with the time pressure of the testing situation, force children to rely even more on their knowledge: they simply do not have sufficient text or time to build up meaning more gradually from what is on the page. As we all know from our ordinary experience of reading, we need a certain amount of time with a text before we are able to engage it on its own terms. Until we reach a certain zone of comfort, we are busy using our stock of knowledge to try and situate the text.

If we return to the polarity units in Chapter 6, we can find many examples of children struggling to make sense of unfamiliar worlds. It is not simply that a particular world may be unfamiliar but the overreliance on lexical polarities makes the passage itself difficult to read. Hence many children skip forward to the tasks to look for clues as to what the passage might mean. But as we have seen, the tasks, too, can embody lexical polarities in a form that is particularly hard to process: not only are children forced to work through an entire paradigm of polarities but the polarities may be presented in a reversed order, either with respect to how they were used in the passage or how they are used more generally. Children may thus be forced, much like adult readers confronting a technical article on lichens that grow above the Arctic Circle, to draw on whatever knowledge they can if they are to get anything out of the text.

In general, children's knowledge about the worlds represented in polarity units is scanty. These worlds tend to be factual, represented either in a descriptive passage (e.g., specific facts about the construction of the George Washington Bridge) or in an expository passage (e.g., generic facts about how food is preserved from the spoiling effects of bacteria). In working with such worlds, children are prone to use whatever knowledge they have in imprecise ways. In trying to make sense out of BACTERIA, for example, a number of children turned to the most familiar object in their environment for preserving food. Rather than attending to a refrigerator's capacity to keep food cold, certain children focused on its tendency to induce a certain wetness. We even came across children from other cultures who associated food preservation with storing things in water.

Before developing the theme of cultural variation in the use of real-world knowledge, we would like to show how even children who possess appropriate real-world knowledge can be misled by it. In GEORGE WASHINGTON BRIDGE, we reported a striking instance of a child who was misled by detailed knowledge of the bridge. This unit describes how those who constructed the bridge did not follow the original plan in which stone was to be placed over the steel towers: once the supporting towers had been built, they were considered too beautiful to cover. In responding to (B), children should choose *steel* as the material the towers are made of. This child, however, chose *steel over stone*: when asked to explain his answer, he referred to the bottom part of each steel tower, which is, in fact, covered with stone. From this vantage point, steel can be considered as *over*—in the sense of "above"—stone. This answer thus accorded not only with his impressive knowledge—he happened to have a view of the bridge from his bedroom window—but it allowed him to preserve the prototypical meaning of *over* as signifying 'a vertical relation.'

This example is admittedly idiosyncratic but on other units a single bit of real-world knowledge led a number of children to select a distractor. An especially vivid example can be found in ALICE AND THE FAWN. In describing how the fawn's eyes looked, many children who knew what a fawn is selected *frightened*. The skittishness they associated with the real-world animal seemingly strengthened their attraction to this distractor. Ironically, children who thought the fawn was a domesticated animal—it was described variously as a dog or duck—were often less attracted to *frightened*: this choice loses much of its appeal if a child thinks of the fawn as an animal accustomed to living around people.

Before leaving the misleading effects of real-world knowledge, we would like to mention briefly a problem that many children experienced: holding on to the prototypical meaning of a word instead of allowing an appropriate contextual meaning to emerge. For example, in responding to a task in RAISINS, children were required to associate the word *sugar* with a natural substance in raisins. Many of them, however, could think of this word only in connection with the artificial product that they scoop out of a bowl. We observed a similar limitation with respect to the word *boat* in CHEE TONG (pp. 152–155) and the word *promise* in ADVERTISING TAILOR (pp. 175–177). This limitation is probably best understood in a developmental context: although all human beings use prototypes in storing their knowledge, children have less experience in adapting these prototypes in order to make sense out of what they read. Test makers need to be cautious about the degree to which they require young children to make such adaptations.

Ethnocultural Variation

As indicated by the earlier example in which children associated water with food preservation in different ways, real-world knowledge is subject to a good deal of ethnocultural variation. Our study has uncovered many examples of children from different backgrounds using different kinds of knowledge in order to make sense of a particular test unit. To illustrate such variation, we will focus on a task in LEARNING TO READ that encouraged children to make use of their real-world knowledge. In responding to (B), children were required to choose *six* as the age of the little girl who is about to go to school. They were supposed to derive this answer from the final sentence of the passage that reports the little girl as thinking that she won't be able to read until she is seven, a year from the present time. Since this information is presented elliptically in the mode of free indirect speech, many children were unable to make sense of it and so were forced to rely on their real-world knowledge. During the interviewing, a number of children said that they chose *six* because that is the age at which children begin school. Other children, particularly African Americans, reported themselves as choosing *four* because they thought of children beginning school at this earlier age. In this instance, the real-world experience of urban African American children worked against them, because so many of them had experienced early exposure to school-like activities in preschool programs such as Headstart. Hence they received no credit for their response, unlike the children who, also using their real-world knowledge, selected *six*.

This contrast in how African American and European American children justified their responses illustrates the subtle ways in which ethnocultural experience can influence children's responses on a reading test. What is particularly disconcerting about this example is that individuals in one ethnocultural group get full credit, but individuals in another group get no credit. Yet individuals in both groups were equally reliant on real-world knowledge as a means of responding to the task.

Given the range of problems that we have delineated, teachers often encourage children to avoid any use of real-world knowledge when they are taking a test. This advice is often encapsulated in a formula such as "just stick to what the passage tells you." Children can become quite timid about using their real-world knowledge and thus not be in a position to respond appropriately to certain tasks (e.g., the one in CHEE TONG that requires children to use their knowledge of a houseboat to infer that it was a boat that provided the shelter).

From the constructivist perspective, students comprehend more efficiently when they increase the number of connections they make between what they read and their existing knowledge and experience. When students do not make such connections, they often fail to establish an appropriate context for what they are reading. This point is well illustrated in an interview with a child about MINNESOTA, a unit in which he missed both tasks. He was quite ahistorical in his thinking about the Indians from whose language the state of Minnesota had been named (a detail that one of the tasks focuses on). He claimed that these Indians were, in fact, able to speak English. As the interview progressed, the child gradually revealed a considerable stock of knowledge which, if he had drawn on it properly, would have allowed him to create an appropriate historical context for the unit. It was as if somehow he was holding this knowledge to the side since he was taking a test. In the best of circumstances, it is not easy for children to bring their knowledge to bear on what they read, but it becomes even more difficult if they are actively encouraged—as they so often are when taking a test—to avoid using it.

In closing this discussion of real-world knowledge, we would like to point out that even though such knowledge plays a crucial role in facilitating reading comprehension, readers do need to be able to distinguish between what comes from their own heads and what comes off the page. In making such a distinction, they are not simply responding to an arbitrary demand of test makers, but rather developing a critical habit of mind that is valuable not only in school but in the larger society: for example, in formulating a critical response to text, readers need to be clear about what can be fairly attributed to the writer. It is the responsibility of schooling to nurture this capacity in readers, and it is altogether fitting that students, once they have sufficiently matured, demonstrate that they possess it. We question, however, whether young children should be required to demonstrate it. In order for them to distinguish between what a text contains and what they bring to it, they must have achieved a certain level of metalinguistic awareness. In the next section we review the considerable evidence that this study has accumulated that most third- and fourth-grade children lack such awareness.

METALINGUISTIC DEMANDS

We introduced the term *metalinguistic* in describing the two tasks in SHOP SIGN, a unit that presents a small-town scene of people gathered around a freshly painted sign. They are excited since the sign promises the opening of a new shop that will sell various kinds of confectionery. This is the only unit in our corpus in which children scored well below chance on both tasks during the pilot testing. It seems evident that their poor performance was directly related to the metalinguistic demands of these tasks. In describing these demands, we can usefully distinguish between the two tasks: (A) is protypically metalinguistic in that it calls for children to focus on a specific signal in the passage that a certain word is not functioning in a normal way: that is to say, the quotation marks placed around *sundries* indicate that it refers to a word rather than a thing. Most children did not, however, interpret the quotation marks in this way. They interpreted the phrase as referring to a real-world entity rather than a word (see pp. 43–45 for a fuller discussion in which we delineate other reasons for children's failure to perform the metalinguistic operation).

By way of contrast, (B) does not focus on any overt metalinguistic signal within the passage itself. Rather this task becomes metalinguistic by virtue of what it asks children to do: to describe what *the story is mainly about*. The target response *a sign* can be selected if children adopt a structural perspective (i.e., if they see that 'sign' is the most pervasive and prominent concept in the passage).

These two tasks exemplify two major kinds of metalinguistic task that will be presented under the headings Passage-Based and Task-Based. The first kind is built around a formal feature within the passage that calls for a metalinguistic operation, whereas the second kind signals a metalinguistic operation by the way in which it is itself structured: in the case of (B), the words *mainly about* cue the seasoned test taker to adopt a structural perspective.

Passage-Based

Some metalinguistic tasks call for sophisticated analysis of a literate—even literary—feature within the passage (perhaps these demands could be even better described as METALITERATE or METALITERARY). We are especially interested in such tasks because they provide evidence that counters a position commonly held by reading specalists: namely, that children can perform well on a reading test with only basic decoding skills to complement their oral experience of language.

The three excerpted units which we discussed in Chapter 3 all reflect a literary tone—indeed, one of them, ALICE AND THE FAWN, is taken directly from Lewis Carroll's *Through the Looking Glass*, and we have already discussed how its evocative prose stimulates children to select a communicative distractor on both tasks (pp. 93–103). The other units both contain formal literary devices that children must properly analyze if they are to respond appropriately to the tasks. BLACK BONNET presents a scene of Miss Esther waiting at a train station for an old lady who does not get off the train. The old lady is initially evoked by a synedoche—*there was no black bonnet with a worn lace veil*—which many children did not understand. Their difficulty in processing such figurative language was increased by a syntactic structure that is itself highly literate: *there was no...*signals that the waiting person was expecting to see the old lady, and the next sentence begins with the contrastive *there was only...*, which signals that the expectation was not met. Our research has demonstrated that most third and fourth graders are not able to analyze either the figurative language or the sophisticated syntax within which it is embedded (pp. 76–78).

LEARNING TO READ presents a scene in which a little girl expresses to her mother the excitement she feels about learning to read as soon as she arrives at school. When the mother cautions her that learning to read may take even a year, the passage shifts abruptly from direct speech to free indirect speech in order to report the little girl's thoughts: *A year? A whole year? Maybe not till she was seven? That would be awful!* This literary mode of representing thought is potentially confusing to children, since familiar language forms are used in an unfamiliar way (e.g., a pronoun is backshifted from first person to third person and a verb tense from present to past). Even when children have well-developed decoding skills, their oral experience of language does not sufficiently prepare them to handle such highly literate features (see pp. 107–109 for discussion of this point).

Test units from other chapters make similar demands. For example, in ADVERTISING TAILOR the figurative expression *hammered out a wardrobe* is especially confusing to children because it so readily invites them to make a literal interpretation (pp. 165–169); and in WHITE CIRCLES the use of figurative expressions such as *like a boiled owl* invites children to assume that a word such as *flying* is used figuratively as well, and they are thus able to picture the woman in a car rather than in an airplane (pp. 209–211). Our research provides a good deal of evidence that children must be able to deal with literate structures if they are to perform well on test units. It is for this reason that we are skeptical about the commonly held notion that children can succeed on a reading test if they have basic decoding skills and a normative stock of oral experience.

Before moving on to metalinguistic demands that are task-based, we would like to call attention to an idiosyncratic task that was especially confusing to children. Minnesota provides the information that the name of the state comes from Indian words meaning "sky-tinted water." In responding to (B), which asks what the Indians were talking about when they said "Minnesota," many children were unable to associate *Indian words* with the single word *Minnesota*, which, for them, is merely the English name of a state, much like New York or Pennsylvania. It is difficult for young children to understand borrowing from a language that they don't know (see pp. 00-00 for vivid examples of children's confusions as they attempt to talk about this metalinguistic problem).

Task-Based

In considering task-based metalinguistic demands, we can begin by returning to (B) in SHOP SIGN, the task that asked children to tell what *the story is mainly about*. Rather than using a structural perspective to select *a sign*, most children focused on content and selected a distractor such as *a shop* or *Mrs. Doyle*, which are, after all, far more promising candidates as to what the story is mainly about. From this perspective, the description of the sign was just a device for getting the story underway.

It is instructive to place SHOP SIGN alongside what we have described as a frame unit, in which a mainly-about task calls for just this kind of perspective (i.e., one that leads the reader to shift from initial rhetorical framing to more substantive material). In the case of a frame unit, the test makers would undoubtedly claim that such a shift was motivated by the passage itself: for example, in JAYS AND CROWS the passage provides clear evidence of a shift from 'birds' to 'sounds.' By the same token, they would claim that though SHOP SIGN may have promised a comparable shift, it did not actually deliver it, and hence readers regard *a sign* as what the story is mainly about. We would claim, however, that children are quite justified, given the presence of the word *story* in the task, in responding to what the passage promises rather than to what it actually delivers. In this sense, they are showing the kind of reader flexibility that frame units are presumably designed to measure. From a constructivist perspective, a reader demonstrates valuable predictive skills in understanding that what the passage conveys is that the real story is yet to come.

The tasks we have classified as acommunicative can also be viewed as metalinguistic. Both recycling and vocabulary-defining tasks call for a metalinguistic focus on a single word or phrase. Both kinds of task resemble a mainly-about task in that it is the task that sets up a metalinguistic operation. These acommunicative tasks are, however, potentially easier for a young child, since they require focus on only a single word or phrase: this kind of metalinguistic activity is common during early years of schooling and children learn to carry it out with relative ease. Their poor performance on these tasks is generally due to another factor: the point of the task is not clearly established and so the presence of a communicative distractor leads children to understand the task as calling for a different kind of response.

TASK STRUCTURE

Throughout this study we have called attention to inconsistencies in how tasks are structured and how they function. We would now like to gather together these inconsistencies and consider them more systematically. We first examine inconsistencies among the tasks themselves before turning to inconsistencies in how tasks are related to passages. Since we will be referring to isolated tasks from many different units, readers are encouraged to use Appendix A (which lists the units in alphabetical order) if they wish to check on particular contexts. Hill and Larsen (1983) provides a more elaborate characterization of task structure that places different kinds of tasks along a communicative/acommunicative continuum (see Pearson & Johnson, 1978, for another useful classification of tasks).

Inconsistencies Among Tasks

We can begin with the most basic inconsistency in task structure: units do not always express their function overtly (i.e., what children are required to do). To illustrate this point, we can examine tasks that call for children to define a vocabulary unit. These tasks are sometimes introduced by formulaic phrasing—*In the story, (the word) "x" means*—that overtly expresses their function (in the second example below *the word* is omitted from the formula since the vocabulary unit to be defined consists of two words):

> In the story, the word "abated" means *died down*. (HURRICANE)
> In the story, "broke into" means *started*. (NERVOUS HORSE)

In other cases, however, vocabulary-defining tasks are not introduced by the formulaic phrasing:

What did Alice try to do to the fawn? *pet it* (ALICE AND THE FAWN)
The story says that trees were *blown over*. (HURRICANE)
Burbank's new plant did not live long in nature because *it was eaten up*.
(SPINELESS CACTUS)

On the surface, these tasks do not resemble those in the first group; yet all three could have used the formula to make clear that they require children to define a lexical unit:

In the story, the word "stroke" means *pet*. (ALICE AND THE FAWN)
In the story, "knocked down" means *blew over*. (HURRICANE)
In the story, "devoured" means *ate up*. (SPINELESS CACTUS)

When we asked 25 fourth-grade children to respond to these three units with the tasks in this form, 18 selected the target response for the first, 19 the target response for the second, and 21 the target response for the third. This impressive rate of success is not surprising, for most children who select an alternative response on these tasks actually know the meaning of the vocabulary item. Indeed, the fact that they know the meaning seems to work against their constituting the task as vocabulary-defining (i.e., knowing a particular vocabulary item prevents children from thinking of it as a likely testing objective). Given the frequent use of the formulaic stem in vocabulary-defining tasks, children may come to rely on it and, whenever it is not used, have difficulty in understanding what the point of the task is. A thoughtful child who develops a systematic approach to test taking is especially vulnerable to such covert tasks.

Let us now consider a task inconsistency that has more to do with the choices than the stem. In most tasks within our corpus, the choices parallel each other in form. Such parallelism reflects the test makers' concern that no particular choice should stand out from the others on purely formal grounds. A common bit of test-taking wisdom passed on in coaching schools is that any choice that stands out is likely to be the target response. Test makers' concern with formal congruence does not, however, prevent their constructing task choices that belong to different grammatical categories. As indicated by the following examples, such formal discontinuity is usually not visible at the language surface and thus easily goes unnoticed (i.e., the grammatical category to which a choice belongs is not necessarily signaled by a separable marker, as indicated by the first example where the suffixes *-ne* and *-ing* signal a verb, the suffix *-s* a noun, and the absence of grammatical marking an adjective):

The green trees were
gone   dying
cedars   hollow (GREEN CEDARS)

The people were surprised when they saw her
owl   blinking
goggles   white circles (WHITE CIRCLES)

Most of the iceberg is
hidden   visible
surface   top (ICEBERG)

As can be seen, none of these tasks is a question, which, as a naturally occurring language form, tends to elicit answers that belong to the same grammatical class. A completion task is not, however, built around any naturally occurring language form, with the consequence that its choices are not necessarily drawn from the same grammatical class. When children deal with grammatically varying completers, they are unable to work paradigmatically with the stem. They are rather forced to reparse it as they move from one completer to the next.

Since this kind of task occurred with a certain frequency in our corpus—it constitutes nearly 20% of the sentence-completion tasks, which themselves outnumber question tasks nearly 2 to 1—it contributed significantly to children's difficulties: in the first task above, for example, children were most attracted to the adjective *hollow* during the pilot testing; since this choice is not especially attractive on substantive grounds, its appeal seems best explained by the fact that an adjective follows the verb *to be* with greater frequency than either a noun or a verb does.

Completion tasks were also the source of another problem—a target proposition that is linguistically ill-formed. We discovered a number of children who rejected target propositions because they did not "sound right":

The people were surprised when they saw her *white circles*. (WHITE CIRCLES)
These bridges are *hung*. (HUNG BRIDGES)

This problem can, once again, be traced to the fact that an incomplete stem and its completers do not have a consistent grammatical relationship as a question and its answers do. It is thus difficult for test makers to come up with four completers, all of which can be integrated with a single incomplete stem into well-formed structures.

We will not recapitulate here the various kinds of syntactic and semantic constraints that the above target propositions violate (see pp. 213-214 for such discussion). We would simply add that a distractor proposition can be ill-formed as well:

Most of the iceberg is *top*. (ICEBERG)
Raisins are made from grapes that have a lot of *varieties*. (RAISINS)

No task proposition—distractor or target—should be ill-formed if the integrity of the multiple-choice format is to be maintained.

Finally, we should note that a task proposition can also be pragmatically ill-formed. Since pragmatic constraints are more delicate, such a proposition does not necessarily strike the ear as awkward. Consider, for example, the following target proposition, which, as can be seen, belongs to a sentence-completion task as well:

The green trees were *cedars*. (GREEN CEDARS)

Although the sentence itself is well-structured, it calls for a rather odd mental operation: readers are to use the color green to identify a particular group of trees as cedars. It is as if they were asked to use the ability to swim to identify a particular group of fish as trout.

Inconsistent Relations Between Task and Passage

Early on in this chapter we made the point that the passage and the tasks together form the text that must be comprehended; it is thus of interest to examine the ways in which cohesion is sustained within this larger text. An interesting point of departure is to examine whether tasks recycle passage information in nominal or pronominal form: recycling tends to be in nominal form, as illustrated by the bracketed material in the following tasks:

Where was [the nest]? *inside a tree* (GREEN CEDARS)
How did [the fawn's eyes] look? *gentle* (ALICE AND THE FAWN)
Most of [the iceberg] is *hidden*. (ICEBERG)

Even though passages are short, they generally introduce a sufficient number of nominals that any use of an isolated pronominal within a task can be confusing.

Nevertheless, such a pronominal is occasionally used in the tasks. In certain instances it may be used to preserve the style of the passage in which a pronominal is introduced without an antecedent. In WHITE CIRCLES, the pronoun *she* occurs at the beginning of both the passage and the first task:

Passage opening: As [she] rolled to a stop...
Task (A):   [She] came into town by *airplane*.

Such stylistic preservation is not, however, reflected in LEARNING TO READ:

Passage opening: [She] looked at the calendar.
Task (A): How old is [the girl] in the story?

The use of *the girl* was unavoidable since *she* could have referred to the only other person introduced in the passage—the girl's mother. In juxtaposing these two units, we catch a glimpse of the different kinds of constraints that determine how tasks sustain cohesive relations with the passage (see Hill & Larsen, 1983, for a more extended discussion of these constraints with respect to verbal structures as well as nominal ones; that discussion focuses on the tense marker and the determiner as well as the pronominal as a source of confusion within tasks).

Given the complexity of these constraints, a pronominal tends not to be used unless it has an immediate antecedent within the task itself (in the following tasks both the pronominal and its antecedent are bracketed):

When [the Indians] said "Minnesota," [they] were talking about *water*. (MINNESOTA)
At first, how long did [the girl] think it would take [her] to learn to read at school? *one day* (LEARNING TO READ)
[The people] were surprised when [they] saw her *white circles*. (WHITE CIRCLES)
[The tailor] was surpised to see how much [he] had promised. (ADVERTISING TAILOR)

In principle, a pronominal whose antecedent is in the same sentence should be easy for children; yet many were confused by the use of *he* in the last task above, aligning it with *Biff* rather than with *the tailor*. They assumed that the tailor would not be surprised by what he himself had done; in order to neutralize children's use of such a pragmatic principle, the reflexive pronominal *himself* could have been inserted after *he*.

In examining how tasks sustain cohesive relations with the passage, we can focus on the choices as well as the stem. Choices also recycle passage nominals, but they tend not to be initiated by *the*, as are recycled nominals in the task stem. Rather they are initiated by *a(n)*, as illustrated by the following tasks:

What was Miss Esther expecting to see?
a lot of people   an old man
a black bonnet   a bird cage (BLACK BONNET)

What was the shelter?

a boat	a stove
a house	an arrangement (CHEE TONG)

This use of the indefinite determiner reflects a basic discourse principle: whenever the person asking a question provides a set of responses, they tend to be presented as indefinite rather than definite.

This principle was violated, however, by a task in SHOP SIGN where three of the choices include *a*, but the other one includes *the*:

What was the mystery?

an appearance	the caramel
a woman	a word (SHOP SIGN)

This violation was apparently motivated by the fact that within the passage caramel was used as a mass noun rather than a count noun. By using only the word *caramel* as a choice, the test makers could have preserved both the mass-noun sense as well as the principle of not using *the* in response to a question; or they could have even used *a caramel* in order to preserve formal equivalence among the four choices. Either strategy would probably have dampened the appeal of this distractor, which was the most attractive choice to both African American and European American children during the pilot testing. The distinctive presence of *the* in this choice probably played some role in this, since *caramel* is not a particularly attractive choice on purely substantive grounds.

Punctuation such as quotation marks can also be examined as a resource for sustaining cohesion: such marks can be used to signal that a task is recycling passage material in verbatim form. Such usage is not, however, common in our corpus, where quotation marks are largely used in vocabulary-defining tasks:

In this story, "called for" means

picked up	telephoned
realized	required (GEORGE WASHINGTON BRIDGE)

Here quotation marks primarily signal the metalinguistic focus described in the previous section, although they can be viewed as secondarily signaling quotation of passage material.

There were only three other uses of quotation marks in the corpus:

When the Indians said "Minnesota," they were talking about *water*.
(MINNESOTA)

Biff "hammered out a wardrobe" by making *home runs*.
(ADVERTISING TAILOR)

The "little grunts" in the story are *noises*. (MOTHER ALLIGATOR)

In the first example, quotation marks signal direct speech; in the second, the use of figurative language. They are not signaling quoted material, since within the passage this figurative expression was used without past tense marking. As for the third example, one of the test makers, when interviewed, claimed that the quotation marks around *little grunts* do, in fact, signal verbatim use of passage material.

This interpretation is, however, difficult to defend, since no other task in our corpus reflects such usage (and nearly all of them recycle at least some passage material in verbatim form). A more convincing interpretation of the quotation marks in this task was offered by a child who claimed that they signaled a special way of "talking about the baby alligators." Since the mother could only hear her babies when they were born, she experiences them only as "little grunts."

In discussing this task, the test maker also pointed out that the distractor *baby alligators*, unlike the target responses *noises*, cannot be substituted for *little grunts* in the passage: such substitution would result in the nonsensical *baby alligators' baby alligators* if the passage phrase *their little grunts* is made explicit. Such a stringent criterion of substitutability is not, however, maintained on other tasks, as illustrated by the following example:

In the story, "broke into" means *started*. (NERVOUS HORSE)

If *started* is substituted for *broke into* within the passage, an ungrammatical sentence results:

*The horse started a canter, then into a full gallop.

We should also note that from a stylistic perspective the target response *noises* does not substitute effectively for *little grunts*. As one girl put it, "The mother didn't hear noises—she heard her babies!" We are sympathetic to her sense of outrage: if substitutability is to be invoked as a criterion, it should be sensitive to style as well as grammar.

The tasks in our corpus are inconsistent not only in their use of quotation marks but also in the way they handle figurative language. We would expect test makers, given their basic orientation, to maintain the literal approach to figurative language that was exemplified in the task we have just examined from ADVERTISING TAILOR:

Biff "hammered out a wardrobe" by making *home runs*.

Here the target response focuses on what Biff really did in order to win the suits that the tailor had promised to give away when he posted the sign on the ballpark fence. Yet a task in BLACK BONNET preserves the figurative meaning of the synedoche that was used in the passage:

What was Miss Esther expecting to see? a black bonnet

A number of children were confused by the fact that the task did not defigure the passage language. When the target response was revealed to one child, his response was an incredulous "but she didn't want to see a black bonnet."

In closing this section, we attend to another task inconsistency that arises from test makers' efforts to maintain formal equivalency among task choices, but which results in a conflict with passage detail. In order to maintain such equivalency, they, at times, set up a task in which the target response recycles only part of the relevant passage information. In ALICE AND THE FAWN, the passage describes the fawn's eyes as *large* and *gentle*; yet the target response for (A) describes the eyes as only *gentle* so that it can parallel the other three choices (each consists of a single adjective). In explaining their rejection of the target response, a number of children emphasized the fact that it was incomplete.

Another example of such a task can be found in HARD LEAD, where the passage ends with the statement that hard lead produces writing that is *thick and dark*. The first task focuses on the kind of writing that soft lead produces, so that skilled test takers expect the target response to be *thin and light*. They are forced, however, to settle for *thin*, an awkward word for describing handwriting (this target proposition is so awkward that it might even be included among those described as ill-formed).

This task can be used to illustrate another kind of task inconsistency: it forces children to extend the passage in selecting a target response, since the first task functions as if it were an additional sentence in the passage:

Final sentence: hard lead ➔ thick and dark writing
First task: soft lead ➔ thin [and light] writing

As we have shown throughout this study, children are often penalized if they extend the passage in responding to a task: for example, in responding to (B) in SHOP SIGN, children receive no credit if they, responding to rhetorical cues in the passage, extend it and select *a shop* or *Mrs. Doyle* as what *the story is mainly about*.

We can thus observe two ways in which this task in HARD LEAD is inconsistent with normative task structure: it forces children, on the one hand, to recycle local detail in partial form and, on the other, to extend the passage. Both of these operations run counter to a basic principle that test makers hold: a task should stimulate only operations that are consistent with a tightly controlled text base. Our corpus has provided a good deal of evidence that test makers, given the complexity of actual task construction, cannot consistently follow this principle. As a result, they end up constructing a wide range of tasks that violate this principle. Ironically, the children most vulnerable to such tasks are likely to be those who have internalized the test makers' overly rigid principle.

POLICY CONSIDERATIONS

We began this research in the hope that it would benefit test makers. We believed that our methods of text analysis would provide useful tools that they could use in developing test material. In our most optimistic moments, we even envisioned developing various heuristics that they might work with in developing passages, tasks, and well-integrated passage-task configurations.

We also believed that our methods of investigating children's responses to prospective test material would prove useful to test makers. From our perspective, they rely too exclusively upon psychometric methods and would benefit from more direct forms of interaction with test takers based on a close analysis of test material. Such analysis is fundamental to our two basic methods—individual interviews and group probes. These methods are useful not only in identifying gender and ethnocultural differences in student responses, but also in uncovering and revising the features of the test material that engender these differences. From our perspective, these methods could provide an important complement to psychometric methods of evaluating prospective test material.

As the study progressed, our perspective began to shift. As an increasing number of problems emerged, we found ourselves thinking less about improving tests and more about whether certain problems were so intractable that these tests, no matter how extensively revised, could not provide reliable and equitable assessment of children's reading comprehension. We finally came to the conclusion that reading tests for young children are so flawed in design and so detrimental to classroom practice that their use should be discontinued. We would now like to lay out our reasons for adopting this position.

The Case Against Reading Tests for Children

We begin with our own study and briefly lay out the case it provides against these tests. We then adopt a broader perspective on how these tests function within schools and the larger society.

Our own study

In stating a case against reading tests for young children, we are well aware that our own study is multifaceted and cannot easily be summarized. In many ways, the case that it makes lies in the cumulative weight of our analyses of 22 test units and children's responses to them. We are also aware that our preceding discussion of passage-task configurations, inferencing, real-world knowledge, metalinguistic demands, and task structure has already made our case. Given the presence of this material, we will simply revisit various constraints that test makers work with in developing test material. It is our conviction that these constraints are so fundamental to the test-making process that they lead inexorably to flawed test material.

To begin with, test makers must produce a test that takes less than an hour so that it will be easy to administer and to allow for children's limited attention span. In addition, they must ensure that different kinds of reading material are adequately represented. These two constraints lead to passages that are brief and decontextualized.

In constructing tasks, test makers must work with two further constraints. On the one hand, they must be able to defend the choice that they designate as the target response. This leads them to construct tasks that do not violate the text base (i.e., the target responses must accord with information that is either directly stated or automatically entailed). On the other hand, they must construct tasks that have sufficient discriminatory power: a task does not make it onto the test unless it elicits a sufficient number of distractor responses. In order to construct genuinely attractive distractors, test makers are inevitably drawn to various kinds of inferences that the passage stimulates. As we have seen, many of the distractors in our own corpus are based on an inference that we describe as either *motivated* or *invited*.

We can thus see how these various constraints conspire to produce a textual configuration that leads young children astray. When they encounter a brief and decontextualized passage, they tend to expand it in order to achieve a coherent world of meaning. Once that expansion is in place, they are primed to select a distractor that accords with this world, unless they have learned to carry out the highly constrained operations that lead to the target response.

In making a case against reading tests for children based on our own study, we are well aware that our corpus consisted of only piloted test material. Rather than revisiting our discussion of the authenticity of this material (pp. 23–25), we will here make two additional points. First, the problems that this study has uncovered can often be traced to the underlying constraints that the test makers work with. As long as they work with these constraints, the problems will remain.

Second, the basic framework of this study has been used productively in many studies of published test material. It has been used to analyze reader response to several widely used tests in this country: the Descriptive Test of Language Skills (DTLS) (Adames, 1987; Bhasin, 1990), the Test of Adult Basic Education (TABE) (Hill & Anderson, 1994; Hill, Anderson, Watt, & Ray, 1989), and the Scholastic Achievement Test (SAT) (Sims-West, 1996). It has also been used to analyze reader response to major tests of English in other countries; for example, the Test of English as a Foreign Language (TOEFL) in Taiwan (Lin, 1993) and in Japan and Chile (Hill & Pike, 1985); the English component of the major entrance exam for universities in Taiwan (Yuan, 1997) and in Japan (Ingulsrud, 1988; Matsumoto, 1997); and British-style tests based on the School Certificate, which have been exported to Nigeria (Parry, 1986) and Zimbabwe (Allen, 1988).

Since the late 1980s, the framework has been used to analyze reader response to not only conventional tests but also those that claim to be communicatively oriented (Chu, 1993; Coyle, 1992; Hayes & McCartney, 1997; Hill, 1992, 1994, 1999; Hill & Larsen, 1992; Hill & Parry, 1988, 1989). These studies have been of particular interest, since they have shown that the basic problems found in the conventional tests remain. Indeed, as Hill and Parry pointed out in their analysis of two versions of the TABE, the problems were often exacerbated in the communicative version built around material such as personal letters and advertisements (in contrast to more neutral material such as expository prose used in the earlier version). Since the communicative material was still followed by tasks that coupled a communicative distractor with an acommunicative target response, it often stimulated students to select the distractor.

These studies of communicatively oriented testing are important, since they show that as long as test makers work with certain underlying constraints, the problems associated with conventional testing not only remain but often become more severe. As we approach the 21st century, it is not clear that test makers, despite their claims of a more communicative approach, are in a position to solve the problems associated with the major genre of reading tests that has dominated the 20th century. It is for this reason that we explore alternatives to this genre in the final section of this chapter.

A broader perspective

Before discontinuing the use of particular tests, it is useful to consider them from a broader perspective: what kinds of functions do they perform within education and the larger society? In addressing this question, we would like to begin with a basic distinction between CLASSROOM-ORIENTED and SYSTEM-ORIENTED FUNCTIONS. In another study (Hill & Larsen, 1992), we describe the major classroom-oriented function as *monitoring student learning* (in using this term, we have in mind not only the monitoring that teachers do of student learning but the self-monitoring that students themselves do).

Such monitoring is often provided by assessment activities that teachers themselves prepare, but externally produced tests increasingly include a diagnostic scheme that claims to perform this function. As Hill (1992) observes, these schemes are highly suspect when they accompany a multiple-choice test, since they classify each task only on the basis of what its target response calls for. Hill goes on to point out that

> anyone who has worked with a multiple-choice format knows that the real demands of a given task are anchored in the total configuration of choices. In effect, the reader has to work through each choice, evaluate what its particular demands are, and then come up with some way of evaluating which choice is, in fact, the most appropriate one. The real point of many tasks...is to force readers to choose between a literal target response and one or more distractors based on richer inferencing. Indeed, test takers are forced to develop an overall tactical approach, no matter how implicit it may remain, for selecting one choice over the others as they move from task to task; and it is their use of such test-taking tactics that is not accounted for in the diagnostic schemes that accompany standardized tests. (1992, p. 23)

We should note that test makers who constructed the Gates-MacGinitie Reading Tests wisely refrained from including such a diagnostic scheme. In explaining this policy, MacGinitie (1973) makes telling arguments against such a scheme.

As for system-oriented functions of testing, they can be placed under three headings: *selecting students, certifying students,* and *monitoring the educational system.* These different functions are not always separable in actual testing practice, but they can be conveniently illustrated by well-known tests used at the secondary level. The first function—selecting students—is associated with the Scholastic Achievement Test (SAT), which is widely used by American colleges and universities in determining which students to accept. The second function—certifying students—is carried out by the test for the General Equivalency Diploma (GED): successful performance on this test is supposed to indicate that an individual possesses the knowledge and skills associated with completing secondary education. The third function—monitoring the educational system—is performed by tests administered by the National Assessment of Educational Progress (NAEP): the results of these tests are used in assessing the performance of the educational system at the national level and, more recently, at the state level as well.

If we turn to the testing of young children's reading comprehension, we might well ask which of these system-oriented functions it serves. Those responsible for such testing often claim that it is not designed to perform any of these functions. In the case of the first two functions, the ordinary use of reading tests for young children bears them out: these tests are not administered at a transition point when students are either certified or selected for further educational opportunities.

The tests are, however, often used, despite test makers' disclaimers, to monitor the educational system. Such monitoring takes place not only at the national and state levels but, in many parts of the country, at lower levels as well. In New York City, for example, the results of these tests—and of math tests—are published annually on a school-by-school basis in *The New York Times*; and even within a school, teachers often feel responsible for the performance of students in their classrooms. It is as if they feel parents, administrators, and other teachers are watching, which, indeed, is often the case. Principals are afraid that their school will receive a low ranking unless individual teachers are motivated to produce high scores on reading tests.

An article in *The New York Times* (Steinberg, 1997) on reading tests for third graders points out the increasing use of these tests to evaluate performance at all levels:

> Schools Chancellor Rudy Crew has said he will use the test scores...to hold the system accountable...to evaluate whether district superintendents...should be rehired, to determine whether struggling schools need more resources, and to identify schools that might benefit from a longer day or year. (B1)

The article includes an interview with Mr. Kessler, a third-grade teacher at P.S. 75, about how reading tests affect what he and other teachers do in the classroom. He describes various preparation activities that range

> from how to sit in one place for an hour (wear comfortable clothes)...to how to handle the questions (read them before reading the passage, to know what to look for). (B3)

Mr. Kessler goes on to say that

> he knows the test is one of the few ways his students' performance, as well
> as his own, his principal's and even the district superintendent's, can be
> measured against the rest of the city's. (B3)

As a consequence, he has "to take it very seriously," even though he
thinks that "it's horrible that this one day of testing means so much,
when there are so many other facts about their [the children's] reading
lives." (B3)

We have quoted from this article at some length because it dramatizes
how reading tests for young children can exercise massive control over
what goes on in the classroom. Rather than reading books that provide
fresh discoveries about the world, children are forced to pore over work-
sheets that simulate reading tests. As children respond to small bits of
decontextualized material followed by multiple-choice tasks, they
respond to text in such a limited way that they run the risk of internaliz-
ing an impoverished model of reading. It is not surprising that such
classroom practices have led many early childhood educators to take a
strong stand against a national reading test.

GUIDELINES FOR TEST MAKERS

Having made our case against reading tests for children, we would
like to restore the perspective with which we began this study—the
one that anticipated the possibility of our work having a positive
influence on test making. We return to this perspective because we
suspect that reading tests for children will remain in use at least for
the next few years: in New York State, these tests are still widely
used, despite recent legislative action that allows for alternative forms
of assessment in early childhood education. The array of forces holding these tests in place is so strong that they will continue to be used
until resistance to their use moves well beyond the school to the
larger society.

In the meantime it is important that we provide guidelines that test
makers can use to minimize the negative effects of an inherently flawed
approach. We have organized our guidelines into those that are concerned with passages and those that are concerned with tasks, but we
would like to emphasize an earlier point—the real text to be comprehended on a reading test is constituted by both the passage and the
tasks.

Constructing Passages

In constructing a passage, test makers should use material that is

1) relatively complete,
2) already written for children of an appropriate age (i.e., test makers should avoid constructing material expressly for a test),
3) not altered in any major way (e.g., in setting up a particular task, test makers should not remove a significant portion of the material),
4) not characterized by
   (a) a sudden shifting from one frame to another
   (b) an inordinate use of
      (i) lexical polarities
      (ii) unfamiliar vocabulary
      (iii) familiar vocabulary with an unfamiliar sense
      (iv) literary language (e.g., free indirect speech).

In following the first guideline, test makers may well have to construct more extended passages: the passages in our corpus usually contain only 3 or 4 short sentences, and most of them, as amply demonstrated, are incomplete in significant ways: for example, all the narrative passages in Part I we identified as truncated, excerpted, or gapped. If these passages had been somewhat longer—for example, even 5 or 6 sentences—their incompleteness could have been substantially reduced. To our way of thinking, it is worth reducing the number of passages, even if this means reduced sampling, in order to achieve greater completeness within each passage.

As for the second guideline, when test makers use actual material, they often have to adapt it in some way: for example, if they follow the fourth guideline, they may have to remove an unfamiliar word or even a familiar one used in an unfamiliar way. Test makers should carry out such adaptations with great care so that they do not compromise the basic integrity of the material (e.g., as they adapt vocabulary, they should be careful to maintain the writer's style).

In general, test makers should keep adaptations of existing material to a minimum. As indicated by the third guideline, they should not take out a significant chunk of text in order to set up a task. In LEAVING HOME (p. 68), we observed how certain information seems to have been removed in order to set up a task. Such a major distortion of text structure can cause young children to be unsure about whether they have properly understood the passage. Such uncertainty, in turn, can undermine their performance in a testing situation.

In closing this section, we would like to comment briefly on the use of pictures with reading passages. As we pointed out in our discussion of

GREEN CEDARS, children are accustomed to reading material that is comprised of both words and pictures. It can thus be argued that tests achieve greater authenticity by introducing such pictures. If test makers do move in this direction, they need to develop explicit guidelines about the degree to which pictures should introduce new information or merely reinforce what is conveyed by the words.

Constructing Tasks

We have already delineated a number of inconsistent patterns in task construction (see pp. 358–366). For the sake of convenience, we here present this material as a set of six guidelines for testmakers (the first three deal with inconsistencies within the tasks, the second three with inconsistent relations with the passage).

1) A task should provide overt representation of its function, especially if that function is acommunicative.
2) Task choices should parallel each other not only in surface form but in the grammatical category to which they belong (e.g., the choices for a sentence-completion task should not be spread across the categories of noun, adjective, and verb).
3) No choice should result in a proposition (target or distractor) that is ill-formed
   (a) from a semantic-syntactic perspective
   (b) from a pragmatic perspective
4) In recycling passage information, a task should be consistent in its use of
   (a) cohesion devices such as determiners, pronominals, or verb tenses
   (b) punctuation such as quotation marks
5) A task should be consistent in whether it presents passage information
   (a) in full or partial form
   (b) from a figurative or literal perspective
6) A task should be consistent in whether or not it extends passage information.

Some of these guidelines are easier to follow than others: for example, the first three are quite manageable, especially if test makers were to discontinue the use of sentence-completion tasks (such tasks generated all the inconsistencies within our corpus that are dealt with under guidelines 2 and 3).[2]

As for the guidelines dealing with relations to the passage, the fourth guideline, especially (a), is more difficult to follow, since the use of cohesion markers within tasks is prone to vary in accordance with the use of such markers within the passage itself: if the passage, for example, uses only pronominals for stylistic reasons, it may be confusing to shift to nominals in the tasks. Nevertheless, it is important that test makers strive for a consistent use of cohesion markers across tasks, since certain test takers, even at an early age, come to rely on such consistency.

Before leaving guidelines for task construction, we would like to lay out briefly a set of three guidelines for constructing a vocabulary-defining task (in effect, we are here realizing the heuristic procedures for test makers that we envisioned at the outset of the study):

1) The vocabulary-defining function should be made explicit (i.e., this accords with the first guideline listed above).
2) The vocabulary item to be defined should be one that children are not likely to know.
3) The context of use should allow children to make sense of the vocabulary item.

If these conditions are not met, a vocabulary-defining task should not be included in a test of reading comprehension. If the point is simply to determine whether children know a certain word, they can be asked to define it apart from a reading passage.

We should note that one test unit within our corpus provides an excellent exemplar of a vocabulary-defining task:

In the story the word "abated" means *died down.* (HURRICANE)

An explicit formula is used, the word *abated* is unfamiliar to children, and the context provides them a clue with which they can figure out the meaning (i.e., in the final sentence of the passage—*Luckily, the mighty storm soon abated*—the word *luckily* provides the necessary clue).

Having laid out these guidelines for test makers, we would like to remind the reader of the basic opposition to reading tests that we set forth earlier: even if test makers strictly follow these guidelines, the basic flaws that we have delineated would still be present; and, of course, the negative effects on classroom practice would continue as well. Nevertheless, these guidelines, if followed, could improve the quality of reading tests for young children; and as long as such tests are used, it is important that they be constructed as carefully as possible.

A final note in concluding this section—test makers could also benefit from some of the methods that we have used in evaluating test material. For example, interviewing children would provide a useful supplement to psychometric methods; such interviewing can uncover a range of problems that a purely statistical method glosses over. We are aware that test makers operate with financial constraints but a judicious use of interviewing could turn out to be cost-effective in the long run: not only would it help test makers uncover problems in proposed test material at an early stage but the very activity by which these problems are uncovered would increase test makers' sensitivity to the various ethnocultural worlds of language, thought, and experience that children bring to text. From our perspective, such sensitivity is perhaps the most important ingredient in the test-making enterprise.

Such interviewing is being experimented with in test-making situations in Asian countries. Yuan (1997) has used interviews to help test makers in Taiwan evaluate test material for the college entrance exam. Wang and Hill (in press) are using interviews and think-aloud protocols to construct short-answer tasks for material used on the College English Test in the People's Republic of China (this test is taken annually by more than two million university students to certify their knowledge and skills in English). The interviews and think-aloud protocols are designed to uncover the inferences that readers make in response to various passages. By introducing these methods in an early stage of test making, the gap between real-world reading and test reading can, in principle, be diminished (i.e., tasks can be built around inferences that readers naturally make).

The Department of Education in this country is proposing such research as part of the development of the national reading test for fourth graders. In examining the specifications for developing such a test, we were surprised to discover that they emphasize think-aloud protocols rather than interviews. On the basis of our own experience, we question whether think-aloud protocols can be used effectively with children of this age.

ALTERNATIVE ASSESSMENT

The last few years have brought a virtual explosion of activities described as ALTERNATIVE ASSESSMENT. We should note at the outset that the use of the word *alternative* suggests that conventional testing continues to exercise a certain dominance. In fact, many forms of alternative assessment still involve testing, although it often calls for test takers to construct their own responses.

As for alternative assessment in early childhood education, testing is often complemented by what Hill and Larsen (1992) have described as DOCUMENTATION. The most familiar kind of documentation involves portfolios, a term generally used to describe a body of student work assembled over time for purposes of evaluation. In our own approach to alternative assessment in early childhood education, we have attempted to maintain a balance between portfolio activities and activities that we describe as TESTLIKE. These two kinds of activities together comprise an assessment model called the Progress Profile. As the name suggests, such an approach is designed to reflect the child's individual development and hence can be referred to as SELF-REFERENCED (in contrast to the NORM-REFERENCED and CRITERION-REFERENCED approaches of conventional testing).[3]

We would like briefly to characterize how the Progress Profile is used to assess the literacy knowledge and skills of young children (it is also used to assess their numeracy knowledge and skills). We will first present testlike activities and then portfolio activities.

Testlike Activities

Testlike activities are those that fall loosely within a testing paradigm, but that do not meet its most strict conditions. In another study (Hill & Larsen, 1992), we have described these conditions in the following way:

1) a single time frame of specified duration,
2) prescribed tasks presented in a stable form,
3) individual responses relatively independent of external resources, and
4) evaluation of individual responses based on a preestablished scheme.[4]

Here is a brief outline of how testlike activities in the Progress Profile fit with these conditions:

1) Children carry out activities in a single time frame, but it is not of a specified duration; they are allowed, within reason, to use as much time as they need (i.e., no attempt is made to use time as a way of showing how efficiently children can respond to tasks).
2) Children do respond to prescribed tasks initially presented in a stable form; if an individual child does not understand a given task or is unable to perform it, the test giver—who is ordinarily the child's teacher—can provide additional information. In fact, the teacher is encouraged to do so. The Progress Profile has been influenced by the model of dynamic assessment developed by Feuerstein (1978), in which teaching and learning are allowed, indeed encouraged, within assessment activities; from Feuerstein's perspective, one of the goals of assessment is to determine how well a child can use relevant information in problem-solving (the evaluation of a child's responses takes into account the specific information that a test giver provides).
3) Although it is the individual child who responds to the activities, the use of external resources is encouraged; for example, in writing a response to what they have read, a child can use a dictionary (i.e., the

basic principle is that children should be in a position to use resources that they ordinarily use in carrying out a particular activity).

4) All children's responses are evaluated, but a preestablished scheme that yields a numerical score is used only for responses to certain tasks (e.g., a comprehension question that calls for factual information); such a scheme is not used to evaluate responses that involve a certain amount of inherent variation (e.g., extending a story). Such responses are, however, evaluated in other ways. In the case of a story extension, the teacher makes notes on the degree to which the extension is motivated by elements in the text base.

We would now like to describe representative activities within the Progress Profile. We can begin by noting that these activities are usually administered at the end of the school year to provide a culminating experience for children. Some schools also administer them at the beginning of the year to provide baseline data. Central to these activities is the child's experience of a book, which reflects our conviction that assessment activities should be concerned with what children ordinarily do. The teacher begins by presenting a collection of small books and encouraging the child to select a particular one. Certain schools have developed a collection for different content areas, such as language arts or social studies; in the language arts we have encouraged teachers to develop a multicultural collection of folktales.

To illustrate how folktales have been used in assessing reading comprehension, we will use a story that was collected among the Hausa people in West Africa. In the original version, the animal is a *dila* "jackal"[5] and the bird a *zal'be* "stork," but in adapting the tale for use with American children, the jackal was changed to the more familiar fox.

One day a fox was eating a chicken when a sharp bone got stuck in his throat. As he began to call for help, he said, "I'll give a reward to anyone who can get this bone out of my throat." A stork came walking along and said, "I'll help you get that bone out." So the stork stuck his head in the fox's mouth and pulled it out.

The fox then turned around and started to walk away. The stork was surprised and so he asked, "Where's my reward?" The fox answered, "Here's your reward: you stuck your head in a fox's mouth and you're still alive."

After reading the story, the children engage in the following testlike activities:

Retelling the story:
Can you tell me in your own words what you just read?

Factual tasks:
Why did the fox need the stork's help?
What did the stork do to help the fox?

Inferential tasks:
Why was the stork able to help the fox?
Do you think the stork got a real reward? Please explain your thinking.

Holistic tasks:
Write an ending to this story in which the stork manages to get something
that (s)he thinks is a real reward. You can either change what the fox did
or add something new that shows the stork getting the kind of reward
(s)he wants.

Experiential tasks:
Describe an experience in which you were disappointed by a reward that
you received. Try to explain why you and the other person differed in
your thinking about a reward.

To illustrate how children respond to the retelling task—which provides an effective foundation for the tasks that follow—we here present
contrasting kinds of retellings, which can be described respectively as
performance style and *summary style.*

> The fox was eating a chicken and he started choking and yelling, "Help!
> Help! I'll give you a reward." And a stork came and helped him. The fox
> didn't give him a reward and...um...the stork yelled, "Where's my
> reward?" The fox said, "You're just lucky to be alive. I didn't bite your
> head off." (11-year-old African American boy)

> The fox was eating and...um...he was eating something and a bone got
> stuck in his throat and after he finished eating it...he felt pain and then he
> went to the stork—I think it was—and the stork helped him with the bone
> and took it out. (10-year-old African American girl)

One major benefit of the Progress Profile is that it allows for legitimate variation in how children respond to a task. Many children whose
language development takes place primarily in oral culture draw on a
more performance-oriented style as they retell a folktale. As we have
seen in this study, when children retell test material, they may use a
familiar formula such as "once upon a time" (see p. 91). Rather than
penalizing children for adopting a performance style (which a testing
paradigm does by requiring them to adopt an acommunicative stance),
the Progress Profile simply records what kind of style a particular child
uses (such information can be useful in the cumulative school record). It
also records the degree to which children include basic plot elements in
their retelling. When teachers listen to children's retelling of this partic-

	yes/no	Comments
STORY STYLE		
Performance		
Summary	✓	hesitant style—use of "I think it was"
STORY ELEMENTS		
fox gets bone stuck in throat	✓	Chicken not mentioned; fox felt pain
fox offers a reward for help		
stork gets bone out	✓	
fox doesn't give reward		
stork asks for reward		
fox explains what reward is		

FIGURE 8.4

ular tale, they provide appropriate checks and comments on a preestablished form. Figure 8.4 shows how this form was used to record the summary offered by the 10-year-old African American girl. As can be seen, the test giver did not check the four story elements that have to do with the reward. She also included brief notes on distinctive aspects of the girl's retelling.

The tasks that follow the retelling are built around the model of comprehension developed by Bloom (1984). The first two kinds of tasks reflect the familiar distinction between literal and inferential comprehension. Rather than setting up a tension between the two—as multiple-choice tasks tend to do—the Progress Profile keeps them separate. One of the inferential tasks asks children to explain their response. In this way, it helps us to determine the degree to which children use the text base in motivating their inference (this information is recorded along with the response itself).

Having responded to the factual and inferential tasks, children are then asked to respond holistically by extending the folktale in some way. The particular way in which children respond to this task often sheds a good deal of light on their understanding of the tale. An 11-year-old African American boy, for example, focused on the stork getting the reward before providing any help (he begins with direct speech expressing the stork's indignation).

"That is not fair. I did you a favor and I don't get anything." The stork left. A couple of days later the fox got a bone stuck in his throat. He went

> back to the stork and asked for help. The stork said, "No." The fox begged and begged so the stork said, "If you give me my reward before I do anything, then I will do it." The fox gave him a reward and he got the bone out of his throat.

It is interesting that this child doesn't bother to specify what the reward is. It is as if the real point of his story is achieved once the fox agrees to give the reward in advance.

The final testlike activity requires children to make a connection between what they have read and their own experience. In responding to this particular folktale, children frequently activate a scenario in which if they get good grades, their parents give them an unwanted book. As one child put it, "they should at least give us something fun for all the hard work."

After children complete this set of comprehension tasks, they carry out a limited set of tasks that focus on literacy conventions: they are asked, for example, (1) to identify specific uses of punctuation such as capitalization or quotation marks and explain how they are being used; (2) to read aloud a short excerpt so that teachers can do a miscue analysis (Goodman, 1976); and (3) to write down a short excerpt that is read aloud so that their knowledge of sound-spelling correspondences can be evaluated. Children's responses to these tasks are evaluated quantitatively according to a preexisting scheme, but it is one designed to take account of appropriate variation: for example, when children write down what they hear, they receive partial credit for any phonetically motivated spelling, even if it is not the correct one (e.g., speakers of African American vernacular receive partial credit for "axed" in place of *asked*).

To our way of thinking, these tasks, though metalinguistic in nature, do not confuse children in the way that metalinguistic tasks often do on reading tests. They do not, for example, force children to carry out metalinguistic analyses as a means of responding to comprehension tasks. We have clearly separated these activities from the comprehension activities that precede them. Moreover, the direct manipulations of language structure that they call for are ones that children are accustomed to doing within normal classroom routines. Combining these two kinds of activities sends a valuable message to both teachers and children—comprehension is at the heart of literacy development but it must not preclude attention to language form.

Why did we decide to include testlike activities in the Progress Profile? There are many answers to this question, but we should perhaps begin with the political context. When we first worked on a model of alternative assessment for a school district, the administrators insisted that we include a component that would yield numerical scores: if we did not meet this condition, they were not willing to discontinue the use of conventional testing. We agreed with this demand because we were glad to have some kind of leverage over the use of such testing: not only did we oppose it for the reasons set out in this study but we had observed in other situations how its continued use undermines efforts to build alternative assessment. Children, teachers, and administrators have difficulty in taking such assessment seriously when conventional testing continues to operate.

Apart from this political context, we wanted to include testlike activities because we felt that they would contribute to the professional development of teachers. To begin with, as teachers work together to develop these activities, they have an opportunity to share their best practices with each other. They also have an opportunity to develop clinical knowledge and skills as they learn to do a miscue analysis or to evaluate sound-spelling correspondences. Moreover, as teachers administer testlike activities, they have an opportunity to make careful observations that carry over into their daily interactions with individual children. It is as if these activities foster development of their capacity to make responsible judgments about children.

From the children's point of view, the close attention that they receive from their teacher can be a rewarding experience that increases their confidence and motivation. We have discovered that children look forward to testlike activities as an opportunity to show what they know and can do; the fact that the teacher is able to help them contributes to their sense of achievement. This feeling contrasts sharply with the fear and intimidation that reading tests often engender.

Portfolio Activities

Within the Progress Profile, portfolio activities around reading vary from school to school, but they generally reflect two components: (1) a journal in which a child's home reading experiences are documented; and (2) written projects based on the child's exploratory reading in different content areas. The first component has been so well-received that we encourage teachers to initiate it as early as kindergarten. As children take home books to read each week, they take along a small notebook in which entries can be made: whoever reads with the child—a parent, a grandparent, an older sibling, or even a visiting friend—writes comments about the child's reading experience (as children progress, they are encouraged to write their own comments as well). When the child brings the notebook back to school, the teacher responds to the entry. In this way, a home–school dialogue is accumulated around the books that the child reads during the course of the year. This journal has the incidental benefit of providing a record of what each child reads at home during the school year; such records can be quite informative at the beginning of a new school year when children move from one teacher to another.

As to written projects in different content areas, these can take a variety of forms. In the language arts, teachers have shown considerable ingenuity in helping children display personal work: the stories children tell and the accompanying pictures they draw are brought together in small books with a pocket inside the cover for a library card. Once these books are completed, they can check them out and read each other's stories at home.

In discussing this activity, Hill (1992) has described various kinds of literacy knowledge that it fosters in children; they learn, for example,

> how an individual book is organized (images and words working together to make meaning) and how books are organized in a library. Here they get early exposure to the alphabetical principle of organization basic to the Western experience of literacy; the alphabet becomes something more for children than a string of letters to recite. But apart from this practical knowledge of literacy, children learn an even more important lesson—that they can bring their personal worlds to the classroom. (pp. 38-39)

Such active assimilation of literacy knowledge and skills is reinforced by portfolio activities as a whole. In order to assemble their portfolios, children are expected to maintain separate files in which they keep track of multiple drafts of various projects. They must then take responsibility for deciding which projects to include in the portfolio and how they will be presented. In preparing an introduction for their portfolios, they must explain not only how these decisions were made but how the portfolio itself is organized. This approach to portfolios develops not only children's literacy skills but their capacity for evaluating their own work. To our way of thinking, developing a capacity for self-monitoring lies at the heart of any good approach to assessment.

We would like to conclude this discussion of alternative assessment on an optimistic, but cautious note. A model such as the Progress Profile offers substantial benefits, but it can be quite difficult to put into place and to sustain. It can place a great deal of strain on local resources: if teachers do not receive strong administrative support, they often find that they are unable to do all that is expected of them.

Moreover, alternative assessment runs the risk of producing so much material that it can be difficult to use. Teachers need to develop ways of first pruning it and then presenting it in an intelligible fashion. Technology will come to play an increasingly useful role in helping teachers to create and transmit an assessment profile for individual children that can be used at school (e.g., by prospective teachers) and at home (by the children themselves as well as their parents). Technology also has the advantage of providing virtual records so that children can eventually take their work home (e.g., picture books). It is ultimately the home that should be the repository of children's work.

Finally, it must be recognized that alternative assessment, at least at this stage of its development, cannot provide quantitative evaluation that achieves a high degree of reliability from a psychometric point of view. As a consequence, it has been subjected to a great deal of criticism from those who are accustomed to the psychometric profile associated with conventional testing. To counter such criticism, it is important that the public be educated on two fronts. First, it must become more aware of what psychometric reliability in conventional testing means: a high degree of reliability can be purchased only at the cost of reducing a complex activity such as reading to a highly circumscribed exercise. The arguments against such an exercise that our study offers must be made with force and clarity in the public domain.

Second, the public needs to learn more about what to expect from alternative assessment. It is not realistic to expect such assessment, given the range and complexity of its various activities, to achieve the kind of reliability associated with conventional testing. Rather the public must be educated to think about reliability in a new way, to associate it with the more comprehensive, and thus more valuable, understanding of individual students that alternative assessment can provide. This new way of thinking is especially important in early childhood education, where the basic role of assessment is to provide a comprehensive understanding of individual children that can be used in facilitating their exploration of knowledge and their development of skills.

NOTES

1. It is for this reason, among others, that we are not altogether convinced of the wisdom of what coaching schools often teach: read the tasks first and then go back to the passage. Such advice may be particularly dangerous for young children who have not developed a firm sense of test-taking norms.

2. We have not set up a separate guideline in which we recommend that sentence-completion tasks be discontinued. We would, however, encourage test makers to give serious consideration to discontinuing such tasks, just as we would encourage them to think about discontinuing the use of the word *story* within a task stem.

3.   The name is borrowed from an assessment model that is used most widely in adult education in the United Kingdom. Holland and Street (1994) use the term *ipsative* (i.e., self-referenced) to characterize this model. Alternative assessment has tended to be used in early childhood education and adult education, two domains in which educators often have greater freedom to experiment.

4.   In addition, the evaluation of the responses must receive institutional sanction. In order to prepare students for a test, a teacher may administer an activity that meets the first four conditions, but this activity does not count as a test, since the teacher's evaluation of student responses is not entered into any official record (for further discussion, see Hill & Larsen, 1992).

5.   Hausa speakers typically describe a *dila* as the *malamin daji* "a clever teacher in the wild."

appendix A

Corpus of Test Units

ADVERTISING TAILOR

An advertising tailor put a sign on the ballpark fence. The sign announced that he would give away a suit of clothes for each home run. Biff took notice. He began to hammer out a wardrobe at such a terrific pace that the owner of the little shop trembled when he heard the news of the game.

A. Biff "hammered out a wardrobe" by
    making a closet   a notice
    home runs   suits

B. The tailor was surprised to see how much he had
    made   trembled
    sold   promised

ALICE AND THE FAWN

The fawn looked at Alice with its large, gentle eyes. It didn't seem at all frightened. "Here, then! Here, then!" Alice said, as she held out her hand and tried to stroke it. It moved back a little and then stood looking at her again.

A. How did the fawn's eyes look?
    sad   tired
    gentle   frightened

B. What did Alice try to do to the fawn?
    help it   pet it
    hug it   hide it

BACTERIA

From the earliest times, people have found ways to keep food from spoiling. The ancient Egyptians kept grain in dry, cool storehouses. They added salt to fish and meat or dried them in the sun. For centuries people have also kept meat from spoiling by smoking it. All of these methods kill bacteria that cause rotting.

A. Which will keep meat from spoiling?
    water   grain
    bacteria   salt

B. Bacteria grow best when food is
    smoked   dry
    warm and damp   cool and dry

BLACK BONNET

The train stopped. Miss Esther stood far back to get away from the smoke and roar. As the cars pulled away, she took a few steps forward to scan the platform. There was no black bonnet with a worn lace veil, no old lady with a burden of bundles. There were only the stationmaster, a boy or two, and a clean-faced bent old man with a bird cage in one hand and an old carpetbag in the other.

A. What was Miss Esther expecting to see?
    a lot of people   an old man
    a black bonnet   a bird cage

B. Miss Esther stepped forward when the
    crowd left   crowd arrived
    train left   train arrived

CHEE TONG

During the day, Chee Tong traveled around the city with his stove. The boatman took his boat up and down the river, but at night he always tied up at the same place. There they met, and together they ate the evening meal, prepared and cooked by Chee Tong. It was a most satisfactory arrangement—the boatman provided shelter, Chee Tong the meals.

A. What did the two men do together?
   cook   go up the river
   tie up   eat

B. What was the shelter?
   a boat   a stove
   a house   an arrangement

CLASS ELECTION

The class became very quiet as Joan opened the last few ballots. The count was 17 to 17. Then she opened the final ballot. "Our new president," she said, "is Jason Brandt."

A. They were voting for
   a new club   club president
   class president   a class name

B. The final count was
   18 to 17   17 to 17
   Jason Brandt   Joan and Jason

GEORGE WASHINGTON BRIDGE

The George Washington Bridge, completed in 1931, spans the Hudson River between New York and New Jersey. The plan for the bridge called for stone coverings over the two towers. But the steel structure itself was beautiful, so the towers stayed as they were.

A. In this story, "called for" means
   picked up   telephoned
   realized   required

B. The finished towers are made of
   stone   steel over stone
   steel   stone over steel

GREEN CEDARS

Far back in the deep woods, the limbs of a large tree stretched gray among the green cedars. Once that tree, too, had been green, but now the leaves were gone, and the tree was dead. Low, near the ground, a black hole opened into the hollow trunk of the tree. Inside the hole a mother bear and her two babies lay on a nest of grass and leaves.

A. The green trees were
    gone   dying
    cedars   hollow

B. Where was the nest?
    inside a tree   on a dead limb
    in a cave   on a green tree

HARD LEAD

Near the top of most pencils there is a symbol, usually a letter or a number. It tells you whether the pencil is soft or hard. If you want your writing to be thick and dark, you select a pencil with a soft lead.

A. You choose a hard lead to make lines that are
    thick   red
    hard   light

B. The letters or numbers near the tops of pencils are
    useless   dates
    symbols   lead

HUNG BRIDGES

Suspension bridges are hung from towers by strong cables. Golden Gate Bridge in San Francisco is one of the world's longest suspension bridges. The world's smallest such bridge may be in the Boston Public Garden. No great ocean liners sail under Tiny Bridge, but Swan Boats do.

A. These bridges are
    towers   long
    small   hung

B. Where is Tiny Bridge?
    in London   in San Francisco
    at Golden Gate   in Boston

HURRICANE

The hurricane dumped huge amounts of rain on the island. Its strong winds knocked down trees and blew away houses. The island's streams and rivers began to overflow, flooding the towns. Luckily, the mighty storm soon abated.

A. The story says that trees were
   flooded   strong
   blown over   blown away

B. In the story, the word "abated" means
   died down   got worse
   rained   blew

ICEBERG

An iceberg is a large chunk of frozen fresh water that floats in the sea. Most of the iceberg is below the surface. Just the top part is visible.

A. Icebergs are made mostly of
   sea water   fresh water
   salt   rock

B. Most of the iceberg is
   hidden   visible
   surface   top

JAYS AND CROWS

It was the season of jays and crows. Their harsh voices pierced the silent air. From everywhere in the woods came the hollow drilling of wood-peckers and the dropping of acorns. Small creatures moved about the floor of the woods noisily. In the dry, crackling ocean of leaves the running squirrel sounded like a man, the hopping sparrow like a dog.

A. This story is mainly about
   birds   voices
   sounds   trees

B. The story says that the air was
   harsh   cold
   silent   clear

LEARNING TO READ

She looked at the calendar. "Only two more days and I go to school. In three days I can read!"

Mama chuckled. "Not quite that soon, dear."

"How many days?"

"Some children learn to read in a few months. Some learn in about a year."

A year? A whole year? Maybe not till she was seven? That would be awful!

A. How old is the girl in this story?

six	four
eight	seven

B. At first, how long did the girl think it would take her to learn to read at school?

three days	one day
a few months	a year

LEAVING HOME

Jim and his family were going away for a week. They took a bus across town to the train station and then settled down for a long trip. First they passed by many tall buildings and busy streets. Later they went by farms and woods. They went through other cities, too, before they reached the little town near the sea.

A. Where is Jim's home?

by the sea	in a little town
on a farm	in a city

B. Most of the trip was by

train	bus
car	boat

MINNESOTA

So much flour and so many dairy products come from Minnesota that it is often called the Bread and Butter State. It is also called the Gopher State because of all the gophers that live in the prairies. The name of the state comes from the Indian words meaning "sky-tinted water."

A. This story is mainly about Minnesota's
    products   prairies
    names   history

B. When the Indians said "Minnesota," they were talking about
    gophers   water
    a state   bread

MOTHER ALLIGATOR

The first time a mother alligator hears her babies, she cannot see them. Their little grunts are coming from a pile of mud and old leaves. That is where the mother alligator laid her eggs many weeks ago.

A. Alligators lay their eggs in
    mud   the night
    water   the winter

B. The "little grunts" in the story are
    old leaves   baby alligators
    eggs   noises

NERVOUS HORSE

Her horse was a little nervous, so she let it trot along slowly. Suddenly, something in the bushes rustled. The horse broke into a canter, then into a full gallop. She held on tightly, talking quietly in order to try to calm it.

A. Which pace is the slowest?
    canter   rustle
    gallop   trot

B. In the story, "broke into" means
    robbed   ran into
    started   tamed

RAISINS

Raisins are made from sweet varieties of grapes. The ripe fruit is usually placed on trays right in the vineyard. There, it dries in the sun. Drying may take several weeks.

A. Raisins are made from grapes that have
    a lot of water   varieties
    skin   sugar

B. What kind of climate is best for raisin-making?
    warm and dry   warm and wet
    cool and dry   cool and wet

SHOP SIGN

Its first appearance sent a flutter of excitement through the street. It was only a shop sign, made up of white lettering on a sky-blue background. It announced that Mrs. Doyle was a dealer in candies, homemade taffies, confectionery, and sundries. The "sundries" was a mystery to most of the admirers of the sign, but they assumed it meant something at least as delicious as caramel.

A. What was the mystery?
    an appearance   the caramel
    a woman   a word

B. The story is mainly about
    candies   a shop
    a sign   Mrs. Doyle

SPINELESS CACTUS

Animals would destroy cactus plants if it were not for their forbidding spines. A plant experimenter, Luther Burbank, produced a spineless variety of prickly-pear cactus. But cattle and other large animals devoured it so rapidly that the spineless cactus did not have a chance to survive long in nature.

A. Burbank's new plant did not live long in nature because it
    was too weak   needed water
    had no seeds   was eaten up

B. Burbank's plant had no
    juice   taste
    spines   fruit

WHITE CIRCLES

As she rolled to a stop in the center of the business district, she quickly was surrounded by townspeople. They were surprised when a woman stood up in the cockpit. When she raised her goggles they were even more surprised. She had been flying into the sun all day and her face was sunburned a bright red except for white circles around her eyes where her goggles had protected her. She blinked out at the assembled population of Hobbs like a boiled owl.

A. She came into town by
airplane   car
motorcycle   parachute

B. The people were surprised when they saw her
owl   blinking
goggles   white circles

Results of Pilot Testing

Appendix B provides the results of the pilot testing for each of the tasks in our corpus. The figures represent the proportion of African American (AA) and European American (EA) third graders who chose each answer (those who did not indicate a choice have been excluded). Because of rounding, the percentages for certain tasks do not add up to 100. The target response for each task is italicized.

Advertising Tailor

	AA	EA		AA	EA
A. a closet	11%	16%	B. made	39%	37%
a notice	29%	28%	trembled	18%	24%
home runs	35%	38%	sold	26%	26%
suits	21%	22%	*promised*	17%	13%

Alice and the Fawn

	AA	EA		AA	EA
A. sad	18%	12%	B. help it	47%	30%
tired	11%	9%	*pet it*	26%	52%
gentle	46%	64%	hug it	18%	10%
frightened	25%	17%	hide it	9%	8%

Bacteria

	AA	EA		AA	EA
A. water	23%	16%	B. smoked	34%	30%
grain	16%	19%	dry	19%	20%
bacteria	28%	20%	*warm and damp*	15%	23%
salt	33%	45%	cool and dry	32%	27%

Black Bonnet

	AA	EA		AA	EA
A. a lot of people	25%	35%	B. crowd left	12%	35%
an old man	32%	16%	crowd arrived	16%	13%
a black bonnet	21%	35%	*train left*	49%	43%
a bird cage	21%	13%	train arrived	23%	9%

Chee Tong

	AA	EA		AA	EA
A. cook	27%	20%	B. *a boat*	34%	42%
go up the river	29%	33%	a stove	24%	20%
tie up	3%	6%	a house	14%	13%
eat	41%	40%	an arrangement	28%	24%

Class Election

	AA	EA		AA	EA
A. a new club	8%	9%	B. *18 to 17*	19%	21%
club president	14%	11%	17 to 17	60%	59%
class president	57%	62%	Jason Brandt	15%	13%
a class name	21%	18%	Joan and Jason	5%	7%

George Washington Bridge

	AA	EA		AA	EA
A. picked up	32%	26%	B. stone	35%	26%
telephoned	20%	21%	steel over stone	8%	17%
realized	20%	20%	*steel*	38%	30%
required	29%	33%	stone over steel	19%	27%

Green Cedars

	AA	EA			AA	EA
A. gone	21%	23%	B. *inside a tree*		44%	59%
dying	31%	31%	on a dead limb		17%	12%
cedars	15%	15%	in a cave		12%	7%
hollow	33%	31%	on a green tree		27%	22%

Hard Lead

	AA	EA			AA	EA
A. thick	32%	38%	B. useless		35%	9%
red	20%	7%	dates		8%	9%
hard	20%	21%	*symbols*		38%	56%
light	29%	34%	lead		19%	26%

Hung Bridges

	AA	EA			AA	EA
A. towers	11%	17%	B. in London		10%	4%
long	30%	32%	in San Francisco		33%	21%
small	36%	20%	at Golden Gate		20%	19%
hung	22%	31%	*in Boston*		36%	55%

Hurricane

	AA	EA			AA	EA
A. flooded	13%	11%	B. *died down*		23%	47%
strong	27%	14%	got worse		37%	17%
blown over	33%	47%	rained		15%	16%
blown away	27%	28%	blew		25%	19%

Iceberg

	AA	EA			AA	EA
A. sea water	40%	31%	B. *hidden*		32%	35%
fresh water	53%	58%	visible		37%	38%
salt	3%	4%	surface		18%	15%
rock	4%	6%	top		15%	9%

Jays and Crows

	AA	EA		AA	EA
A. birds	52%	43%	B. harsh	10%	20%
voices	15%	18%	cold	27%	18%
sounds	26%	30%	*silent*	31%	36%
trees	7%	9%	clear	32%	26%

Learning to Read

	AA	EA		AA	EA
A. *six*	26%	40%	B. three days	42%	49%
four	23%	14%	*one day*	19%	17%
eight	10%	5%	a few months	16%	16%
seven	41%	41%	a year	23%	18%

Leaving Home

	AA	EA		AA	EA
A. by the sea	32%	23%	B. *train*	43%	56%
in a little town	32%	34%	bus	27%	27%
on a farm	12%	9%	car	18%	9%
in a city	24%	35%	boat	12%	7%

Minnesota

	AA	EA		AA	EA
A. products	30%	46%	B. gophers	34%	31%
prairies	20%	30%	*water*	26%	28%
names	25%	22%	a state	22%	25%
history	15%	12%	bread	17%	16%

Mother Alligator

	AA	EA		AA	EA
A. *mud*	64%	78%	B. old leaves	23%	16%
the night	17%	8%	baby alligators	49%	63%
water	6%	7%	eggs	25%	17%
the winter	13%	6%	*noises*	3%	4%

Nervous Horse

	AA	EA		AA	EA
A. *canter*	19%	17%	B. robbed	27%	13%
rustle	14%	41%	ran into	37%	16%
gallop	28%	22%	*started*	17%	16%
trot	39%	19%	tamed	19%	55%

Raisins

	AA	EA		AA	EA
A. water	23%	16%	B. *warm and dry*	57%	61%
varieties	47%	62%	warm and wet	13%	11%
skin	12%	7%	cool and dry	17%	15%
sugar	18%	14%	cool and wet	13%	13%

Shop Sign

	AA	EA		AA	EA
A. an appearance	36%	31%	B. candies	23%	28%
the caramel	36%	34%	a shop	22%	14%
a woman	22%	20%	*a sign*	23%	17%
a word	7%	16%	Mrs. Doyle	32%	40%

Spineless Cactus

	AA	EA		AA	EA
A. was too weak	41%	30%	B. juice	27%	20%
needed water	27%	32%	taste	11%	15%
had no seeds	9%	10%	*spines*	37%	44%
was eaten up	24%	28%	fruit	25%	21%

White Circles

	AA	EA		AA	EA
A. *airplane*	33%	47%	B. owl	20%	11%
car	33%	26%	blinking	24%	18%
motorcycle	11%	10%	goggles	31%	45%
parachute	23%	17%	*white circles*	25%	25%

Glossary

This glossary groups together terms that are conceptually related as subentries under a main entry (e.g., all the different kinds of tasks are entered as subentries under the main entry TASKS). In order to help a reader find subentries, they are cross-referenced to the main entries, as illustrated by the first six entries below.

ACOMMUNICATIVE TASK: see TASKS

ALTERNATIVE ASSESSMENT: see TESTING AND ASSESSMENT

ANAPHORA/ANAPHORIC: see COHESION

ANCHORED: see DEIXIS/DEICTIC

ARROW: see COHESION

AUTOMATED INFERENCE: see INFERENCE

BACKING-INTO-THE-ANSWER STRATEGY: see RESPONSE STRATEGY

BACKSHIFTING: a change in language form that occurs when a writer moves from direct speech to free indirect speech (e.g., *will* becomes *would* or *I* becomes *she*)

BISERIAL CORRELATION: see PSYCHOMETRICS

CANONICAL PARAGRAPH: a paragraph structure with an initial topic sentence followed by sentences that support or develop a main idea (this idealized structure is often taught, though erroneously, as the most frequently recurring paragraph)

CATAPHORA/CATAPHORIC: see COHESION

CLASSROOM-ORIENTED FUNCTIONS: see FUNCTIONS OF TESTING AND ASSESSMENT

CHOICES/RESPONSES: the answers provided in a multiple-choice task from among which a student must select one

COHESION: the various connections between presupposing elements (e.g., a pronominal) and presupposed elements (e.g., a nominal) that run through a text

ANAPHORA/ANAPHORIC: a cohesive relationship in which a word such as a pronominal presupposes information introduced earlier in the text

ARROW: the presupposing element (e.g., a pronominal) in a cohesive relationship

CATAPHORA/CATAPHORIC: a cohesive relationship in which a word such as the demonstrative *this* presupposes information that occurs later in the text

COHESIVE FRAME: a linguistic framework built around various cohesive relationships

COHESIVE MARKER: the arrow or target in a cohesive relationship

COHESIVE RELATIONSHIP: a connection between cohesive markers

TARGET: the presupposed element (e.g., a nominal) in a cohesive relationship

COHESIVE FRAME: see COHESION

COHESIVE MARKER: see COHESION

COHESIVE RELATIONSHIP: see COHESION

COMMUNICATIVE DISTRACTOR: see DISTRACTOR

COMMUNICATIVE CONFIGURATION: see PASSAGE/TASK CONFIGURATION

COMMUNICATIVE TASK: see TASK

COMPLETER: a word or phrase used to complete a stem in a completion task

COMPLETER STEM: see STEM

COMPLETION TASK: see TASK

CONTENT FRAME: see FRAME

CONVENTIONAL TESTING: see TESTING AND ASSESSMENT

COVERT TASK: see TASK

CRITERION-REFERENCED TESTING: see TESTING AND ASSESSMENT

DEICTICALLY ANCHORED: see DEIXIS/DEICTIC

DEICTICALLY UNANCHORED: see DEIXIS/DEICTIC

DEIXIS/DEICTIC: language use dependent on the immediate communicative situation, especially the spatiotemporal location of the language user(s) (also referred to as DEICTICALLY ANCHORED or simply ANCHORED)

DYNAMIC MODE: an interpretive mode associated with the non-deictic use of language as well as the deictic use of in-tandem imagery

EXCLUSIVE MODE: an interpretive mode in which either the beginning point or the end point of a temporal field (or both) is excluded

INCLUSIVE MODE: an interpretive mode in which either the beginning point or the end point of a temporal field (or both) is included

IN-TANDEM IMAGERY: deictic imagery in which the language user(s) and the spatial or temporal field are both oriented toward a further point

MIRROR IMAGERY: deictic imagery in which the language user(s) and the spatial or temporal field are oriented toward each other

NON-DEICTIC: language use not dependent on the immediate communicative situation, especially the spatio-temporal location of the language user(s) (also referred to as DEICTICALLY UNANCHORED or simply UNANCHORED)

NOW ANCHORING: a deictic interpretation of consecutive temporal units in which they are both anchored in the language user(s)' temporal location

NOW-THEN ANCHORING: a deictic interpretation of consecutive temporal units in which the first is anchored in the language user(s)' temporal location and the second begins where the first one ends

STATIC MODE: an interpretive mode associated with the deictic use of language (especially mirror imagery)

DESPERATION STRATEGY: see RESPONSE STRATEGY

DISCOURSE: language used to achieve interaction (written as well as spoken)

DISCOURSE FRAME: see FRAME

DISTRACTOR: a task choice designated as incorrect by test makers

COMMUNICATIVE DISTRACTOR: a distractor that leads children astray by encouraging them to construct a situation model that extends beyond the text base

ELLIPTICAL DISTRACTOR: a distractor presented in a compressed form by the omission of words, which can lead a test taker to make alternative interpretations (the stem may be elliptical as well)

REAL-WORLD-KNOWLEDGE DISTRACTOR: a distractor that leads children astray by encouraging them to use their real-world knowledge

REPETITION DISTRACTOR: a distractor that repeats a word or words from the passage

SYMPTOMATIC DISTRACTOR: a distractor that was viewed, on the basis of earlier research, as indicative of a problematical interaction with a test unit (during interviews with individual children, the researchers focused on these distractors)

DISTRACTOR PROPOSITION: see TASK PROPOSITION

DOCUMENTATION: alternative assessment that provides either samples or records of student work

DYNAMIC ASSESSMENT: an approach to assessment in which the test giver provides help to students when they need it (such help can be factored into the evaluation of their performance)

DYNAMIC MODE: see DEIXIS/DEICTIC

ELIMINATE-IF-EQUAL STRATEGY: see RESPONSE STRATEGY

ELLIPTICAL DISTRACTOR: see DISTRACTOR

EXCERPTED PASSAGE: see PASSAGE

EXCLUSIVE MODE: see DEIXIS/DEICTIC

EXPANDED NARRATIVE: see NARRATIVE

EXPERIENTIAL INFERENCE: see INFERENCE

EXTENDED INFERENCE: see INFERENCE

EXTENDED SITUATION MODEL: see SITUATION MODEL

FACTUAL NARRATIVE: see NARRATIVE

FICTIONAL NARRATIVE: see NARRATIVE

FOCUSED TASK: see TASK

FRAME: the set of mental associations and expectations activated by a text

CONTENT FRAME: a frame based on the content of a passage (such a frame may need to be abandoned in light of later content)

DISCOURSE FRAME: a frame based on the way in which a passage is organized rather than on its content

INITIAL FRAME: the first frame formed by test takers as they work through a passage (such a frame needs to be suppressed in order to deal successfully with a frame configuration)

INTERPRETIVE FRAME: the particular expectations that the style of a passage leads the reader to adopt (e.g, whether the text should be interpreted holistically or only for detail)

FRAME UNIT: see UNIT

FRAME CONFIGURATION: see PASSAGE/TASK CONFIGURATION

FREE INDIRECT SPEECH (Fr.: *style indirect libre*): a literary technique for representing a stream of thought from an external point of view (e.g., the use of third-person instead of first-person pronominals to represent internal speech)

FUNCTIONS OF TESTING AND ASSESSMENT: the major purposes for which testing and assessment are used in education

CLASSROOM-ORIENTED FUNCTIONS: purposes that support classroom teaching and learning (e.g., monitoring students' work or developing their capacity to evaluate their own work)

SYSTEM-ORIENTED FUNCTIONS: purposes that support the educational system at large (e.g., certifying students, selecting students for further educational opportunities, or monitoring how well the educational system is performing)

GAP-JUMPING: see POLARITY RESPONSES

GAPPED PASSAGE: see PASSAGE

HISTORICAL NARRATIVE: see NARRATIVE

INCLUSIVE MODE: see DEIXIS/DEICTIC

INERTIA PRINCIPLE: a principle whereby readers assume that referential frames will be maintained in the absence of any signal to the contrary

INFERENCE: a reader response stimulated by the text base

AUTOMATED INFERENCE: an inference directly entailed by the text base

INVITED INFERENCE: an inference more loosely associated with the text base than a motivated inference

META-INFERENCE: an inference that test takers make about what a particular multiple-choice task is calling for

MOTIVATED INFERENCE: an inference that normatively expands the text base

EXTENDED INFERENCE: an inference not normatively associated with the text base

INFERENTIAL TASK: see TASK

INFORMATION-RECYCLING TASK: see TASK

INITIAL FRAME: see FRAME

IN-TANDEM IMAGERY: see DEIXIS/DEICTIC

INTERPRETIVE FRAME: see FRAME

INTRODUCER: a marker that indicates a turn in a dialogue (after the speakers' identities and the order of their exchanges are established, such a marker is often omitted until the turn-taking pattern shifts)

INVITED INFERENCE: see INFERENCE

INVITED SITUATION MODEL: see SITUATION MODEL

KNOWLEDGE PROBE: see PROBES

KNOWLEDGE-BUILDING COMPREHENSION: a mode of comprehension in which test takers are able to work out the meaning of what they have read and integrate it into their permanent stock of knowledge (see SYMBOL-MANIPULATING COMPREHENSION)

LANGUAGE-DEPENDENT INFORMATION: see SOURCES OF INFORMATION

LOCALIST HYPOTHESIS: a semantic theory in which the spatial domain is viewed as providing templates for meaning in other domains

LEXICAL POLARITY: a relation between two words that are semantically opposed to each other (see POLARITY RESPONSES)

LITERAL TASK: see TASK

LITERATE REGISTER: see REGISTER

MARKED: see MARKEDNESS

MARKEDNESS: a feature of natural languages in which the positive pole in an opposing pair is more widespread in its use (e.g., *tall* is used rather than *short* in syntactic structures such as *I am as x as she is* and *How x is she?*), and so the negative pole is considered as marked

MARKED: the negative pole of an opposing pair (e.g., *short*), which is more restricted in its use

UNMARKED: the positive pole of an opposing pair (e.g., *tall*), which is more widespread in its use

META-INFERENCE: see INFERENCE

METALINGUISTIC TASK: see TASK

METALITERATE TASK: see TASK

METALITERARY TASK: see TASK

MIRROR IMAGERY: see DEIXIS/DEICTIC

MOTIVATED INFERENCE: see INFERENCE

MOTIVATED SITUATION MODEL: see SITUATION MODEL

NARRATIVE: a text structure based on temporally sequenced events

   EXPANDED NARRATIVE: a narrative based on an incomplete sequence of temporal events that the reader expands in order to achieve a more complete story

   FACTUAL NARRATIVE: a narrative based on factual information

   FICTIONAL NARRATIVE: a narrative based on imagined information

   HISTORICAL NARRATIVE: a narrative based on historical information

   NARRATIVE EXPANSION: the process of a reader using inferences to expand an incomplete story

NARRATIVE-DESCRIPTIVE: a test makers' category that includes both narrative and descriptive text structures

NARRATIVE EXPANSION: see NARRATIVE

NON-DEICTIC: see DEIXIS/DEICTIC

NORM-REFERENCED TESTING: see TESTING AND ASSESSMENT

NOW ANCHORING: see DEIXIS/DEICTIC

NOW-THEN ANCHORING: see DEIXIS/DEICTIC

ORAL REGISTER: see REGISTER

OVERT TASK: see TASK

PARADIGM/PARADIGMATIC: the use of words such that a contrastive rather than an integrative relationship is formed between the words (see SYNTAGM/SYNTAGMATIC)

PARALLELISM: a literary technique in which sequential structures are identical except for a contrasting element (e.g., *There was no black bonnet; there was only...*)

PASSAGE: the text part of a unit

   EXCERPTED PASSAGE: a passage that lacks an appropriate beginning or ending

   GAPPED PASSAGE: a passage that lacks information to which readers are accustomed on the basis of past experience with similar texts

   TRUNCATED PASSAGE: a passage that lacks an appropriate ending

PASSAGE-INDEPENDENT STRATEGY: see RESPONSE STRATEGY

PASSAGE-TASK CONFIGURATION: a major pattern formed by a passage and one or more tasks

COMMUNICATIVE CONFIGURATION: a communicatively oriented passage combined with a task in which the target response is acommunicative and one or more distractors is communicative

FRAME CONFIGURATION: a passage that shifts rapidly from one frame to another combined with a task in which a distractor is based on the initial frame

POLARITY CONFIGURATION: a passage built around/containing multiple lexical polarities combined with a task in which one or more distractors is based on these polarities

PERFORMANCE PROBE: see PROBES

POLARITY CONFIGURATION: see PASSAGE-TASK CONFIGURATION

POLARITY RESPONSES: major kinds of responses to a polarity task

GAP-JUMPING: a response to a polarity task in which a test taker uses textual information, no matter how slight, to shift from one lexical pole to another

POLARIZATION: a process whereby a reader infers an interpretive frame that opposes a textually based one (e.g., the climate must have been wet since it took the grapes a long time to dry)

WIRE-CROSSING: a response to a polarity task in which a test taker inadvertently reverses lexical polarities

POLARITY UNIT: see UNIT

POLARIZATION: see POLARITY RESPONSES

POLYSEMIC: a word (especially a high-frequency one) that is used in a wide variety of contexts and thus tends to cover large, diffuse areas of meaning (it acquires a precise sense only in a particular context)

PREDICATED SEQUENCE: order of events or states within a represented world (see TEXT SEQUENCE)

PROBE: an experimental task designed by the researchers to investigate specific aspects of test takers' interactions with a test unit

KNOWLEDGE PROBE: a probe designed to investigate what test takers know about some particular feature (e.g., a vocabulary word) of a test unit (i.e., it focuses on their real-world schemas)

PERFORMANCE PROBE: a probe designed to investigate test takers' responses when a test unit is presented in a different way (i.e., it focuses on their textual schemas)

PROCESS DESCRIPTION: a text structure based on the description of sequential processes in an established routine (e.g., the first part may present materials to be processed and the second part the processes used to create a product from these materials)

PSYCHOMETRICS: the use of statistical techniques in the construction and validation of instruments that measure mental abilities

BISERIAL CORRELATION: a statistical technique that correlates the performance of test takers on existing test material with their performance on prospective material

TEST RELIABILITY: the degree to which a test is consistent in measuring whatever it does measure

TEST VALIDITY: the degree to which a test measures what it is supposed to measure

QUESTION TASK: see TASK

QUESTION STEM: see STEM

READER FLEXIBILITY: various kinds of flexibility that children must demonstrate in responding to frame units, polarity units, and register units

REAL-WORLD KNOWLEDGE: knowledge about how the world functions

REAL-WORLD-KNOWLEDGE DISTRACTOR: see DISTRACTOR

REAL-WORLD SCHEMA: see SCHEMA

READER-DEPENDENT INFORMATION: see SOURCES OF INFORMATION

REGISTER: use of language that accords with the communicative situation

ORAL REGISTER: use of language that accords with a relatively informal situation

LITERATE REGISTER: use of language that accords with a relatively formal situation

REGISTER UNIT: see UNIT

REPETITION DISTRACTOR: see DISTRACTOR

REPETITION RESPONSE: a response that repeats material from the passage

RESPONSE STRATEGY: various strategies that test takers use to respond to test units (these strategies do not necessarily operate at a conscious level)

BACKING-INTO-THE-ANSWER STRATEGY: a strategy in which test takers eliminate all but one choice

DESPERATION STRATEGY: a strategy that test takers use when they become so confused that they have no idea what a task calls for (e.g., they may latch onto any word repeated from the passage)

ELIMINATE-IF-EQUAL STRATEGY: a strategy based on the notion that if two or more choices have equal validity, the correct answer must be another choice

PASSAGE-INDEPENDENT STRATEGY: a strategy by which test takers make a choice based on their real-world knowledge rather than on passage content

SOUNDS-RIGHT STRATEGY: a strategy by which test takers evaluate a choice according to whether it contains language that seems to be structurally in tact

STICK-TO-THE-PASSAGE STRATEGY: a strategy by which test takers attempt to follow the admonition to work only with what is in the passage and not use outside knowledge

SUBSTITUTION STRATEGY: a strategy by which test takers substitute choices for words in the passage in an attempt to find one that fits well enough to be selected

SCHEMA: a formalized representation of a generic situation that allows one to anticipate the course of events that should unfold in that type of situation

    REAL-WORLD SCHEMA: a schema based on real-world experience (e.g., a vacation schema)

    TEXTUAL SCHEMA: a schema based on past experiences of various text structures (e.g., descriptive or expository structures)

SELF-REFERENCED ASSESSMENT: see TESTING AND ASSESSMENT

SITUATION MODEL: a situation that a reader constructs from a text base (see TEXT BASE)

    EXTENDED: a non-normative situation that a reader constructs from a text base (i.e., one based on at least one extended inference)

    MOTIVATED: a normative situation that a reader constructs from a text base (i.e., one based on at least one motivated inference)

    INVITED: a quasi-normative situation that a reader constructs from a text base (i.e., one based on at least one invited inference)

SOUNDS-RIGHT STRATEGY: see RESPONSE STRATEGY

SOURCES OF INFORMATION: the various sources of information that a reader uses in comprehending text

    LANGUAGE-DEPENDENT INFORMATION: information that inheres in language elements independent of their role in the text

    READER-DEPENDENT INFORMATION: information that the reader must infer from the text base

    TEXT-DEPENDENT INFORMATION: information that is directly stated in the text or which can be automatically inferred

STAGED: information that is in a discourse-prominent position

STANDARDIZED TESTING: see TESTING AND ASSESSMENT

STATIC MODE: see DEIXIS/DEICTIC

STEM: the initiating part of a task (i.e., the task with the choices removed)

    COMPLETER STEM: the initiating part of a completer task that must be completed by one of the task choices

    QUESTION STEM: the initiating part a question task that must be completed by one of the task choices

STICK-TO-THE-PASSAGE STRATEGY: see RESPONSE STRATEGY

SUBSTITUTION STRATEGY: see RESPONSE STRATEGY

SYMBOL-MANIPULATING COMPREHENSION: a mode of comprehension in which test takers process passage information at a surface level (i.e., they manipulate the language as verbal symbols in order to complete a task, but do not develop a deeper understanding of what the passage means) (see KNOWLEDGE-BUILDING COMPREHENSION)

SYMPTOMATIC DISTRACTOR: see DISTRACTOR

SYNCRETISM: the tendency of children to assimilate new detail into an existing frame even if it does not readily fit

SYNEDOCHE: a literary technique in which a subject is referred to by one of its constituent details or parts (e.g., a black bonnet to represent an old lady)

SYNTAGM/SYNTAGMATIC: the role played by an individual word in relation to other words in a sentence such that a meaningful whole is formed (see PARADIGM/PARADIGMATIC)

SYSTEM-ORIENTED FUNCTIONS: see FUNCTIONS OF TESTING AND ASSESSMENT

TARGET: see COHESION

TARGET RESPONSE: the task choice designated as correct by the test makers (see DISTRACTORS)

TARGET PROPOSITION: see TASK PROPOSITION

TASK: a problem that the test taker must solve after having read the passage (i.e., it consists of a stem and four choices from which the test taker must select an answer)

ACOMMUNICATIVE TASK: a task that requires the test taker to use language for purposes counter to everyday communicative norms (e.g., to recycle information)

COMMUNICATIVE TASK: a task that requires a meaningful inference to be drawn from the passage

COMPLETION TASK: a task consisting of an incomplete statement and four choices designed to complete that statement

COVERT TASK: an acommunicative task that does not contain any explicit indication as to what its purpose is

FOCUSED TASK: an overt task in which the reader can know that the task is vocabulary-defining

INFERENTIAL TASK: a task based on what a passage implies rather than what is explicitly stated

INFORMATION-RECYCLING TASK: a task that requires the test taker to restate or paraphrase passage information (see LITERAL TASK)

LITERAL TASK: a task that requires the test taker to restate or paraphrase passage information (see INFORMATION-RECYCLING TASK)

METALINGUISTIC TASK: an acommunicative task that requires the test taker to analyze language structure (e.g., a mainly-about task based on the most pervasive and prominent information in the passage)

METALITERATE TASK/METALITERARY TASK: an acommunicative task that requires the test taker to analyze a literate feature associated with the literary use of language (e.g., *style indirect libre*)

OVERT TASK: an acommunicative task that contains a formula indicating the purpose of the task as vocabulary-defining or information-recycling

QUESTION TASK: a task that consists of a question and four choices representing possible answers

UNFOCUSED TASK: an overt task in which the reader can know that the task is acommunicative, but not whether it is vocabulary-defining or information-recycling

VOCABULARY-DEFINING TASK: a task that requires the test-taker to define a word in the context of the passage

TASK PROPOSITION: a stem combined with any one of the four choices (i.e., the target response or the distractors)

TARGET PROPOSITION: a stem combined with the target response

DISTRACTOR PROPOSITION: a stem or question combined with a distractor

TEST RELIABILITY: see PSYCHOMETRICS

TEST VALIDITY: see PSYCHOMETRICS

TESTING AND ASSESSMENT: various activities used to evaluate student knowledge and skills

ALTERNATIVE ASSESSMENT: an approach that emphasizes documentation activities (e.g., portfolios) and testlike activities as an alternative to standardized testing

CONVENTIONAL TESTING: the standardized forms of testing that have become dominant in modern societies

CRITERION-REFERENCED TESTING: a form of testing in which individual performance is evaluated according to pre-established criteria

NORM-REFERENCED TESTING: a form of testing in which individual performance is evaluated according to the norms of performance of a larger group

SELF-REFERENCED ASSESSMENT (IPSATIVE): a form of assessment in which individual performance is evaluated according to prior performances of that individual

STANDARDIZED TESTING: a modern approach to testing built largely around multiple-choice tasks and psychometric techniques that measure student performance on these tasks

TRADITIONAL TESTING: various activities used to evaluate student knowledge and skills before the development of standardized testing (e.g., essay writing)

TESTLIKE: activities that deviate in one or more ways from conventional testing

TEST UNIT: see UNIT

TEXT BASE: information that is directly stated or which can be automatically inferred (see SITUATION MODEL)

TEXT-DEPENDENT INFORMATION: see SOURCES OF INFORMATION

TEXT SEQUENCE: the order of actions, events, or states within the text (see PREDICATED SEQUENCE)

TEXTUAL SCHEMA: see SCHEMA

TRADITIONAL TESTING: see TESTING AND ASSESSMENT

TRUNCATED PASSAGE: see PASSAGE

UNANCHORED: see DEIXIS/DEICTIC

UNFOCUSED TASK: see TASK

UNMARKED: see MARKEDNESS

UNIT (also described as TEST UNIT): the combination of a passage and multiple-choice tasks

   FRAME UNIT: a unit that leads readers to construct one frame, but then abandon it in light of subsequent information

   POLARITY UNIT: a unit that requires readers to handle multiple pairs of lexical polarities with limited context to support overlapping and indeterminate meanings

   REGISTER UNIT: a unit that requires readers to shift from an evocative register in the passage to an analytic one in the tasks

UNIT LEAKAGE: a process in which knowledge or associations activated by a test unit affect the interpretation of other units

VOCABULARY-DEFINING TASK: see TASK

WIRE-CROSSING: see POLARITY RESPONSES

References

Abubakar, A. T. (1985). *The acquisition of 'front' and 'back' among Hausa children: A study in deixis.* Unpublished doctoral dissertation, Teachers College, Columbia University, New York.

Adames, J. A. (1987). *A study of the reading process of selected English as a second language college students.* Unpublished doctoral dissertation, Teachers College, Columbia University, New York.

Allen, K. (1988). *The development of a test of communicative competence for speakers of English as a second language in Zimbabwe.* Unpublished doctoral dissertation, Teachers College, Columbia University, New York.

Aronowitz, R. (1984). Reading tests as texts. In D. Tannen (Ed.), *Coherence in spoken and written discourse* (pp. 43–62). Norwood, NJ: Ablex.

Aronson, E., & Farr, R. (1988). Issues in assessment. *Journal of Reading, 32,* 174–177.

Banfield, A. (1982). *Unspeakable sentences.* London: Routledge & Kegan Paul.

Bennett, C. (1976). *Spatial and temporal uses of English prepositions: An essay in stratificational semantics.* London: Longman.

Bereiter, C., & Englemann, S. (1966). *Teaching disadvantaged children in the preschool.* Englewood Cliffs, NJ: Prentice-Hall.

Bhasin, J. (1990). *The demands of main idea tasks in reading comprehension tests and the strategic responses of bilingual poor comprehenders.* Unpublished doctoral dissertation, Teachers College, Columbia University, New York.

Black, J., & Bower, G. (1980). Story understanding as problem-solving. *Poetics, 9,* 223–250.

Bloom, B. S. (1956). *Taxonomy of educational objectives.* New York: Longman.

Braddock, R. (1974). The frequency and placements of topic sentences in expository prose. *Research in the Teaching of English, 8,* 287–302.

Briggs, C. (1986). *Learning how to ask: A sociolinguistic appraisal of the role of the interview in social science research.* Cambridge, UK: Cambridge University Press.

Calfee, R. C. (1987). The school as a context for assessment of literacy. *The Reading Teacher, 40,* 738–744.

Chu, H. (1993). *Assessing Chinese kindergarten children in New York City.* Unpublished doctoral dissertation, Teachers College, Columbia University, New York.

Clark, M. J., & Grandy, J. (1984). *Sex differences in the academic performance of scholastic aptitude test takers.* New York: College Entrance Examination Board.

Collins, A., Brown, J., & Larkin, K. (1980). Inference in text understanding. In R. J. Spiro, B. C. Bruce, & W. F. Brewer (Eds.), *Theoretical issues in reading comprehension* (pp. 385–407). Hillsdale, NJ: Lawrence Erlbaum.

Cooper, W., & Ross, J. (1975). Word order. In R. Grossman, L. J. San, & T. Vance, (Eds.), *Papers from the parasession on functionalism* (pp. 63–111). Chicago: Chicago Linguistic Society.

Coyle, M. (1992). *The New Jersey high school proficiency test in writing: A pragmatic face on an autonomous model.* Unpublished doctoral dissertation, Teachers College, Columbia University, New York.

Cruse, D. A. (1986). *Lexical semantics.* Cambridge, UK: Cambridge University Press.

Dale, E., & O'Rourke, J. (1976). *The living word vocabulary: The words we know: A national vocabulary inventory.* Elgin, IL: Field Enterprises Education.

Dorans, N. J., & Kulick, E. (1983). *Assessing unexpected differential item performance of female candidates on SAT and TSE forms administered in December 1977: An application of the standardization approach.* Princeton, NJ: Educational Testing Service.

Duckworth, E. (1987). *"The having of wonderful ideas" and other essays on teaching and learning.* New York: Teachers College Press.

Feuerstein, R. (1972). Cognitive assessment of the socioculturally deprived child and adolescent. In L. J. Cronbach & P. Drenth (Eds.), *Mental tests and cultural adaptation* (pp. 265–275). The Hague, The Netherlands: Mouton.

Feuerstein, R. (1977). Mediated learning experience: A theoretical basis for cognitive human modifiability during adolescence. In P. Mittler (Ed.), *Research to practice in mental retardation. Vol. II* (pp. 105–115). Baltimore: University Park Press.

Feuerstein, R. (1978). The ontogeny of learning. In M. Brazier (Ed.), *Brain mechanisms in memory and learning.* New York: Raven Press.

Fillmore, C. J. (1997). *Lectures on deixis.* New York: Cambridge University Press.

Fillmore. C. J. (1982). Ideal readers and real readers. In D. Tannen, (Ed.), *Analyzing discourse: Text and talk* (pp. 248–270). Washington, DC: Georgetown University Press.

Fillmore, C., & Kay, P. (1983). *Text-semantic analysis of reading comprehension tests.* Berkeley: University of California, Institute of Human Learning.

Flower, L., & Hayes, J. R. (1980). The cognition of discovery: Defining a rhetorical problem. *College Composition and Communication, 31,* 21–32.

Freedle, R. (Ed.) (1977). *Discourse production and comprehension.* Norwood, NJ: Ablex.

Freedle, R. O., & Duran, R. P. (1987). *Cognitive and linguistic analyses of test performance.* Norwood, NJ: Ablex.

Garcia, G. E. (1988). *Factors influencing English reading test performance of Spanish-English bilingual children.* Unpublished doctoral dissertation, University of Illinois, Urbana-Champaign.

Gardner, H. (1991). *The unschooled mind.* New York: Basic Books.

Goodman, K. (1986). *What's whole in whole language?* Portsmouth, NH: Heinemann Educational Books.

Goodman, K. (1976). Miscue analysis: Theory and reality in reading. In J. E. Merritt (Ed.), *New horizons in reading: Proceedings of the Fifth International Reading Association World Congress on Reading* (pp. 15–26). Newark, DE: International Reading Association.

Green, G. (1983). *Some remarks on how words mean.* Bloomington, IN: Indiana University Linguistics Club.

Halliday, M. A. K., & Hasan, R. (1976). *Cohesion in English.* London: Longman.

Haney, W., & Scott, L. (1987). Talking with children about tests: An exploratory study of test item ambiguity. In R. O. Freedle & R. P. Duran (Eds.), *Cognitive and linguistic analyses of test performance* (pp. 298–368). Norwood, NJ: Ablex.

Hayes, T., & McCartney, N. (1993). *Progressive Achievement Tests of Reading.* Unpublished manuscript.

Herzog, M., Weinreich, U., & Labov, W. (1968). Empirical foundations for a theory of language change. In W. Lehmann & Y. Malkiel (Eds.), *Directions for historical linguistics* (pp. 95–188). Austin: University of Texas Press.

Hill, C. (1974). Spatial perception and linguistic encoding: A case study in Hausa and English. *Studies in African Linguistics, 4,* 135–148.

Hill, C. (1975a). Sex-based differences in cognitive processing of spatial relations among bilingual students in Niger. *Working Papers in Linguistics: Patterns in Language, Culture, and Society* (Ohio State University), *19,* 185–198.

Hill, C. (1975b). Variation in the use of 'front' and 'back' by bilingual speakers. *Proceedings of the Berkeley Linguistics Society, 1,* 196–206.

Hill, C. (1977a). *Urban minority students, language, and reading.* Arlington, VA: Center for Applied Linguistics.

Hill, C. (1977b). A review of the language deficit position: Some sociolinguistic and psycholinguistic perspectives. *IRCD Bulletin, 12,* 4.

Hill, C. (1978). Linguistic representation of spatial and temporal orientation. *Proceedings of the Berkeley Linguistics Society, 4,* 524–538.

Hill, C. (1982). Up/down, front/back, left/right: A contrastive study of Hausa and English. In J. Weissenborn & W. Klein (Eds.), *Here and there: Cross-linguistic studies on Deixis and demonstration.* Amsterdam: John Benjamins Press.

Hill, C. (1991a). Recherches interlinguistiques en orientation spatiale. *Communications, 53,* 171–207.

Hill, C. (1991b). *Spatial and temporal orientation: African and African American continuities* (LC Report 91–1). New York: Teachers College, Columbia University, Literacy Center.

Hill, C. (1992, April). *Testing and assessment: An ecological approach.* Inaugural lecture for the Arthur I. Gates Chair in Language and Education. New York: Teachers College, Columbia University.

Hill, C. (1995). Testing and assessment: An applied linguistics perspective. *Educational Assessment, 2,* 179–212.

Hill, C. (1998). *Static and dynamic frames of communication: The semiotics of spatiotemporal orientation.* Unpublished manuscript.

Hill, C. (1999). A national reading test for fourth graders: A missing component in the policy debate. In B. Preseissen (Ed.), *Teaching for intelligence I* (pp. 125–152). Chicago: Skylight.

Hill, C. (in press). Constructivist assessment in early childhood education. In B. Preseissen (Ed.), *Teaching for intelligence II.* Chicago: Skylight.

Hill, C., & Anderson, L. (1993). The interview as a research tool. *New Ideas in Psychology, 11,* 111–125.

Hill, C., Anderson, L., Watt, Y., & Ray, S. (1989). *Reading assessment in adult education: Local detail versus textual gestalt* (LC Report 89-2). New York: Teachers College, Columbia University, Literacy Center.

Hill, C., & Larsen, E. (1983). *What reading tests call for and what children do.* (Final Report for NIE Grant G-78-0095). Washington, DC: National Institute of Education.

Hill, C., & Larsen, E. (1992). *Assessment in secondary education: A critical review of emerging practices.* Berkeley: University of California, National Center for Research in Vocational Education.

Hill, C., & Parry, K. (1988). *Reading assessment: Autonomous and pragmatic models of literacy* (LC Report 88-2). New York: Teachers College, Columbia University, Literacy Center.

Hill, C., & Parry, K. (1989). Autonomous and pragmatic models of literacy: Reading assessment in adult education. *Linguistics and Education, 1,* 233–283.

Hill, C., & Parry, K. (1992). The test at the gate: Models of literacy in reading assessment. *TESOL Quarterly, 26*: 433–461.

Hill, C., & Parry, K. (1994). *From testing to assessment: English as an international language.* Harlow, UK: Longman.

Hill, C., & Pike, L. (1985). *A comparison of cloze substitutions in English texts by native speakers of English, Spanish, and Japanese.* Unpublished manuscript.

Ho, Y. M. (1997). *Textual orientation and problem solving in mainland China and Taiwan.* Unpublished manuscript, Teachers College, Columbia University, New York.

Hoffman, B. (1964). *The tyranny of testing.* New York: Crowell-Collier.

Holland, D., & Street, B. (1994). Assessing adult literacy in the United Kingdom: The progress profile. In C. Hill & K. Parry (Eds.), *From testing to assessment: English as an international language* (pp. 241–249). Harlow, UK: Longman.

Hymes, D. (1962). The ethnography of speaking. In T. Gladwin & W. Sturtevant (Eds.), *Anthropology and human behavior.* Washington, DC: Anthropological Society of Washington.

Ingulsrud, J. E. (1988). *Testing in Japan: A discourse analysis of reading comprehension items.* Unpublished doctoral dissertation, Teachers College, Columbia University, New York.

Isma'il, T. (1979). *Cross-cultural variation in spatial and temporal constructs*. Unpublished doctoral dissertation, Teachers College, Columbia University, New York.

Jencks, C., & Phillips, M. (Eds.). (1998). *The Black-White test score gap*. Washington, DC: Brookings Institution Press.

Johnston, P. (1984). *Reading comprehension assessment: A cognitive basis*. Newark, DE: International Reading Association.

Ji, J. (1998). *Spatiotemporal orientation among Chinese-speaking immigrants in metropolitan New York*. Unpublished doctoral dissertation, Teachers College, Columbia University, New York.

Kimmel, S., & MacGinitie, W. (1981). *Hypothesis testing in reading comprehension*. New York: Teachers College, Columbia University, Research Institute for the Study of Learning Disabilities.

Labov, W. (1970). The logic of nonstandard English. In F. Williams (Ed.), *Language and poverty*. Chicago: Markham.

Lakoff, G., & Johnson, M. (1980). *Metaphors we live by*. Chicago: University of Chicago Press.

Langer, J. A. (1987). The construction of meaning and the assessment of comprehension: An analysis of reader performance on standardized test items. In R. O. Freedle & R. P. Duran (Eds.), *Cognitive and linguistic analyses of test performance* (pp. 225–244). Norwood, NJ: Ablex.

Lin, H. S. (1993). *A TOEFL coaching school in Taiwan*. Unpublished doctoral dissertation, Teachers College, Columbia University, New York.

Lyons, J. (1977). *Semantics* (Vol. 2) Cambridge, UK: Cambridge University Press.

MacGinitie, W. H. (1973). *Assessment problems in reading*. Newark, DE: International Reading Association.

MacGinitie, W. H. (1978a). *Gates-MacGinitie reading tests* (2nd ed.). Boston: Houghton Mifflin.

MacGinitie, W. H. (1978b). *Teachers manual: Gates-MacGinitie reading tests* (2nd ed.). Boston: Houghton Mifflin.

Martin, P. (1987). *A historical approach to phrasal verbs*. Unpublished doctoral dissertation, Teachers College, Columbia University, New York.

Matsumoto, K. (1997). *The approach of coaching schools to the JFSAT*. Unpublished manuscript, Teachers College, Columbia University, New York.

McKenna, S., & Hill, C. (1997). *Language and deictic imagery: African and African American continuities*. Unpublished manuscript.

Medina, N., & Neill, D. M. (1990). *Fallout from the testing explosion* (3rd ed.). Boston: National Center for Fair and Open Testing.

Mishler, E. (1986). *Research interviewing: Context and narrative*. Cambridge, MA: Harvard University Press.

Nix, D., & Schwartz, M. (1979). Toward a phenomenology of reading comprehension. In R. O. Freedle (Ed.), *New directions in discourse processing* (pp. 183–196). Norwood, NJ: Ablex.

Olson, D. R. (1977). From utterance to text: The bias of language in speech and writing. *Harvard Educational Review, 2*, 109–178.

Parry, K. (1986). *Readers in context: A study of northern Nigerian students and school certificate texts.* Unpublished doctoral dissertation, Teachers College, Columbia University, New York.

Pearson, P., & Johnson, D. (1978). *Teaching reading comprehension.* New York: Holt, Rinehart, & Winston.

Pearson, P. D., & Valencia, S. (1987). Assessment, accountability, and professional prerogative. In J. E. Readence & R. S. Baldwin (Eds.), *Research in literacy: Merging perspectives* (pp. 3–16). Rochester, NY: National Reading Conference.

Piaget, J. (1926). *Language and thought of the child.* New York: Harcourt, Brace & Co.

Quirk, R., Greenbaum, S., Leech, G., & Svartik, J. (1985). *A comprehensive grammar of the English language.* New York: Longman.

Rodgers, P. C., Jr. (1966). A discourse-centered rhetoric of the paragraph. *College Composition and Communication, 17,* 2–11.

Rosch, E. (1977). Human categorization. In N. Warren (Ed.), *Studies in cross-cultural psychology* (pp. 84–102). London: Academic.

Rosser, P. (1989). *The SAT gender gap: Identifying the causes.* Washington, DC: Center for Women Policy Studies.

Sims-West, N. E. (1996). *An investigation of gender differences on the Scholastic Aptitude Test of verbal ability.* Unpublished doctoral dissertation, Teachers College, Columbia University, New York.

Smith, F. (1994). *Understanding reading: A psycholinguistic analysis of reading and learning to read* (5th ed.). Hillsdale, NJ: Erlbaum.

Steinberg, J. (1997, April 18). Testing whether New York City's children make the grade as readers. *The New York Times,* pp. B1, B3.

Tanz, C. (1980). *Studies in the acquisition of deictic terms.* Cambridge, UK: Cambridge University Press.

Trabasso, T. (1981). On the making of inferences during reading and their assessment. In J. T. Guthrie (Ed.), *Comprehension and teaching: Research reviews* (pp. 56–75). Newark, DE: International Reading Association.

van Dijk, T. A., & Kintsch, W. (1983). *Strategies of discourse comprehension.* New York: Academic.

Wang, H., & Hill, C. (in press). Short-answer questions in testing reading comprehension in College English. In T. Yenren (Ed.), *Teaching English in the 21st century.* Nanjing, China: Nanjing University Press.

Wei, Y. (1996). *Linguistic representation of spatial and temporal orientation: Structured variation among Chinese university students.* Unpublished doctoral dissertation, Teachers College, Columbia University, New York.

Yuan, Y. P. (1997). *Reader response to the Taiwan Joint College Entrance Examination: English Reading Section.* Unpublished doctoral dissertation, Teachers College, Columbia University, New York.

Author Index

Subject Index

repetition distractor, 39, 98, 113. *See also* distractors
repetition strategy, p. 39. *See also* response strategies
response strategies
  backing-into-the-answer strategy, 83, 238, 254
  desperation strategy, 39
  eliminate-if-equal strategy, 47, 63–64
  passage-independent strategy, 113
  repetition strategy, 39
  sounds-right strategy, 38, 241, 360–361
  stick-to-the-passage strategy, 39, 153
  substitution strategy, 328–329

S
schema
  real-world schema, 17
  textual schema, 17
Scholastic Achievement Test, 5, 368. *See also* tests
self-referenced assessment (ipsative), 376. *See also* alternative assessment
situation model, 9. *See also* text base
  extended, 11, 346, 349
  motivated, 11, 96–97, 156–158, 346–348, 367
  invited, 11, 96, 99, 346–350, 367
sounds-right strategy, 38, 241, 360–361. *See also* response strategies
sources of information
  language-dependent information, 167–169
  reader-dependent information, 167–169
  text-dependent information, 167–169
staged information, 50
standardized testing, 5, 332n
  biserial correlation, 4–5, 24, 29n
  criterion-referenced testing, 5, 376
  norm-referenced testing, 5, 376
  psychometrics, 4–5
Stanford Achievement Test, 326
static mode, 226–228, 344–345. *See also* deixis/deictic
stick-to-the-passage strategy, 39, 153. *See also* response strategies

substitution strategy, 328–329. *See also* response strategies
summary style of recall, 378–379. *See also* recall of passages
symbol-manipulating comprehension, 264–266, 345–346. *See also* modes of comprehension
symptomatic distractor, 16. *See also* distractors
syncretism, 149, 183, 340. *See also* inertia principle
synedoche, 77–81. *See also* figurative language
system-oriented functions of assessment, 369–371. *See also* functions of testing and assessment

T
tasks
  acommunicative task, 93–96, 98–103, 129–143, 340
  communicative task, 340
  covert task, 94–95, 129–140
  experiential task, 378
  factual task, 378
  focused task, 94–95, 129–140
  holistic task, 378
  inferential task, 378
  information-recycling task, 93–95, 205–206, 249–258, 261–264, 273–277, 304–310, 316–318
  metalinguistic task, 51, 98, 191–193, 340, 355–358
  metaliterate task, 356
  metaliterary task, 356
  overt task, 94–95
  unfocused task, 94–95
  vocabulary-defining task, 93–95, 99–102, 129–143, 284–292, 326, 331n
task structure, 358–366
  inconsistencies among tasks, 358–361
  inconsistent relations between passages and tasks, 361–366
Test of Adult Basic Education, 368. *See also* tests